SCHAUM'S OUTLINE OF

THEORY AND PROBLEMS

of

DATA STRUCTURES
WITH C++

•

JOHN R. HUBBARD, Ph.D.

Professor of Mathematics and Computer Science
University of Richmond

•

SCHAUM'S OUTLINE SERIES

McGRAW-HILL

New York   San Francisco   Washington, D.C.   Auckland   Bogota′ Caracas
Lisbon   London   Madrid   Mexico City   Milan   Montreal
New Delhi   San Juan   Singapore   Sydney   Tokyo   Toronto

JOHN R. HUBBARD is Professor of Mathematics and Computer Science at the University of Richmond. He received his Ph.D. from The University of Michigan (1973) and has been a member of the Richmond faculty since 1983. His primary interests are in numerical algorithms and database systems. Dr. Hubbard is the author of several other books, including *Schaum's Outline of Programming with C++, Schaum's Outline of Programming with Java*, and *Schaum's Outline of Fundamentals of Computing with C++.*

Schaum's Outline of Theory and Problems of

DATA STRUCTURES WITH C++

1 2 3 4 5 6 7 8 9 10 11 12 13 14 15 16 17 PRS PRS 0 9 8 7 6 5 4 3 2 1 0

ISBN 0-07-135345-3

Sponsoring Editor: Barbara Gilson
Production Supervisor: Elizabeth Strange
Editing Supervisor: Maureen Walker

Library of Congress Cataloging-in-Publication Data

Hubbard, J. R. (John Rast), date
   Schaum's outline of theory and problems of data structures with C++ / John R. Hubbard.
     p. cm. − − (Schaum's outline series)
   ISBN 0-07-135345-3
   1. C++ (Computer program language) 2. Data structures (Computer science) I. Title:
Theory and problems of data structures with C++. II. Title. III. Series.

  QA76.73.C153 H815 2000
  005.13'3 − − dc21
                               00–022981
                                CIP

McGraw-Hill

A Division of The McGraw-Hill Companies

Preface

Like all Schaum's Outline Series books, this is intended to be used primarily for self study, preferably in conjunction with a regular course in data structures using the C++ programming language.

The book includes over 200 examples and problems. The author firmly believes that the principles of data structures can be learned from a well-constructed collection of examples with complete explanations. This book is designed to provide that support.

Source code for all the examples and problems in this book may be downloaded from the author's Web sites: `http://www.richmond.edu/~hubbard`, `http://www.jhubbard.net`, or `http://www.projectEuclid.net`. These sites also contain any corrections and addenda for the book.

I wish to thank all my friends, colleagues, students, and the McGraw-Hill staff who have helped me with the critical review of this manuscript. Special thanks to my wife, Anita Hubbard for her advice, encouragement, and supply of creative problems for this book. Many of the original ideas used here are hers.

JOHN R. HUBBARD
Richmond, Virginia

Dedicated to the memory of my parents:

Sara Rast Hubbard and Willard Wright Hubbard III

Contents

Chapter 1

Review of C++

This chapter reviews the essential features of C++. For more detail see the books **[Stroustrup2]** and **[Hubbard1]** listed in Appendix A.

1.1 THE STANDARD C++ PROGRAMMING LANGUAGE

The C++ programming language was invented by Bjarne Stroustrup in 1980 while he was building a distributed computing system. He based it upon the C programming language which had been invented in 1972 by Dennis Ritchie at Bell Labs. The name C was used because the language was a successor to a language named B, a typeless programming language invented by Ken Thompson as a successor to a language named BCPL (Basic Combined Programming Language) which was invented by Martin Richards in 1967. The name C++ was used to suggest an incremented C. Stroustrup incremented C by adding classes. Indeed, he first named the language "C with Classes." The classes feature, which facilitates object-oriented programming, came from the Simula programming language, developed in the early 1960s.

In 1998, the C++ programming language was standardized by the International Standards Organization (ISO) and by the American National Standards Institute (ANSI). This new standard includes the Standard Template Library (STL) developed originally by Alexander Stepanov in 1979. The term "Standard C++" refers to this standardized version of the language.

EXAMPLE 1.1 The Standard C++ "Hello World" Program

```
#include <iostream>    // defines the std::cout and std::endl objects
int main()
{ // prints "Hello, World!"
  std::cout << "Hello, World!" << std::endl;
}
Hello, World!
```

The *preprocessor directive* on the first line tells the C++ compiler to include the definitions from the *standard header* file `iostream` that is part of the *Standard C++ Library*. It defines the `cout` object and the `endl` object in the `std` namespace. The *scope resolution operator* `::` is used to indicate the location of those definitions.

EXAMPLE 1.2 Using the Standard `std` Namespace

```
#include <iostream>    // defines the std::cout and std::endl objects
using namespace std;   // renders the std:: prefix unnecessary
int main()
{ // prints "Hello, World!"
  cout << "Hello, World!" << endl;
}
Hello, World!
```

The using declaration on the second line adds the name std to the local scope, obviating the std::
scope resolution prefix on the cout and endl objects.

All the remaining programs in this book are assumed to begin with the following two lines:

```
#include <iostream>
using namespace std;
```

If you are using a pre-Standard compiler, use this single line instead:

```
#include <iostream.h>
```

EXAMPLE 1.3 The Quadratic Formula

```
#include <cmath>   // defines the sqrt() function
int main()
{ // implements the quadratic formula
  double a, b, c;
  cout << "Enter the coefficients of a quadratic equation:\n";
  cout << "\ta: ";   cin >> a;
  cout << "\tb: ";   cin >> b;
  cout << "\tc: ";   cin >> c;
  cout << "The equation is: " << a << "*x*x + " << b
       << "*x + " << c << " = 0\n";
  double d = b*b - 4*a*c;   // discriminant
  double sqrtd = sqrt(d);
  double x1 = (-b + sqrtd)/(2*a);
  double x2 = (-b - sqrtd)/(2*a);
  cout << "The solutions are:\n";
  cout << "\tx1 = " << x1 << endl;
  cout << "\tx2 = " << x2 << endl;
  cout << "Check:\ta*x1*x1 + b*x1 + c = " <<   a*x1*x1 + b*x1 + c;
  cout << "\n     \ta*x2*x2 + b*x2 + c = " <<   a*x2*x2 + b*x2 + c;
}
```

On the first run we input 2, 1, and –3 to solve the quadratic equation $2x^2 + x - 3 = 0$:

```
Enter the coefficients of a quadratic equation:
        a: 2
        b: 1
        c: -3
The equation is: 2*x*x + 1*x + -3 = 0
The solutions are:
        x1 = 1
        x2 = -1.5
Check:  a*x1*x1 + b*x1 + c = 0
        a*x2*x2 + b*x2 + c = 0
```

The program computes the correct solutions, 1 and –1.5, and then checks them by substituting them back
into the quadratic expression to get 0.

On the second run we input 2, 1, and 3 to solve the quadratic equation $2x^2 + x + 3 = 0$:

The program outputs the symbol nan for the solutions x_1 and x_2 and for the resulting check calculation.
That symbol stands for "not a number." It resulted from the fact that the discriminant $d = b^2 - 4ac < 0$.
Consequently, the call sqrt(d) to the square root function failed, returning the value nan. That is a
valid value for float and double variables. But it is *idempotent*: when combined arithmetically with
any other value, the resulting value is also nan.

```
Enter the coefficients of a quadratic equation:
        a: 2
        b: 1
        c: 3
The equation is: 2*x*x + 1*x + 3 = 0
The solutions are:
        x1 = nan
        x2 = nan
Check:  a*x1*x1 + b*x1 + c = nan
        a*x2*x2 + b*x2 + c = nan
```

1.2 CONDITIONALS

We can improve the program in Example 1.3 by using an `if` statement to handle the negative discriminant case separately.

EXAMPLE 1.4 A More Robust Implementation of the Quadratic Formula

```cpp
#include <cmath>  // defines the function sqrt() function
int main()
{ // implements the quadratic formula
  double a, b, c;
  cout << "Enter the coefficients of a quadratic equation:" << endl;
  cout << "\ta: ";  cin >> a;
  cout << "\tb: ";  cin >> b;
  cout << "\tc: ";  cin >> c;
  cout << "The equation is: " << a << "*x*x + " << b
       << "*x + " << c << " = 0\n";
  double d = b*b - 4*a*c;  // discriminant
  if (d < 0)
  { cout << "The discriminant, d = " << d
         << " < 0, so there are no real solutions.\n";
    return 0;
  }
  double sqrtd = sqrt(d);
  double x1 = (-b + sqrtd)/(2*a);
  double x2 = (-b - sqrtd)/(2*a);
  cout << "The solutions are:\n";
  cout << "\tx1 = " << x1 << endl;
  cout << "\tx2 = " << x2 << endl;
  cout << "Check:";
  cout << "\ta*x1*x1 + b*x1 + c = " <<  a*x1*x1 + b*x1 + c;
  cout << "\n\ta*x2*x2 + b*x2 + c = " <<  a*x2*x2 + b*x2 + c;
}
```

On the same input, 2, 1, and 3, to attempt to solve the quadratic equation $2x^2 + x + 3 = 0$, this version gives more informative output. When the discriminant $d < 0$, the program prints a diagnostic message and then exits by the `return 0` statement.

```
Enter the coefficients of a quadratic equation:
        a: 2
        b: 1
        c: 3
The equation is: 1*x*x + 2*x + 3 = 0
The discriminant, d = -8 < 0, so there are no real solutions.
```

The `if` statement is a *conditional*; its action depends upon the value of a condition, which is a boolean expression. C++ also has a `switch` statement. Its action depends upon the value of an integer expression.

EXAMPLE 1.5 A Simple Calculator Simulation

```
int main()
{ // performs arithmetic on integers
  int m, n;
  cout << "Enter two integers: ";   cin >> m >> n;
  char op;
  cout << "Enter an operator (+,-,*,/,%): ";   cin >> op;
  cout << "\t" << m << op << n << " = ";
  switch (op)
  { case '+': cout << m + n; break;
    case '-': cout << m - n; break;
    case '*': cout << m * n; break;
    case '/': cout << m / n; break;
    case '%': cout << m % n;
  }
}
```

The `op` variable holds one character. Since `char` is an integral type, it can be used to control the `switch` statement.

```
Enter two integers: 30 7
Enter an operator (+,-,*,/,%): %
        30%7 = 2
```

In this run, the value of `op` is the character `'%'`, so the statements that follow `case '/'`: execute.

Note the need for `break` statements within the cases of the `switch` statement. Without them, control would "fall through," executing all the cases after the one selected.

In addition to the `if` and the `switch` statements, C++ also has the *conditional expression operator* for conditional execution. Its syntax is

    (condition ? value1 : value2)

Its value is **value1** if **condition** is true, and **value2** if **condition** is false.

EXAMPLE 1.6 The Conditional Expression Operator

```
int main()
{ // prints the maximum of two given integers
  int m, n;
  cout << "Enter two integers: ";   cin >> m >> n;
  cout << "Their maximum is " << ( m>n ? m : n );
}
```

```
Enter two integers: 44 33
Their maximum is 44
```

1.3 OPERATORS

An *operator* is a function that takes one or more expressions as input and returns an expression that uses a special infix symbol instead of the usual functional notation. For example, the operator "+" is written "22 + 44" instead of "+(22, 44)". The values that the operator operates on are called its *operands*. The operands of "22 + 44" are 22 and 44.

The five *arithmetic operators* are: +, -, *, /, %. These are all *binary operators*, which means that they have two operands. The + and - operators also have unary versions, meaning only one operand.

The arithmetic operators can be combined with the standard assignment operator (=) to produce five more *assignment operators*: +=, -=, *=, /=, %=. For example,

```
x *= y;
```
means multiply x by y.

The six *relational operators* are: <, >, <=, >=, ==, !=. These have the same meanings as the corresponding mathematical operators $<$, $>$, $\leq$, $\geq$, $=$, and $\neq$.

Don't confuse the equality operator == with the assignment operator =. In mathematics, both operators are represented by the equals sign =. In C++, these two operators have very different effects. The equality operator == tests for equality of expressions; it changes no values and returns either `true` or `false`. The assignment operator = assigns the vlue of the expression on its right to the object on its left and returns that value. Using the assignment operator in a condition is one of the most common errors made by C++ programmers:

```
if (n = 0) ++k;   // ERROR: assignment operator used by mistake
```
The expression (n = 0) evaluates to 0, which is then interpreted to mean `false`. The author of that code probably meant to write

```
if (n == 0) ++k;   // correct usage
```
The three *logical operators* are: &&, ||, !. These are also called *boolean operators* because both their operands and their resulting values are *boolean expressions* (expressions of type `bool`).

The && and || operators allow for "short circuiting," which means that their second operand is not evaluated unless necessary. For example,

```
if (x == 0 || y/x > 1) ++k;   // OK: will not crash if x is 0
```
Evaluating the expression y/x > 1 would generate a run-time error (program "crash") if the value of x were 0. But if it is, the first operand will evaluate to `true`, causing the second operand to be ignored. Similarly,

```
if (x != 0 && y/x > 1) ++k;   // OK: will not crash if x is 0
```
is also safe because here the second operand will be ignored if the first evaluates to `false`.

Every operator expression has a value and a type. For example, the value of the expression

```
n = 44
```
is 44 and has type `int`. That allows operators to be chained, like this:

```
k = m += n = 44;
```
This means: (1) assign 44 to n; (2) add that value (44) to m; assign that value to k. Chaining assignment operators works from right to left. On the other hand, chaining arithmetic operators and chaining input/output operators work from left to right:

```
z = 88 - x + y;                          // the "-" is evaluated before the "+"
cout << x << ", " << y << ", " << z << "\n";
```

Operators follow standard precedence rules that determine the order of evaluation when several operators are used in the same expression. For example, `*` has higher precedence than `+`, so in the expression `x + y * z`, the expression `y * z` will be evaluated first. And `<` has higher precedence than `||`, so in the expression `(x<4 || y<8)`, the expressions `x<4` and `y<8` will be evaluated first. The following table groups all the C++ operators according to their precedence levels, from highest (`::`) to lowest (`,`).

Precedence of Operators

`::`
`.`, `->`, `[]`, `()`, `++` (post-increment), `--`(post-decrement), `typeid`, `dynamic_cast`, `static_cast`, `reinterpret_cast`, `const_cast`
`~`, `!`, `+`, `-` (unary), `++` (pre-increment), `--`(pre-decrement), `new`, `delete`, `&` (reference), `*` (dereference), `sizeof`
`.*`, `->*`
`*` (multiply), `/`, `%`
`+`, `-` (binary)
`<<`, `>>`
`<`, `>`, `<=`, `>=`
`==`, `!=`
`&` (bitwise AND)
`^` (bitwise XOR)
`|` (bitwise OR)
`&&`
`||`
`=`, `+=`, `-=`, `*=`, `/=`, `%=`, `<<=`, `>>=`, `&=`, `|=`, `^=`
`?:`
`throw`
`,`

These precedence rules can be overridden by using parentheses. For example, in the expression `x * (y + z)`, the expression `y + z` will be evaluated first.

1.4 ITERATION

To *iterate* means to repeat one or more statements until a certain condition is true. This process is called *iteration*. C++ has four mechanisms for producing iteration: the `goto` statement, the `do` statement, the `while` statement, and the `for` statement.

EXAMPLE 1.7 Using a `goto` Loop to Sum Reciprocals

This program computes and prints the sum $1 + 1/2 + 1/3 + \cdots + 1/100$.

```
int main()
{ const int N=100;
  double sum=0.0;
  int x=1;
  repeat: sum += 1.0/x++;
  if (x<=N) goto repeat;
  cout << "The sum of the first " << N << " reciprocals is " << sum;
}
```
The sum of the first 100 reciprocals is 5.18738

The expression `repeat:` on the fifth line is called a *label*. It locates a line in the program to which execution control can be diverted, as it is on the next line, by means of a `goto` statement. The effect here is that the statement

```
sum += 1.0/x++;
```
is executed repeatedly as long as the condition `(x<=N)` is true. Thus, the values 1.0/1, 1.0/2, 1.0/3, $\cdots$ are added to `sum` until the value of x exceeds 100.

Note the use of the `const` keyword on the second line. This specifies that the integer N is a constant and prevents its value from being changed. (C++ programmers usually capitalize all the letters of a constant identifier.)

EXAMPLE 1.8 Using a do...while Loop to Sum Reciprocals

```
int main()
{ const int N=100;
  double sum=0.0;
  int x=1;
  do sum += 1.0/x++;
  while (x <= N);
  cout << "The sum of the first " << N << " reciprocals is " << sum;
}
```
The sum of the first 100 reciprocals is 5.18738

This program is the same as the program in Example 1.7 except that the keywords **do** and **while** are used in place of the **repeat** label and the **goto** keyword. The effect is the same.

EXAMPLE 1.9 Using a while Loop to Sum Reciprocals

```
int main()
{ const int N=100;
  double sum=0.0;
  int x=1;
  while (x <= N)
    sum += 1.0/x++;
  cout << "The sum of the first " << N << " reciprocals is " << sum;
}
```
The sum of the first 100 reciprocals is 5.18738

This program is the same as the program in Example 1.8 except that the keyword `do` is not used and the `while` condition is placed ahead of the statement to be repeated. The effect is the same.

EXAMPLE 1.10 Using a `for` Loop to Sum Reciprocals

```
int main()
{ const int N=100;
  double sum=0.0;
  for (int x=1; x <= N; x++)
    sum += 1.0/x;
  cout << "The sum of the first " << N << " reciprocals is " << sum;
}
The sum of the first 100 reciprocals is 5.18738
```

This program is the same as the program in Example 1.9 except that the keyword `while` is replaced with the keyword `for` and the three expressions `int x=1`, `x <= N`, and `x++` are placed together in a control descriptor delimited by parentheses. The effect is the same.

Like any other statement or block of statements, a loop may be inserted in another loop. The result is called *nested loops*.

EXAMPLE 1.11 Using Nested `for` Loops to Print a Triangle of Stars

```
int main()
{ const int N=10;
  for (int i=0; i<N; i++)
  { for (int j=0; j<2*N; j++)
      if (j<N-i || j>N+i) cout << " ";
      else cout << "*";
    cout << "\n";
  }
}
          *
         ***
        *****
       *******
      *********
     ***********
    *************
   ***************
  *****************
 *******************
```

The outer `for` loop prints one line on each iteration. The inner `for` loop prints one character, either a blank or a star, on each iteration.

1.5 FUNCTIONS

A *function* is a subprogram that can be called (invoked) from another function and can return a value to it. Every C++ program is required to begin with the `main()` function. Relegating separate tasks to separate functions is a fundamental programming technique that leads to simpler and more efficient programs.

EXAMPLE 1.12 Using a Separate Function

```
void printRow(const int, const int);   // prototype

int main()
{ const int N=10;
  for (int i=0; i<N; i++)
    printRow(i,N);
}
void printRow(const int row, const int N)  // implementation
{ for (int j=0; j<2*N; j++)
    if (j<N-row || j>N+row) cout << " ";
    else cout << "*";
  cout << "\n";
}
```

This program has the same results as that in Example 1.11. It has relegated the task of printing one row to the separate `printRow()` function. This is a `void` function because it does not return anything to `main()`. It has two `int` parameters: `row` and `N`. They are passed values from the arguments `i` and `N`.

The function is declared by the one-line prototype above `main()`, and it is defined by its complete implementation below `main()`. Note that the prototype omits the parameter names (optional) and ends with a semicolon (required).

Notice that both parameters are declared to be `const`. It is good programming practice to declare as `const` any object that is intended not to be changed.

EXAMPLE 1.13 A `power()` Function

```
double power(const double, const int);

int main()
{ cout << "power(2,0) = " << power(2,0) << "\n";
  cout << "power(2,1) = " << power(2,1) << "\n";
  cout << "power(2,2) = " << power(2,2) << "\n";
  cout << "power(2,3) = " << power(2,3) << "\n";
  cout << "power(2,-3) = " << power(2,-3) << "\n";
  cout << "power(2.01,3) = " << power(2.01,3) << "\n";
}

double power(const double x, int n)
{ double y=1.0;
  for (int i=0; i<n; i++)   // if n>0, y = x*x*...*x (n times)
    y *= x;
  for (int i=0; i>n; i--)   // if n<0, y = 1/x*x*...*x (n times)
    y /= x;
  return y;
}
power(2,0) = 1
power(2,1) = 2
power(2,2) = 4
power(2,3) = 8
power(2,-3) = 0.125
power(2.01,3) = 8.1206
```

The call `power(x,n)` returns the value of x^n. Notice that if n is 0, neither loop executes; otherwise exactly one loop executes.

The program in Example 1.13 is a *test driver*. Its only purpose is to test the function. All functions should be tested with a test driver.

1.6 STRINGS

A *string* is a sequence of characters. Its *length* is the number of characters it contains. If the string is empty, then its length is 0; otherwise its length is a positive integer.

Standard C++ has a built-in `string` class. The following examples illustrate some of its functionality.

EXAMPLE 1.14 The `length()` and `substr()` Functions

```
int main()
{ string s="ABCDEFGH";
  cout << "s = [" << s << "]\n";
  cout << "s.length() = " << s.length() << "\n";
  cout << "s.substr(2,4) = [" << s.substr(2,4) << "]\n";
}
s = [ABCDEFGH]
s.length() = 8
s.substr(2,4) = [CDEF]
```

The `length()` function, when applied to a string using the dot operator this way, returns the length of that string.

The `substr()` function returns a substring of that string. When called like this

```
s.substr(k,len)
```

it extracts `len` characters after skipping the first `k` characters.

EXAMPLE 1.15 Reading Words from the Standard Input Stream `cin`

```
int main()
{ string word;
  while (cin >> word)
    cout << "\t[" << word << "] " << word.length() << "\n";
}
Now is the winter of our discontent
        [Now] 3
        [is] 2
        [the] 3
        [winter] 6
        [of] 2
        [our] 3
        [discontent] 10
```

When the input operator `>>` is applied to a string, it reads as a word all the characters up to the next white space character (blank, newline, *etc.*) after skipping over any current white space.

EXAMPLE 1.16 Comparing Words

```
int main()
{ const string s1 = "COMPUTE";
  const string s2 = "COMPUTER";
  const string s3 = "COMPUTABLE";
  const string s4 = "COMPUTARE";
  printComparison(s1,s2);
  printComparison(s1,s3);
  printComparison(s1,s4);
  printComparison(s2,s2);
  printComparison(s3,s4);
}

void printComparison(const string s1, const string s2)
{ if (s1 < s2) cout << s1 << " < " << s2 << "\n";
  else if (s1 == s2) cout << s1 << " == " << s2 << "\n";
  else cout << s1 << " > " << s2 << "\n";
}
```
```
COMPUTE < COMPUTER
COMPUTE > COMPUTABLE
COMPUTE > COMPUTARE
COMPUTER == COMPUTER
COMPUTABLE < COMPUTARE
```

Strings are compared *lexicographically* (*i.e.*, according to their dictionary ordering). The string `"COMPUTABLE"` is less than the string `"COMPUTARE"` because their first seven characters match, and the eighth character of the first string (`'B'`) comes before the eighth character of the second string (`'R'`). The string `"COMPUTE"` is less than the string `"COMPUTER"` because the first string is a proper substring of the second.

The `string` class has two concatenation operators: `+` and `+=`. The `+` operator creates a new string that is the concatenation of its two operands. The `+=` operator appends the right operand to the left operand.

EXAMPLE 1.17 Concatenating Strings

```
int main()
{ const string s = "Pease-porridge ";
  string nurseryRhyme = s + "hot, " + s + "cold,\n";
  nurseryRhyme += s + "in the pot, nine days old.";
  cout << nurseryRhyme;
}
```
```
Pease-porridge hot, Pease-porridge cold,
Pease-porridge in the pot, nine days old.
```

The `string` class has a `find()` function that searches for substrings.

EXAMPLE 1.18 Searching for Substrings

```
int main()
{ const string str = "Mississippi";
  const string substr = "issi";
  cout << "str.find(substr) = " << str.find(substr) << "\n";
  cout << "str.find(substr,2) = " << str.find(substr,2) << "\n";
  cout << "str.find(substr,8) = " << str.find(substr,8) << "\n";
  cout << "           UINT_MAX = " << UINT_MAX << "\n";
}
str.find(substr) = 1
str.find(substr,2) = 4
str.find(substr,8) = 4294967295
           UINT_MAX = 4294967295
```

The call str.find(substr) returns the first starting position in str of the substring substr. The call str.find(substr,2) returns the first starting position in str of the substring substr after the first 2 characters. The call str.find(substr,8) returns a large integer (UINT_MAX) indicating that the substring was not found after the first 8 characters.

Note that the unsigned int constant UINT_MAX is defined in the <limits> header which must be included in the program in Example 1.18.

1.7 FILES

In Standard C++, input from and output to a text file is similar to input from cin and output to cout.

EXAMPLE 1.19 Capitalizing Words in a File

```
#include <ctype.h>    // defines isalpha() function
#include <fstream>    // defines ifstream and ofstream classes
int main()
{ ifstream infile("input.txt");
  ofstream outfile("output.txt");
  string line;
  while (getline(infile,line))
  { for (int i=0; i<line.length(); i++)
      if (i==0 || line[i-1] == ' ' && isalpha(line[i]))
        line[i] = toupper(line[i]);
    outfile << line << endl;
  }
}
```

input.txt

```
we hold these truths to be self-evident,
that all men are created equal, that they
are endowed by their creator with certain
unalienable rights, that among these are
life, liberty, and the pursuit of happiness
```

output.txt

```
We Hold These Truths To Be Self-evident,
That All Men Are Created Equal, That They
Are Endowed By Their Creator With Certain
Unalienable Rights, That Among These Are
Life, Liberty, And The Pursuit Of Happiness
```

The infile and outfile objects are streams that represent the external text files input.txt and output.txt. The call getline(infile,line) reads one line of text from the input.txt file into the string object line and returns true (unless the end of the file has been reached in which case it returns `false`). The `for` loop then capitalizes each word in that `line` object. Then the line is output to the `output.txt` file.

Review Questions

1.1   What is the purpose of the preprocessor directive `#include <iostream>`?

1.2   What is the purpose of the following statement?
    `using namespace std;`

1.3   What is the purpose of the preprocessor directive `#include <cmath>`?

1.4   What is the purpose of the `break` statement in a `switch` statement?

1.5   How is the expression (`m>n ? m : n`) evaluated?

1.6   What is an operator?

1.7   What is an arithmetic operator?

1.8   What is an assignment operator?

1.9   What is a relational operator?

1.10 What is a logical operator?

1.11 Does the order of the operands matter in the following statement?
    `if (x == 0 || y/x > 1) ++k;   // OK: will not crash if x is 0`

1.12 What is a label in C++?

1.13 What are the differences between a `do...while` loop and a `while` loop?

1.14 What are nested loops?

1.15 What is a test driver?

1.16 What does "lexicographic order" mean?

1.17 What is the purpose of the preprocessor directive `#include <limits>`?

1.18 What is the purpose of the preprocessor directive `#include <ctype.h>`?

1.19 What is the purpose of the preprocessor directive `#include <fstream>`?

Problems

1.1   Write a program that prints the maximum of four given integers. For example:
```
Enter four integers: 44 33 66 55
Their maximum is 66
```

1.2   Write a program that prints the median of five given integers. For example:
```
Enter five integers: 44 33 66 55 77
Their median is 55
```

1.3   Modify the program in Example 1.5 on page 4 so that it gives the correct solution when $a = 0$.

1.4   Write and run a program that inputs a letter and then prints the musical syllable that represents that letter as a tone on the diatonic scale: "do" for C, "re" for D, "mi" for E, "fa" for F, "so" for G, "la" for A, and "ti" for B. Use a `switch` statement.

1.5   Write and test a program that plays the game of "rock, paper, scissors." In this game, each of two players simultaneously say (or display a hand symbol representing) either "rock," "paper," or "scissors." The winner is the one whose choice beats that of the other. The rules are: paper beats (wraps) rock, rock beats (breaks) scissors, and scissors beat (cut) paper. Use enumerations for the choices and for the results. Use the `rand()` function defined in the standard header `<cstdlib>` to generate a random choice for the computer.

```
Choose either rock, scissors, or paper (R/S/P): S
I chose rock.
I won.
```

1.6   Write and test a program that inputs a dollar amount and then prints the tax due on that annual income, according to the following 1998 U.S. Tax Rate Schedule:

Schedule X

If the amount on Form 1040, line 37, is: Over—	But not over—	Enter on Form 1040, line 38	of the amount over—
$0	$22,100	15%	$0
22,100	53,500	$3,315.00 + 28%	22,100
53,500	115,000	12,107.00 + 31%	53,500
115,000	250,000	31,172.00 + 36%	115,000
250,000	-------	79,772.00 + 39.6%	250,000

1.7   Write a program that amortizes a loan, like this:

```
Enter amount of loan (in $): 1000
Enter monthly payment (in $): 200
Enter interest rate (as a %): 7.5

Month  Interest    Amount
-----  --------    -------
  0                1000.00
  1      6.25       806.25
  2      5.04       611.29
  3      3.82       415.11
  4      2.59       217.70
  5      1.36        19.06
  6      0.12         0.00
-----  --------    ------
```

1.8   Use a pair of nested `for` loops to print a diamond of stars, like this:

```
   *
  ***
 *****
*******
 *****
  ***
   *
```

1.9   Use a pair of nested `for` loops to print an "X" of stars, like this:

```
*       *
 *     *
  *   *
   * *
    *
   * *
  *   *
 *     *
*       *
```

1.10   Write and run a program that prints the multiplication table for integers from 1 to 12.

1.11   Write and test a function that converts Fahrenheit temperatures to Celsius. For example, `celsius(212)` would return `100`.

1.12   Write and test a function that returns $n!$ (factorial). For example, `factorial(5)` would return `120`. Use the fact that each number is the sum of the two above it.

1.13   Write and test a program that computes e^x for a given value of x, using the formula

$$e^x = 1 + \frac{x}{1} + \frac{x^2}{2!} + \frac{x^3}{3!} + \frac{x^4}{4!} + \frac{x^5}{5!} + \cdots$$

1.14   Write and test a function that implements the following algorithm (known as the *Babylonian Algorithm*) to compute the square root of $x > 0$.

  1. Let $y = 1$.
  2. If $x > 2$, let $y = x/2$.
  3. Let $y = (y + x/y)/2$ (the average of y and x/y).
  4. If y^2 is not close enough to x, repeat step 3.
  5. Return y.

1.15   Write and test a function that returns the *integral binary logarithm* of a given positive number (the number of times it can be divided in two). For example, `f(500)` would return `9`.

1.16   Write and test a boolean function that determines whether a given year is a leap year. Under our current (Gregorian) calendar, a year is a leap year if it is divisible by 400 or if it is divisible by 4 but not by 100. For example, the years 1996 and 2000 are leap years, but the years 1900 and 1999 are not.

1.17   Write and test a boolean function that determines whether a given positive integer is prime.

1.18   Write and test a function that returns the sum of the digits of a positive integer. For example, `digitSum(49205)` would return `20`.

1.19   Write and test a function that reverses the digits of a positive integer. For example, `reverse(49205)` would return `50294`.

1.20   Write and test a function that returns a string that is the reverse of the string passed to it. For example, `reverse("COMPUTER")` would return `"RETUPMOC"`.

1.21   Write and test a boolean function that determines whether a given string is a palindrome (using only its capitalized letters). For example, the call `isPalindrome("Able was I, ere I saw elba.")` would return true.

1.22   Write and test a program that right-justifies a text file.

Answers to Review Questions

1.1   The preprocessor directive `#include <iostream>` is needed whenever the standard output stream object `cout` or the standard input stream object `cin` is used because they are defined in the `<iostream>` header file.

1.2   Without the statement `using namespace std;` the standard output stream object `cout` would have to be referred to as `std::cout`, and the standard input stream object `cin` would have to be referred to as `std::cin`.

1.3   The preprocessor directive `#include <cmath>` is needed whenever any of the standard mathematical functions such as `sqrt()` are used because they are defined in the `<cmath>` header file. (See Example 1.3 on page 2.)

1.4   Without including a `break` statement after each case in a `switch` statement, all the statements after the `case` selected would execute. (See Example 1.5 on page 4.)

1.5   The expression (`m>n ? m : n`) is evaluated to the value of `m` if the condition `m>n` is true; otherwise it is evaluated to the value of `n`. It is called the *conditional expression operator*.

1.6 An *operator* is a function whose name is a symbol such as + that is used in infix notation like this: x + 5. Its arguments (*e.g.*, x and 5) are called *operands*.

1.7 An *arithmetic operator* is an operator such as + whose operands and result all have a numeric type.

1.8 An *assignment operator* is an operator such as += that is formed from another operator and the assignment operator. It applies the other operator with the right operand to the left operand.

1.9 A *relational operator* is an operator such as == that evaluates equality or order.

1.10 A *logical operator* is one that applies a logical connective such as "OR" to its two boolean operands resulting in another boolean expression.

1.11 The order of the operands in the statement
```
if (y/x > 1 || x == 0) ++k;   // OK: will not crash if x is 0
```
does matter. If the value of x is 0, that statement will crash, but the following version will not:
```
if (x == 0 || y/x > 1) ++k;   // OK: will not crash if x is 0
```

1.12 In C++, a *label* is an identifier followed by a colon and used as a prefix to a statement. Labels are necessary to designate the destination of a goto statement. (See Example 1.7 on page 6.)

1.13 In a do...while loop the control condition is at the end of the loop; in a while loop it is at the beginning. Consequently, a do...while loop must always iterate at least once, but it has the advantage of being able to initialize any control variables inside the loop.

1.14 A *nested loop* is a loop placed inside another loop. (See Example 1.11 on page 8.)

1.15 A *test driver* is a program whose only purpose is to test a function or class. (See Example 1.13 on page 9.)

1.16 The phrase *lexicographic order* refers to the usual dictionary ordering of words and strings. (See Example 1.16 on page 11.)

1.17 The preprocessor directive #include <limits> defines the standard constants that hold the minimum and maximum values of the numeric types. (See Example 1.18 on page 12.)

1.18 The preprocessor directive #include <ctype.h> defines certain character processing functions such as isalpha() and toupper(). (See Example 1.19 on page 12.)

1.19 The preprocessor directive #include <fstream> defines the ifstream and ofstream classes needed for file processing. (See Example 1.19 on page 12.)

Solutions to Problems

1.1 Prints the maximum of four given integers:
```cpp
int main()
{ int n1, n2, n3, n4;
  cout << "Enter four integers: ";
  cin >> n1 >> n2 >> n3 >> n4;
  int max=n1;
  if (n2 > max) max = n2;
  if (n3 > max) max = n3;
  if (n4 > max) max = n4;
  cout << "Their maximum is " << max << "\n";
}
```

1.2 Prints the median of five given integers:
```cpp
int main()
{ int n, n1, n2, n3;
  cout << "Enter five integers: ";
  cin >> n;
  n1 = n;
  cin >> n;
  if (n < n1) { n2 = n1; n1 = n; }
  else n2 = n;   // now n1 <= n2
  cin >> n;
```

```
      if (n < n1) { n3 = n2; n2 = n1; n1 = n; }
      else if (n < n2) { n3 = n2; n2 = n; }
      else n3 = n;  // now n1 <= n2 <= n3
      cin >> n;
      if (n < n1) { n3 = n2; n2 = n1; n1 = n; }
      else if (n < n2) { n3 = n2; n2 = n; }
      else if (n < n3) n3 = n;   // now n1 <= n2 <= n3 <= other n
      cin >> n;
      if (n < n1) { n3 = n2; n2 = n1; n1 = n; }
      else if (n < n2) { n3 = n2; n2 = n; }
      else if (n < n3) n3 = n;   // now n1 <= n2 <= n3 <= other n's
      cout << "Their median is " << n3 << "\n";
    }
```

1.3   Implements the quadratic formula:

```
      #include <cmath>   // defines the sqrt() function
      #include <iostream>
      using namespace std;
      int main()
      { // implements the quadratic formula
        double a, b, c;
        cout << "Enter the coefficients of a quadratic equation:" <<
      endl;
        cout << "\ta: ";   cin >> a;
        cout << "\tb: ";   cin >> b;
        cout << "\tc: ";   cin >> c;
        cout << "The equation is: " << a << "*x*x + " << b
            << "*x + " << c << " = 0\n";
        if (a == 0.0)
        { if (b == 0.0)
            if (c == 0.0) cout << "Every x satisfies that equation.\n";
            else cout << "No x satisfies that equation.\n";
          else cout << "The unique solution is: x = " << -c/b << endl;
          return 0;
        }
        double d = b*b -     *c;   // discriminant
        if (d < 0)
        { cout << "The discriminant, d = " << d
              << " < 0, so there are no real solutions.\n";
          return 0;
        }
        double sqrtd = sqrt(d);
        double x1 = (-b + sqrtd)/(2*a);
        double x2 = (-b - sqrtd)/(2*a);
        cout << "The solutions are:\n";
        cout << "\tx1 = " << x1 << endl;
        cout << "\tx2 = " << x2 << endl;
        cout << "Check:";
        cout << "\ta*x1*x1 + b*x1 + c = " <<  a*x1*x1 + b*x1 + c;
        cout << "\n\ta*x2*x2 + b*x2 + c = " <<  a*x2*x2 + b*x2 + c;
      }
```

1.4   Prints syllable for a given tone on the diatonic scale:

```
      int main()
      { // prints the syllable for a given tone:
        char tone;
        string syllable;
        cout << "Enter the tone (e.g. G): ";
```

```
      cin >> tone;
      switch (tone)
      { case 'A': syllable = "la";  break;
        case 'B': syllable = "ti";  break;
        case 'C': syllable = "do";  break;
        case 'D': syllable = "re";  break;
        case 'E': syllable = "mi";  break;
        case 'F': syllable = "fa";  break;
        case 'G': syllable = "so";  break;
        default : syllable = "error";
      }
      cout << "The syllable for " << tone << " is \""
           << syllable << "\".\n";
```

1.5   Simulates the game of "rock, scissors, paper":

```
      #include <cstdlib> // defines the rand() function
      #include <iostream>
      using namespace std;
      enum Choice {PAPER, SCISSORS, ROCK};
      enum Result {YOU, ME, TIE};
      int main()
      { // each player makes a choice:
        Choice yours, mine;
        Result winner = YOU;
        string s;
        cout << "Choose either rock, scissors, or paper (R/S/P): ";
        cin >> s;
        switch (s[0])
        { case 'R': case 'r': yours = ROCK;      break;
          case 'S': case 's': yours = SCISSORS;  break;
          case 'P': case 'p': yours = PAPER;     break;
          default:  yours = ROCK;
        }  int n = rand();  // generates a random integer
        int n = rand();  // generates a random integer
        switch (n%3)
        { case 0: mine = PAPER;     cout << "I chose paper.\n";
      break;
          case 1: mine = SCISSORS;  cout << "I chose scissors.\n";
      break;
          case 2: mine = ROCK;      cout << "I chose rock.\n";
        }
        if (yours == mine) winner = TIE;
        if (yours == PAPER && mine == SCISSORS
          || yours == SCISSORS && mine == ROCK
          || yours == ROCK && mine == PAPER) winner = ME;
        switch (winner)
        { case YOU: cout << "You won!\n"; break;
          case  ME: cout << "I won.\n";   break;
          case TIE: cout << "We tied.\n";
        }
      }
```

1.6   Computes U.S. federal income tax:

```
      #include <iostream>
      using namespace std;
      int main()
      { // prints tax due on annual income:
        const float BRACKET1 =  22100;
```

```cpp
      const float BRACKET2 =   53500;
      const float BRACKET3 = 115000;
      const float BRACKET4 = 250000;
      const float RATE1 = 0.15;
      const float RATE2 = 0.28;
      const float RATE3 = 0.31;
      const float RATE4 = 0.36;
      const float RATE5 = 0.396;
      const float BASE2 = 3315.00;
      const float BASE3 = 12107.00;
      const float BASE4 = 31172.00;
      const float BASE5 = 79772.00;
      float income, tax;
      cout << "Enter taxable income: ";
      cin >> income;
      if       (income <= BRACKET1) tax = RATE1*income;
      else if (income <= BRACKET2) tax = BASE2 +
   RATE2*(income-BRACKET1);
      else if (income <= BRACKET3) tax = BASE3 +
   RATE3*(income-BRACKET2);
      else if (income <= BRACKET4) tax = BASE4 +
   RATE4*(income-BRACKET3);
      else                         tax = BASE5 + RATE5*(income-BRACKET4);
      cout << "Your tax on $" << income << " is $" << tax;
```

1.7   Amortizes a loan:

```cpp
      #include <iomanip>      // defines setw() function
      #include <iostream>     // defines cin and cout objects
      using namespace std;   // obviates the std:: prefix
      int main()
      { double amount, payment, rate, interest;
        cout << "Enter amount of loan (in $): ";   cin >> amount;
        cout << "Enter monthly payment (in $): ";   cin >> payment;
        cout << "Enter interest rate (as a %): ";   cin >> rate;
        rate /= 100;  // convert from percentage to decimal
        rate /= 12;    // convert annual rate to monthly rate
        cout << setw(6) << "\n Month  Interest     Amount\n";
        cout << setw(6) <<    " -----  --------    -------\n";
        cout << setiosflags(ios::fixed|ios::showpoint) << setpreci-
   sion(2);
        cout << setw(6) << 0 << setw(20) << amount << "\n";
        for (int month=1; amount>0; month++)
        { interest = rate*amount;
          amount += interest;
          amount -= payment;
          cout << setw(6) << month
               << setiosflags(ios::fixed|ios::showpoint)
               << setprecision(2)
               << setw(10) << interest
               << setw(10) << (amount>0?amount:0) << "\n";
        }
        cout << setw(6) << " -----  --------    ------\n";
      }
```

1.8   Prints a diamond of stars:

```cpp
      int main()
      { const int N=5;
        for (int i=0; i<=2*N; i++)
```

```
      { for (int j=0; j<=2*N; j++)
          if (i<=N)
              if (j<N-i || j>N+i) cout << " ";
              else cout << "*";
          else
              if (j<i-N || j>3*N-i) cout << " ";
              else cout << "*";
          cout << "\n";
      }
  }
```

1.9   Prints an "X" of stars:

```
  int main()
  { const int N=5;
    for (int i=0; i<=2*N; i++)
    { for (int j=0; j<=2*N; j++)
        if (i<=N)
            if (j<N-i || j>N+i) cout << " ";
            else cout << "*";
        else
            if (j<i-N || j>3*N-i) cout << " ";
            else cout << "*";
        cout << "\n";
    }
  }
```

1.10   Prints a multiplication table:

```
  #include <iomanip.h>
  #include <iostream>
  using namespace std;
  int main()
  { setiosflags(ios::right);
    const int N=12;
    for (int x=1; x <= N; x++)
    { for (int y=1; y <= N; y++)
        cout << setw(5) << x*y;
      cout << endl;
    }
  }
```

1.11   Tests a function that converts Fahrenheit to Celsius:

```
  #include <iostream>
  using namespace std;
  float celsius(float);
  int main()
  { for (int x=2; x<232; x += 10)
      cout << x << "\t" << celsius(x) << "\n";
  }
  float celsius(float x)
  { return 5.0/9.0*(x-32);
  }
```

1.12   Tests the factorial function:

```
  #include <iostream>
  using namespace std;
  int factorial(int);
  int main()
  { for (int n=0; n<12; n++)
      cout << n << "\t" << factorial(n) << "\n";
  }
```

```
    int factorial(int n)
    { int f=1;
      for (int i=2; i<=n; i++)
        f *= i;
      return f;
    }
```

1.13 Computes e^x:

```
    #include <iomanip.h>
    #include <iostream>
    using namespace std;
    int main()
    { const double TOL=5e-15;   // maximal round-off error
      double x;
      cout << "Enter x: ";
      cin >> x;
      double t=1, y=1;
      int n=0;
      while(t>TOL || -t>TOL)
      { t *= x/++n;
        y += t;
        cout << setw(16) << n << ":"
             << setprecision(15) << setw(20) << y << "\n";
      }
    }
```

1.14 Implements the Babylonian Algorithm for computing the square root:

```
    #include <iomanip.h>
    #include <iostream>
    using namespace std;
    double f(double);
    int main()
    { for (double x=0.0; x<=2.0; x += 0.25)
      { double y = f(x);
        cout << setw(6)  << x << setw(10) << y << setw(6)  << y*y <<
"\n";
      }
    }
    double f(double x)
    { const double TOL=5e-15;
      if (x<=0) return 0.0;
      double y = (x>2?x/2:1);
      do { y = (y + x/y)/2; }
      while (x>y*y+TOL || y*y>x+TOL);
      return y;
    }
```

1.15 Tests the binary logarithm:

```
    #include <iostream>
    using namespace std;
    int lg(double);
    int main()
    { cout << "lg(1) = " << lg(1) << "\n";
      cout << "lg(2) = " << lg(2) << "\n";
      cout << "lg(3) = " << lg(3) << "\n";
      cout << "lg(4) = " << lg(4) << "\n";
      cout << "lg(5) = " << lg(5) << "\n";
      cout << "lg(100) = " << lg(100) << "\n";
      cout << "lg(1000) = " << lg(1000) << "\n";
```

```
      cout << "lg(100000) = " << lg(1000000) << "\n";
    }
    int lg(double x)
    { int y=0;
      while (x>1)
      { x /= 2;
        ++y;
      }
      return y;
    }
```

1.16 Tests the leap year function:

```
    #include <iostream>
    using namespace std;
    bool isLeap(int);
    int main()
    { cout << "isLeap(1900) = " << isLeap(1900) << "\n";
      cout << "isLeap(1996) = " << isLeap(1996) << "\n";
      cout << "isLeap(1999) = " << isLeap(1999) << "\n";
      cout << "isLeap(2000) = " << isLeap(2000) << "\n";
    }
    bool isLeap(int y)
    { if (y%400==0) return true;
      if (y%100==0) return false;
      if (y%4==0) return true;
      return false;
    }
```

1.17 Tests the primality function:

```
    #include <iostream>
    using namespace std;
    bool isPrime(int);
    int main()
    { const int N=500;
      for (int n=0; n<N; n++)
        if (isPrime(n)) cout << n << "\t";
    }
    bool isPrime(int n)
    { if (n<2) return false;
      if (n==2) return true;
      if (n%2==0) return false;
      for (int d=3; d<n; d += 2)
        if (n%d==0) return false;
      return true;
    }
```

1.18 Tests the sum of digits function:

```
    #include <iostream>
    using namespace std;
    int digitSum(int);
    int main()
    { int n;
      cout << "Enter a positive integer: ";  cin >> n;
      cout << "digitSum(n) = " << digitSum(n) << "\n";
    }
    int digitSum(int n)
    { int sum=0;
      while (n>0)
      { sum += n%10;
```

```
        n /= 10;
      }
      return sum;
    }
```

1.19   Tests the reverse digits function:

```
      #include <iostream>
      using namespace std;
      int reverse(int);
      int main()
      { int n;
        cout << "Enter a positive integer: ";  cin >> n;
        cout << "reverse(n) = " << reverse(n) << "\n";
      }
      int reverse(int n)
      { int r=0;
        while (n>0)
        { r = 10*r + n%10;
          n /= 10;
        }
        return r;
      }
```

1.20   Tests the reverse string function:

```
      #include <iostream>
      using namespace std;
      string reverse(string);
      int main()
      { string s;
        cout << "Enter a string: ";
        cin >> s;
        cout << "reverse(" << s << ") = " << reverse(s) << "\n";
      }
      string reverse(string s)
      { string r=s;
        int len=s.length();
        for (int i=0; i<len; i++)
          r[i] = s[len-1-i];
        return r;
      }
```

1.21   Tests for palindromes:

```
      #include <ctype.h>    // defines isalpha() and toupper()
      #include <iostream>
      using namespace std;
      bool isPalindrome(string);
      int main()
      { string s;
        cout << "Enter a string: ";
        while (getline(cin,s))
        { cout << "The string \"" << s;
          if (isPalindrome(s)) cout << "\" is a palindrome!\n";
          else cout << "\" is a not palindrome.\n";
          cout << "Enter another string: ";
        }
      }
      bool isPalindrome(string s)
      { string ss=s;
        int k=0;
```

```
          for (int i=0; i<s.length(); i++)  // extract k letters
            if (isalpha(s[i])) ss[k++]=toupper(s[i]);
          s = ss.substr(0,k);  // use only first k characters
          for (int i=0; i<k/2; i++)
            if (ss[i] != ss[k-1-i]) return false;
          return true;
        }
```

1.22   Right-justifies a text file:

```
        #include <fstream>
        using namespace std;
        int main()
        { const int WIDTH=60;
          ifstream in("Butler.txt");
          ofstream out("Butler.justified.txt");
          string s;
          while (getline(in,s))
            out << string(WIDTH-s.length(),' ') << s << "\n";
        }
```

Chapter 2

Pointers and Arrays

2.1 POINTERS

The declarations
```
int n=44;
string s="Hello";
```
declare the variable n initialized to the value 44 and the string object s initialized to the value "Hello". Variables and objects are sequences of bytes in memory that have associated names and types. The identifier n is the name of an integer of type int, and the identifier s is the name of an object of type string. The *address* of a variable or object is the address of its first byte of memory storage. Addresses are usually expressed as hexadecimal numerals. In the picture above, the address of the variable n would be 0x18ff24b8 and the address of the object s would be 0x18ff24bc.

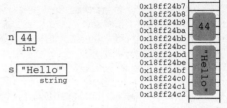

A *pointer* is a variable whose value either is 0 or is the address of some other variable or object. If its value is 0, we say the pointer is *null*. Otherwise, we say that the pointer *points* to the variable or object whose address it stores. An uninitialized pointer is called a *dangling pointer*. Like any other uninitialized variable its value is unpredictable.

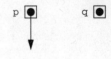

A pointer's type is "pointer to *xxxx*", where *xxxx* is the type of the variable or object to which it points. The identifier for "pointer *xxxx*" is *xxxx**. for example:
```
int* p;          // a dangling pointer
int* q=0;        // a null pointer
int* pn=&n;      // points to n
string* ps=&s;   // points to s
```
The picture at right is a common way to represent pointers. Note that the dangling pointer p points at nothing, and the null pointer q is unable to point.

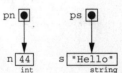

EXAMPLE 2.1 Pointers

```
int main()
{ int n=44;
  string s="Hello";
  cout << "&n = " << &n << "\n";
  cout << "&s = " << &s << "\n";
  int* p;          // declares p to be a dangling pointer to int
  int* q=0;        // initializes the pointer q to be null
  int* pn=&n;      // initializes the pointer pn with the address of n
```

25

```
    string* ps=&s;  // initializes the pointer ps with the address of s
    cout << "p =  " << p << "\n";
    cout << "q =  " << q << "\n";
    cout << "pn = " << pn << "\n";
    cout << "ps = " << ps << "\n";
}
&n = 0x18ff24b8
&s = 0x18ff24bc
p =  0x2007e9a4
q =  0x00000000
pn = 0x18ff24b8
ps = 0x18ff24bc
```

The symbol & is called the *reference operator*. When used as a prefix to the name x of a variable or object, the resulting expression &x evaluates to the memory address of x. Consequently, & is also called the "address of" operator.

EXAMPLE 2.2 Dereferencing Pointers

```
int main()
{ int n=66;
  string s="Goodbye";
  int* pn=&n;     // initializes the pointer pn with the address of n
  string* ps=&s;  // initializes the pointer ps with the address of s
  cout << "pn = " << pn << "\n";
  cout << "ps = " << ps << "\n";
  int m=*pn;      // initializes m with the int to which pn points
  string t=*ps;   // initializes t with the string to which ps points
  cout << "m = " << m << "\n";
  cout << "t = " << t << "\n";
}
pn = 0x0065fdf8
ps = 0x0065fdfc
m = 66
t = Goodbye
```

The symbol * is called the *dereference operator*. When used as a prefix to the name p of a pointer, the resulting expression *p evaluates to the value of the variable or object to which p points.

2.2 DERIVED TYPES

Each of the symbols & and * have two distinct roles in C++. When used as prefixes on identifiers, as in &n and *pn, these symbols represent operators: the reference operator and the dereference operator, respectively. But they are also used as suffixes on types, like this:

```
int* p;
void swap(int&, int&);
```
In this roll, these symbols are not operators. Instead, they define derived types.

A *derived type* is a type that is derived from another type. For example:

```
int* p;              // declares p to have type pointer to int
int& x;              // declares x to have type reference to int
const int C=99;      // declares C to have type const int
int f();             // deflares f to be a function that returns int
int a[];             // declares a to have type array of int
```

Here, p, x, C, f(), and a[] all have types that are derived from type int. But each of these derived types is distinctly different from the int type.

2.3 REFERENCES

A *reference* is an alias, a synonym for an existing variable or object. A reference has type *xxxx&*, where *xxxx* is the type of the variable or object which it names. Like constants, references must be initialized.

EXAMPLE 2.3 Using References

```
int main()
{ int n=44;
  int& rn=n;                 // declares rn to be a reference for n
  cout << "n = " << n << "\n";
  cout << "rn = " << rn << "\n";
  n *= 2;                    // double n, and rn
  cout << "n = " << n << "\n";
  cout << "rn = " << rn << "\n";
  rn /= 2;                   // halves rn, and n
  cout << "n = " << n << "\n";
  cout << "rn = " << rn << "\n";
}
```

```
n = 44
rn = 44
n = 88
rn = 88
n = 44
rn = 44
```

There is only one int in this program. It is declared on the first line to be named n. The second line declares rn to be a reference to n, which means that it is just another name for the same variable. Consequently, when n is doubled, so is rn. And when rn is halved, so is n.

2.4 PASSING BY REFERENCE

When a function parameter is declared to have a reference type, we say that its arguments are *passed by reference*. The effect is that the parameter becomes an alias for whatever argument is passed to it, and therefore any change made to the parameter is also made to that argument.

If the parameter's type is not a reference type, then the parameter acts like a local variable. After being initialized with the value of the argument or expression passed to it, it is independent of the argument. Its scope is limited to the body of the function, and therefore any change made to it has no effect outside of the function. This is called *passing by value*.

EXAMPLE 2.4 Passing by Value and by Reference

```
void f(int,int&);

int main()
{ int m=22;
  int n=44;
  cout << "m = " << m << "\n";
  cout << "n = " << n << "\n";
  f(m,n);
  cout << "m = " << m << "\n";
  cout << "n = " << n << "\n";
}

void f(int x, int& y)
{ x += 1000;      // adds 1000 to x
  y *= 1000;      // multiplies y by 1000
}
m = 22
n = 44
m = 22
n = 44000
```

The function f() changes the values of both of its parameters. But only the change on y affects its argument because it is passed by reference.

Passing by value is safer than passing by reference because it prevents the unintentional changing of the argument. But it has the disadvantage of having to duplicate the argument. When an object is passed to a function that should not change it, it should be passed *by constant reference*. This has the advantage of preventing unintentional changes to the argument without the disadvantage of duplicating it.

EXAMPLE 2.5 Passing by Constant Reference

```
#include <ctype.h>     // defines toupper() function
string toUpper(const string&);

int main()
{ string name;
  cout << "Enter your name: ";
  cin >> name;
  cout << "Hello, " << toUpper(name) << "!\n";;
}
string toUpper(const string& s)
{ string ss(s);
  for (int i=0; i<s.length(); i++)
    ss[i] = toupper(s[i]);  // copies the uppercase version of s[i]
  return ss;
}
Enter your name: Hillary
Hello, HILLARY!
```

The `toUpper()` function returns an uppercase version of the string passed to it. Since that string could be a large object, it is better to pass it by reference so that it doesn't get duplicated. But the function is not intended to modify that string, so it should be passed by constant reference.

2.5 NULL POINTER EXCEPTIONS

Anyone who uses Windows computers has probably encountered the alert panels shown below. This is the result of an attempt to dereference a dangling pointer or a null pointer. Such an attempt causes a run-time error. In C++, this throws an "exception" which then crashes the program because there was no code to "handle" the exception.

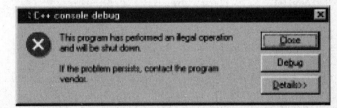

EXAMPLE 2.6 Attempting to Dereference an Uninitialized Pointer

This program causes a run-time error:
```
int main()
{ string* ps;
  cout << "*ps = " << *ps << "\n";    // ERROR: ps is not initialized
}
```
The exception is thrown when the operating system attempts to evaluate the expression `*ps`. The pointer ps is not initialized so it is a dangling pointer: it points to nothing. So the dereference operator `*` cannot be applied to `ps`. It's the same kind of mistake as attempting to divide by zero, with the same outcome: the program crashes!

To avoid the serious error illustrated in Example 2.6, always initialize pointer variables, like this:
```
string name("Erika");
string* p=&name;
```

2.6 THE `new` AND `delete` OPERATORS

The objects declared in all the previous examples have been bound to the scope in which they are declared. That means that the object exists only within the block in which it is declared.

EXAMPLE 2.7 Attempting to Dereference a Null Pointer

This program causes a run-time error:
```
int main()
{ string* p;  // WARNING: pointer p is not initialized
  if (2+2==4)
  { string name("Erika");  // name is local to this block
```

```
    p = &name;
    cout << "Now p points to " << *p << "\n";
  }
  cout << "Now p points to " << *p << "\n";   // ERROR
}
```
```
Now p points to Erika
Now p points to fB
```

This program has the same error as in Example 2.6. The string `name` is bound to the scope of the function `if` block. It does not exist outside of that block, so p remains a dangling pointer and should be dereferenced.

EXAMPLE 2.8 Using the `new` Operator

```
string* f();
int main()
{ string* ps=f();
  cout << "*ps = " << *ps << "\n";    // OK: the string is still alive
}
string* f()
{ string* ps = new string("Hello");
  return ps;                          // ps points to a global string object
}
```
```
*ps = Hello
```

The `new` operator creates the `string` object at run-time, so it will remain alive throughout the life of the program itself.

The syntax for invoking the `new` operator is

  *Xxxxx** p = new *Xxxx*();

where *Xxxx* is a class. (See Chapter 3.) The expression `new Xxxx()` calls the class constructor to create the new object and then returns a pointer to it. The resulting object is *anonymous*; it has no name. It is accessed using `*p`, or `*q` where q is any other pointer to the string that equals p.

In some cases it is important to terminate the existence of a run-time object before the end of the program. The `delete` operator does that.

EXAMPLE 2.9 Using the `delete` Operator

```
int main()
{ string* p = new string("Goodbye");
  cout << "p = " << p << "\n";
  cout << "*p = " << *p << "\n";
  delete p;
  cout << "p = " << p << "\n";
  cout << "*p = " << *p << "\n";   // ERROR: ps is dangling
}
```
```
p = 0x004307a0
*p = Goodbye
p = 0x004307a0
*p =
```

Attempting to dereference a deleted pointer will fail and may cause the program to crash.

The `delete` operator should be applied only to pointers that have been returned by the `new` operator.

2.7 ARRAYS

An *array* is a sequence of contiguous storage locations all of which can be accessed by the single array name followed by an integer subscript called the *index* of the array. If a is the name of the array, then its elements are accessed using `a[0]`, `a[1]`, `a[2]`, `a[3]`, *etc*. The number of elements in the array is called its *dimension*. In C++, the array index always begins with 0.

EXAMPLE 2.10 An Array of Strings

```
int main()
{ string a[4];   // an array of 4 strings
  a[0] = "Microsoft";
  a[1] = "Oracle";
  a[2] = "Inprise";
  a[3] = "IBM";
  for (int i=0; i<4; i++)
    cout << "a[" << i << "] = " << a[i] << "\n";
}
a[0] = Microsoft
a[1] = Oracle
a[2] = Inprise
a[3] = IBM
```

Arrays are usually processed with `for` loops.

Arrays can be initialized when they are declared using an *initializer list*.

EXAMPLE 2.11 Using an Initializer List to Initialize an Array

```
int main()
{ string a[] = {"Exxon","Shell","Texaco","BP"};
  for (int i=0; i<4; i++)
    cout << "a[" << i << "] = " << a[i] << "\n";
}
a[0] = Exxon
a[1] = Shell
a[2] = Texaco
a[3] = BP
```

Notice that the array dimension can be omitted when an initializer list is used. The compiler will set the dimension equal to the number of elements in the list.

2.8 DYNAMIC ARRAYS

An array that is declared as in Example 2.10 or Example 2.11 is called a *static array* because it is allocated at compile-time. The dimension must be a constant integer.

The `new` operator can be used to create a *dynamic array* whose dimension may be a variable integer. Dynamic arrays are allocated at run-time.

EXAMPLE 2.12 Using a Dynamic Array

```
int main()
{ int n;
  cout << "How many children do you have? ";
  cin >> n;
  string* child = new string[n];
  cout << "Please give me the names of your " << n
       << " children:\n";
  for (int i=0; i<n; i++)
  { cout << "\t" << i+1 << ": ";
    cin >> child[i];
  }
  cout << "They are " << child[0];
  for (int i=1; i<n; i++)
  { cout << ", " << child[i];
  }
  cout << "\n";
}
```

```
How many children do you have? 4
Please give me the names of your 4 children:
        1: Sara
        2: John
        3: Andrew
        4: Michael
They are Sara, John, Andrew, Michael
```

Notice that the name of a dynamic array is a pointer to its element type.

The syntax for declaring a dynamic array is

```
xxxx* a = new xxxx[n];
```

where *xxxx* is the element type, and *n* is the dimension of the array, which may be any integer expression.

2.9 PASSING AN ARRAY TO A FUNCTION

An array parameter can be declared like this:

```
void sort(double a[], int size);
```

But in C++, an array name is actually a constant pointer to its first element. So an array parameter can also be declared like this:

```
void sort(double* a, int size);
```

The two forms are equivalent. Either way, the function is called by passing the array name as the argument, like this:

```
sort(a, 100);
```

EXAMPLE 2.13 Finding the Maximum Element of an Array

```
int main()
{ int a[] = {44, 77, 33, 66, 55, 88, 22};
  cout << "max(a,7) = " << max(a,7) << "\n";
}
int max(int* a, int n)
{ int m=a[0];
  for (int i=1; i<n; i++)
    if (a[i] > m) m = a[i];
  return m;
}
```

```
max(a,7) = 88
```

2.10 MULTIDIMENSIONAL ARRAYS

Multidimensional arrays are declared the same way as one-dimensional arrays:

```
double m[5][4];  // a two-dimensional array
int x[4][2][4][3][2];  // a five-dimensional array
```

They can also be initialized the same way:

```
int c[2][3] = { {22,66,88}, {55,77,44} };
```

Notice that a two-dimensional array can be regarded as an array of arrays.

When processing a multidimensional array, it is usually helpful to use a `typedef` to define the array type, especially if it has to be passed to a function.

EXAMPLE 2.14 Processing a Two-Dimensional Array

This program tests a function that swaps two columns of a 2×3 array of `int`s:

```
#include <iostream>
using namespace std;
const int ROWS=2;
const int COLS=3;
typedef int Array[ROWS][COLS];  // defines the type Array
void swapCols(Array,int,int);
void print(const Array);

int main()
{ Array a = { {11,33,55}, {22,44,66} };
  print(a);
  swapCols(a,1,2);
  print(a);
}

void swapCols(Array a, int c1, int c2)
{ for (int i=0; i<ROWS; i++)
```

```
    { int temp=a[i][c1];
      a[i][c1] = a[i][c2];
      a[i][c2] = temp;
    }
  }

void print(const Array a)
{ for (int i=0; i<ROWS; i++)
  { for (int j=0; j<COLS; j++)
      cout << a[i][j] << " ";
    cout << "\n";
  }
  cout << "\n";
}
```

```
11 33 55
22 44 66

11 55 33
22 66 44
```

The typedef defines `Array` to be the type for arrays of `int`s with `ROWS` rows and `COLS` columns. Those two constants are defined to be 2 and 3. The call `swapCols(a,1,2)` function interchanges column 1 with column 2 (which are the second and third columns since numbering begins with 0).

Review Questions

2.1 What is a pointer?

2.2 What is a dangling pointer?

2.3 What is a null pointer?

2.4 What is a reference?

2.5 Why must a reference always be initialized?

2.6 What's wrong with the following declaration?

```
    int& r=44;
```

2.7 How can you tell when a numeric literal is a memory address?

2.8 What are the two uses of the `&` symbol in C++?

2.9 What are the two uses of the `*` symbol in C++?

2.10 What does the reference operator do?

2.11 What does the dereference operator do?

2.12 What is the difference between passing an argument by reference and passing it by value?

2.13 What is the difference between passing an argument by reference and passing it by constant reference?

2.14 Why can't a literal argument be passed by reference [*e.g.*, `f(22)`]?

2.15 Why can't a general expression be passed by reference [*e.g.*, `f(2*x+3)`]?

2.16 What does the `new` operator do?

2.17 What does the `delete` operator do?

2.18 What is the difference between a static array and a dynamic array?

Problems

2.1   Write and test a function that returns the minimum value of an array of integers.

2.2   Write and test a function that returns the last index of the maximum value of an array of integers.

2.3   Write and test a function that appends one array of integers to another.

2.4   Write and test a function that adds arrays of integers element-wise.

2.5   Write and test a function that rotates an array of integers a given number of positions.

2.6   Write and test a boolean function that determines whether a given array is sorted.

2.7   Write and test a function that performs a perfect shuffle on an array of integers. The *perfect shuffle* of a sequence is obtained by interleaving its first half with its second half, always moving the middle card to the front. For example, the perfect shuffle of $\{1, 2, 3, 4, 5, 6, 7, 8\}$ is $\{5, 1, 6, 2, 7, 3, 8, 4\}$.

2.8   Write and test a function that returns the minimal number of perfect shuffles required to restore an array of a given size to its original order. (See Problem 2.7.) For example $f(7) = 3$ because it takes 6 perfect shuffles to restore an array of 7 elements to its original order: $\{1, 2, 3, 4, 5, 6, 7\} \rightarrow \{5, 1, 6, 2, 7, 3, 8, 4\} \rightarrow \{7, 5, 3, 1, 8, 6, 4, 2\} \rightarrow \{8, 7, 6, 5, 4, 3, 2, 1\}$ $\rightarrow \{4, 8, 3, 7, 2, 6, 1, 5\} \rightarrow \{2, 4, 6, 8, 1, 3, 5, 7\} \rightarrow \{1, 2, 3, 4, 5, 6, 7, 8\}$. (Use the solution to Problem 2.6.)

2.9   Write and test a function that returns the mean of the elements of an array of type `double`. The (arithmetic) *mean* of a sequence of n numbers is the number m defined by the formula

$$m = \frac{x_0 + x_1 + x_2 + \cdots + x_{n-1}}{n}$$

2.10 Write and test a function that returns the standard deviation of the elements of an array of type `double`. The *standard deviation* of a sequence of n numbers $x_0, x_1, x_2, ..., x_{n-1}$ is the number s given by the formula

$$s = \frac{\sqrt{(x_0 - m)^2 + (x_1 - m)^2 + (x_2 - m)^2 + \cdots + (x_{n-1} - m)^2}}{n}$$

where m is their mean. (See Problem 2.10.)

2.11 Write and test a program that implements the *Sieve of Eratosthenes* for finding prime numbers. This algorithm uses an array `p[]` of type `bool`, setting `p[k]` true if and only if k is prime. It does that by initializing all `p[k]` to be true for k > 1, and then resetting those `p[k]` to false where k has a nontrivial divisor.

2.12 Write and test a function that merges two sorted arrays of integers, combining them into a third sorted array.

2.13 Write and test a function that reverses the order of an array of pointers to strings.

2.14 Write and test a function that duplicates an array of pointers to strings.

2.15 Write and test a function that is passed an array of string pointers and returns a new array of pointers to duplicate strings.

2.16 Write and test a function that tallies the frequencies of the 26 letters (without regard to case) in a given string.

2.17 Write and test a function that implements the following algorithm (known as the *Horner's Method*) to evaluate a polynomial $p(x) = a_0 + a_1 x + a_2 x^2 + a_3 x^3 + \cdots + a_n x^n$ by using its equivalent form $p(x) = a_0 + x(a_1 + x(a_2 + x(a_3 + \cdots + x(a_n) \cdots)))$. For example, the polynomial $p(x) = 5 - 8x + 4x^3$ would be evaluated as $p(x) = 5 + x(-8 + x(0 + x(4)))$.

2.18 Write a program that prints *Pascal's triangle* of binomial coefficients, like this:

```
                          1
                       1     1
                    1     2     1
                 1     3     3     1
              1     4     6     4     1
           1     5    10    10     5     1
        1     6    15    20    15     6     1
     1     7    21    35    35    21     7     1
     1     8    28    56    70    56    28     8     1
  1     9    36    84   126   126    84    36     9     1
1    10    45   120   210   252   210   120    45    10     1
1    11    55   165   330   462   462   330   165    55    11     1
1    12    66   220   495   792   924   792   495   220    66    12     1
```

2.19 Write and test a function that returns the trace of a square matrix. A *matrix* is a two-dimensional array. A *square matrix* is a matrix that has the same number of rows and columns. The *diagonal* of a square matrix `a[][]` is the sequence of elements `a[0][0]`, `a[1][1]`, `a[2][2]`, *etc.* The *trace* of a square matrix is the sum of its diagonal elements.

2.20 Write and test a function that transposes a square matrix. The *transpose* of a matrix is the matrix obtained by reflecting it about its diagonal, so that the rows of the resulting matrix are the columns of the given matrix, and *vice versa*.

2.21 Write and test a function that returns the inner product of two arrays of the same size. The *inner product* (also called the *scalar* or *dot product*) of two arrays $\{a_0, a_1, a_2, \ldots, a_{n-1}\}$ and $\{b_0, b_1, b_2, \ldots, b_{n-1}\}$ is the number c defined by the formula

$$c = a_0b_0 + a_1b_1 + a_2b_2 + \cdots + a_{n-1}b_{n-1}$$

2.22 Write and test a function that obtains the outer product of two arrays. The *outer product* of two arrays $\{a_0, a_1, a_2, \ldots, a_{n-1}\}$ and $\{b_0, b_1, b_2, \ldots, b_{n-1}\}$ is the matrix $\{c_{ij}\}$ whose *ij*th element c_{ij} (*i.e.*, the element in row i and column j) is defined by the formula

$$c_{ij} = a_{ij}b_{ij}$$

2.23 Write and test a function that obtains the product of two matrices. The *matrix product* of two matrices $\{a_{ij}\}$ and $\{b_{ij}\}$ is the matrix $\{c_{ij}\}$ whose *ij*th element c_{ij} (*i.e.*, the element in row i and column j) is defined by the formula

$$c_{ij} = a_{i0}b_{0j} + a_{i1}b_{1j} + a_{i2}b_{2j} + \cdots + a_{i, n-1}b_{n-1, j}$$

Note that this is the inner product of the *i*th row of $\{a_{ij}\}$ and the *j*th column of $\{b_{ij}\}$. (See Problem 2.21.)

Answers to Review Questions

2.1 A *pointer* is a variable whose value is the memory address of an object.

2.2 A *dangling pointer* is a pointer that has not been initialized or has been de-allocated with the `delete` operator. (See Example 2.6 on page 29.)

2.3 A *null pointer* is a pointer whose value is 0 (*i.e.*, the address `0x0`). Since this address will be outside the process space of any running program, it is invalid and any attempt to dereference the pointer will cause a run-time error (*i.e.*, the program will crash). (See Example 2.7 on page 29.)

2.4 A *reference* is a synonym for an existing object. (See Example 2.3 on page 27.)

2.5 References must be initialized because they are synonyms for existing objects.

2.6 That declaration is invalid because the reference is being initialized with a literal. It should be a name, like this:

```
    int& r=n;
```

2.7   Numeric literals that are memory addresses are expressed in hexadecimal, like this: `0x18c5b4`.

2.8   As a prefix, the `&` symbol is used for the reference operator on objects. As a suffix, it is used to designate the "reference to" derived type.

2.9   As a prefix, the `*` symbol is used for the dereference operator on pointers. As a suffix, it is used to designate the "pointer to" derived type.

2.10   Applied to an object, the *reference operator* returns the memory address of that object. (See Example 2.1 on page 25.)

2.11   Applied to a pointer, the *dereference operator* returns the object to which that pointer points. (See Example 2.2 on page 26.)

2.12   When an argument is passed to a function parameter by value, the parameter becomes an independent local variable for the function, initialized with the value of that argument, so changes to the parameter have no effect upon the argument. When it is by reference, the parameter becomes a synonym for that argument, so any change to the parameter is a change to the argument. (See Example 2.4 on page 28.)

2.13   Passing an argument by constant reference is the same as passing it by reference except that the former cannot be changed. (See Example 2.5 on page 28.)

2.14   A literal argument cannot be passed by reference because literals are constants but arguments passed by reference must be able to be changed.

2.15   A general expression cannot be passed by reference because it does not store any values but arguments passed by reference must have a value that can be changed.

2.16   The `new` operator allocates memory space to objects during run-time. (See Example 2.8 on page 30 and Example 2.12 on page 32.)

2.17   The `delete` operator de-allocates memory space during run-time. (See Example 2.9 on page 30.)

2.18   A *static array* is allocated at compile time and is declared like this:
```
    double a[N];   // N must be a constant
```
A *dynamic array* is allocated at run-time and is declared like this:
```
    double* a = new double[n];   // n may be a variable
```

Solutions to Problems

2.1   Tests a function that returns the minimum value of an array:
```
    #include <iostream>
    using namespace std;
    int min(int*,int);
    int main()
    { int a[] = {66,44,88,11,77,33,99,55,22};
      cout << "min(a,9) = " << min(a,9) << "\n";
    }
    int min(int* a, int n)
    { int m=a[0];
      for (int i=1; i<n; i++)
        if (a[i]<m) m = a[i];
      return m;
    }
```

2.2   Tests a function that returns the last index of the maximum value of an array:
```
    #include <iostream>
    using namespace std;
    int lastIndexOfMax(int*,int);
    int main()
    { int a[] = {66,44,88,11,77,33,88,55,22};
      int j = lastIndexOfMax(a,9);
      cout << "lastIndexOfMax(a,9) = " << j << "\n";
```

```
        cout << "a[lastIndexOfMax(a,9)] = " << a[j] << "\n";
      }
      int lastIndexOfMax(int* a, int n)
      { int j=0;
        for (int i=1; i<n; i++)
          if (a[i]>=a[j]) j = i;
        return j;
      }
```

2.3 Tests a function that appends one array to another:

```
      #include <iostream>
      using namespace std;
      int* append(int*,int,int*,int);
      void print(int*,int);
      int main()
      { int a[] = {11,22,33,44,55};
        int b[] = {66,77,88,99};
        print(a,5);
        print(b,4);
        int* c = append(a,5,b,4);
        print(c,9);
      }
      int* append(int* a, int m, int* b, int n)
      { int* c = new int[m+n];
        for (int i=0; i<m; i++)
          c[i] = a[i];
        for (int i=m; i<m+n; i++)
          c[i] = b[i-m];
        return c;
      }
      void print(int* a, int n)
      { cout << "{" << a[0];
        for (int i=1; i<n; i++)
          cout << "," << a[i];
        cout << "}\n";
      }
```

2.4 Tests a function that adds two arrays:

```
      #include <iostream>
      using namespace std;
      int* sum(int*,int,int*,int);
      void print(int*,int);  // same function as in Problem 2.3
      int main()
      { int a[] = {11,22,33,44,55};
        int b[] = {88,77,66};
        print(a,5);
        print(b,3);
        int* c = sum(a,5,b,3);
        print(c,5);
      }
      int* sum(int* a, int m, int* b, int n)
      { int* aa, * bb;  // aa is the shorter array
        int mm, nn;
        if (m<n) aa=a, bb=b, mm=m, nn=n;
        else     aa=b, bb=a, mm=n, nn=m;
        int* c = new int[nn];
        for (int i=0; i<mm; i++)
          c[i] = aa[i] + bb[i];
```

```
        for (int i=mm; i<nn; i++)
          c[i] = bb[i];
        return c;
    }
```

2.5   Tests a function that rotates an array:

```
    #include <iostream>
    using namespace std;
    void rotate(int*,int,int);
    void print(int*,int);  // same function as in Problem 2.3
    int main()
    { int a[] = {11,22,33,44,55,66,77,88,99};
      print(a,9);
      rotate(a,9,2);
      print(a,9);
    }
    void rotate(int* a, int n, int k)
    { int* temp = new int[9];  // dynamic array
      for (int i=0; i<k; i++)
        temp[i] = a[n-k+i];
      for (int i=k; i<n; i++)
        temp[i] = a[i-k];
      for (int i=0; i<n; i++)
        a[i] = temp[i];
    }
```

2.6   Tests a function that determines whether a given array is sorted:

```
    #include <iostream>
    using namespace std;
    bool isSorted(int*,int);
    int main()
    { { int a[] = {11,22,33,44};
        cout << "isSorted(a,4) = " << isSorted(a,4) << "\n";
      }
      { int a[] = {44,11,22,33};
        cout << "isSorted(a,4) = " << isSorted(a,4) << "\n";
      }
    }
    bool isSorted(int* a, int n)
    { for (int i=1; i<n; i++)
        if (a[i-1] > a[i]) return false;
      return true;
    }
```

2.7   Tests a function that shuffles an array:

```
    ##include <iostream>
    using namespace std;
    void shuffle(int*,int);
    void print(int*,int);  // same function as in Problem 2.3
    int main()
    { int a[] = {11,22,33,44,55,66,77,88,99};
      print(a,9);
      shuffle(a,9);
      print(a,9);
    }
    void shuffle(int* a, int n)
    { int* temp = new int[n];  // dynamic array
      for (int i=0; i<n/2; i++)
        temp[2*i+1] = a[i];
```

```
          for (int i=n/2; i<n; i++)
            temp[2*(i-n/2)] = a[i];
          for (int i=0; i<n; i++)
            a[i] = temp[i];
        }
```

2.8   Tests a function that returns the minimal number of shuffles needed to restore an array of a given size
        to its original order:

```
        #include <iomanip>  // defines setw() function
        #include <iostream>
        using namespace std;
        int minShuffles(int);
        void shuffle(int*,int);
        int main()
        { for (int n=2; n<20; n++)
            cout << setw(4) << n << ". " << minShuffles(n) << "\n";
        }
        bool isSorted(int*,int);  // same function as in Problem 2.6
        int minShuffles(int n)
        { int* a = new int[n];  // dynamic array
          for (int i=0; i<n; i++)
            a[i] = i;
          int count=0;
          do
          { shuffle(a,n);
            ++count;
          } while (!isSorted(a,n));
          return count;
        }
```

2.9   Tests a function that returns the mean average of an array:

```
        #include <iostream>
        using namespace std;
        double mean(double*,int);
        int main()
        { double a[] = {11,22,33,44,55};
          cout << "mean(a,4) = " << mean(a,4) << "\n";
          cout << "mean(a,5) = " << mean(a,5) << "\n";
        }
        double mean(double* a, int n)
        { double sum=0;
          for (int i=0; i<n; i++)
            sum += a[i];
          return sum/n;
        }
```

2.10   Tests a function that returns the standard deviation of an array:

```
        #include <cmath>  // defines sqrt() function
        #include <iostream>
        using namespace std;
        double stdDev(double*,int);
        int main()
        { { double a[] = {100,200,300,400,500};
          cout << "stdDev(a,1) = " << stdDev(a,1) << "\n";
          cout << "stdDev(a,2) = " << stdDev(a,2) << "\n";
          cout << "stdDev(a,3) = " << stdDev(a,3) << "\n";
          cout << "stdDev(a,4) = " << stdDev(a,4) << "\n";
          cout << "stdDev(a,5) = " << stdDev(a,5) << "\n";
        }
```

```
        { double a[] = {400,100,300,500,200};
          cout << "stdDev(a,5) = " << stdDev(a,5) << "\n";
        }
      }
      double mean(double*,int);   // same function as in Problem 2.9
      double stdDev(double* a, int n)
      { double m=mean(a,n);
        double sum=0;
        for (int i=0; i<n; i++)
          sum += (a[i]-m)*(a[i]-m);
        return sqrt(sum/n);
      }
```

2.11   The Sieve of Eratosthenes:

```
      #include <iomanip>  // defines setw() function
      #include <iostream>
      using namespace std;
      int main()
      { const int N=1000;
        bool p[N]={false};       // initializes all elements to false
        p[2] = p[3] = true;      // 2 and 3 are the first two primes
        for (int n=5; n<N; n += 2) // even numbers >2 are not prime
        { p[n] = true;                          // assume n is prime
          double sqrtn=sqrt(n);      // need only check div <=sqrt(k)
          for (int d=3; d<=sqrtn; d++)
            if (n%d==0)        // n has a divisor, so it is not prime
            { p[n] = false;
              break;                             // go on to next n
            }
        }
        for (int n=0; n<N; n++)
          if (p[n]) cout << setw(5) << n;
          else if (n%50==0) cout << "\n";
      }
```

2.12   Tests a function that merges two sorted arrays:

```
      #include <iostream>
      using namespace std;
      int* merge(int*,int,int*,int);
      void print(int*,int);  // same function as in Problem 2.3
      int main()
      { int a[] = {11,44,55,88};
        int b[] = {22,33,66,77,99};
        print(a,4);
        print(b,5);
        int* c = merge(a,4,b,5);
        print(c,9);
      }
      int* merge(int* a, int m, int* b, int n)
      { int* c = new int[m+n];
        for (int i=0, j=0, k=0; k<m+n; k++)
          c[k] = a[i]<b[j] ? a[i++] : b[j++];
        return c;
      }
```

2.13   Tests a function that reverses an array of string pointers:

```
      #include <iostream>
      using namespace std;
      void reverse(string**,int);
```

```
      void print(string**,int);
      int main()
      { string s[] = { "Italy", "Korea", "Spain", "China", "Japan" };
        string* a[] = { &s[0], &s[1], &s[2], &s[3], &s[4] };
        print(a,5);
        reverse(a,5);
        print(a,5);
      }
      void reverse(string** a, int n)
      { for (int i=0; i<n/2; i++)
        { string* temp = a[i];
          a[i] = a[n-1-i];
          a[n-1-i] = temp;
        }
      }
      void print(string** a, int n)
      { for (int i=0; i<n; i++)
          cout << *a[i] << " ";
        cout << "\n";
      }
```

2.14 Tests a function that duplicates an array of string pointers:

```
      #include <iostream>
      using namespace std;
      string** copy(string**,int);
      void print(string**,int);  // same function as in Problem 2.13
      int main()
      { string s[] = { "Italy", "Korea", "Spain", "China", "Japan" };
        string* a[] = { &s[0], &s[1], &s[2], &s[3], &s[4] };
        string** aa = copy(a,5);
        print(a,5);
        print(aa,5);
        *a[2]="India";
        print(a,5);
        print(aa,5);
      }
      string** copy(string** a, int n)
      { string** c = new string*[n];  // allocate the n pointers
        for (int i=0; i<n; i++)
          c[i] = a[i];  // sets new pointers to existing strings
        return c;
      }
```

2.15 Tests a function that duplicates an array of pointers to duplicated strings:

```
      #include <iostream>
      using namespace std;
      string** copy(string**,int);
      void print(string**,int);  // same function as in Problem 2.13
      int main()
      { string s[] = { "Italy", "Korea", "Spain", "China", "Japan" };
        string* a[] = { &s[0], &s[1], &s[2], &s[3], &s[4] };
        string** aa = copy(a,5);
        print(a,5);
        print(aa,5);
        *a[2]="India";
        print(a,5);
        print(aa,5);
      }
```

```
string** copy(string** a, int n)
{ string** c = new string*[n];   // allocate the n pointers
  for (int i=0; i<n; i++)
    c[i] = new string(*a[i]);   // sets new pointers to new strings
  return c;
}
```

2.16 Tallies frequencies:

```
#include <ctype.h>   // defines toupper() and isalpha() functions
#include <iostream>
using namespace std;
int* tally(string);
void print(int*,int);   // same function as in Problem 2.3
int main()
{ string s="ABCDEFG ABCDE! ABC*5= abcabc. aaAA xyz";
  int* t = tally(s);
  print(t,26);
}

int* tally(string s)
{ const int N=26;        // 26 letters in the Latin alphabet
  int* t = new int[N];   // one counter for each letter
  for (int n=0; n<N; n++)
    t[n] = 0;
  for (int i=0; i<s.length(); i++)
    if (isalpha(s[i])) ++t[toupper(s[i])-'A'];
  return t;
}
```

2.17 Implements Horner's Method to evaluate a polynomial:

```
#include <iomanip.h>
#include <iostream>
using namespace std;
double p(double*,int,double);
int main()
{ double a[] = {16,-32,24,-8,1};   // p(x) = (x-2)^4
  for (int x=0; x<=4; x++)
  { cout << setw(6)  << x << setw(10) << p(a,4,x) << "\n";
  }
}

double p(double* a, int n, double x)
{ double y=a[n];
  for (int i=n-1; i>=0; i--)
    y = y*x + a[i];
  return y;
}
```

2.18 Prints Pascal's Triangle:

```
#include <iomanip.h>
#include <iostream>
using namespace std;
int main()
{ const int N=12;
  int c[N+1][N+1];
  for (int i=0; i<=N; i++)
    c[i][0] = c[i][i] = 1;
  for (int i=2; i<=N; i++)
    for (int j=1; j<i; j++)
      c[i][j] = c[i-1][j-1] + c[i-1][j];
  for (int i=0; i<=N; i++)
```

```
      { cout << "\n" << string(2*(N-i),' ');
        for (int j=0; j<=i; j++)
          cout << setw(4) << c[i][j];
      }
    }
```

2.19 Tests a function that returns the trace of a matrix::

```
      #include <iomanip.h>   // defines the setw() function
      #include <iostream>
      using namespace std;
      const int N=3;
      typedef int Matrix[N][N];   // defines the type Matrix
      int trace(Matrix);
      void print(const Matrix);
      int main()
      { Matrix a = { {11,22,33}, {44,55,66}, {77,88,99} };
        print(a);
        cout << "trace(a) = " << trace(a) << "\n";
      }
      int trace(Matrix m)
      { int sum=0;
        for (int i=0; i<N; i++)
          sum += m[i][i];
        return sum;
      }
      void print(const Matrix m)
      { for (int i=0; i<N; i++)
        { for (int j=0; j<N; j++)
            cout << setw(4) << m[i][j];
          cout << "\n";
        }
        cout << "\n";
      }
```

2.20 Tests a function that transposes a matrix:

```
      #include <iomanip.h>   // defines the setw() function
      #include <iostream>    // defines the swap() function
      using namespace std;
      const int N=3;
      typedef int Matrix[N][N];   // defines the Matrix type
      void transpose(Matrix&);
      void print(const Matrix);   // same as defined in Problem 2.19
      int main()
      { Matrix a = { {11,22,33}, {44,55,66}, {77,88,99} };
        print(a);
        transpose(a);
        print(a);
      }
      void transpose(Matrix& m)
      { for (int i=0; i<N; i++)
          for (int j=0; j<i; j++)
            swap(m[i][j],m[j][i]);
      }
```

2.21 Tests a function that returns the inner product of two arrays:

```
      #include <iostream>
      using namespace std;
      int innerProduct(int*,int*,int);
      void print(int*,int);   // same function as in Problem 2.3
```

```
int main()
{ int a[] = {11,22,33,44};
  int b[] = {40,30,0,-10};
  print(a,4);
  print(b,4);
  cout << "innerProduct(a,b,4) = " << innerProduct(a,b,4) << "\n";
}
int innerProduct(int* a, int* b, int n)
{ int sum=0;
  for (int i=0; i<n; i++)
    sum += a[i]*b[i];
  return sum;
}
```

2.22 Tests a function that computes the outer product of two arrays:

```
#include <iomanip.h>  // defines the setw() function
#include <iostream>
using namespace std;
const int N=4;
typedef int Matrix[N][N];  // defines the Matrix type
void outerProduct(Matrix&,int*,int*);
void print(int*,int);  // same function as in Problem 2.3
void print(const Matrix);  // same as defined in Problem 2.19
int main()
{ int a[] = {11,22,33,44};
  int b[] = {40,30,0,-10};
  Matrix m;
  print(a,N);
  print(b,N);
  outerProduct(m,a,b);
  print(m);
}
void outerProduct(Matrix& m, int* a, int* b)
{ for (int i=0; i<N; i++)
    for (int j=0; j<N; j++)
      m[i][j] = a[i]*b[j];
}
```

2.23 Tests a function that returns the product of two matrices:

```
#include <iomanip.h>  // defines the setw() function
#include <iostream>
using namespace std;
const int N=2;
typedef int Matrix[N][N];  // defines the Matrix type
void multiply(Matrix&,Matrix,Matrix);
void print(const Matrix);  // same as defined in Problem 2.19
int main()
{ Matrix a = { {2,4}, {3,5} };
  Matrix b = { {3,0}, {6,-1} };
  Matrix c;
  multiply(c,a,b);
  print(a);
  print(b);
  print(c);
}
void multiply(Matrix& c, Matrix a, Matrix b)
{ for (int i=0; i<N; i++)
    for (int j=0; j<N; j++)
```

```
{ c[i][j] = 0;
  for (int k=0; k<N; k++)
    c[i][j] += a[i][k]*b[k][j];
}
}
```

Chapter 3

Classes

In object-oriented programming languages such as C++, a *class* is a user-defined type that includes data members and functions. A class is a data type for objects.

3.1 A `Point` CLASS

The first three examples illustrate a simple class whose objects represent points in the cartesian plane.

EXAMPLE 3.1 Interface for the `Point` Class

```
class Point
{ public:
    Point(double=0.0,double=0.0);      // default constructor
    Point(const Point&);                // copy constructor
    ~Point();                           // destructor
    Point& operator=(const Point&);     // assignment operator
    double x() const;                   // accessor function
    double y() const;                   // accessor function
    string toString() const;
  protected:
    double _x, _y;
};
```

This code would be saved in a *header file* named Point.h. It is called the *interface* for the class because it is the part of the class that programmers need in order to use the class in their client programs. It is also that part of the class that the compiler needs to compile statements that use the class.

This class declaration has seven member functions and two data members. The member functions are named Point(double,double), Point(const Point&), operator=(), ~Point(), x(), y(), and toString(). The data members are named _x and _y. Notice that the function members are declared to be public and the data members are declared to be protected. That means that client programs can use the member functions, but they have no direct access to the data members. [They will have indirect read-only access to the data through the accessor functions x() and y().]

The first two function members are *constructors*. The first constructor is the *default constructor*. It is invoked by default whenever an object is constructed by a declaration like this:

    Point p2(7.2,4.9);   // constructs an object for the point (7.2,4.9)

Since both of its parameters have default values, it can also be invoked like this:

    Point p1(7.2);   // constructs an object for the point (7.2,0.0)
    Point p0;   // constructs an object for the point (0.0,0.0)

The default constructor is also invoked to construct anonymous objects, like this:

    p1 = Point(7.2);   // constructs an object for the point (7.2,0.0)

The second constructor is the *copy constructor*. It is invoked when an existing object is to be duplicated by constructing a copy of it.

47

The third member function is the class *destructor*. It is invoked automatically when the object goes out of scope.

The fourth member function is the overloaded *assignment operator*. It is invoked like this:

```
p0 = p1;
```

The fifth and sixth member functions are *accessor functions*. They give indirect access to an object's protected data, like this:

```
double x1 = p1.x();   // assigns the value of p1._x to x1
```

The last member function returns a string that represents the object. It could be used like this:

```
string s1 = p1.toString();   // initializes s1 to "(7.2,0.0)"
```

It is useful to include a `toString()` function in every class. (This is done automatically in Java.)

Notice that the `const` keyword is used at the end of the declarations of the read-only member functions `x()`, `y()`, and `toString()`. It is good "defensive programming" practice to declare as constant functions that are not intended to change the state of the objects to which they are bound. By doing so, the programmer gains extra assistance from the compiler which will consequently prohibit the addition of code in the function that would change the object's state.

In C++, the declaration for the copy constructor, the destructor, and the assignment operator for a class X must have the form

```
X(const X&);              // copy constructor
~X();                     // destructor
X& operator=(const X&);   // assignment operator
```

If either of these or the default constructor is not declared explicitly in the class definition, the compiler will automatically create one for the class.

EXAMPLE 3.2 Test Driver for the `Point` Class

Here is a simple test driver program for the `Point` class defined in Example 3.1:

```
int main()
{ Point p0;                   // invokes default constructor
  cout << "p0 = " << p0.toString() << "\n";
  Point p1(5,-2);             // invokes default constructor
  cout << "p1 = " << p1.toString() << "\n";
  Point p2=p1;                // invokes copy constructor
  cout << "p2 = " << p2.toString() << "\n";
  p0 = p1;                    // invokes assignment operator
  cout << "p0 = " << p0.toString() << "\n";
  cout << "p0.x() = " << p0.x() << "\n";
  cout << "p0.y() = " << p0.y() << "\n";
}
```

Its output is

```
p0 = (0,0)
p1 = (5,-2)
p2 = (5,-2)
p0 = (5,-2)
p0.x() = 5
p0.y() = -2
```

EXAMPLE 3.3 Implementation for the `Point` Class

Here is an implementation for the class defined in Example 3.1:

```
    Point::Point(double x, double y) : _x(x), _y(y) { }
    Point::Point(const Point& p) : _x(p._x), _y(p._y) { }
    Point::~Point() { }
    Point& Point::operator=(const Point& p)
    { _x = p._x;
      _y = p._y;
      return *this;
    }
    double Point::x() const { return _x; }
    double Point::y() const { return _y; }
    string Point::toString() const
    { ostringstream output;
      output << "(" << _x << "," << _y << ")";
      return output.str();
    }
```

The bodies of the two constructors and the destructor are empty. Both constructors do their work through their *initialization lists*. For example, the initialization list for the copy constructor

```
    Point::Point(const Point& p) : _x(p._x), _y(p._y) { }
```

is shown in bold here. This definition is equivalent to

```
    Point::Point(const Point& p)
    { _x = p._x;
      _y = p._y;
    }
```

Note that this body is nearly the same as the assignment operator's. The main difference between a copy constructor and an assignment operator is that the former creates the object before assigning to it.

Only constructors can have initialization lists.

Also note that default values for parameters are given in the interface but not the implementation.

The `toString()` function uses a *string stream* to accumulate its output. This is the object named `output` of type `ostringstream`. Use of that class requires the directive

```
    #include <sstream>  // defines the ostringstream class
```

Output is put into an `ostringstream` object by means of the output operator `<<` the same way as with the `cout` stream object. The advantage of a string stream is that the output is saved in a buffer string which can be accessed with the `str()` member function like this:

```
    return output.str();
```

3.2 INSTANCES, IMPLICIT ARGUMENTS, AND THE this POINTER

The declaration

```
    Point p1(5,-2);
```

creates a `Point` object named `p1` and initializes its data members to 5.0 and –2.0. We can visualize the resulting object as shown here.

The process of constructing an object is called *instantiation*, and the resulting object is called an *instance* of the class. The object `p1` is an instance of the `Point` class.

The expression `p1.toString()` in the statement

```
    cout << "p1 = " << p1.toString() << "\n";
```

calls the `toString()` function. As a call of a class member function, it must be bound to an instance of its class. This call is bound to the instance `p1`. The instance to which a call is bound is called the *implicit argument* of the call. The object p1 is the implicit argument of the call `p1.toString()`. The names `_x` and `_y` in the statement

```
        output << "(" << _x << "," << _y << ")";
```
refer to the implicit argument's data. So in this example, _x means p1._x whose value is 5.0.

In any class member function, the keyword this can be used to refer to the implicit argument. The variable this is always a pointer to that instance of the class. So *this is always a reference to the implicit argument. The overloaded assignment operator, which is required to return a reference to an instance of the class, always returns the reference *this. That makes it possible to chain assignments this way:

```
        p4 = p3 = p2 = p1 = Point(2.9,6.1);
```
Each call to the assignment operator returns a reference to the current implicit argument which then becomes the implicit argument of the next call in the chain.

3.3 COMPILING CLASSES AND THEIR CLIENT PROGRAMS

There are several ways to compile a class and its client programs. The simplest way is to put the class interface, the client program, and the class implementation all together in the same file, as shown here. In this case, the three parts should be placed in that order: interface, program, implementation.

```
test_Point.cpp
#include <iostream>
#include <sstream>
using namespace std;

class Point
{ // ...
   // class interface
   // ...
};

int main()
{ // ...
   // client program
   // ...
}

Point::Point(double x, double y) : _x(x), _y(y) { }
   // ...
   // class implementation
   // ...
```

For greater flexibility, the class interface and implementation may be placed in a separate *header file*, as shown below. Note that the name of the header file, Point.h, must be named in the directive

```
    #include "Point.h"
```
which is placed at the beginning of the file of each client program that uses the class.

```
test_Point.cpp
#include "Point.h"

int main()
{ // ...
   // client program
   // ...
}
```

```
Point.h
#include <iostream>
#include <sstream>
using namespace std;

class Point
{ // ...
   // class interface
   // ...
};

Point::Point(double x, double y) : _x(x), _y(y) { }
   // ...
   // class implementation
   // ...
```

The compiler will insert the entire contents of the Point.h file into the test_Point.cpp file at the location of the #include "Point.h" directive. Note that the other two directives and the using statement are not needed in the test_Point.cpp file because they will be inserted from the Point.h file.

The advantage of separating the class definition from its client programs is that it can be compiled separately, once. Then that compiled code needs only to be linked with the separately compiled programs that use it.

A third way to compile a class definition is to place its implementation in a separate file. This is illustrated in the figure below. Here, the interface of the Point class is in the header file

Point.h ("`.h`" stands for "header"), and its implementation is in the file `Point.cpp`. This allows better "information hiding."

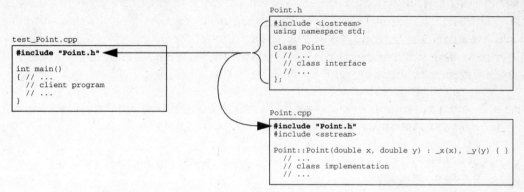

The implementation file can be compiled separately and the resulting (unreadable) binary code can be shipped to a client together with the header file, keeping the source code for the implementation secret. All the client needs to use the class is the interface information provided by the header file along with the actual machine code that will be linked to the compiled client programs.

Note that both `.cpp` files have to `#include` the `Point.h` header file. Consequently, from the point of view of the compiler, that three-file configuration is equivalent to this two-file alternative:

```
test_Point.cpp

#include <iostream>
using namespace std;

class Point
{ // ...
   // class interface
   // ...
};

int main()
{ // ...
   // client program
   // ...
}
```

```
Point.cpp

#include <iostream>
#include <sstream>
using namespace std;

class Point
{ // ...
   // class interface
   // ...
};

Point::Point(double x, double y) : _x(x), _y(y) { }
   // ...
   // class implementation
   // ...
```

It is possible to place the definitions of the class's members within the class definition itself instead of keeping the implementation separate. This is illustrated in the following example.

EXAMPLE 3.4 Placing the Class Implementation inside its Definition

This is a complete, self-contained program that is equivalent to the combined code from the previous three examples:

```
#include <iostream>
#include <sstream>  // defines the ostringstream class
using namespace std;

class Point
{ public:
    Point(double x=0.0, double y=0.0) : _x(x), _y(y) { }
    Point(const Point& p) : _x(p._x), _y(p._y) { }
    ~Point() { }
    Point& operator=(const Point& p)
```

```
        { _x = p._x;
          _y = p._y;
          return *this;
        }
      double x() const { return _x; }
      double y() const { return _y; }
      string toString() const
      { ostringstream output;
        output << "(" << _x << "," << _y << ")";
        return output.str();
      }
    protected:
      double _x, _y;
  };

  int main()
  { Point p0;                      // invokes default constructor
    cout << "p0 = " << p0.toString() << "\n";
    Point p1(5,-2);               // invokes default constructor
    cout << "p1 = " << p1.toString() << "\n";
    Point p2=p1;                   // invokes copy constructor
    cout << "p2 = " << p2.toString() << "\n";
    p0 = p1;                       // invokes assignment operator
    cout << "p0 = " << p0.toString() << "\n";
    cout << "p0.x() = " << p0.x() << "\n";
    cout << "p0.y() = " << p0.y() << "\n";
  }
```

Obviously, this method is much more succinct than the method used in the previous examples.

Placing the implementation of a class within its definition as in Example 3.4 is generally advisable only when a single programmer wants a compact, complete, self-contained program. Larger projects in the "real world" usually adhere to the information-hiding principles exemplified by the three separate files at the top of page 50.

When placing a class definition in a separate header file, it is good defensive programming practice to "wrap" the class definition within a #ifndef directive, like this:

```
#ifndef POINT_H
#define POINT_H
// ...
// class definition
// ...
#endif  // POINT_H
```

This assures that, if the code for the class definition indirectly gets included more than once in a program, the compiler will not attempt to compile it more than once. (A repeated attempt causes an error.) The directive

```
#ifndef POINT_H
```

tells the compiler to ignore all the code between that line and the next occurrence of an #endif directive if the symbol POINT_H has already been defined. The directive

```
#define POINT_H
```

defines that symbol. So the first time the compiler encounters this "wrapper" of directives it will define the `POINT_H` symbol, and then on any successive encounters it will ignore all the code wrapped by it.

Using an `#ifndef` directive wrapper then, here is the preferred configuration for the `Point` class and its test driver:

```
test_Point.cpp

#include "Point.h"

int main()
{ // ...
  // client program
  // ...
}
```

```
Point.h

#ifndef POINT_H
#define POINT_H

#include <iostream>
using namespace std;

class Point
{ // ...
  // class interface
  // ...
};

#endif  //POINT_H
```

```
Point.cpp

#include "Point.h"
#include <sstream>
using namespace std;

Point::Point(double x, double y) : _x(x), _y(y) { }
  // ...
  // class implementation
  // ...
```

3.4 FRIEND FUNCTIONS

A *friend function* in a class is a nonmember function that has access to the `protected` (and `private`) members of the class. It is declared using the `friend` keyword. Friend functions are usually declared as alternatives to member functions when one wants the implicit parameter to be explicit. The overloaded output operator is the most common example.

EXAMPLE 3.5 Overloading the Output Operator in the `Point` Class

```
class Point
{   friend ostream& operator<<(ostream&, const Point&);
  public:
    Point(double=0.0,double=0.0);          // default constructor
    Point(const Point&);                   // copy constructor
    Point& operator=(const Point&);        // assignment operator
    double x() const;
    double y() const;
    string toString() const;
  protected:
    double _x, _y;
};
ostream& operator<<(ostream& ostr, const Point& point)
{ return ostr << point.toString();
}
```
With this additional function, clients can output `Point` objects like this:

```
cout << "p0=" << p0 << ", p1=" << p1 << ", and p2=" << p2 << "\n";
```
obtaining output like this:

```
    p0=(0,0),  p1=(1,0),  and p2=(5,-2)
```
This allows `Point` objects to be output the same way that we output `int`s and `string`s.

3.5 A `Line` CLASS

The next example illustrates a class whose instances represent lines in the cartesian plane.

EXAMPLE 3.6 Interface for the `Line` Class

```
    class Line
    { public:
        Line(double=1.0,double=1.0);        // two-intercept form of a line
        Line(const Point&, double=0.0);       // point-slope form of a line
        Line(const Point&, const Point&);      // two-point form of a line
        Line(double,double,double);     // general form of a line
        Line(const Line&);              // copy constructor
        ~Line();                        // destructor
        Line& operator=(const Line&);   // assignment operator
        double xCoef() const;
        double yCoef() const;
        double cTerm() const;
        string toString() const;
      protected:
        double _a, _b, _c;      // coefficients in general form: ax+by+c=0
    };
```
This class has five constructors. Two of them use the `Point` class.

The first constructor is the default constructor. It could be used like this:
```
    Line line1;        // x + y = 1
    Line line2(7);     // x + 7y = 7
    Line line3(7,5);   // 5x + 7y = 35
```
The two parameters for this constructor represent the two intercepts of the line. So `line3` has x-intercept $(7, 0)$ and y-intercept $(0, 5)$, so its equation is $7x + 5y = 35$. The default intercepts are $(1, 0)$ and $(0, 1)$.

The second constructor uses the point-slope form of a line. It could be used like this:
```
    Line line4(Point(1,6),-2);   // 2x + y = 8
```
This constructs the line through the point $(1, 6)$ with slope -2. Its equation is $2x + y = 8$.

The third constructor uses the 2-point form of a line. It could be used like this:
```
    Line line5(Point(1,6),Point(-1,5));   // x - 2y = 11
```
This constructs the line through the point $(1, 6)$ with slope 1/2. Its equation is $x - 2y = -11$.

The fourth constructor uses the general 3-parameter form of the equation of a line: $Ax + By + C = 0$. It could be used like this:
```
    Line line6(2,3,6);   // 2x + 3y = -6
```
This constructs the line whose general equation is $2x + 3y + 6 = 0$.

The class has three accessor functions: `xCoef()`, `yCoef()`, and `cTerm()`, one for each of the three data members _a, _b, and _c.

Note that this interface should be preceded with the directive
```
    #include "Point.h"
```
since it uses the `Point` class.

EXAMPLE 3.7 Test Driver for the Line Class

```
int main()
{ Point p1(4,1);
  cout << "p1 = " << p1 << "\n";
  Line line1(2,3,6);
  cout << "line1: " << line1 << "\n";
  Line line2(-2,12);
  cout << "line2: " << line2 << "\n";
  Line line3(p1,3);
  cout << "line3: " << line3 << "\n";
  Point p2(0,5);
  cout << "p2 = " << p2 << "\n";
  Line line4(p1,p2);
  cout << "line4: " << line4 << "\n";
}
p1 = (4,1)
line1: 2x + 3y + 6 = 0
line2: 12x + -2y + 24 = 0
line3: 3x + -1y + -11 = 0
p2 = (0,5)
line4: 4x + 4y + -20 = 0
p2 is on line4
line4: 4x + 4y + -20 = 0
```

EXAMPLE 3.8 Implementation of the Line Class

```
ostream& operator<<(ostream& ostr, const Line& line)
{ return ostr << line.toString();
}
Line::Line(double x0, double y0) : _a(y0), _b(x0), _c(-x0*y0) { }
Line::Line(const Point& p, double m)
  : _a(m), _b(-1), _c(p._y-m*p._x) { }
Line::Line(const Point& p, const Point& q)
  : _a(q._y-p._y), _b(p._x-q._x), _c(q._x*p._y-p._x*q._y) { }
Line::Line(double a, double b, double c) : _a(a), _b(b), _c(c) { }
Line::Line(const Line& l) : _a(l._a), _b(l._b), _c(l._c) { }
Line::~Line() { }
Line& Line::operator=(const Line& line)
{ _a = line._a;
  _b = line._b;
  _c = line._c;
  return *this;
}
double Line::xCoef() const { return _a; }
double Line::yCoef() const { return _b; }
double Line::cTerm() const { return _c; }
string Line::toString() const
{ ostringstream out;
  out << _a << "x + " << _b << "y + " << _c << " = 0";
  return out.str();
}
```

3.6 A CLASS FOR RANDOM NUMBERS

Computer simulation is one of the most important applications of computing today. It is essential to most forms of scientific research, especially physical and biomedical research. It is also essential to engineering applications, from exploration for natural resources to weather prediction. Computer simulation requires a mechanism for modeling unpredictable behavior. This is done by means of random number generators.

EXAMPLE 3.9 Interface for the Random Class

Here is a class whose instances generate random numbers:

```
class Random
{ public:
    Random(unsigned long=0);
    void reset_seed(unsigned long=0);
    int integer(unsigned long=ULONG_MAX,unsigned long=1);
    double real();
  private:
    unsigned long _seed;  // INVARIANT: 0 <= _seed < ULONG_MAX
    void randomize();
};
```

The data member _seed is used to generate each random number. After each generation, it is automatically rescrambled to disguise any detectable pattern. It is initialized either by the constructor or by the computer's system clock. The latter method ensures that repeated runs of the same program will almost certainly produce different sequences of random numbers.

EXAMPLE 3.10 Test Driver for the Random Class

```
int main()
{ Random random;
  for (int i=0; i<25; i++)
    cout << random.integer(100) << " ";
  cout << "\n";
  for (int i=0; i<8; i++)
    cout << random.real() << " ";
  cout << "\n";
  int count[5]={0};
  for (int j=0; j<100000; j++)
    ++count[random.integer(4,0)];
  for (int i=0; i<5; i++)
    cout << "count[" << i << "] = " << count[i] << "\n";
}
```

The call random.integer(100) returns a random integer in the range 1 to 100. The call random.real() returns a random decimal number in the range 0 to 1. The call random.integer(4,0) returns a random integer in the range 0 to 4. That call is made 100,000 times and the results are tallied in the count[] array.

The output for one run is shown below. Out of 10,000 calls to random.integer(4,0), the value 3 was returned 20,011 times. That is very close to the expected 20%. Each of the other four values also was returned nearly 20% of the time.

```
43 83 42 14 40 50 97 23 84 37 45 72 4 16 50 63 92 36 42 87 41 11 4 36 87
0.937592 0.858781 0.652112 0.88836 0.0598571 0.237993 0.682301 0.32947
count[0] = 20044
count[1] = 19748
count[2] = 20035
count[3] = 20011
count[4] = 20162
```

EXAMPLE 3.11 Implementation of the Random Class

```
Random::Random(unsigned long seed) : _seed(seed)
{ if (seed == 0) _seed = time(NULL);
  randomize();
}
void Random::reset_seed(unsigned long seed)
{ _seed = seed;
  if (seed == 0) _seed = time(NULL);
  randomize();
}
int Random::integer(unsigned long hi,unsigned long lo)
{ // returns a random integer in the range lo to hi
  randomize();
  return (_seed/10)%(hi-lo+1) + lo;
}
double Random::real()
{ // returns a random real number in the range 0.0 to 1.0
  randomize();
  return double(_seed)/ULONG_MAX;
}
void Random::randomize()
{ _seed = (1103515245*_seed+123456789)%ULONG_MAX;
}
```

The call `time(NULL)` returns an integer that represents the number of seconds elapsed since some past reference time. This call requires the header `<ctime>` to be included:

```
#include <ctime>  // defines the time() function
```

The expression `(_seed/10)%(hi-lo+1) + lo` uses the current value of `_seed` to produce an integer in the range `lo` to `hi`. It is divided by 10 first to eliminate the alternation of odd and even numbers. The expression `(1103515245*_seed+123456789)%ULONG_MAX` produces an integer in the range 0 to 4,294,967,294 (`ULONG_MAX` – 1). The expression `(1103515245*_seed+123456789)` scrambles the seed.

3.7 STATIC MEMBERS

A *static* class member (data or function) is a member that has exactly one instance for the entire class. A *nonstatic* member has a separate instance for each object instantiated from the class. Members which characterize the class itself or which do not require separate instances for separate objects should be declared to be static with the `static` keyword.

EXAMPLE 3.12 Interface for the `Card` Class

Here is a class whose objects represent ordinary playing cards:
```
class Card
{   friend ostream& operator<<(ostream&, const Card&);
  public:
    enum Rank { TWO, THREE, FOUR, FIVE, SIX, SEVEN, EIGHT, NINE,
                TEN, JACK, QUEEN, KING, ACE };
    enum Suit { CLUB, DIAMOND, HEART, SPADE };
    Card(Rank=ACE,Suit=SPADE);        // default constructor
    Card(int,int);                    // constructor
    Card(const Card&);                // copy constructor
    ~Card();                          // destructor
    Rank rank() const;
    Suit suit() const;
    bool isFaceCard() const;
    int count() const;
    string toString() const;
    string abbr() const;
    bool operator<(const Card&) const;
    bool operator>(const Card&) const;
    bool operator<=(const Card&) const;
    bool operator>=(const Card&) const;
    bool operator==(const Card&) const;
    bool operator!=(const Card&) const;
  private:
    Rank _rank;
    Suit _suit;
    static int _count[15][4];
};
```
The array `_count[][]` is used to keep a count of how many cards of each kind exist (*i.e.*, have been instantiated). For example, if the value of `_count[12][3]` is 2, then 2 aces of spades have been created (constructed). This variable is declared `static` because we need only one instance of it for the entire class.

EXAMPLE 3.13 Implementation of the `Card` Class

Here are implementations for some of the `Card` class members:
```
Card::Card(Rank rank, Suit suit) : _rank(rank), _suit(suit)
{ ++_count[_rank][_suit];
}

Card::~Card()
{ --_count[_rank][_suit];
}

int Card::count() const
{ return _count[_rank][_suit];
}

bool Card::operator<(const Card& card) const
```

```
  { return _rank<card._rank || _rank==card._rank && _suit<card._suit;
  }
```

```
    int Card::_count[15][4]={{0}};
```
Note first how the static array `_count[][]` is defined and initialized in the implementation. Even though the code for it here is nearly the same as in the interface, the definition here is required. The code for `_count[][]` in the interface only declares the member; it does not define it.

Each time a card is created (in a constructor) the `_count[][]` array is incremented for that card. The destructor decrements that card's counter. The nonstatic   `count()`   function returns the number of existing cards for its implicit argument.

EXAMPLE 3.14 Test Driver for the `Card` Class

```
    int main()
    { Card c1;
      cout << "c1 = " << c1 << ", c1.count() = " << c1.count() << "\n";
      Card c2;
      cout << "c2 = " << c2 << ", c2.count() = " << c2.count() << "\n";
      cout << "c1 = " << c1 << ", c1.count() = " << c1.count() << "\n";
      { Card c3;
        cout << "c3 = " << c3 << ", c3.count() = " << c3.count() << "\n";
      }
      cout << "c1 = " << c1 << ", c1.count() = " << c1.count() << "\n";
      Card c4(Card::SIX,Card::HEART);
      cout << "c4 = " << c4 << ", c4.count() = " << c4.count() << "\n";
    }
```
```
    c1 = ace of spades, c1.count() = 1
    c2 = ace of spades, c2.count() = 2
    c1 = ace of spades, c1.count() = 2
    c3 = ace of spades, c3.count() = 3
    c1 = ace of spades, c1.count() = 2
    c4 = six of hearts, c4.count() = 1
```
Notice how the enumeration literals `SIX` and `HEART` are referenced in the test driver:
```
    Card c4(Card::SIX,Card::HEART);
```
An enumeration literal is actually a `static const int`. As a static member, when referenced outside the class it must be prefixed with `Card::`.

3.8 COMPOSITION

When one class is used as the type of a member variable for another class, we say that the latter class is *composed* with the former class.

EXAMPLE 3.15 A Class for Decks of Cards

```
    class Deck
    { public:
        Deck();
        void print() const;
        void shuffle() const;
      protected:
```

```
    Card** _card;  // an array of pointers
    static const int _SIZE;
    static Random _random;  // random number generator
};
```

Here the Deck class is composed with the Card class and the Random class.

Also note that this Deck class has two private static members: the const int _SIZE and the Random object _random.

EXAMPLE 3.16 Test Driver for the Deck Class

```
int main()
{ Deck deck;
  deck.print();    // prints all 52 cards
  deck.shuffle();  // shuffles the deck
  deck.print();
  deck.shuffle();
  deck.print();
}
```

```
AS KS QS JS TS 9S 8S 7S 6S 5S 4S 3S 2S
AH KH QH JH TH 9H 8H 7H 6H 5H 4H 3H 2H
AD KD QD JD TD 9D 8D 7D 6D 5D 4D 3D 2D
AC KC QC JC TC 9C 8C 7C 6C 5C 4C 3C 2C

AC 3S KS AD 2S AH KC 4H AS 9C TC 8H 7H
KD KH 9H QD 5S 2H JH 9S 8C QS 7D 6D TH
JC 3D 5D QC TS 9D JD JS 4D 7S 8D 3H 8S
TD 2C 2D 4C 6C 5C 5H 4S 6H 6S 3C 7C QH

AD 3H 8C QD 2C 6D TS 7S 2H TH 3C 2D 3S
7D 5C 7C AS AC 4S 8H 6C 4H KC 8D 7H 4D
9C 9D 5S JD QS 6H 9S KS 5H TD 2S 8S 5D
KH QC QH 4C AH KD 6S JH TC JS 3D JC 9H
```

EXAMPLE 3.17 Implementation for the Deck Class

```
Deck::Deck()
{ _card = new Card*[_SIZE];
  int r=13, s=3;
  for (int i=0; i<_SIZE; i++)
  { if (r==0)
    { r = 12;
      s = (s-1)%4;
    }
    else --r;
    _card[i] = new Card(r,s);
  }
}
void Deck::print() const
{ for (int i=0; i<_SIZE; i++)
    cout << _card[i]->abbr() << (i%13==12?"\n":" ");
  cout << "\n";
}
```

```
      void Deck::shuffle() const
      { for (int i=0; i<_SIZE; i++)
        { int j = _random.integer(_SIZE)-1;
          Card* p = _card[i];
          _card[i] = _card[j];
          _card[j] = p;
        }
      }
      const int Deck::_SIZE=52;
      Random Deck::_random;
```

Notice how the two static members are initialized in the interface. The const int _SIZE is initialized with the initializer =52. The Random object _random is initialized by the default constructor.

The default constructor constructs all 52 Card objects with the statement

```
      _card[i] = new Card(r,s);
```

which invokes the Card constructor. Prior to that for loop, it first allocated the dynamic array _card with the statement

```
      _card = new Card*[_SIZE];
```

This makes _card an array of 52 pointers to Card objects.

The shuffle() function swaps each of the 52 Card pointers in the _card array with another one selected at random using the Random object _random.

3.9 INHERITANCE

An important feature of object-oriented programming is that new classes can be derived from existing classes. If a new class is simply an extension of an old class, only adding new data members and/or new member functions, then it can inherit the definition of the old class, thereby obviating the need to replicate its code. The new class is called a *subclass* of the old class. If Y is a subclass of X, we also call Y a *derived class* of the *base class* X.

EXAMPLE 3.18 Monte Carlo Simulation to Approximate Pi

The mathematical constant π (pi) is defined to be the ratio of the circumference to the diameter of a circle. This irrational number is approximately 3.1416. There are many classic algorithms for computing more accurate approximations. One method, called *Monte Carlo simulation*, is based upon the geometric facts that π is

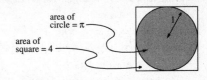

equal to the area of a circle of radius 1 and that the area of its circumscribing square is 4. So the ratio of area of the circle to that of the square is π/4, and thus the probability that a point selected at random in the square hits the interior of the circle is also π/4. So if we select a large number of points in the square at random, the fraction of them that fall within the circle should be approximately π/4.

Here is a program that selects 10,000,000 points at random from the square and counts how many of them hit the interior of the circle:

```
      int main()
      { const int SHOTS=10000000;   // 10M
        int hits=0;
        for (int i=0; i<SHOTS; i++)
        { RandomPoint p0(1,1,-1,-1);   // -1 <= x <= 1 and -1 <= y <= 1
          double x = p0.x();
          double y = p0.y();
```

```
      if (x*x+y*y<1) ++hits;
   }
   cout << "SHOTS = " << SHOTS << "\n";
   cout << "hits = " << hits << "\n";
   cout << "pi = " << 4.0*hits/SHOTS << "\n";
}
SHOTS = 10000000
hits = 7854654
pi = 3.14186
```

The approximation 3.14186 is off by only 0.00027, less than 0.01%.

The Monte Carlo simulation in Example 3.18 required the use of a RandomPoint class. Instances of that class should be points in the cartesian plane whose coordinates are selected at random from the range −1 to 1. The object-oriented solution to this problem is to extend our Point class.

EXAMPLE 3.19 The **RandomPoint** Class

Here are the interface and implementation for a RandomPoint class:

```
class RandomPoint : public Point
{ // instances represent randomly selected points in the plane
   public:
      RandomPoint(double=1.0,double=1.0,double=0.0,double=0.0);
   protected:
      double _x1, _x2, _y1, _y2;
      static Random _random;
};
```

The code **: public Point** appended to the class declaration tells the compiler that this class is to be a subclass of the Point class. So this new class inherits the three member functions [x(), y(), and toString()] and the two data members (_x and _y) from the Point class, extending it by adding its own default constructor and five new data members (_x1, _x2, _y1, _y2, and _random).

The constructor takes four arguments: the bounds (_x1, _x2, _y1, and _y2) on the coordinates for the random points. In the program in Example 3.18, we set those bounds to be −1 and 1 for both x and y, making all the random points fall within the circumscribing square.

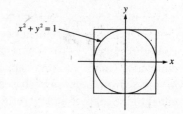

The other data member is the static random number generator _random. Defining this to be static means that only one random number generator will be created for the entire class, instead of one for each instance of the class. If it were not static, then the program would have to create 10,000,000 random number generators.

EXAMPLE 3.20 Test Driver for the **RandomPoint** Class

```
int main()
{ RandomPoint p0;
   cout << "p0 = " << p0 << "\n";
   RandomPoint p1(100,400);
   cout << "p1 = " << p1 << "\n";
```

```
    RandomPoint p2(1000,60000,2000,80000);
    cout << "p2 = " << p2 << "\n";
}
```

```
p0 = (0.22508,0.0406549)
p1 = (45.4084,260.726)
p2 = (1913.5,71656)
```

EXAMPLE 3.21 Implementation of the `RandomPoint` Class

```
RandomPoint::RandomPoint(double x2, double y2, double x1, double y1)
   : _x2(x2), _y2(y2), _x1(x1), _y1(y1)
{ double x = _random.real();
  _x = (_x2 - _x1)*x + _x1;
  double y = _random.real();
  _y = (_y2 - _y1)*y + _y1;
}
Random RandomPoint::_random;
```

The `RandomPoint` constructor uses the `static` `_random` object to generate two random numbers, x and y. The `Random` class specifies that these will be in the range 0 to 1. They are then scaled to fall within their required bounds. The following derivation shows that those are the correct scaling equations:

$$0 \le x \le 1$$

$$(x_2 - x_1)(0) \le (x_2 - x_1)(x) \le (x_2 - x_1)(1)$$

$$0 \le (x_2 - x_1)x \le x_2 - x_1$$

$$x_1 \le (x_2 - x_1)x + x_1 \le x_2$$

If $0 \le x \le 1$, then $x_1 \le (x_2 - x_1)x \le x_2$ for any x_1 and x_2, so `(_x2 - _x1)*x + _x1` is between `_x1` and `_x2`.

Note that the `static` `_random` object must be defined in the class implementation, separately from its declaration in the class interface.

Inheritance is often called an "is a" relationship. For example a `RandomPoint` object is a `Point` object. This characterization is used to distinguish inheritance from composition, which is called a "has a" relationship. For example, a `RandomPoint` object has a `Random` object, as a data member. The `RandomPoint` class inherits from the `Point` class and is composed with the `Random` class.

In this chapter we have declared all nonpublic members to be `protected`. This means that they are not accessible from client programs or other classes, except derived classes. Protected members are accessible from derived classes. To prevent access from derived classes, members should be declared to be `private` instead of `protected`.

Review Questions

3.1   What is a class in C++?

3.2   What is a class interface?

3.3   What is a class implementation?

3.4   What is a constructor?

3.5   What is a default constructor?

3.6   What is a copy constructor?

3.7   What is a destructor?

3.8   What is an overloaded assignment operator?

3.9   What is the difference between a class's copy constructor and its assignment operator?

3.10 What is an initialization list?

3.11 What is an accessor function?

3.12 What is an implicit argument?

3.13 What is a default argument?

3.14 What is a static member?

3.15 What is a subclass?

3.16 What is the meaning of the keyword `const` when appended to the header of a class member function?

3.17 What is the meaning of the keyword `this` when used in the implementation of a class member function?

3.18 What is the value in placing a class definition in a separate header file?

3.19 What is the value in placing the implementation of a class definition in a separate file?

3.20 Why can't we add a sixth constructor to the `Line` class (Example 3.6 on page 54) that uses the slope-intercept form of a line ($y = mx + b$)?

3.21 What is the difference between inheritance and composition?

3.22 What is the difference between an "is a" relationship and a "has a" relationship?

3.23 What is the difference among `public`, `protected`, and `private` members of a class?

Problems

3.1   Modify the `Point` class so that the default constructor prints "DEFAULT CONSTRUCTOR INVOKED", the copy constructor prints "COPY CONSTRUCTOR INVOKED", and the assignment operator prints "ASSIGNMENT OPERATOR INVOKED". Then test it with a test driver to see when each of these member functions is invoked.

3.2   Add the following member functions to the `Point` class:
```
double magnitude() const;  // polar coordinate r
double amplitude() const;  // polar coordinate θ
```
Use the formulas

$$r = \sqrt{x^2 + y^2}$$

$$\theta = \operatorname{atan}(y/x)$$

3.3   Add the following member function to the `Point` class:
```
void rotate(double);
```
This rotates the point counterclockwise about the origin by the given angle.

Use the formulas

$$x = r\cos\theta$$

$$y = r\sin\theta$$

where r and θ are the polar coordinates for the point. (See Problem 3.2.)

3.4   Add the following `friend` function to the `Point` class (Example 3.1 on page 47):
```
friend Point operator-(const Point&);
```
This function returns the negative of the given point. For example, if `p` represents the point $(5, -2)$, then `-p` would represent the point $(-5, 2)$.

3.5   Add the following `friend` functions to the `Point` class:

```
friend Point operator+(const Point&, const Point&);
friend Point operator-(const Point&, const Point&);
```
These functions return the sum and the difference of the two given points.

3.6   Add the following `friend` functions to the `Point` class:
```
friend Point operator*(const double, const Point&);
friend Point operator/(const Point&, const double);
```
These functions multiply and divide the given point by a given number.

3.7   Add the following `friend` function to the `Point` class (Example 3.1 on page 47):
```
friend double distance(const Point&, const Point&);
```
This function returns the distance between the two given points. Use the formula
$$d = \sqrt{(x_1 - x_2)^2 + (y_1 - y_2)^2}$$

3.8   Add the following static constant to the `Point` class:
```
static const Point ORIGIN;   // the point (0,0)
```

3.9   Add the following member functions to the `Line` class (Example 3.6 on page 54):
```
double slope() const;
double xIntercept() const;
double yIntercept() const;
```
Use the following formulas for a line whose general form is $ax + by + c = 0$:
$$m = \frac{-a}{b}$$

$$x_0 = \frac{-c}{a}$$

$$y_0 = \frac{-c}{b}$$

3.10   Add the following member functions to the `Line` class (Example 3.6 on page 54):
```
bool isHorizontal() const;
bool isVertical() const;
```

3.11   Add the following member functions to the `Line` class (Example 3.6 on page 54):
```
double distanceTo(Point&) const;
```
Use this formula for the distance from a point to a line:
$$d = \frac{|ax + by + c|}{\sqrt{x^2 + y^2}}$$

3.12   Add the following member functions to the `Line` class (Example 3.6 on page 54):
```
bool contains(Point&) const;
```

3.13   Add the following `friend` functions to the `Line` class (Example 3.6 on page 54):
```
friend bool areParallel(Line&,Line&);
friend bool arePerpendicular(Line&,Line&);
```
Use the conditions $a_1 b_2 = b_1 a_2$ and $a_1 a_2 + b_1 b_2 = 0$ for the parallelism and perpendicularity of two lines whose general forms are $a_1 x + b_1 y + c_1 = 0$ and $a_2 x + b_2 y + c_2 = 0$.

3.14   Add the following `friend` function to the `Line` class (Example 3.6 on page 54):
```
friend double angle(Line&,Line&);
```
Use this formula for the angle between two lines with slopes m_1 and m_2:
$$\theta = \operatorname{atan}\left(\frac{m_2 - m_1}{1 + m_1 m_2}\right)$$

The special cases where the lines are either horizontal or vertical must be handled separately.

3.15   Add the following static constants to the `Line` class:
```
static const Line X_AXIS;   // the line y = 0
static const Line Y_AXIS;   // the line x = 0
```

```
static const Line DIAGONAL;   // the line y = x
```
3.16 Add the following member functions to the `Point` class:
```
double distanceTo(Line&) const;
```
(See Problem 3.11.)

3.17 Add the following member functions to the `Point` class:
```
bool isOn(Line&) const;
```
3.18 Replace the default constructor in the `Line` class (Example 3.6 on page 54) with one that uses the slope-intercept form ($y = mx + b$) of a line instead of the two-intercept form.

3.19 Finish the implementation of the `Card` class (Example 3.13 on page 58) and then test it.

3.20 Show how the interface of the `RandomPoint` class would look without using inheritance.

3.21 Implement and test a `RandomLine` class that uses the `Random` class (Example 3.12 on page 58) to extend the `Line` class (Example 3.6 on page 54) the same way that the `RandomPoint` class (Example 3.19 on page 62) extends the `Point` class (Example 3.1 on page 47).

3.22 Write and run a program that prints the system clock time once per second for 10 seconds. Use a `for` loop to force 1-second delays. Experiment to determine the correct length of the `for` loop; it will depend upon the speed of your computer and the statement(s) you put in the loop.

3.23 Implement and test a `Purse` class whose instances represent coin purses containing pennies, nickels, dimes, and quarters. Include member functions for inserting and removing a given amount of cash. Enforce the class invariant that the total number of coins is minimal.

Answers to Review Questions

3.1 A *class* is an encapsulation of data and functions that forms a data type for objects. C++ allows programmers to define their own classes, thereby extending the language itself.

3.2 The *interface* of a class is that part of the class's code that is needed by the compiler to compile programs that use the class. It consists of the declarations of the class's member functions and data members. It may also contain other declarations and definitions.

3.3 The *implementation* of a class contains the rest of the class's code that was left out of its declaration. It completes the definitions of its member functions by including their bodies. The compiled code of any program that uses the class must be linked with the compiled code of the class implementation before an executable program can be created.

3.4 A *constructor* is a member function of a class that is invoked to construct new objects (instances) of the class. A constructor has the same name as the class itself and it has no return type.

3.5 A *default constructor* is a class constructor that can be invoked with no arguments. It either has no parameters or all of its parameters have default values. The compiler will create a default constructor automatically if it is omitted by the programmer.

3.6 A *copy constructor* is a class constructor that is invoked to construct a new object that is to be a copy of an existing object. It has a single parameter of type `const` reference. The compiler will create a copy constructor automatically if it is omitted by the programmer.

3.7 A *destructor* is a member function of a class that is invoked when its implicit parameter goes out of scope. A constructor has the same name as the class itself, preceded by the tilde (~) character, and it has no return type. The compiler will create a destructor automatically if it is omitted by the programmer.

3.8 An *overloaded assignment operator* is a class member function that is invoked whenever one instance of the class is assigned to another. Its prototype is
```
Object& operator=(const Object&);
```
for a class named `Object`. The compiler will create an assignment operator automatically if it is omitted by the programmer.

3.9   The copy constructor is used to copy an existing object into a new object; the assignment operator is used to copy an existing object into another existing object.

3.10   An *initialization list* is a list of expressions of the form `_x(x)`, where `x` is a parameter of a class constructor and `_x` is a data member of the class. That expression is equivalent to the initialization `_x = x` of the data member. Initialization lists are used only in constructors. They are appended to the constructor's header, preceded by a colon (`:`). For example, `_x(x), _y(y)` is an initialization list for the default constructor on the first line of the implementation of the `Point` class defined in Example 3.1 on page 47.

3.11   An *accessor function* is a class member function that provides read-only access to a data member of the class. For example, the member functions `x()` and `y()` are accessor functions in the default construct of the `Point` class defined in Example 3.1 on page 47.

3.12   When a class member function is called, it must be bound to some instance of that class. That object is called the *implicit argument* of the call. For example, the `Point` object p0 in the call `p0.y()` on the last line of the test driver program in Example 3.2 on page 48 is the implicit argument of that call.

3.13   A *default argument* is a member function parameter value that is specified in the parameter list of the function's declaration and is used as the value of the corresponding parameter if its corresponding argument is omitted. For example, the value 0.0 is the default argument for both parameters in the default construct of the `Point` class defined in Example 3.1 on page 47.

3.14   A *static member* is a class member (data or function) that will have exactly one instance for all instances of the class. (Nonstatic members have separate instances for each instance of the class.) So a static member is a characteristic of the class itself instead of the class's objects. Static members have no implicit argument, so they are referenced by prefixing their names with `X::`, where X is the name of the class itself.

3.15   A class Y is a *subclass* of a class X if Y inherits from X. That means that Y is declared like this:

```
class Y : public X
```

Consequently, the members (functions and data) of X are also members of Y.

3.16   A `const` member function is declared by appending the `const` keyword to its header. Such functions are prohibited from changing the state (*i.e.*, the data members) of the function call's implicit argument.

3.17   When used in the implementation of a class member function, the keyword `this` is a pointer to the implicit argument when the function is called. For example, on the last line of the implementation of the assignment operator in Example 3.3 on page 48, `this` points to the object to which the point p is being assigned. The statement

```
return *this;
```

returns a reference to that object, thereby allowing chained assignments for instances of the `Point` class.

3.18   The advantage of placing a class definition in a separate header file is that its code needs to be stored only once, even though it may be used by many different programs.

3.19   The advantage of placing a class implementation in a separate file (as illustrated on page 50) is that it allows the implementation to be "hidden" from clients who use the class. The implementation file can be compiled separately allowing the class to be distributed as a pair of files: its readable header file, which contains only the class interface, and its compiled implementation file in (unreadable) binary form.

3.20   We cannot add a sixth constructor to the `Line` class (Example 3.6 on page 54) that uses the slope-intercept form of a line because its parameter list would be `(double,double)`, and we already have a constructor with that parameter list. Overloading requires unique parameter lists.

3.21   If class Y inherits from class X, then Y has the same members (functions and data) as X. On the other hand, if Y is composed with Z, then Y simply has a data member of type Z. For example,

```
class Y : public X
{ Z _z;
}
```

3.22 Inheritance is an "is a" relationship. Composition is an "has a" relationship. In the example in Problem 3.21, Y is an X and has a Z.

3.23 Class members that are declared to be private are accessible only from within the class itself (or from friend classes and functions). Class members that are declared to be protected are accessible only from within the class itself (or from friend classes and functions) and from derived classes. Class members that are declared to be public are accessible everywhere.

Solutions to Problems

3.1 Modified implementations of Point class functions:

```
Point::Point(double x, double y) : _x(x), _y(y)
{ cout << "DEFAULT CONSTRUCTOR INVOKED ON " << *this << "\n";
}
Point::Point(const Point& p) : _x(p._x), _y(p._y)
{ cout << "COPY CONSTRUCTOR INVOKED ON " << *this << "\n";
}
Point::~Point()
{ cout << "DESTRUCTOR INVOKED ON " << *this << "\n";
}
Point& Point::operator=(const Point& point)
{ cout << "ASSIGNMENT OPERATOR INVOKED ON " << *this << "\n";
  _x = point._x;
  _y = point._y;
  return *this;
}
```

Test driver:

```
int main()
{ Point p0;  // invokes default constructor
  Point p1(1);  // invokes default constructor
  Point p2=p1;  // initialization invokes copy constructor
  p1 = Point(5,-2);  // assignment invokes assignment operator
}
DEFAULT CONSTRUCTOR INVOKED ON (0,0)
DEFAULT CONSTRUCTOR INVOKED ON (1,0)
COPY CONSTRUCTOR INVOKED ON (1,0)
DEFAULT CONSTRUCTOR INVOKED ON (5,-2)
ASSIGNMENT OPERATOR INVOKED ON (1,0)
DESTRUCTOR INVOKED ON (5,-2)
DESTRUCTOR INVOKED ON (1,0)
DESTRUCTOR INVOKED ON (5,-2)
DESTRUCTOR INVOKED ON (0,0)
```

3.2 Implementations of extra member functions of the Point class:

```
double Point::magnitude() const { return sqrt(_x*_x+_y*_y); }
double Point::amplitude() const { return atan(_y/_x); }
```

3.3 Implementation of another member function of the Point class:

```
void Point::rotate(double alpha)
{ double r = magnitude();
  double theta = amplitude() + alpha;
  _x = r*cos(theta);
  _y = r*sin(theta);
}
```

3.4 Implementation of a friend function of the Point class:

```
Point operator-(const Point& point)
```

```
              { return Point(-1*point._x,-1*point._y);
              }
```

3.5   Implementation of more `friend` functions for the `Point` class:

```
         Point operator+(const Point& p1, const Point& p2)
         { return Point(p1._x+p2._x,p1._y+p2._y);
         }
         Point operator-(const Point& p1, const Point& p2)
         { return Point(p1._x-p2._x,p1._y-p2._y);
         }
```

3.6   Implementation of more `friend` functions for the `Point` class:

```
         Point operator*(const double coef, const Point& point)
         { return Point(coef*point._x,coef*point._y);
         }
         Point operator/(const Point& point, const double divisor)
         { return Point(point._x/divisor,point._y/divisor);
         }
```

3.7   Implementation of another `friend` function for the `Point` class:

```
         double distance(const Point& p1, const Point& p2)
         { float dx=(p1._x-p2._x);
           float dy=(p1._y-p2._y);
           return sqrt(dx*dx+dy*dy);
         }
```

3.8   Definitions of a static constant for the `Point` class:

```
         const Point Point::ORIGIN(0,0);
```

3.9   Implementation of more member functions for the `Line` class:

```
         double Line::slope() const { return -_a/_b; }
         double Line::xIntercept() const { return -_c/_a; }
         double Line::yIntercept() const { return -_c/_b; }
```

3.10   Implementation of more member functions for the `Line` class:

```
         bool Line::isHorizontal() const { return (_a == 0); }
         bool Line::isVertical() const { return (_b == 0); }
```

3.11   Implementation of another member function for the `Line` class:

```
         double Line::distanceTo(Point& p) const
         { return abs(_a*p._x+_b*p._y+_c)/sqrt(_a*_a+_b*_b);
         }
```

3.12   Implementation of another member function for the `Line` class:

```
         bool Line::contains(Point& p) const
         { return (_a*p.x() + _b*p.y() + _c == 0);
         }
```

3.13   Implementation of more `friend` functions for the `Line` class:

```
         bool areParallel(Line& line1, Line& line2)
         { return (line1._a*line2._b == line1._b*line2._a);
         }
         bool arePerpendicular(Line& line1, Line& line2)
         { return (line1._a*line2._a + line1._b*line2._b == 0);
         }
```

3.14   Implementation of another `friend` function for the `Line` class:

```
         double angle(Line& line1, Line& line2)
         { const double PI=3.1415926535897932;
           if (areParallel(line1,line2)) return 0;
           if (arePerpendicular(line1,line2)) return PI/2;
           if (line1.isVertical()) return atan(-1.0/line2.slope());
           if (line2.isVertical()) return atan(-1.0/line1.slope());
           double m1 = line1.slope();
           double m2 = line2.slope();
```

```
          return atan((m2-m1)/(1+m1*m2));
      }
```

3.15 Definitions of static constants for the Line class:

```
      const Line Line::X_AXIS(0,1,0);
      const Line Line::Y_AXIS(1,0,0);
      const Line Line::DIAGONAL(1,-1,0);
```

3.16 Implementation of another member function for the Point class:

```
      double Point::distanceTo(Line& line) const
      { double a = line._a;
        double b = line._b;
        double c = line._c;
        return abs(a*_x+b*_y+c)/sqrt(a*a+b*b);
      }
```

3.17 Implementation of another member function for the Point class:

```
      bool Point::isOn(Line& line) const
      { double a = line._a;
        double b = line._b;
        double c = line._c;
        return (a*_x + b*_y + c == 0);
      }
```

3.18 Replacement for the default constructor for the Line class:

```
      Point::Point(double m, double b) : _a(m), _b(-1), _c(b) { }
```

3.19 Complete implementation for Card class:

```
      ostream& operator<<(ostream& ostr, const Card& card)
      { return ostr << card.toString();
      }
      Card::Card(Rank rank, Suit suit) : _rank(rank), _suit(suit)
      { ++_count[_rank][_suit];
      }
      Card::Card(int r, int s) : _rank(Rank(r)), _suit(Suit(s))
      { ++_count[_rank][_suit];
      }
      Card::Card(const Card& card) : _rank(card._rank),
      _suit(card._suit)
      { ++_count[_rank][_suit];
      }
      Card::~Card() { --_count[_rank][_suit]; }
      Card::Rank Card::rank() const { return _rank; }
      Card::Suit Card::suit() const { return _suit; }
      bool Card::isFaceCard() const { return (_rank > NINE); }
      int Card::count() const { return _count[_rank][_suit]; }
      string Card::toString() const
      { string str;
        switch (_rank)
        { case TWO:   str = "two of ";   break;
          case THREE: str = "three of ";   break;
          case FOUR:  str = "four of ";   break;
          case FIVE:  str = "five of ";   break;
          case SIX:   str = "six of ";   break;
          case SEVEN: str = "seven of ";   break;
          case EIGHT: str = "eight of ";   break;
          case NINE:  str = "nine of ";   break;
          case TEN:   str = "ten of ";   break;
          case JACK:  str = "jack of ";   break;
          case QUEEN: str = "queen of ";   break;
          case KING:  str = "king of ";   break;
```

```
      default:     str = "ace of ";
    }
    switch (_suit)
    { case CLUB:     str += "clubs";       break;
      case DIAMOND: str += "diamonds";   break;
      case HEART:    str += "hearts";      break;
      default:       str += "spades";
    }
    return str;
}
string Card::abbr() const
{ string str;
    switch (_rank)
    { case TWO:    str = "2";   break;
      case THREE: str = "3";   break;
      case FOUR:  str = "4";   break;
      case FIVE:  str = "5";   break;
      case SIX:   str = "6";   break;
      case SEVEN: str = "7";   break;
      case EIGHT: str = "8";   break;
      case NINE:  str = "9";   break;
      case TEN:   str = "T";   break;
      case JACK:  str = "J";   break;
      case QUEEN: str = "Q";   break;
      case KING:  str = "K";   break;
      default:     str = "A";
    }
    switch (_suit)
    { case CLUB:     str += "C";  break;
      case DIAMOND: str += "D";  break;
      case HEART:    str += "H";  break;
      default:       str += "S";
    }
    return str;
}
bool Card::operator<(const Card& card) const
{ return _rank<card._rank || _rank==card._rank &&
_suit<card._suit;
}
bool Card::operator>(const Card& card) const
{ return _rank>card._rank || _rank==card._rank &&
_suit>card._suit;
}
bool Card::operator<=(const Card& card) const
{ return _rank<=card._rank || _rank==card._rank &&
_suit<=card._suit;
}
bool Card::operator>=(const Card& card) const
{ return _rank>=card._rank || _rank==card._rank &&
_suit>=card._suit;
}
bool Card::operator==(const Card& card) const
{ return _rank == card._rank && _suit == card._suit;
}
bool Card::operator!=(const Card& card) const
{ return _rank != card._rank || _suit != card._suit;
```

```
        }
        int Card::_count[15][4]={{0}};
```

3.20 Without using inheritance to extend the Point class, the interface for the RandomPoint class would be:

```
class RandomPoint
{ // instances represent randomly selected points in the plane
  public:
    RandomPoint(double=0.0,double=0.0);   // default constructor
    RandomPoint(double,double,double,double);
    double x() const;
    double y() const;
    string toString() const;
  protected:
    double _x, _y, _x1, _x2, _y1, _y2;
    static Random _random;
};
```

Notice that the default arguments of the previous version of the RandomPoint class's default constructor have to be removed to avoid conflicting with the original Point class's default constructor, now redefined to be the RandomPoint class's default constructor. (The copy constructor, destructor, and assignment operator are omitted because the corresponding versions created by the compiler will be the same.)

3.21 Interface for RandomLine class:

```
class RandomLine : public Line
{ // instances represent randomly selected lines in the cartesian
plane
  public:
    RandomLine();
  protected:
    static Random _random;
};
```

Implementation for RandomLine class:

```
RandomLine::RandomLine()
{ _a = _random.real();
  _b = _random.real();
  _c = _random.real();
}
Random RandomLine::_random;
```

Test driver for RandomLine class:

```
int main()
{ RandomLine line0;
  cout << "line0: " << line0 << "\n";
  RandomLine line1;
  cout << "line1: " << line1 << "\n";
  line0 = RandomLine();
  cout << "line0: " << line0 << "\n";
}
```

```
line0: 0.74368x + 0.372701y + 0.548289 = 0
line1: 0.124666x + 0.872231y + 0.545966 = 0
line0: 0.636143x + 0.82803y + 0.218931 = 0
```

3.22 Prints the system clock time once per second for 10 seconds:

```
#include <ctime>   // defines the time() function
#include <iostream>
using namespace std;
int main()
{ for (int i=0; i<10; i++)
```

```
{ cout << "time(NULL) = " << time(NULL) << "\n";
  for (int j=0; j<20000; j++)
    time(NULL);
}
```
```
time(NULL) = 928670401
time(NULL) = 928670402
time(NULL) = 928670403
time(NULL) = 928670404
time(NULL) = 928670405
time(NULL) = 928670406
time(NULL) = 928670407
time(NULL) = 928670408
time(NULL) = 928670409
time(NULL) = 928670410
```

3.23 Interface for Purse class:

```
#ifndef PURSE_H
#define PURSE_H
#include <iostream>
using namespace std;
class Purse
{ // instances represent purses containing coins
  public:
    Purse(int=0,int=0,int=0,int=0);
    int pennies() const;
    int nickels() const;
    int dimes() const;
    int quarters() const;
    float value() const;
    void insert(float);
    void remove(float);
    float empty();
    bool isEmpty() const;
  private:
    int _pennies;
    int _nickels;
    int _dimes;
    int _quarters;
    void reduce();
    //   INVARIANTS: 0 <= _pennies < 5
    //               0 <= _nickels < 2
    //               0 <= dimes < 3
    //               0 <= _quarters
};
#endif  // PURSE_H
```

Implementation for Purse class:

```
#include "Purse.h"
Purse::Purse(int pennies, int nickels, int dimes, int quarters)
   : _pennies(pennies), _nickels(nickels), _dimes(dimes),
     _quarters(quarters)
{ reduce();
}
int Purse::pennies() const { return _pennies; }
int Purse::nickels() const { return _nickels; }
int Purse::dimes() const { return _dimes; }
int Purse::quarters() const { return _quarters; }
```

```
float Purse::value() const
{ return 0.01*_pennies + 0.05*_nickels + 0.10*_dimes
                       + 0.25*_quarters;
}
void Purse::insert(float dollars)
{ _pennies += int(100*dollars);
  reduce();
}
void Purse::remove(float dollars)
{ _pennies -= int(100*dollars);
  reduce();
}
float Purse::empty()
{ float v = value();
  _pennies = _nickels = _dimes = _quarters = 0;
  return v;
}
bool Purse::isEmpty() const
{ return !(_pennies || _nickels || _dimes || _quarters);
}
void Purse::reduce()
{ int v = int(100*value());
  if (v < 0.00)
  { empty();
    return;
  }
  _quarters = v/25;
  v %= 25;
  _dimes = v/10;
  v %= 10;
  _nickels = v/5;
  v %= 5;
  _pennies = v;
}
```

Test driver for Purse class:

```
#include <iomanip>
#include "Purse.h"
void print(Purse);
int main()
{ Purse purse(20,10,10,5);
  print(purse);
  purse.insert(0.97);
  print(purse);
  purse.remove(1.14);
  print(purse);
  purse.remove(3.33);
  print(purse);
}
void print(Purse purse)
{ cout << "purse.value() = " << purse.value() << "\n\n";
  if (purse.isEmpty()) cout << "  The purse is empty.\n";
  else cout << setw(3) << purse.pennies()  << " pennies   = "
            << 0.01*purse.pennies() << "\n"
            << setw(3) << purse.nickels()  << " nickels   = "
            << 0.05*purse.nickels() << "\n"
            << setw(3) << purse.dimes()    << " dimes     = "
```

```
                        << 0.10*purse.dimes() << "\n"
                        << setw(3) << purse.quarters() << " quarters  = "
                        << 0.25*purse.quarters() << "\n\n";
    }
```

```
purse.value() = 2.95
  0 pennies   = 0
  0 nickels   = 0
  2 dimes     = 0.2
 11 quarters  = 2.75

purse.value() = 3.92
  2 pennies   = 0.02
  1 nickels   = 0.05
  1 dimes     = 0.1
 15 quarters  = 3.75

purse.value() = 2.78
  3 pennies   = 0.03
  0 nickels   = 0
  0 dimes     = 0
 11 quarters  = 2.75

purse.value() = 0
  The purse is empty.
```

Chapter 4

Recursion

A *recursive* function is one that calls itself. Recursion is a powerful programming technique that allows elegantly simple solutions to difficult problems. But it can also be misused, producing inefficient code.

4.1 THE FACTORIAL FUNCTION

n	$n!$
0	1
1	1
2	2
3	6
4	24
5	120
6	720
7	5,040
8	40,310
9	362,880

The *factorial* function is defined mathematically by

$$n! = \begin{cases} 1, & \text{if } n = 0 \\ n(n-1)!, & \text{if } n > 0 \end{cases}$$

This is a recursive definition because the factorial "recurs" on the right side of the equation. The function is defined in terms of itself. The first 10 values of the factorial function are shown at right. Evidently this function grows rapidly.

EXAMPLE 4.1 Recursive Implementation of the Factorial Function

When a function is defined recursively, its implementation is usually a direct translation of the mathematics into code:

```
long f(int n)
{ if (n < 2) return 1;   // basis
  return n*f(n-1);        // recursion
}
```

Note that we use `long` for the return type to accommodate the large values.

Here is a simple little test driver for the factorial function:

```
int main()
{ for (int n=0; n<10; n++)
    cout << "f(" << n << ") = " << f(n) << endl;
}
```

It should print the same values as shown in the table above.

EXAMPLE 4.2 Iterative Implementation of the Factorial Function

The factorial function is also easy to implement iteratively:

```
long f(int n)
{ long f=1;
  for (int i=2; i<=n; i++)
    f *= i;
  return f;
}
```

Note that the function header is identical to that used in Example 4.1, only the body is different. This allows us to use the same test driver for both implementations. The output should be the same.

4.2 TRACING A RECURSIVE CALL

Tracing by hand the execution of code is an essential process.

EXAMPLE 4.3 Tracing the Recursive Factorial Function

Here is a trace of the call f(5) to the recursive factorial function defined in Example 4.1:

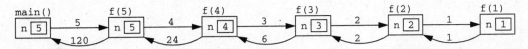

The call originates in the main() function, passing 5 to the f() function. There, the value of the parameter n is 5, so it calls f(4), passing 4 to the f() function. There the value of the parameter n is 4, so it calls f(3), passing 3 to the f() function. This process continues (recursively) until the call f(1) is made from within the call f(2). There, the value of the parameter n is 1, so it returns 1 immediately, without making any more calls. Then the call f(2) returns 2*1 = 2 to the call f(3). Then the call f(3) returns 3*2 = 6 to the call f(4). Then the call f(4) returns 4*6 = 24 to the call f(5). Finally, the call f(5) returns the value 120 to main().

The trace in Example 4.3 shows that the call f(n) to the recursive implementation of the factorial function will generate $n-1$ recursive calls. This is clearly very inefficient compared to the iterative implementation in Example 4.2.

4.3 THE FIBONACCI SEQUENCE

The *Fibonacci sequence* is 1, 1, 2, 3, 5, 8, 13, 21, 34, 55, ... Each number after the second is the sum of the two preceding numbers. This is a naturally recursive definition:

$$F_n = \begin{cases} 0, & \text{if } n = 0 \\ 1, & \text{if } n = 1 \\ F_{n-1} + F_{n-2}, & \text{if } n > 1 \end{cases}$$

n	F_n
0	0
1	1
2	1
3	2
4	3
5	5
6	8
7	13
8	21
9	34
10	55
11	89
12	144
13	233
14	377

EXAMPLE 4.4 Recursive Implementation of the Fibonacci Function

This implementation of the Fibonacci function is logically equivalent to a direct translation of the mathematical definition given above. Since $F_n = n$ for $n < 2$, we can simplify it with a single if statement.

```
long fib(int n)
{ if (n < 2) return n;        // basis
  return fib(n-1) + fib(n-2); // recursion
}
```

EXAMPLE 4.5 Tracing the Recursive Fibonacci Function

The Fibonacci function (Example 4.4) is more heavily recursive than the factorial function (Example 4.1) because it includes two recursive calls. The consequences can be seen from the trace of the call fib(5), shown below. The call originates in the main() function, passing 5 to the fib() function. There, the value of the parameter n is 5, so it calls fib(4) and fib(3), passing 4 and 3, respectively. Each of these calls then makes two more recursive calls, continuing down to the basis calls f(1) and f(0). Each of these basis calls returns 1. The recursive calls then return the sum of the two values returned to them, ultimately resulting in the value 8 being returned to main().

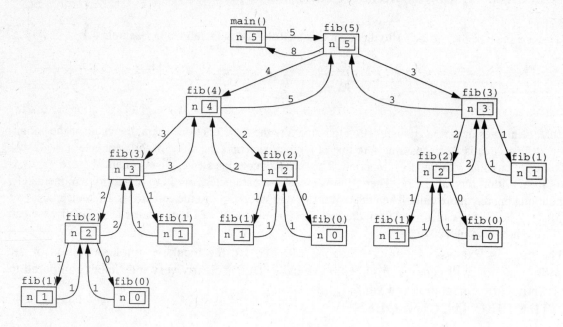

4.4 BINOMIAL COEFFICIENTS

The *binomial coefficients* are the coefficients that result from the expansion of a binomial expression of the form $(x + 1)^n$. For example,

$$(x + 1)^6 = x^6 + 6x^5 + 15x^4 + 20x^3 + 15x^2 + 6x + 1$$

The 7 coefficients generated here are 1, 6, 15, 20, 15, 6, and 1.

The French mathematician Blaise Pascal (1623-1662) discovered a recursive relationship among the binomial coefficients. By arranging them in a triangle, he found that each interior number is the sum of the two directly above it:

```
                              1
                          1       1
                      1       2       1              Column 2
                  1       3       3       1
              1       4       6       4       1
          1       5      10      10       5       1
Row 6 →   1       6     (15)     20      15       6       1
      1       7      21      35      35      21       7       1
  1       8      28      56      70      56      28       8       1
```

For example, $15 = 5 + 10$.

Let $c(n, k)$ denote the coefficient in row number n and column number k (counting from 0). For example, $c(6, 2) = 15$. Then Pascal's recurrence relation can be expressed as

$$c(n, k) = c(n-1, k-1) + c(n-1, k), \text{ for } 0 < k < n$$

For example, when $n = 6$ and $k = 2$, $c(6, 2) = c(5, 1) + c(5, 2)$.

EXAMPLE 4.6 Recursive Implementation of the Binomial Coefficient Function

```
long c(int n, int k)
{ if (k == 0 or k == n) return 1;   // basis
  return c(n-1,k-1) + c(n-1,k);     // recursion
}
```

The basis for the recursion covers the left and right sides of the triangle, where $k = 0$ and where $k = n$.

The binomial coefficients are the same as the *combination* numbers used in combinatorial mathematics and computed explicitly by the formula

$$c(n, k) = \frac{n!}{k!(n-k)!} = \left(\frac{n}{1}\right)\left(\frac{n-1}{2}\right)\left(\frac{n-2}{3}\right) \cdots \left(\frac{n-k+1}{k}\right)$$

In this context, the combination is often written $c(n, k) = \binom{n}{k}$ and is pronounced "n choose k." For example, "8 choose 3" is $\binom{8}{3} = (8/1)(7/2)(6/3) = 56$.

EXAMPLE 4.7 Iterative Implementation of the Binomial Coefficient Function

This version implements the explicit formula given above. The expression on the right consists of k factors, so it is computed by a loop iterating k times:

```
long c(int n, int k)
{ long c = 1;
  for (int j=1; j <= k; j++)
    c = c*(n-j+1)/j;
  return c;
}
```

4.5 THE EUCLIDEAN ALGORITHM

The *Euclidean Algorithm* computes the greatest common divisor of two positive integers. Appearing as Proposition 2 in Book VII of Euclid's *Elements* (c. 300 B.C.), it is probably the oldest recursive algorithm. As originally formulated by Euclid, it says to subtract repeatedly the smaller number n from the larger number m until the resulting difference d is smaller than n. Then repeat the same steps with d in place of n and with n in place of m. Continue until the two numbers are equal. Then that number will be the greatest common divisor of the original two numbers.

```
 494
-130
 364
-130
 234
-130    130
 104   -104    104
         26    -26
                78
               -26
                52
               -26
                26
```

The example on the right applies this algorithm to find the greatest common divisor of 494 and 130 to be 26. This is correct because $494 = 26 \cdot 19$ and $130 = 26 \cdot 5$.

EXAMPLE 4.8 Recursive Implementation of the Euclidean Algorithm

Each step in the algorithm simply subtracts the smaller number from the larger. This is done recursively by calling either gcd(m,n-m) or gcd(m-n,n):

```
long gcd(long m, long n)
{ if (m == n) return n;                    // basis
    else if (m < n) return gcd(m,n-m);     // recursion
    else return gcd(m-n,n);                // recursion
}
```

For example, the call gcd(494,130) recursively calls gcd(364,130), which recursively calls gcd(234,130), which recursively calls gcd(104,130), which recursively calls gcd(104,26), which recursively calls gcd(78,26), which recursively calls gcd(52,26), which recursively calls gcd(26,26), which returns 26. That value 26 is then successively returned all the way back up the chain to the original call gcd(494,130) which returns it to its caller.

4.6 INDUCTIVE PROOF OF CORRECTNESS

Recursive functions are usually proved correct by the principle of *mathematical induction*. (See Appendix B.) This principle states that an infinite sequence of statements can be proved to be true by verifying that (*i*) the first statement is true, and (*ii*) the truth of every other statement in the sequence can be derived from the assumption that its preceding statements are true. Part (*i*) is called the *basis step* and part (*ii*) is called the *inductive step*. The assumption that the preceding statements are true is called the *inductive hypothesis*.

EXAMPLE 4.9 Proof that the Recursive Factorial Function is Correct

To prove that the recursive implementation of the factorial function (Example 4.1 on page 76) is correct, we first verify the basis. The call f(0) returns the correct value 1 because of the first line

```
if (n < 2) return 1;
```

Next, we assume that the function returns the correct value for all integers less than some $n > 0$. Then the second line

```
return n*f(n-1);
```

will return the correct value $n!$ because (by the inductive hypothesis) the call f(n-1) will return $(n-1)!$ and $n! = n \cdot (n-1)$.

Note that we are using the *strong* principle of mathematical induction here (also called the *second* principle). In this version, the inductive hypothesis allows us to assume that *all* the preceding statements are true. In the *weak* (or *first*) principle, we are allowed to assume that only the single preceding statement is true. But since these two principles are equivalent (*i.e.*, they are both valid methods of proof), it is usually better to apply strong induction.

EXAMPLE 4.10 Proof that the Euclidean Algorithm is Correct

We can use (strong) induction to prove that the Euclidean algorithm (Example 4.8 on page 80) is correct. If m and n are equal, then that number is their greatest common divisor. So the function returns the correct value in that case because of the line

```
    if (m == n) return n;
```

If m and n are not equal, then the function returns either gcd(m,n-m) or gcd(m-n,n). To see that this too is the correct value, we need only realize that all three pairs (m,n), (m,n-m), and (m-n,n) will always have the same greatest common divisor. This fact is a theorem from number theory. It is proved in Appendix B.

4.7 COMPLEXITY ANALYSIS OF RECURSIVE ALGORITHMS

The complexity analysis of a recursive algorithm depends upon the solubility of its recurrence relation. The general technique is to let $T(n)$ be the number of steps required to carry out the algorithm on a problem of size n. The recursive part of the algorithm translates into a recurrence relation on $T(n)$. Its solution is then the complexity function for the algorithm.

EXAMPLE 4.11 Complexity Analysis of the Recursive Factorial Function

Let $T(n)$ be the number of recursive calls made from the initial call f(n) to the function in Example 4.1 on page 76. Then $T(0) = T(1) = 0$, because if $n < 2$ no recursive calls are made. If $n > 1$, then the line

```
    return n*f(n-1);
```

executes, making the recursive call f(n-1). Then the total number of recursive calls is 1 plus the number of calls that are made from f(n-1). That translates into the recurrence relation

$$T(n) = 1 + T(n-1)$$

The solution to this recurrence is

$$T(n) = n-1, \text{ for } n > 0$$

This conclusion is obtained in two stages: first we *find* the solution; then we use induction to *prove* that it is correct.

n	$T(n)$
0	0
1	0
2	1
3	2
4	3
5	4
6	5

The simplest technique for finding the solution to a recurrence relation is to make a table of values and look for a pattern. This recurrence relation says that each value of $T(n)$ is 1 more than the previous value. So the solution $f(n) = n-1$ is pretty obvious.

Now to prove that $T(n) = n-1$ for all $n > 0$, let $f(n) = n-1$ and apply the (weak) principle of mathematical induction. The basis case is where $n = 1$. In that case, $T(n) = T(1) = 0$ and $f(n) = f(1) = (1) - 1 = 0$. For the inductive step, we assume that $T(n) = f(n)$ for some $n > 0$ and then deduce from that assumption that $T(n+1) = f(n+1)$:

$$T(n+1) = 1 + T(n) = 1 + f(n) = 1 + (n-1) = n$$
$$f(n+1) = (n+1) - 1 = n$$

That completes the proof.

Now that we have determined that the complexity function for this recursive implementation of the factorial function $T(n) = n-1$, we can conclude that this implementation "will run in $O(n)$ time." This means that its execution time will be proportional to the size of its argument n. If it takes 3 milliseconds to compute 8!, then it should take about 6 milliseconds to compute 16!.

4.8 DYNAMIC PROGRAMMING

In most cases, recursion is very inefficient because of its frequent function calls. So an iterative implementation may be better if it is not too complex. Another alternative is to implement the recurrence relation by storing previously computed values in an array instead of recomputing them with recursive function calls. This method is called *dynamic programming*.

EXAMPLE 4.12 Dynamic Programming Implementation of the Fibonacci Function

```
long fib(int n)
{ if (n < 2) return n;
  long* f = new long[n];  // dynamic array
  f[0] = 0;
  f[1] = 1;
  for (int i=2; i<n; i++)  // store Fibonacci numbers
    f[i] = f[i-1] + f[i-2];
  return f[n-1] + f[n-2];
}
```

This implementation uses a dynamic array f[] of n long integers to store the first n Fibonacci numbers.

4.9 THE TOWERS OF HANOI

We have seen important examples of functions that are more naturally defined and more easily understood using recursion. For some problems, recursion is the only reasonable method of solution

The Towers of Hanoi game is a classic example of a problem whose solution demands recursion. The game consists of a board with three vertical pegs labeled "A," "B," and "C," and a sequence of *n* disks with holes in their centers. The radii of the 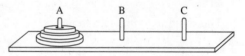 disks are in an arithmetic progression (*e.g.*, 5 cm, 6 cm, 7 cm, 8 cm, . . .) and are mounted on peg A. The rule is that no disk may be above a smaller disk on the same peg. The objective of the game is to move all the disks from peg A to peg C, one disk at a time, without violating the rule.

The general solution to the Towers of Hanoi game is naturally recursive:

- Part I: move the smaller *n* – 1 disks from peg A to peg B.
- Part II: move the remaining disk from peg A to peg C.
- Part III: move the smaller *n* – 1 disks from peg B to peg C.

The first and third steps are recursive: apply the complete solution to *n* – 1 disks. The basis to this recursive solution is the case where *n* = 0: in this case, do nothing.

The solution for the case of *n* = 1 disk is:

1. Move the disk from peg A to peg C.

The solution for the case of *n* = 2 disks is:

1. Move the top disk from peg A to peg B.
2. Move the second disk from peg A to peg C.
3. Move the top disk from peg B to peg C.

The solution for the case of $n = 3$ disks is:

1. Move the top disk from peg A to peg C.
2. Move the second disk from peg A to peg B.
3. Move the top disk from peg C to peg B.
4. Move the remaining disk from peg A to peg C.
5. Move the top disk from peg B to peg A.
6. Move the second disk from peg B to peg C.
7. Move the top disk from peg A to peg C.

Here, steps 1–3 constitute Part I of the general solution, step 4 constitutes Part II, and steps 5–7 constitute Part III.

Since the general recursive solution requires the substitution of different peg labels, it is better to use variables. Then, naming this three-step algorithm $hanoi(n, x, y, z)$, it becomes:

- Part I: move the smaller $n-1$ disks from peg x to peg z.
- Part II: move the remaining disk from peg x to peg y.
- Part III: move the smaller $n-1$ disks from peg z to peg y.

The general solution is implemented in the next example.

EXAMPLE 4.13 The Towers of Hanoi Puzzle

```
void hanoi(int n, char x, char y, char z)
{ if (n == 1)   // basis
    cout << "Move top disk from peg " << x << " to peg " << z << "\n";
  else          // recursion
  { hanoi(n-1,x,z,y);
    hanoi(1,x,y,z);
    hanoi(n-1,y,x,z);
  }
}
```

The solution for 4 disks is produced by the call

```
hanoi(4,'A','B','C');
```

The output is

```
Move top disk from peg A to peg B
Move top disk from peg A to peg C
Move top disk from peg B to peg C
Move top disk from peg A to peg B
Move top disk from peg C to peg A
Move top disk from peg C to peg B
Move top disk from peg A to peg B
Move top disk from peg A to peg C
Move top disk from peg B to peg C
Move top disk from peg B to peg A
Move top disk from peg C to peg A
Move top disk from peg B to peg C
Move top disk from peg A to peg B
Move top disk from peg A to peg C
Move top disk from peg B to peg C
```

4.10 MUTUAL RECURSION

When a function calls itself, it is called *direct recursion*. Another form of recursion is when a function calls other functions that call other functions that eventually call the original function. This is called *indirect recursion*. Its most common form is when two functions call each other. This is called *mutual recursion*.

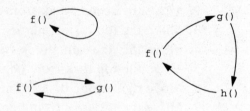

EXAMPLE 4.14 The sine and cosine Functions by Mutual Recursion

The sine and cosine functions from trigonometry can be defined in several different ways, and there are several different algorithms for computing their values. The simplest (although not the most efficient) is via mutual recursion. It is based upon the identities

$$\sin 2\theta = 2 \sin\theta \cos\theta$$

$$\cos 2\theta = 1 - 2(\sin\theta)^2$$

and the two Taylor polynomials

$$\sin x \approx x - x^3/6$$

$$\cos x \approx 1 - x^2/2$$

which are close approximations for small values of x.

```
double s(double x)
{ if (-0.005 < x && x < 0.005) return x - x*x*x/6;   // basis
  return 2*s(x/2)*c(x/2);                            // recursion
}

double c(double x)
{ if (-0.005 < x && x < 0.005) return 1.0 - x*x/2;   // basis
  return 1 - 2*s(x/2)*s(x/2);                        // recursion
}
```

This works because on each recursive call x is divided by 2 so eventually it reaches the basis criterion (-0.005 < x && x < 0.005) which stops the recursion. When x is that small, the Taylor polynomials give accurate results to 15 decimal places.

Review Questions

4.1 A recursive function must have two parts: its *basis*, and its *recursive part*. Explain what each of these is and why it is essential to recursion.

4.2 How many recursive calls will the call f(10) to the recursive factorial function (Example 4.1 on page 76) generate?

4.3 How many recursive calls will the call fib(6) to the recursive Fibonacci function (Example 4.4 on page 77) generate?

4.4 What are the advantages and disadvantages of implementing a recursive solution instead of an iterative solution?

4.5 What is the difference between direct recursion and indirect recursion?

Problems

4.1   Write and test a recursive function that returns the sum of the squares of the first n positive integers.

4.2   Write and test a recursive function that returns the sum of the first n powers of a base b.

4.3   Write and test a recursive function that returns the sum of the first n elements of an array.

4.4   Write and test a recursive function that returns the maximum among the first n elements of an array.

4.5   Write and test a recursive function that returns the maximum among the first n elements of an array, using at most lg n recursive calls. (Recall that lg is the binary logarithm $\log_2$. See Appendix B.)

4.6   Write and test a recursive function that returns the power x^n.

4.7   Write and test a recursive function that returns the power x^n, using at most 2 lg n recursive calls.

4.8   Write and test a recursive function that returns the integer binary logarithm of an integer n (*i.e.*, the number of times n can be divided in two).

4.9   Write and test a recursive boolean function that determines whether a string is a palindrome. (A *palindrome* is a string of characters that is the same as the string obtained from it by reversing its letters.)

4.10   Write and test a recursive function that prints an input string in reverse.

4.11   Write and test a recursive function that returns a string that contains the binary representation of a positive integer.

4.12   Write and test a recursive function that returns a string that contains the hexadecimal representation of a positive integer.

4.13   Write and test a recursive function that prints all the permutations of the first n characters of a string. For example, the call `print("ABC",3)` would print

```
ABC
ACB
BAC
BCA
CBA
CAB
```

4.14   Implement the recursive Ackermann function:

$$a(0, n) = 1$$
$$a(1, 0) = 2$$
$$a(m, 0) = m + 2, \text{ if } m > 1$$
$$a(m, n) = a(a(m - 1, n), n - 1), \text{ if } m > 0 \text{ and } n > 0$$

4.15   Implement the Fibonacci function iteratively (without using an array).

4.16   Prove Pascal's recurrence relation (page 79).

4.17   Trace the recursive implementation of the Euclidean Algorithm (Example 4.8 on page 80) on the call `gcd(385, 231)`.

4.18   Implement the Euclidean Algorithm (page 79) iteratively.

4.19   Implement the recursive Euclidean Algorithm (Example 4.8 on page 80) using the integer remainder operator % instead of repeated subtraction.

4.20   Implement the Euclidean Algorithm iteratively using the integer remainder operator % instead of repeated subtraction.

4.21 Use mathematical induction to prove that the recursive implementation of the Fibonacci function (Example 4.4 on page 77) is correct.

4.22 Use mathematical induction to prove that the recursive function in Problem 4.4 is correct.

4.23 Use mathematical induction to prove that the recursive function in Problem 4.5 is correct.

4.24 Use mathematical induction to prove that the recursive function in Problem 4.8 is correct.

4.25 Use mathematical induction to prove that the recursive function in Problem 4.13 is correct.

4.26 The *computable domain* of a function is the set of inputs for which the function can produce correct results. Determine empirically the computable domain of the factorial function implemented in Example 4.1 on page 76.

4.27 Determine empirically the computable domain of the `sum(b,n)` function implemented in Problem 4.2, using $b = 2$.

4.28 Determine empirically the computable domain of the Fibonacci function implemented in Example 4.4 on page 77.

4.29 Determine empirically the computable domain of the recursive binomial coefficient function (Example 4.6 on page 79).

4.30 The Towers of Hanoi program performs 7 disk moves for 3 disks. How many disk moves are performed for:
a. 5 disks?
b. 6 disks?
c. n disks?

4.31 Show the recursive call tree for the call `hanoi(4,'A','B','C')` in Example 4.13 on page 83.

4.32 Determine empirically the computable domain of the Ackermann function (Problem 4.14).

4.33 Use mutual recursion to implement the hyperbolic sine and hyperbolic cosine functions. Use these formulas:

$$\sinh 2\theta = 2\sinh\theta\cosh\theta$$

$$\cosh 2\theta = 1 + 2(\sinh\theta)^2$$

$$\sinh x \approx x + x^3/6$$

$$\cosh x \approx 1 + x^2/2$$

4.34 Implement the tangent function recursively using the formulas

$$\tan 2x = \frac{2\tan x}{1 - (\tan x)^2}$$

$$\tan x \approx x + \frac{1}{3}x^3$$

4.35 Implement a recursive function that evaluates a polynomial $a_0 + a_1 x + a_2 x^2 + \cdots + a_n x^n$ where the $n+1$ coefficients a_i are passed to the function in an array along with the degree n.

Answers to Review Questions

4.1 The basis of a recursive function is its starting point in its definition and its final step when it is being called recursively; it is what stops the recursion. The recursive part of a recursive function is the assignment that includes the function on the right side of the assignment operator, causing the function to call itself; it is what produces the repetition. For example, in the factorial function, the basis is $n! = 1$ if $n = 0$, and the recursive part is $n! = n(n-1)$ if $n > 0$.

4.2   The call `factorial(10)` will generate 10 recursive calls.

4.3   The call `f(6)` to the Fibonacci function will generate $14 + 8 = 22$ recursive calls because it calls `f(5)` and `f(4)` which generate 14 and 8 recursive calls, respectively.

4.4   A recursive solution is often easier to understand than its equivalent iterative solution. But recursion runs more slowly than iteration.

4.5   Direct recursion is where a function calls itself. Indirect recursion is where a group of functions call each other.

Solutions to Problems

4.1   A recursive function that returns the sum of the first n squares:
```
long sum(int n)
{ if (n == 0) return 0;     // basis
    return sum(n-1) + n*n;   // recursion
}
```

4.2   A recursive function that returns the sum of the first n powers of a base b:
```
double sum(double b, int n)
{ if (n == 0) return 1;      // basis
    return 1 + b*sum(b,n-1);  // recursion
}
```
Note that this solution implements Horner's method: $1 + b*(1 + b*(1 + b*(1 + \cdots + b)))$.

4.3   A recursive function that returns the sum of the first n elements of an array:
```
double sum(double a[], int n)
{ if (n == 0) return 0.0;    // basis
    return sum(a,n-1) + a[n-1];  // recursion
}
```

4.4   A recursive function that returns the maximum among the first n elements of an array:
```
double max(double a[], int n)
{ if (n == 1) return a[0];   // basis
    double m = max(a,n-1);      // recursion
    if (a[n-1] > m) return a[n-1];
    else return m;
}
```

4.5   A recursive function that returns the maximum among the first n elements of an array and makes no more than $\lg n$ recursive calls:
```
double max(double a[], int n)
{ if (n == 1) return a[0];        // basis
    int n1 = n/2;
    int n2 = n - n1;
    double m1 = max(a,n1);          // recursion on a[0:n1-1]
    double m2 = max(a+n1,n2);       // recursion on a[n1:n-1]
    return ( m1 > m2 ? m1 : m2 );   // = max{m1,m2}
}
```

4.6   A recursive function that returns the power x^n:
```
double pow(double x, int n)
{ if (n == 0) return 1.0;   // basis
    return x*pow(x,n-1);      // recursion
}
```

4.7   A recursive function that returns the power x^n and makes no more than $\lg n$ recursive calls:
```
double pow(double x, int n)
{ if (n == 0) return 1.0;    // basis
    double p = pow(x,n/2);
    if (n%2 == 0) return p*p;  // recursion (n even)
```

```
      else return x*p;                    // recursion (n odd)
   }
```

4.8   A recursive function that returns the integer binary logarithm of *n*:
```
      int lg(long n)
      { if (n == 1) return 0.0;    // basis
        return 1 + lg(n/2);        // recursion
      }
```

4.9   A recursive function that determines whether a string is a palindrome:
```
      bool isPalindrome(string s)
      { int len = s.length();
        if (len == 1) return true;               // basis
        if (len == 2) return (s[0] == s[1]);     // basis
        return isPalindrome(s.substr(1,len-2));  // recursion
      }
```

4.10   A recursive function that echos an input string in reverse:
```
      void reverse()
      { char c;
        cin.get(c);
        if (c == '\n') return;   // basis
        reverse();               // recursion
        cout << c;
      }
```

4.11   A recursive function that converts decimal to binary:
```
      string binary(int n)
      { string s;
        if (n%2 == 0) s = "0";
        else s = "1";
        if (n < 2) return s;       // basis
        return binary(n/2) + s;    // recursion
      }
```

4.12   A recursive function that converts decimal to hexadecimal:
```
      string hexadecimal(long n)
      { string s = hex(n%16);
        if (n < 16) return s;            // basis
        return hexadecimal(n/16) + s;    // recursion
      }
      string hex(int n)
      { if (n == 0)  return "0";
        if (n == 1)  return "1";
        if (n == 2)  return "2";
        if (n == 3)  return "3";
        if (n == 4)  return "4";
        if (n == 5)  return "5";
        if (n == 6)  return "6";
        if (n == 7)  return "7";
        if (n == 8)  return "8";
        if (n == 9)  return "9";
        if (n == 10) return "A";
        if (n == 11) return "B";
        if (n == 12) return "C";
        if (n == 13) return "D";
        if (n == 14) return "E";
        else         return "F";
      }
```

4.13   A recursive function that prints permutations:
```
      void print(string s, string pre="")
```

```
{ int n = s.length();
  if (n == 1) cout << pre + s << endl;              // basis
  else
    for (int i=0; i < n; i++)
    { char temp = s[i];
      s[i] = s[0];
      s[0] = temp;
      print(s.substr(1,n-1), pre + s.substr(0,1));  // recursion
    }
}
```

4.14 The Ackermann function:

```
int ackermann(int m, int n)
{ if (m == 0) return 1;                   // basis
  if (n == 0)
    if (m == 1) return 2;                 // basis
    else return m + 2;                    // basis
  return ackermann(ackermann(m-1,n), n-1); // recursion
}
```

4.15 Iterative implementation of the Fibonacci function:

```
long fib(int n)
{ if (n < 2) return n;
  long f0=0, f1=1, f=f0+f1;
  for (int i=2; i<n; i++)
  { f0 = f1;
    f1 = f;
    f = f0 + f1;
  }
  return f;
}
```

4.16 Consider the relationship $c(8, 3) = 56 = 35 + 21 = c(7, 3) + c(7, 2)$ from the expansion of $(x + 1)^8$:

$$
\begin{aligned}
(x + 1)^8 &= (x + 1)(x + 1)^7 \\
&= (x + 1)(x^7 + 7x^6 + 21x^5 + 35x^4 + 35x^3 + 21x^2 + 7x + 1) \\
&= x^8 + 7x^7 + 21x^6 + 35x^5 + 35x^4 + 21x^3 + 7x^2 + x \\
&\quad + x^7 + 7x^6 + 21x^5 + 35x^4 + 35x^3 + 21x^2 + 7x + 1 \\
&= x^8 + 8x^7 + 28x^6 + 56x^5 + 70x^4 + 56x^3 + 28x^2 + 7x + 1
\end{aligned}
$$

The coefficient $c(8, 3)$ is for the x^5 term which is $35x^5 + 21x^5 = 56x^5$. The sum $35x^5 + 21x^5$ came from $x(35x^4)$ and $1(21x^5)$. So those coefficients are $35 = c(7,3)$ and $21 = c(7,2)$.

The general proof is based upon the same argument: $c(n,k)$ is the coefficient of the term x^k in the expansion of $(x + 1)^n$. Since $(x + 1)^n = (x + 1)(x + 1)^{n-1}$, that term comes from the sum

$$(x)(c(n-1, k-1)x^{k-1}) + (1)(c(n-1, k)x^k) = (c(n-1, k-1) + c(n-1, k))x^k$$

Therefore $c(n, k) = c(n-1, k-1) + c(n-1, k)$.

4.17 Trace of the call `gcd(616, 231)`:

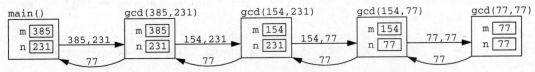

4.18 Iterative implementation of the Euclidean algorithm:

```
long gcd(long m, long n)
{ while (m != n)  // INVARIANT: gcd(m,n)
```

```
        if (m < n) n -= m;
        else m -= n;
      return n;
    }
```

4.19 Recursive implementation of the Euclidean algorithm using the remainder operator:

```
long gcd(long m, long n)
{ if (m == 0) return n;              // basis
  if (n == 0) return m;              // basis
  else if (m < n) return gcd(m,n%m);  // recursion
  else return gcd(m%n,n);            // recursion
}
```

4.20 Iterative implementation of the Euclidean algorithm using the remainder operator:

```
long gcd(long m, long n)
{ while (n > 0)   // INVARIANT: gcd(m,n)
  { long r = m%n;
    m = n;
    n = r;
  }
  return m;
}
```

4.21 To prove that the recursive implementation of the Fibonacci function is correct, first verify the basis. The calls `fib(0)` and `fib(1)` return the correct values 0 and 1 because of the first line

```
    if (n < 2) return n;
```

Next, we assume that the function returns the correct values for all integers less than some $n > 1$. Then the second line

```
    return fib(n-1) + fib(n-2);
```

will return the correct value $n!$ because (by the inductive hypothesis) the calls `fib(n-1)` and `fib(n-2)` return the correct values for F_{n-1} and F_{n-2}, respectively, and $F_n = F_{n-1} + F_{n-2}$ by definition. Note that the basis here required the verification of the first *two* steps in the sequence because the recurrence relation $F_n = F_{n-1} + F_{n-2}$ applies only for $n > 1$.

4.22 If $n = 1$, then the basis executes, returning `a[0]` which is the maximum element because it is the only element. If $n > 1$, then the function correctly computes the maximum m of the first $n-1$ elements (by the inductive hypothesis). If `(a[m-1] > m)`, then `a[m-1]` is returned, and that is the largest because it is larger than the largest of all the others. Otherwise, m is returned, and that is the largest because `a[m-1]` is not larger.   **Q.E.D.**

4.23 If $n = 1$, then the basis executes, returning `a[0]` which is the maximum element because it is the only element. If $n > 1$, then the function correctly computes the maxima m1 and m2 of the first and second halves of the array (by the inductive hypothesis). One of these two numbers is the correct maximum for the entire array. The larger is returned.   **Q.E.D.**

4.24 If $n = 1$, then the basis executes, returning 0 which is the number of times n can be divided in two. If $n > 1$, then the function correctly computes the number of times $n/2$ can be divided in two (by the inductive hypothesis). This is 1 less than the number of times n can be divided in two, so the value returned, `1 + lg(n/2)`, is correct.   **Q.E.D.**

4.25 If $n = 1$, then the string has only one character and the function prints it and returns. If $n > 1$, then the `for` loop iterates n times. On each iteration, it swaps the first character with the ith character and then prints all the permutations of the given string that begin with that character. The inductive hypothesis guarantees that this works because

4.26 For the factorial function implemented in Example 4.1 on page 76, integer overflow occurs on the return type `long` with $n = 13$ on the author's computer. So the computable domain for this function is $0 \le n \le 12$.

4.27 For the `sum(b,n)` function implemented in Problem 4.2 on page 85 with b = 2, floating point overflow occurs on the return type `double` with $n = 1{,}023$ on the author's computer. So the computable domain for this function is $0 \le n \le 1{,}022$.

4.28 For the Fibonacci function implemented in Example 4.4 on page 77, the overhead from the recursive calls degrades the run-time performance noticeably after $n = 36$ on the author's computer. So the computable domain for this function is about $0 \le n \le 40$.

4.29 For the binomial coefficient function implemented in Example 4.3 on page 77, the overhead from the recursive calls degrades the run-time performance noticeably after $n = 25$ on the author's computer. So the computable domain for this function is about $0 \le n \le 30$.

4.30 The Towers of Hanoi program performs:

a. 31 moves for 5 disks;

b. 63 moves for 6 disks;

c. 2^n moves for n disks.

4.31 The call tree for Example 4.13 on page 83:

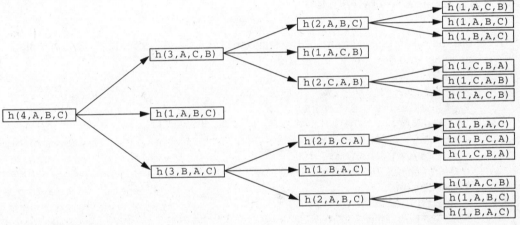

4.32 For the Ackerman function implemented in Problem 4.14 on page 85, exceptions are thrown for $m = 17$ when $n = 2$, for $m = 5$ when $n = 3$, for $m = 4$ when $n = 4$, and for $m = 3$ when $n = 5$. So the computable domain for this function is restricted to $0 \le m \le 16$ when $n = 2$, to $0 \le m \le 4$ when $n = 3$, to $0 \le m \le 3$ when $n = 4$, and to $0 \le m \le 2$ when $n = 5$.

4.33 Mutually recursive implementations of the hyperbolic sine and cosine functions:

```
double s(double x)
{ if (-0.005 < x && x < 0.005) return x + x*x*x/6;   // basis
  return 2*s(x/2)*c(x/2);                             // recursion
}
double c(double x)
{ if (-0.005 < x && x < 0.005) return x + x*x*x/2;   // basis
  return 1 + 2*s(x/2)*s(x/2);                         // recursion
}
```

4.34 Recursive implementation of the tangent function:

```
double t(double x)
{ if (-0.005 < x && x < 0.005) return x + x*x*x/3;   // basis
  return 2*t(x/2)/(1 - t(x/2)*t(x/2));                // recursion
}
```

4.35 Recursive evaluation of a polynomial function:

```
double p(double* c, double x, int n)
{ if (n == 0) return c[0];        // basis
  return p(c,x,n-1)*x + c[n];     // recursion
}
```

Chapter 5

Stacks

A *stack* is a container that implements the last-in–first-out (LIFO) protocol. That means that the only accessible object in the container is the last one among them that was inserted. A stack of books is a good analogy: you can't read any book in the stack without first removing the books that are stacked on top of it.

5.1 THE `stack` INTERFACE

Here are the essential members of the standard C++ `stack` container class template:
```
template <class T> class stack
{ public:
    stack();                              // default constructor
    stack(const stack&);                  // copy constructor
    ~stack();                             // destructor
    stack& operator=(const stack&);       // assignment operator
    int size() const;               // returns number of elements
    bool empty() const;                // returns true iff empty
    T& top();                          // returns the top element
    void push(const T&);        // inserts given element on top
    void pop();                        // removes top element
    //...
};
```
This class is defined in the standard `<stack>` header.

5.2 USING `stack` OBJECTS

As a template, the interface given above can be used only by specifying the type of object that is to be stored in its instances. For example:
```
stack<int> s1;      // s1 is a stack of integers
stack<double> s2;   // s2 is a stack of double precision numbers
stack<string> s3;   // s3 is a stack of strings
stack<Card> s4;     // s4 is a stack of cards
```
The symbol `T` in the interface code stands for the type of object being stored. So the declaration
```
    T& top();
```
means that the `top()` function returns a reference to the element that is on top of the stack. For example,
```
    cout << s1.top();
```
would print the integer that is on the top of stack `s1`, and
```
    s3.top() = "McGraw-Hill";
```
would change the top element of stack `s3` to the string assigned to it. Similarly,
```
    s2.push(3.14159);
```

would insert that number on the top of stack s2.

EXAMPLE 5.1 Using a Stack of Strings

This illustrates the push(), pop(), size(), empty(), and top() functions.

```
#include <iostream>
#include <stack>  // defines the stack<T> class template
using namespace std;

int main()
{ stack<string> s;  // s is a stack of strings
  s.push("first");
  s.push("second");
  s.push("third");
  s.push("fourth");
  cout << "s.size() = " << s.size() << "\n";
  while (!s.empty())
  { cout << "s.top() = " << s.top() << "\n";
    s.pop();
  }
  cout << "s.size() = " << s.size() << "\n";
}
```

```
s.size() = 4
s.top() = fourth
s.top() = third
s.top() = second
s.top() = first
s.size() = 0
```

The program pushes four strings on the stack s. Then after checking the size of the stack, it uses a while loop to pop them off the stack. Note that the elements of a stack are always removed in the reverse order from which they were inserted.

Note that in this implementation, the top() and pop() functions are independent. Some authors define the pop() function to return the removed element. But this Standard C++ implementation does not: pop() is a void function, returning nothing. To access the removed element, one must call the top() function before calling the pop() function.

5.3 APPLICATIONS OF STACKS

Although the stack data structure is one of the simplest, it is essential in certain important applications. Some of these are illustrated in the following examples.

An arithmetic expression is said to be in *postfix* notation (also called *reverse Polish notation*, or *RPN*) if each operator is placed after its operands. For example, the postfix expression for 3*(4+5) is 3 4 5 + *. (The expression 3*(4+5) is called an *infix expression*.) Postfix expressions are easier to process by machine than infix. Calculators that process postfix expressions are called *RPN calculators*.

EXAMPLE 5.2 An RPN Calculator

This program parses postfix expressions, performing the indicated arithmetic. It uses two stacks, one to accumulate the operators and one to accumulate the operands.

```cpp
int main()
{ stack<char> oprtr;      // stack for operators
  stack<double> oprnd;    // stack for operands
  string input;
  bool quit=false;
  double x, y;
  while (!quit)
  { cout << "RPN> ";   // user prompt
    cin >> input;
    switch (input[0])
    { case 'Q':  case 'q':
        quit = true;
        break;
      case '+':
        y = oprnd.top();
        oprnd.pop();
        x = oprnd.top();
        oprnd.pop();
        cout << "\t" << x << "+" << y << " = " << x+y << "\n";
        oprnd.push(x+y);
        break;
      case '-':
        y = oprnd.top();
        oprnd.pop();
        x = oprnd.top();
        oprnd.pop();
        cout << "\t" << x << "-" << y << " = " << x-y << "\n";
        oprnd.push(x-y);
        break;
      case '*':
        y = oprnd.top();
        oprnd.pop();
        x = oprnd.top();
        oprnd.pop();
        cout << "\t" << x << "*" << y << " = " << x*y << "\n";
        oprnd.push(x*y);
        break;
      case '/':
        y = oprnd.top();
        oprnd.pop();
        x = oprnd.top();
        oprnd.pop();
        cout << "\t" << x << "/" << y << " = " << x/y << "\n";
        oprnd.push(x/y);
        break;
      default:
        istringstream in(input);  // converts input to stream
```

```
          in >> x;                          // reads double from stream
          oprnd.push(x);
     }
   }
}
```

```
RPN> 3
RPN> 4
RPN> 5
RPN> +
        4+5 = 9
RPN> *
        3*9 = 27
RPN> 10
RPN> /
        27/10 = 2.7
RPN> 1
RPN> -
        2.7-1 = 1.7
RPN> Q
```

This run processes the postfix expression 3 4 5 + * 10 / 1 - which represents the infix expression 3*(4+5)/10-1. The output is shown at the top of the next page. Each intermediate calculation is printed: 4+5 = 9, 3*9 = 27, 27/10 = 2.7, and 2.7–1 = 1.7.

On each iteration of the while loop, the program prints the RPN> prompt and then reads an input string. It uses the first character of that string to decide which course of action to take. If it is a 'Q', then the program terminates. If it is a '+', '-', '*', or '/', then it takes the action required by the operator of that name. Otherwise, it assumes that the input is a numeric operand. In that case, it uses a stringstream to read the numeric value into the variable x and then pushes it onto the operand stack.

When one of the four operators is input, it pops the last two numbers off the operand stack, performs the indicated arithmetic operation, prints the result, and then pushes it onto the operand stack.

Human readers tend to prefer infix to postfix notation for arithmetic expressions. The following example converts a given infix expression to postfix.

EXAMPLE 5.3 Converting Infix to Postfix

```
int main()
{ stack<char> op;      // stack for operators
  string s;
  cout << "Enter an infix expression: ";
  getline(cin,s);
  istringstream in(s);   // convert input to stringstream
  char c;
  while (in >> c)
  { if (c=='+' || c=='-' || c=='*' || c=='/') op.push(c);
    else if (c==')')
    { cout << op.top() << " ";
      op.pop();
    }
    else if (c>='0' && c<= '9')
    { in.putback(c);
      int n;
```

```
        in >> n;
        cout << n << " ";
      }
    }
    cout << op.top() << endl;
  }
```

```
Enter an infix expression: 30*(40+50)
30 40 50 + *
```

The input is read into the string s and then converted into the istringstream object in. An istringstream object is like a string that allows the input operator >> to extract information from it the same way that it extracts information from input streams such as cin.

On its first iteration, the while loop extracts the character 3 from the stream into c. Since it fails the first two if tests but passes the third (c>='0' && c<= '9'), it puts the 3 back into the stream so it can read it with the second character as the integer 30, which it then outputs. On its second iteration, it extracts the * character from the stream into c. Since it passes the first if tests (c=='*'), it pushes the * onto the op stack so it can be output later. On the third iteration, the character (is extracted from the stream into c. Since it fails all three if tests, it is ignored. On the fourth iteration, the integer 40 is extracted by the same mechanism that extracted 30 on the first iteration: reading the 4 first to detect that an integer is coming, putting it back, and then reading the complete integer. The 40 is output. On the next iteration, the + character is read and pushed onto the stack. Then the 50 is read and output. Finally, the) character is read, causing the + to be popped and printed, and then the * to be popped and printed.

Note that this version requires the input expression to be completely parenthesized.

Here is another sample run:

```
Enter an infix expression: (80-30)*(40+(10*50))
80 30 - 40 10 50 * + *
```

5.4 REMOVING RECURSION

A computer's operating system executes a recursive function by using a stack to store the current run-time state each time it makes a recursive call. Then each time it returns from a recursive call, it pops the top state off the run-time stack so it can continue where it left off. Since stacks are used by the operating system to execute a recursive function, it stands to reason that the programmer should be able to rewrite a recursive function so that it uses an explicit stack instead of making recursive calls.

EXAMPLE 5.4 Iterative Towers of Hanoi

```
    void hanoi(int,char,char,char);

    int main()
    { hanoi(3, 'A', 'B', 'C');
    }

    struct Quad
    { Quad() {}
      Quad(int n, char a, char b, char c) : _n(n), _x(a), _y(b), _z(c) {}
      int _n;
      char _x, _y, _z;
    };
```

```
    void hanoi(int n, char x, char y, char z)
    { stack<Quad> s;
      s.push(Quad(n,x,y,z));
      while (!s.empty())
      { Quad q = s.top();
        s.pop();
        n = q._n;
        x = q._x;
        y = q._y;
        z = q._z;
        if (n == 1)
          cout << "Move top disk from peg " << q._x
               << " to peg " << q._z << "\n";
        else
        { s.push(Quad(n-1,y,x,z));
          s.push(Quad(1,x,y,z));
          s.push(Quad(n-1,x,z,y));
        }
      }
    }
```

This function produces the same output as the one in Example 4.13 on page 83:

```
Move top disk from peg A to peg C
Move top disk from peg A to peg B
Move top disk from peg C to peg B
Move top disk from peg A to peg C
Move top disk from peg B to peg A
Move top disk from peg B to peg C
Move top disk from peg A to peg C
```

It uses a stack instead of recursion.

The Quad structure is used to hold a quadruple containing an integer and three characters. Each recursive call is replaced with a push onto the stack of a Quad object that holds the current state: the number _n of disks to be moved, and the names _a, _b, _c, of the disks.

5.5 CONTIGUOUS IMPLEMENTATION

Here is an implementation of a Stack class template using a dynamic array.

EXAMPLE 5.5 Dynamic Array Implementation of the Stack Class Template

```
    template <class T>
    class Stack
    { public:
        Stack();
        Stack(const Stack&);
        ~Stack();
        Stack& operator=(const Stack&);
        int size() const;          // returns number of elements in this
        bool empty() const;        // returns true iff this is empty
        T& top();                  // returns the top element
        void push(const T&);       // inserts given element on top
```

```
    void pop();              // removes element from top
  protected:
    T* _;                    // dynamic array for stack elements
    int _size;               // number of elements in stack
    int _cap;                // number of elements in array
    static const int _CAP=4; // initial capacity
    void rebuild();          // moves all stack elements to new array
};

template <class T>
Stack<T>::Stack() : _(new T[_CAP]), _size(0), _cap(_CAP)
{
}

template <class T> Stack<T>::Stack(const Stack& s)
  : _(new T[s._cap]), _size(s._size), _cap(s._cap)
{ for (int i=0; i<_cap; i++)
    _[i] = s._[i];
}

template <class T> Stack<T>::~Stack()
{ delete [] _;
}

template <class T> Stack<T>& Stack<T>::operator=(const Stack& s)
{ _ = new T[s._cap];
  _size = s._size;
  _cap = s._cap;
  for (int i=0; i<_cap; i++)
    _[i] = s._[i];
}

template <class T> int Stack<T>::size() const
{ return _size;
}

template <class T> bool Stack<T>::empty() const
{ return _size == 0;
}

template <class T> T& Stack<T>::top()
{ return _[_size-1];
}

template <class T> void Stack<T>::pop()
{ --_size;
}

template <class T> void Stack<T>::push(const T& x)
{ if (_size == _cap) rebuild();
  _[_size++] = x;
}
```

```
template <class T> void Stack<T>::rebuild()
{ _cap *= 2;   // double the capacity of the storage array
  T* temp = new T[_cap];
  for (int i=0; i<_size; i++)
    temp[i] = _[i];
  delete [] _;
  _ = temp;
}
```

EXAMPLE 5.6 Testing the Contiguous Implementation

Here is a test driver for the Stack class template implemented in Example 5.5:

```
template <class T> void print(Stack<T>);

int main()
{ Stack<string> s;     print(s);
  s.push("first");     print(s);
  s.push("second");    print(s);
  s.push("third");     print(s);
  s.pop();             print(s);
  s.push("fourth");    print(s);
  s.push("fifth");     print(s);
  s.push("sixth");     print(s);
}

template <class T>
void print(Stack<T> s)
{ cout << "size=" << s.size();
  if (s.size()>0)
  { cout << ", top=" << s.top() << ": (" << s.top();
    s.pop();
    while (!s.empty())
    { cout << "," << s.top();
      s.pop();
    }
    cout << ")";
  }
  cout << "\n";
}
```

```
size=0
size=1, top=first: (first)
size=2, top=second: (second,first)
size=3, top=third: (third,second,first)
size=2, top=second: (second,first)
size=3, top=fourth: (fourth,second,first)
size=4, top=fifth: (fifth,fourth,second,first)
size=5, top=sixth: (sixth,fifth,fourth,second,first)
```

The diagram on the next page shows a trace of this run.

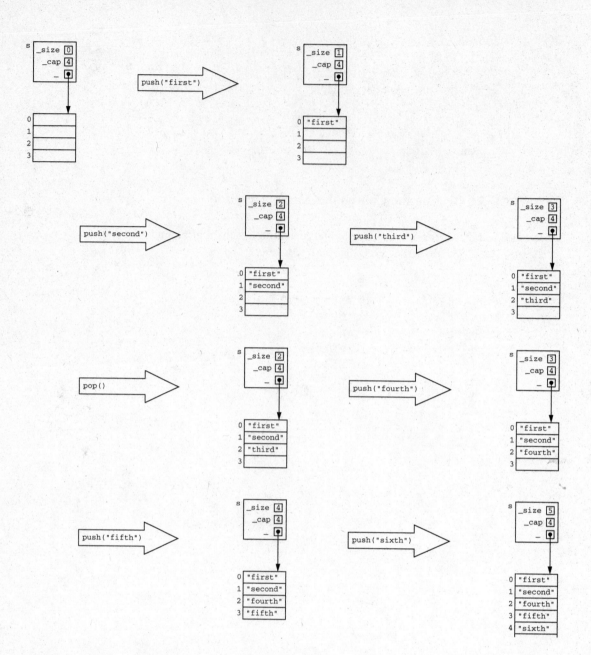

5.6 LINKED IMPLEMENTATION

Here is an implementation of the `Stack` class template using a linked list.

EXAMPLE 5.7 Linked Implementation of the `Stack` Class

```
template <class T>
class Stack
{ public:
    Stack();
```

```
      Stack(const Stack&);
      ~Stack();
      Stack& operator=(const Stack&);
      int size() const;      // returns number of elements
      bool empty() const;    // returns true iff this is empty
      T& top();              // returns the top element
      void push(const T&);   // inserts given element on top
      void pop();            // removes element from top
  protected:
      class Node
      { public:
          Node(const T& data, Node* next=0) : _data(data), _next(next) {}
          T _data;
          Node* _next;
      };
      Node* _top;
      int _size;
};

template <class T> Stack<T>::Stack() : _top(0), _size(0)
{
}

template <class T>
Stack<T>::Stack(const Stack& s) : _top(0), _size(s._size)
{ if (_size==0) return;
  Node* pp=0;
  for (Node* p=s._top; p; p = p->_next)
    if (p==s._top) pp = _top = new Node(p->_data);
    else pp = pp->_next = new Node(p->_data);
}

template <class T> Stack<T>::~Stack()
{ while (_top)
  { Node* p=_top;
    _top = _top->_next;
    delete p;
  }
}

template <class T> int Stack<T>::size() const
{ return _size;
}

template <class T> bool Stack<T>::empty() const
{ return _size == 0;
}

template <class T> T& Stack<T>::top()
{ return _top->_data;
}
template <class T> void Stack<T>::pop()
```

```
{ Node* p=_top;
  _top = _top->_next;
  delete p;
  --_size;
}
template <class T> void Stack<T>::push(const T& x)
{ if (_size==0) _top = new Node(x);
  else _top = new Node(x,_top);
  ++_size;
}
```

EXAMPLE 5.8 Testing the Linked Implementation

Here is a test driver for the Stack class template implemented in Example 5.7:

```
template <class T>
void print(Stack<T>);                 // prints a copy of given stack

int main()
{ Stack<string> s;          print(s);
  s.push("first");    print(s);
  s.push("second");   print(s);
  s.push("third");    print(s);
  s.pop();            print(s);
  s.push("fourth");   print(s);
  s.push("fifth");    print(s);
}

template <class T>
void print(Stack<T> s)
{ cout << "size=" << s.size();
  if (s.size()>0)
  { cout << ",\ttop=" << s.top() << ":\t(" << s.top();
    s.pop();
    while (!s.empty())
    { cout << "," << s.top();
      s.pop();
    }
    cout << ")";
  }
  cout << "\n";
}
```

```
size=0
size=1, top=first:        (first)
size=2, top=second:       (second,first)
size=3, top=third:        (third,second,first)
size=2, top=second:       (second,first)
size=3, top=fourth:       (fourth,second,first)
size=4, top=fifth:        (fifth,fourth,second,first)
```

The diagram on the next page shows a trace of this run.

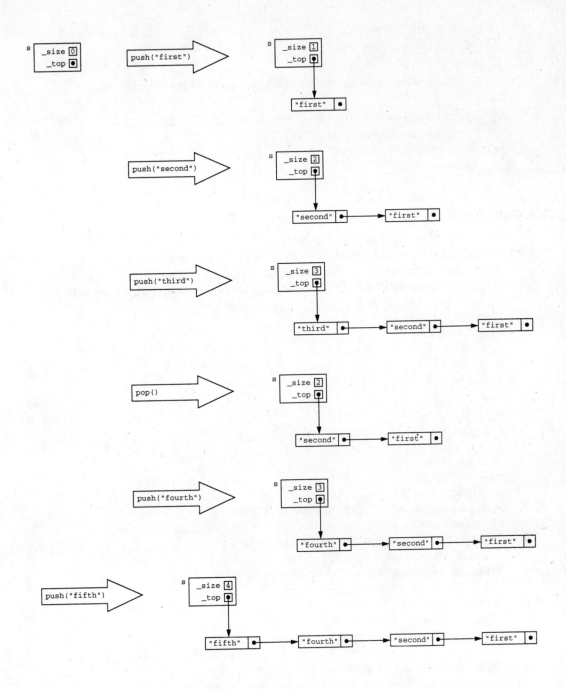

Review Questions

5.1 Why are stacks called "LIFO" structures?

5.2 Would it make sense to call a stack
   a. a "LILO" structure?
   b. a "FILO" structure?

5.3 What are the advantages and disadvantages of the linked implementation of a stack relative to the contiguous implementation?

5.4 What is "prefix" notation?
5.5 What is "infix" notation?
5.6 What is "postfix" notation?
5.7 Determine whether each of the following is true about postfix expressions:
  a. $x\,y + z + = x\,y\,z + +$
  b. $x\,y + z - = x\,y\,z - +$
  c. $x\,y - z + = x\,y\,z + -$
  d. $x\,y - z - = x\,y\,z - -$

Problems

5.1 Write the following function template:
```
template <class T> void reverse(Stack<T>&);
// reverses the contents of the given stack;
```
5.2 Trace the following code, showing the contents of the stack s after each call:
```
stack<char> s;
s.push('A');
s.push('B');
s.push('C');
s.pop();
s.pop();
s.push('D');
s.push('E');
s.push('F');
s.pop();
s.push('G');
s.pop();
s.pop();
s.pop();
```
5.3 Write the following member function for stacks:
```
T& bottom();        // returns the bottom element
```
5.4 Use a stack to implement the following function:
```
bool isPalindrome(string s);
```
5.5 Write the following overloaded equality operator for stacks:
```
bool Stack::operator==(const Stack&);
```
5.6 Write the following member function for stacks:
```
void Stack::clear();  // empties this stack
```
5.7 Write the following member function for stacks:
```
void Stack::popBottom();  // removes the bottom element
```
5.8 Write the following overloaded equality operator for stacks:
```
bool Stack::operator+=(const Stack&);
// pushes the contents of the given stack onto this stack;
```
5.9 Translate each of the following infix expressions into prefix, and then evaluate it:
  a. (6*4)/(7 - (3 + 2))
  b. (6*4)/((7 - 3) + 2))
  c. (2 + 7)*(8/(6 - (3 + 1)))
  d. (2 + 7)*(8/((6 - 3) + 1))
5.10 Translate into postfix each of the expressions given in Problem 5.9, and then evaluate it.
5.11 Translate each of the following prefix expressions into infix, and then evaluate it:
  a. * - 9 + 2 3 - 7 1
  b. * + - 9 2 3 - 7 1

    c. / + * 3 8 4 + 6 - 3 2
    d. / + 4 * 3 8 + - 3 2 6

5.12 Translate each of the following postfix expressions into infix, and then evaluate it:

    a. 4 5 * 6 - 7 / 8 +
    b. 4 5 6 * 7 8 + / -
    c. 6 5 4 3 2 1 - + / + *
    d. 6 5 * 4 3 2 + 1 - / +

5.13 Use the standard C++ `vector` class to implement the `Stack` interface.

5.14 Use the standard C++ `list` class to implement the `Stack` interface.

Answers to Review Questions

5.1 Stacks are called "LIFO" structures because the last element that is inserted into a stack is always the first element to be removed. "LIFO" is an acronym for "Last-In–First-Out."

5.2 *a.* No, because a "LILO" structure would mean "Last-In–First-Out" which is just the opposite of the "Last-In–First-Out" protocol.

    b. Yes, because "First-In–Last-Out" is the same as a "Last-In–First-Out" protocol.

5.3 The linked implementation is more efficient than the contiguous implementation because it uses all its allocated storage. When a contiguous stack calls its `rebuild()` function, it doubles the amount of memory allocated to the stack, even though it only need one more element at that moment. Also, that rebuilding operation will take some time because it has to copy the complete stack into new storage locations. The linked implementation does require extra storage for each link. But on most computers, a pointer requires only 4 bytes, so the storage overhead for pointers is likely to be insignificant. Moreover, the linked implementation releases memory (by the `delete` operator) with each call to `pop()`, so it never occupies more memory than it needs.

5.4 The prefix notation for arithmetic expressions places binary operators ahead of both of their operands. For example, the expression "$x + 2$" is written "$+ \, x \, 2$" in prefix notation. The standard functional notation used in mathematics uses prefix notation: $f(x)$, $\sin x$, *etc.*

5.5 The infix notation for arithmetic expressions places binary operators between their operands. Infix notation is the usual format for arithmetic expressions, *e.g.*, "$x + 2$".

5.6 The postfix notation for arithmetic expressions places binary operators after both of their operands. For example, the expression "$x + 2$" is written "$x \, 2 \, +$" in postfix notation. The factorial function in mathematics uses postfix notation: $n!$.

5.7 *a.* True, because $(x + y) + z = x + (y + z)$.

    b. True, because $(x + y) - z = x + (y - z)$.

    c. False, because $(x - y) + z \neq x - (y + z)$.

    d. False, because $(x - y) - z \neq x - (y - z)$.

Solutions to Problems

5.1 A function template to reverse the contents of a stack:

```
template <class T> void reverse(Stack<T>& s)
{ Stack<T> ss=s;
  while (!s.empty())
    s.pop();
  while (!ss.empty())
  { s.push(ss.top());
    ss.pop();
  }
}
```

5.2   Trace:

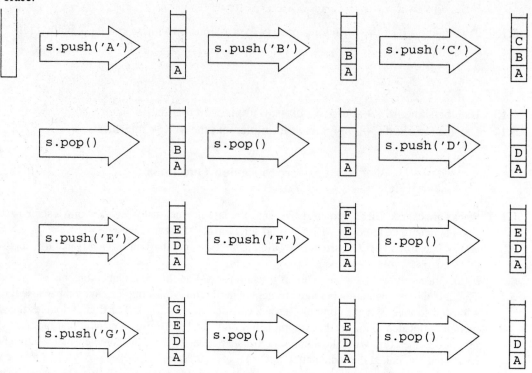

5.3   This version of the solution defines the `bottom()` function in a subclass of an instance of the standard `stack` class template, using `char` for the template parameter:

```
class Stack : public stack<char>
{ public:
    char& bottom();
};
```

char& Stack::bottom()

```
{ Stack s;
  while (!empty())
  { s.push(top());
    pop();
  }
  push(s.top());
  s.pop();
  char& c=top();
  while (!s.empty())
  { push(s.top());
    s.pop();
  }
  return c;
}
```

5.4
```
bool isPalindrome(const string s)
{ stack<char> stack;
  for (int i=0; i<s.length(); i++)
    stack.push(s[i]);
  for (int i=0; i<s.length(); i++)
    if (stack.top() != s[i]) return false;
    else stack.pop();
  return true;
}
```

5.5   ```
bool Stack::operator==(const Stack s)
{ Stack s1=s, s2=*this;
    while (!s1.empty())
        if (s1.top() != s2.top()) return false;
        else
        { s1.pop();
          s2.pop();
        }
    return true;
}
```

**5.6**     ```
void Stack::clear()
{ while (!empty())
    pop();
}
```

5.7   ```
void Stack::popBottom()
{ Stack s;
    while (!empty())
    { s.push(top());
      pop();
    }
    s.pop();
    while (!s.empty())
    { push(s.top());
      s.pop();
    }
}
```

**5.8**     ```
bool Stack::operator+=(const Stack& s)
{ Stack ss=s, s2;
    while (!ss.empty())
    { s2.push(ss.top());
      ss.pop();
    }
    while (!s2.empty())
    { push(s2.top());
      s2.pop();
    }
}
```

5.9   *a.* / * 6 4 - 7 + 3 2 = 12
     b. / * 6 4 + - 7 3 2 = 4
     c. * + 2 7 / 8 - 6 + 3 1 = 36
     d. * + 2 7 / 8 + - 6 3 1 = 18

5.10 *a.* 6 4 * 7 3 2 + - / = 12
     b. 6 4 * 7 3 - 2 + / = 4
     c. 2 7 + 8 6 3 1 + - / * = 36
     d. 2 7 + 8 6 3 - 1 + / * = 18

5.11 *a.* (9 - (2 + 3))*(7 - 1) = 24
     b. ((9 - 2) + 3)*(7 - 1) = 60
     c. (3*8 + 4)/(6 + (3 - 2)) = 4
     d. (4 + 3*8)/((3 - 2) + 6) = 4

5.12 *a.* (4*5 - 6)/7 + 8 = 10
     b. 4 - 5*6/(7 + 8) = 2
     c. 6*(5 + 4/(3 + (2 - 1)) = 36
     d. 6*5 + 4/((3 + 2) - 1) = 31

5.13   Using the standard C++ vector class to implement the Stack interface:

```cpp
template <class T>
class Stack
{ public:
    Stack();
    Stack(const Stack&);
    ~Stack();
    Stack& operator=(const Stack&);
    int size() const;        // returns number of elements in this
    bool empty() const;      // returns true iff this is empty
    T& top();                // returns the top element
    void push(const T&);     // inserts given element on top
    void pop();              // removes element from top
  protected:
    vector<T> _;             // vector for stack elements
};

template <class T>
Stack<T>::Stack()
{
}

template <class T>
Stack<T>::Stack(const Stack& s) : _(s._)
{
}

template <class T>
Stack<T>::~Stack()
{
}

template <class T>
Stack<T>& Stack<T>::operator=(const Stack& s)
{ _ = s._;
}

template <class T>
int Stack<T>::size() const
{ return _.size();
}

template <class T>
bool Stack<T>::empty() const
{ return _.empty();
}

template <class T>
T& Stack<T>::top()
{ return _.back();
}

template <class T>
void Stack<T>::pop()
{ _.pop_back();
}
```

```
template <class T>
void Stack<T>::push(const T& x)
{ _.push_back(x);
}
```

5.14 The `list` implementation of the `Stack` class template is the same as the `vector` implementation because the member functions that we need have the same prototypes in the two standard classes. The only change is the declaration of the protected data container named "_":

```
template <class T>
class Stack
{ public:
    Stack();
    Stack(const Stack&);
    ~Stack();
    Stack& operator=(const Stack&);
    int size() const;        // returns number of elements in this
    bool empty() const;      // returns true iff this is empty
    T& top();                // returns the top element
    void push(const T&);     // inserts given element on top
    void pop();              // removes element from top
  protected:
    list<T> _;               // vector for stack elements
};
```

Chapter 6

Queues

A *queue* is a container that implements the first-in–first-out (FIFO) protocol. That means that the only accessible object in the container is the one among them that was inserted first. A good analogy is a group of people waiting in line for a movie: the next one admitted is the person in the line who got there ahead of everyone else.

6.1 THE `queue` INTERFACE

Here are the essential members of the standard C++ `queue` container class template:

```
template <class T> class queue
{ public:
    queue();                              // default constructor
    queue(const queue&);                  // copy constructor
    ~queue();                             // destructor
    queue& operator=(const queue&);       // assignment operator
    int size() const;                     // returns number of elements
    bool empty() const;                   // returns true iff is empty
    T& front();                           // returns the element in front
    T& back();                            // returns the element in back
    void push(const T&);                  // inserts given element at back
    void pop();                           // removes element from front
    //...
};
```

This class is defined in the standard `<queue>` header.

6.2 USING `queue` OBJECTS

As a template, the interface given above can be used only by specifying the type of object that is to be stored in its instances. For example:

```
queue<int> q1;             // q1 is a queue of integers
queue<string> q2;          // q2 is a queue of strings
queue<Person> q3;          // p3 is a queue of Person objects
queue< stack<int> > q4;    // q4 is a queue of integer stacks
```

The symbol T in the interface code stands for the type of object being stored. So the declaration

```
    T& front();
```

means that the `front()` function returns a copy of the element that is in the front of the queue, and

```
    T& back();
```

means that the `back()` function returns a copy of the element that is in the back. For example,

```
    cout << q1.front();
```

would print the integer that is in the back of queue q1, and

```
    q2.back() = "Microsoft";
```
would change the element in the back of queue q3 to the string assigned to it. Similarly,
```
    q3.push(newton);
```
would insert the `Person` object named `newton` at the back of queue q3, and
```
    q4.pop();
```
would remove the integer stack object that is in the front of queue q4.

EXAMPLE 6.1 Using a queue of Strings

This complete program illustrates the `push()`, `pop()`, `size()`, `empty()`, `front()`, and `back()` functions:

```
#include <iostream>
#include <queue>   // defines the queue<T> class template
using namespace std;
template <class T> void print(const queue<T>&);

int main()
{ queue<string> q;       print(q);
  q.push("Jean");        print(q);
  q.push("Stefan");      print(q);
  q.pop();               print(q);
  q.push("Paul");        print(q);
  q.push("Jessica");     print(q);
  q.push("David");       print(q);
  q.pop();               print(q);
}

template <class T> void print(const queue<T>& q)
{ queue<T> qq=q;   // creates a local copy of q
  cout << "size=" << qq.size();
  if (qq.empty()) cout << "; the queue is empty.";
  else
  { cout << "; front=" << qq.front()
         << ", back=" << qq.back()
         << ": (" << qq.front();
    qq.pop();
    while (!qq.empty())
    { cout << ", " << qq.front();
      qq.pop();
    }
    cout << ").";
  }
  cout << "\n";
}
```

```
size=0; the queue is empty.
size=1; front=Jean, back=Jean: (Jean).
size=2; front=Jean, back=Stefan: (Jean, Stefan).
size=1; front=Stefan, back=Stefan: (Stefan).
size=2; front=Stefan, back=Paul: (Stefan, Paul).
size=3; front=Stefan, back=Jessica: (Stefan, Paul, Jessica).
size=4; front=Stefan, back=David: (Stefan, Paul, Jessica, David).
size=3; front=Paul, back=David: (Paul, Jessica, David).
```

After Jean and Stefan enter the queue, Jean leaves. Then Paul, Jessica, and David enter the queue and then Stefan leaves.

The `print()` function shows the current state of the queue that is passed to it. Note that because it is a nonmember function, it must change the queue in order to print its contents. This is due to the fact that only member functions have access to elements that are not at the front or back of the queue. But the parameter q is passed by `const` reference, so the function is unable to change it. So it uses the copy constructor to make a temporary duplicate that can be changed and printed.

6.3 APPLICATIONS OF QUEUES

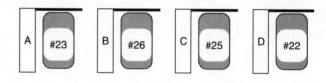

Queues are widely used in simulations. In any situation where the rate at which users' demands for services can exceed the rate at which those services can be supplied, queues are normally used.

The following example could be modified to simulate customers waiting in line at a bank, computer print jobs waiting in a printer queue, or Internet message packets waiting to be routed.

EXAMPLE 6.2 A Toll Plaza Simulation

This program simulates the process of cars waiting in line and being served at a highway toll plaza. We assume there are 4 toll booths and one line of cars that feed into them. Time is measured in "ticks" that represent tenths of a second so that time variables can be declared as `ints` that can be incremented and decremented. The time between car arrivals and the time that it takes for a car to be served at a toll booth are exponentially distributed random variables. In this simulation we set the average time between arrivals to be 2 seconds (20 ticks) and the average service time to be 16 seconds (160 ticks). The program uses 3 classes: the `Exp` class whose objects generate exponentially distributed random numbers, the `Car` class whose objects represent cars in the simulation, and the `TollBooth` class whose objects represent the four toll booths.

```
const int BOOTHS=4;      // 4 toll booths
const int TICKS=600;     // 60 seconds = 1 minute
const float IAT=20;      // average arrival every 2 seconds
const float ST=80;       // average 8 seconds per service
class Exp : public Random
{ public:
    Exp(float mean) : _mean(mean) {}
    float time() { return -_mean*log(1.0-real()); }
  private:
    float _mean;
};
```

```
    class Car
    {   friend class TollBooth;
        friend ostream& operator<<(ostream& ostr, const Car& car)
        { ostr << "#" << car._id << "(" << car._arrive
                << "," << car._service << "," << car._server
                << "," << car._exit << ")";
          return ostr;
        }
        static int _count;
      public:
        Car(int time=0) : _id(_count++), _arrive(time),
          _service(0), _remaining(0.0), _exit(0) {}
        int id() { return _id; }
        bool finished() { return _remaining <= 0.0; }
      protected:
        int _id;
        int _arrive;
        int _service;
        float _remaining;
        int _exit;
        char _server;
    };

    class TollBooth
    {   static Exp _service;   // generates random service times
      public:
        TollBooth() : _serving(false), _p(0) {}
        void setId(char ch) { _id = ch; }
        bool isServing() { return _serving; }
        Car& car() { return *_p; }
        void enter(Car* p, int time)
        { _serving = true;
          _p = p;
          p->_service = time;
          p->_remaining = _service.time();
          p->_server = _id;
        }
        void serviceCar() { _p->_remaining -= 1.0; }
        void vacate(int time)
        { _serving = false;
          _p->_exit = time;
        }
      private:
        char _id;
        bool _serving;
        Car* _p;
    };

    int Car::_count = 0;            // initializes Car counter
    Exp TollBooth::_service(ST);   // initializes _service generator
```

```
int main()
{ vector<TollBooth> booth(BOOTHS);
  for (int i=0; i<BOOTHS; i++)
    booth[i].setId('A'+i);   // name booths as 'A', 'B', 'C', etc.
  queue<Car*> line;
  Exp arrival(IAT);          // generates random arrival intervals
  float timeToNextArrival=0.0;
  for (int t=0; t<TICKS; t++, timeToNextArrival -= 1.0)
  { if (timeToNextArrival <= 0.0)  // a car has arrived
    { Car* p = new Car(t);         // construct new Car object
      line.push(p);                // move car to back of line
      timeToNextArrival = arrival.time();
    }
    for (int i=0; i<BOOTHS; i++)
      if (booth[i].isServing())
      { Car& car=booth[i].car();
        booth[i].serviceCar();
        if (car.finished())
        { booth[i].vacate(t);       // move car out of booth
          cout << car << "\n";
        }
      }
      else if (!line.empty())       // move front car to booth
      { Car* p=line.front();
        booth[i].enter(p,t);
        line.pop();
      }
  }
}
```

The Exp class is defined to be a subclass of the Random class (page 384). The Random::real() function returns numbers x that are uniformly distributed in the interval $0 \le x < 1$. The Exp::time() function uses that function to generate numbers t that are exponentially distributed with mean value _mean. The exponential density function is shown at right. The value c is the reciprocal of the mean. This distribution is the standard mathematical model used to simulate events that occur at random times.

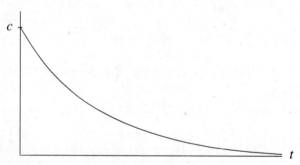

The Car class produces objects that represent cars at the toll booth plaza. Each Car object stores an identification number _id, the time _arrive (in ticks) when it arrived at the plaza, the time _service when it arrived at a toll booth, the time _exit when it left the toll booth, the character _server that identifies the toll booth that served the car, and an integer _remaining that is used to count down the time ticks until the toll booth has finished serving the car. The class uses a static counter _count to generate identification numbers for the cars (car #1, car #2, etc.).

The TollBooth class instantiates objects that represent the toll booths. The main program uses a vector of four TollBooth objects. Each object stores an identification letter _id (booth A, booth B, etc.), a flag _serving to determine whether the booth is currently serving a customer, and a pointer _p to the car that it is serving. The class has three mutator functions: enter() which is called when a car arrives at the toll booth, `serviceCar()` which is called once at each tick during which the booth is serving its car, and `vacate()` which is called when its car leaves the toll booth.

The main program first initializes the vector `booth` of four `TollBooth` objects, the queue `line` of `Car` pointers, the `Exp` random number generator `arrival` that will generate interarrival times for the cars, and the integer `timeToNextArrival` that records how long before the next car arrives. Then it begins the main timing loop which iterates once for each 0.1 second click of the clock. If it is time for a new car to arrive, it constructs one and inserts it at the back of the `line` queue. Then it checks each of the four toll booths. If it is serving a car, then it calls that booth's `serviceCar()` function to update the car's data members and then check whether it is time for the car to leave the booth. If it is not serving a car and if there are cars waiting in the `line` queue, then it moves the front car to that booth.

The output consists of one line for each car that leaves a toll booth. It shows the car's identification number, the time the car arrived at the toll plaza, the time that it entered a toll booth, the name of that toll booth, and the time that it left the toll booth. The rows are printed in the order in which the cars left their toll booths:

```
#3(38,38,C,123)
#2(24,24,B,143)
#1(0,0,A,195)
#5(73,124,C,247)
#4(48,48,D,254)
#6(88,144,B,262)
#7(102,196,A,824)
```

Here is a graphic summary of this run:

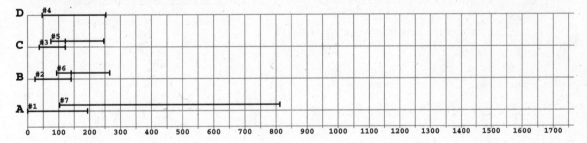

6.4 CONTIGUOUS IMPLEMENTATION

Here is an implementation of a `queue` class template using a dynamic array.

EXAMPLE 6.3 Dynamic Array Implementation of the `queue` Class Template

```
template <class T>
class queue
{ public:
    queue();
    queue(const queue&);
    ~queue();
    queue& operator=(const queue&);
    int size() const;            // returns number of elements in this
    bool empty() const;          // returns true iff this is empty
    T& back();                   // returns the back element
    T& back();                   // returns the back element
    void push(const T&);         // inserts given element on back
```

```
    void pop();                    // removes element from back
  protected:
    T* _;                          // dynamic array for queue elements
    int _size;                     // number of elements in queue
    int _cap;                      // number of elements in array
    static const int _CAP=4;       // initial capacity
    void rebuild();                // moves all queue elements to new array
};
template <class T>
queue<T>::queue() : _(new T[_CAP]), _size(0), _cap(_CAP)
{
}

template <class T> queue<T>::queue(const queue& s)
  : _(new T[s._cap]), _size(s._size), _cap(s._cap)
{ for (int i=0; i<_cap; i++)
    _[i] = s._[i];
}

template <class T> queue<T>::~queue()
{ delete [] _;
}

template <class T> queue<T>& queue<T>::operator=(const queue& s)
{ _ = new T[s._cap];
  _size = s._size;
  _cap = s._cap;
  for (int i=0; i<_cap; i++)
    _[i] = s._[i];
}

template <class T> int queue<T>::size() const
{ return _size;
}

template <class T> bool queue<T>::empty() const
{ return _size == 0;
}

template <class T> T& queue<T>::front()
{ return _[_size-1];
}

template <class T> T& queue<T>::back()
{ return _[_size-1];
}

template <class T> void queue<T>::pop()
{ --_size;
}
```

```
template <class T> void queue<T>::push(const T& x)
{ if (_size == _cap) rebuild();
  _[_size++] = x;
}

template <class T> void queue<T>::rebuild()
{ _cap *= 2;   // double the capacity of the storage array
  T* temp = new T[_cap];
  for (int i=0; i<_size; i++)
    temp[i] = _[i];
  delete [] _;
  _ = temp;
}
```

EXAMPLE 6.4 Testing the Contiguous Implementation

Here is a test driver for the Stack class template implemented in Example 5.5 on page 97:

```
int main()
{ queue<string> s;      print(s);
  s.push("first");      print(s);
  s.push("second");     print(s);
  s.push("third");      print(s);
  s.pop();              print(s);
  s.push("fourth");     print(s);
  s.push("fifth");      print(s);
  s.push("sixth");      print(s);
}

template <class T>
void print(queue<T> s)
{ cout << "size=" << s.size();
  if (s.size()>0)
  { cout << ", back=" << s.back() << ": (" << s.back();
    s.pop();
    while (!s.empty())
    { cout << "," << s.back();
      s.pop();
    }
    cout << ")";
  }
  cout << "\n";
}
size=0
size=1, back=first: (first)
size=2, back=second: (second,first)
size=3, back=third: (third,second,first)
size=2, back=second: (second,first)
size=3, back=fourth: (fourth,second,first)
size=4, back=fifth: (fifth,fourth,second,first)
size=5, back=sixth: (sixth,fifth,fourth,second,first)
```

The diagram on the next page shows a trace of this run.

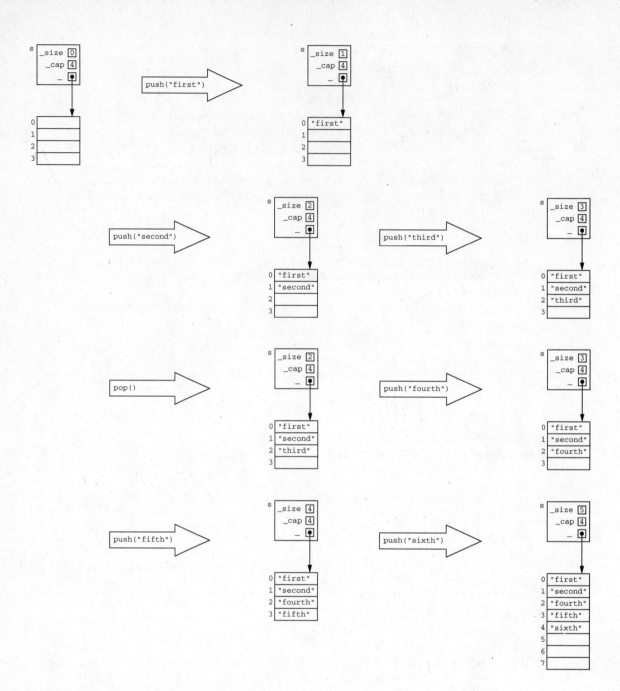

6.5 LINKED IMPLEMENTATION

Here is an implementation of the queue class template using a linked list.

EXAMPLE 6.5 Linked Implementation of the queue Class

```
template <class T>
class Queue
{ public:
```

```
        Queue();
        Queue(const Queue&);
        ~Queue();
        Queue& operator=(const Queue&);
        int size() const;        // returns number of elements
        bool empty() const;      // returns true iff this is empty
        T& front();              // returns the front element
        T& back();               // returns the back element
        void push(const T&);  // inserts given element at back
        void pop();           // removes element from front
    protected:
        class Node
        { public:
            Node(const T& x, Node* next=0) : _(x), _next(next) {}
            T _;
            Node* _next;
        };
        Node* _front, _back;
        int _size;
};
template <class T> Queue<T>::Queue() : _back(0), _size(0)
{
}

template <class T>
Queue<T>::Queue(const Queue& s) : _back(0), _size(s._size)
{ if (_size==0) return;
  Node* pp=0;
  for (Node* p=s._back; p; p = p->_next)
    if (p==s._back) pp = _back = new Node(p->_);
    else pp = pp->_next = new Node(p->_);
}

template <class T> Queue<T>::~Queue()
{ while (_back)
  { Node* p=_back;
    _back = _back->_next;
    delete p;
  }
}

template <class T> int Queue<T>::size() const
{ return _size;
}

template <class T> bool Queue<T>::empty() const
{ return _size == 0;
}

template <class T> T& Queue<T>::front()
{ return _front->_;
}
```

```
template <class T> T& Queue<T>::back()
{ return _back->_;
}

template <class T> void Queue<T>::push(const T& x)
{ if (_size==0) _front = _back = new Node(x);
  else _back = _back->_next = new Node(x);
  ++_size;
}

template <class T> void Queue<T>::pop()
{ Node* p=_front;
  _front = _front->_next;
  delete p;
  --_size;
}
```

EXAMPLE 6.6 Testing the Linked Implementation

The program shown in Example 6.4 on page 117 has the same effect on the linked implementations. Here is what happens when the program runs:

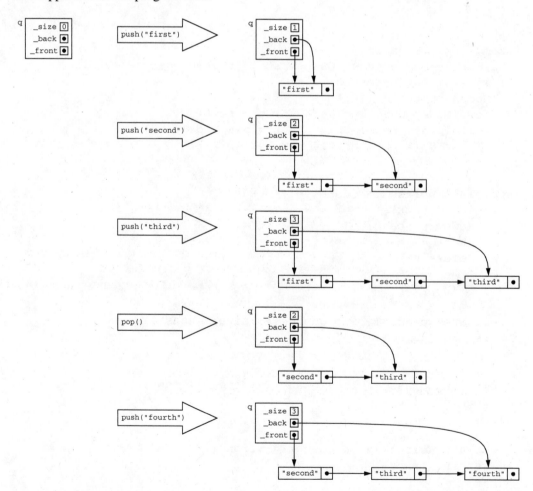

Review Questions

6.1   Why are queues called "LIFO" structures?

6.2   Would it make sense to call a queue
        a. a "LILO" structure?
        b. a "FILO" structure?

6.3   What are the advantages and disadvantages of the linked implementation of a queue relative
        to the contiguous implementation?

Problems

6.1   Trace the following code, showing the contents of the queue q after each call:

```
queue<char> s;
q.push('A');
q.push('B');
q.push('C');
q.pop();
q.pop();
q.push('D');
q.push('E');
q.push('F');
q.pop();
q.push('G');
q.pop();
q.pop();
q.pop();
```

6.2   Write the following function template:

```
template <class T> void reverse(queue<T>&);
// reverses the contents of the given queue;
```

6.3   Write the following overloaded equality operator for queues:

```
bool queue::operator==(const queue&);
```

6.4   Write the following member function for queues:

```
void queue::clear();  // empties this queue
```

6.5   Write the following overloaded equality operator for queues:

```
bool queue::operator+=(const queue&);
// pushes the contents of the given queue onto this queue;
```

6.6   Use the standard C++ list class to implement the queue interface.

6.7   Modify the program in Example 6.2 on page 112 so that it computes and prints each of the
        following statistics. Test it on a 1-hour run (36,000 ticks).
        a. the average number of cars in the line waiting for service;
        b. the average waiting time in line;
        c. the average service time among all cars served;
        d. the average service time duration for each toll booth;
        e. the percent of time that each toll booth server is idle.

Answers to Review Questions

6.1   Queues are called "FIFO" structures because the first element that is inserted into a queue is always the first element to be removed. "FIFO" is an acronym for "First-In–First-Out."

6.2   *a.* Yes, because a "LILO" structure would mean "Last-In–Last-Out" which is just the same as a "First-In–First-Out" protocol.

   b. No, because a "FILO" structure would mean "First-In–Last-Out" which is the opposite of the "First-In–First-Out" protocol

6.3   The relative advantages of the linked implementation for queues is the same as that for stacks. (See Problem 5.3 on page 103.)

Solutions to Problems

6.1   Trace:

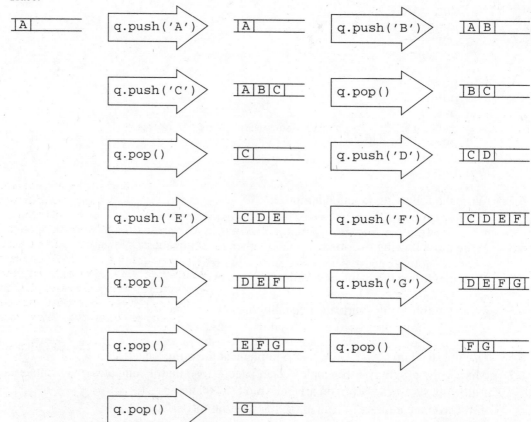

6.2   A function template to reverse the contents of a queue:

```
template <class T> void reverse(queue<T>& s)
{ queue<T> ss=s;
  while (!s.empty())
    s.pop();
  while (!ss.empty())
  { s.push(ss.back());
    ss.pop();
  }
}
```

6.3
```
bool queue::operator==(const queue s)
{ queue s1=s, s2=*this;
  while (!s1.empty())
    if (s1.back() != s2.back()) return false;
    else
    { s1.pop();
      s2.pop();
    }
  return true;
}
```

6.4
```
void queue::clear()
{ while (!empty())
    pop();
}
```

6.5
```
bool queue::operator+=(const queue& s)
{ queue ss=s, s2;
  while (!ss.empty())
  { s2.push(ss.back());
    ss.pop();
  }
  while (!s2.empty())
  { push(s2.back());
    s2.pop();
  }
}
```

6.6   Using the standard C++ `list` class to implement the `queue` interface:
```
template <class T>
class Queue
{ public:
    Queue();                                // default constructor
    Queue(const Queue&);                    // copy constructor
    ~Queue();                                    // destructor
    Queue& operator=(const Queue&);        // assignment operator
    int size() const;              // returns number of elements
    bool empty();                     // returns true iff is empty
    T& front();                 // returns the element in front
    T& back();                   // returns the element in back
    void push(const T&);        // inserts given element at back
    void pop();                   // removes element from front
  protected:
    list<T> _;                        // vector for queue elements
};
template <class T>
Queue<T>::Queue()
{
}
template <class T>
Queue<T>::Queue(const Queue& s) : _(s._)
{
}
template <class T>
Queue<T>::~Queue()
{
}
```

```
template <class T>
Queue<T>& Queue<T>::operator=(const Queue& s)
{ _ = s._;
}
template <class T>
int Queue<T>::size() const
{ return _.size();
}
template <class T>
bool Queue<T>::empty() const
{ return _.empty();
}
template <class T>
T& Queue<T>::front()
{ return _.front();
}
template <class T>
T& Queue<T>::back()
{ return _.back();
}
template <class T>
void Queue<T>::pop()
{ _.pop_front();
}
template <class T>
void Queue<T>::push(const T& x)
{ _.push_back(x);
}
```

6.7
```
void queue::clear()
class Car
{   friend class TollBooth;
    friend ostream& operator<<(ostream& ostr, const Car& car)
    { ostr << "#" << car._id << "(" << car._arrive
           << "," << car._service << "," << car._server
           << "," << car._exit << ")";
      return ostr;
    }
    static int _count;
  public:
    Car(int time=0) : _id(_count++), _arrive(time),
      _service(0), _remaining(0.0), _exit(0) {}
    int id() { return _id; }
    int arrived() { return _arrive; }
    int served() { return _service; }
    bool finished() { return _remaining <= 0.0; }
    int timeInLine() { return int(_service) - _arrive; }
    int serviceTime() { return _exit - int(_service); }
  protected:
    int _id;
    int _arrive;
    int _service;
    float _remaining;
    int _exit;
    char _server;
};
```

```
class TollBooth
{   static Exp _service;   // generates random service times
  public:
    TollBooth() : _serving(false), _p(0) {}
    char id() { return _id; }
    void setId(char ch) { _id = ch; }
    bool isServing() { return _serving; }
    Car& car() { return *_p; }
    void enter(Car* p, int time)
    { _serving = true;
      _p = p;
      p->_service = time;
      p->_remaining = _service.time();
      p->_server = _id;
    }
    void serviceCar() { _p->_remaining -= 1.0; }
    void vacate(int time)
    { _serving = false;
      _p->_exit = time;
    }
  private:
    char _id;
    bool _serving;
    Car* _p;
};

int Car::_count = 0;          // initializes Car counter
Exp TollBooth::_service(ST);   // initializes _service generator

int main()
{ ofstream fout("Simulation.out");
  float sumLineLength=0.0;
  float sumTimeInLine=0.0;
  int numCarsInLine=0;
  float sumServiceTime[BOOTHS]={0.0};
  int numCarsServed[BOOTHS]={0};
  vector<TollBooth> booth(BOOTHS);
  for (int i=0; i<BOOTHS; i++)
    booth[i].setId('A'+i);   // name booths as 'A', 'B', 'C', etc.
  queue<Car*> line;
  Exp arrival(IAT);           // generates random arrival intervals
  float timeToNextArrival=0.0;
  for (int t=0; t<TICKS; t++, timeToNextArrival -= 1.0)
  { if (timeToNextArrival <= 0.0)  // a car has arrived
    { Car* p = new Car(t);         // construct new Car object
      line.push(p);                // move car to back of line
      timeToNextArrival = arrival.time();
    }
    for (int i=0; i<BOOTHS; i++)
      if (booth[i].isServing())
      { Car& car=booth[i].car();
        booth[i].serviceCar();
        if (car.finished())
        { booth[i].vacate(t);      // move car out of booth
          fout << car << "\n";
          sumServiceTime[i] += car.serviceTime();
```

```
                ++numCarsServed[i];
            }
        }
    else if (!line.empty())           // move front car to booth
    { Car* p=line.front();
        booth[i].enter(p,t);
        line.pop();
        sumTimeInLine += p->timeInLine();
        ++numCarsInLine;
    }
  sumLineLength += line.size();
}
cout << "\nAverage number of cars in line: "
    << sumLineLength/TICKS;
cout << "\nAverage time in line: "
    << sumTimeInLine/numCarsInLine/10 << " seconds.";
float sumST=0.0;
int numCS=0;
for (int i=0; i<BOOTHS; i++)
  cout << "\nNumber of cars served by booth " << booth[i].id()
      << ": "   << numCarsServed[i];
for (int i=0; i<BOOTHS; i++)
{ cout << "\nAverage service time for booth " << booth[i].id()
      << ": " << sumServiceTime[i]/numCarsServed[i]/10
      << " seconds.";
  sumST += sumServiceTime[i];
  numCS += numCarsServed[i];
}
cout << "\nAverage service time per car: "
    << sumST/numCS/10 << " seconds.";
for (int i=0; i<BOOTHS; i++)
  cout << "\nBooth " << booth[i].id() << " idle: "
      << int(100-100*sumServiceTime[i]/TICKS) << "% of time.";
cout << "\n";
}
```

Chapter 7

Lists

A *list* is a sequential container that can insert and delete elements locally in *constant time*; *i.e.*, at a rate  that is independent of the size of the container. It is the preferred data structure for applications that do not need random access. A good analogy is a train of box cars: any car can be removed simply by disconnecting it from its two neighbors and then reconnecting them.

7.1 THE list INTERFACE

Here are the essential members of the standard C++ list container class template:

```
template <class T> class list
{ public:
    list();                              // default constructor
    list(const list&);                   // copy constructor
    list(int, const T&=T());             // auxiliary constructor
    list(int);                           // auxiliary constructor
    list(iterator,iterator);             // auxiliary constructor
    ~list();                             // destructor
    list& operator=(const list&);        // assignment operator
    void assign(int, const T&=T());      // assigns a given value
    void assign(iterator,iterator);      // copies elements' values
    void resize(int);                    // changes size of list
    void swap(list&);                    // swaps elements
    bool empty() const;                  // returns true iff empty
    int size() const;                    // returns number of elements
    iterator begin();                    // locates first element
    iterator end();                      // locates dummy end element
    T& front();                          // accesses the first element
    T& back();                           // accesses the last element
    void push_front(const T&);           // inserts element at beginning
    void pop_front();                    // removes first element
    void push_back(const T&);            // inserts element at end
    void pop_back();                     // removes last element
    iterator insert(iterator, const T&=T());     // inserts element
    void insert(iterator,int, const T&=T());     // inserts elements
    void insert(iterator,iterator,iterator);     // inserts elements
    iterator erase(iterator);            // removes element
    iterator erase(iterator,iterator);   // removes elements
    void remove(const T&);               // removes elements
    void clear();                        // removes all the elements
    void reverse();                      // reverses the elements
    void unique();                       // removes all duplicates
    void merge(list&);                   // merges sorted lists
    void splice(iterator,list&);   // inserts elements from other list
```

```
        void splice(iterator,list&,iterator);
        void splice(iterator,list&,iterator,iterator);
    };
```

This includes essentially all the member functions of the `vector` class except the subscript operator and the `at()` function.

7.2 USING `list` OBJECTS

EXAMPLE 7.1 Using a List of Strings

```
    #include <iostream>
    #include <list>                // defines list<T> class template
    using namespace std;
    typedef list<string> List;   // defines List type
    typedef List::iterator It;   // defines It type
    void print(List&);           // prints a copy of given List

    int main()
    { List cars;
      cars.push_back("sugar");    print(cars);
      cars.push_back("dates");    print(cars);
      cars.push_back("wheat");    print(cars);
      cars.push_front("beans");   print(cars);
      cars.push_front("clams");   print(cars);
      cars.sort();                print(cars);
    }

    void print(List& list)
    { cout << "size=" << list.size();
      if (list.size() == 0) cout << ":\t()\n";
      else
      { It it=list.begin();
        cout << ":\t(" << *it++;
        while (it != list.end())
          cout << "," << *it++;
        cout << ")\n";
      }
    }
```

```
size=1:  (sugar)
size=2:  (sugar,dates)
size=3:  (sugar,dates,wheat)
size=4:  (beans,sugar,dates,wheat)
size=5:  (clams,beans,sugar,dates,wheat)
size=5:  (beans,clams,dates,sugar,wheat)
```

The `print()` function uses an iterator to traverse the list and print its elements.

7.3 ITERATORS

An *iterator* is an object that is capable of moving down (or up) a list from one element to the next. It is the alternative to a subscript on an array or vector. Just as subscripts are the natural mechanism for processing arrays, iterators are the natural mechanism for processing lists.

EXAMPLE 7.2 Using List Iterators

This code is inserted at the end of `main()` in Example 7.1:

```
It it1=cars.begin();        // it1 points to beans car
++it1;                      // now it1 points to clams car
*it1 = "ducks";             // changes clams to ducks car
print(cars);                // now it1 points to ducks car
cars.insert(it1,3,"beer");  // adds 3 beer cars
print(cars);                // it1 still points to ducks car
It it2=cars.end();          // it2 points to dummy end element
--it2;                      // now it2 points to wheat car
--it2;                      // now it2 points to sugar car
--it2;                      // now it2 points to dates car
cars.erase(it2);            // removes dates car
print(cars);                // now it2 is undefined
it2=it1;                    // now it2 points to ducks car
++it1;                      // now it1 points to sugar car
++it1;                      // now it1 points to wheat car
cars.splice(it2,cars,it1);  // moves wheat in front of ducks
print(cars);                // now it1 is undefined
```

```
size=5:  (beans,clams,dates,sugar,wheat)
size=5:  (beans,ducks,dates,sugar,wheat)
size=8:  (beans,beer,beer,beer,ducks,dates,sugar,wheat)
size=7:  (beans,beer,beer,beer,ducks,sugar,wheat)
size=7:  (beans,beer,beer,beer,wheat,ducks,sugar)
```

The dereference operator `*` allows access to the data in the element located by the cursor, allowing that data to be read or written. The `insert()` function inserts one or more new elements in front of the element located by the given cursor. The `erase()` function deletes the element located by the given cursor. The `splice()` function moves one or more elements from the position of the second iterator to the position of the first iterator.

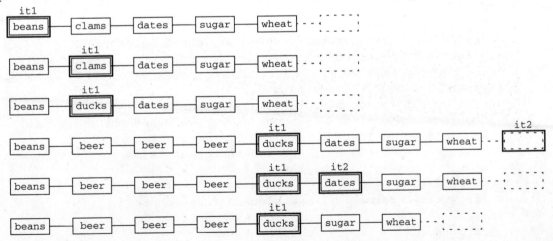

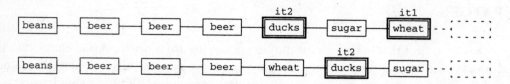

There are three fundamental operators that can be performed on a sequential container such as a list: access (read and write), remove, and insert. Iterators are used to determine where an operatoion is to be performed. On a sequence of n elements, there are n places where an access can be performed, n places where a removal can occur, and $n+1$ places where an insertion can occur. Accesses and removals are done on the element located by the iterator. Insertions are performed immediately *in front* of the iterator. Elements are appended to the end of a sequence by inserting in front of the dummy end element.

7.4 APPLICATIONS

EXAMPLE 7.3 A `Polynomial` Class Interface

A *polynomial* is a mathematical function of the form $p(x) = a_n x^n + a_{n-1} x^{n-1} + \cdots + a_2 x^2 + a_1 x + a_0$, where n is a nonnegative integer and the $n+1$ constants $a_n, a_{n-1}, \ldots, a_2, a_1, a_0$ are real numbers. The constant n is called the *degree* of the polynomial and the constants $a_n, a_{n-1}, \ldots, a_2, a_1, a_0$ are called its *coefficients*. For example, $p(x) = 2x^7 - 8x^3 + 5x^2 + 9$ is a polynomial of degree 7 with coefficients 2, –8, 5, and 9. Its value at $x = 2$ is $p(2) = 2(2)^7 - 8(2)^3 + 5(2)^2 + 9 = 256 - 64 + 20 + 9 = 221$.

Polynomials can be implemented as sequences of pairs, each pair containing the coefficient and the exponent of one term. For example, the polynomial $p(x) = 2x^7 - 8x^3 + 5x^2 + 9$ can be implemented by the 4-element list { (2, 7), (–8, 3), (5, 2), (9, 0) }.

```
class Polynomial
{ protected:
    struct Term
    { friend ostream& operator<<(ostream&, const Term&);
      Term(double=0.0,unsigned=0);
      bool operator==(const Term&) const;
      bool operator<(const Term&) const;
      double _coef;
      unsigned _exp;
    };
  public:
    friend ostream& operator<<(ostream&, const Polynomial&);
    friend Polynomial operator*(const double, const Polynomial&);
    friend Polynomial operator+(const Polynomial&, const Polynomial&);
    Polynomial(double=0,unsigned=0);
    bool operator==(const Polynomial&) const;
    double operator()(double) const;   // evaluates the polynomial
    long degree() const;
    unsigned terms() const;   // the number of terms in the polynomial
    static const Polynomial ZERO;   // p(x) = 0
  protected:
    list<Term> _terms;   // one element for each term
    long _degree;        // maximum exponent
    void reduce();       // collect terms
```

```
    typedef list<Term> TermList;
    typedef list<Term>::iterator It;
    typedef list<Term>::const_iterator CIt;
};
```

The Term structure is defined to be protected inside the Polynomial class so that it is accessible only from within the class or from friends of the class. It has two data members: _coef for the coefficient and _exp for the exponent of the term. It also defines a constructor, an overloaded output operator, and two overloaded relational operators. We defined Term as a struct instead of a class simply because all of its members are public which is the default for structs.

Besides the definition of the Term structure, this Polynomial class defines two constructors, six overloaded operators, two accessor functions, the static constant ZERO, the two data members _terms and _degree, the protected utility function reduce(), and three typedefs. The overloaded function call operator (operator()()) is ised to evaluate the polynomial at a given number. The only purpose of the protected typedefs is to make the class's implementation code (Example 7.4) to be a little more readable.

If p is a Polynomial object representing the polynomial $p(x) = 4x^7 - x^2$, then p could be visualized as

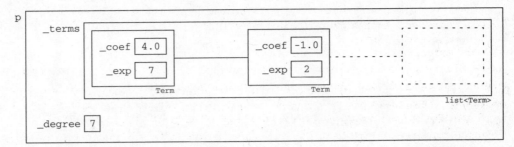

The Polynomial object p has two data members: a list<Term> object named _terms and a long int named _degree. The list<Term> object _terms is a sequence of two Term objects. The picture also shows the dummy end element returned by _terms.end().

EXAMPLE 7.4 Implementation of the Polynomial Class

```
#include "Polynomial.h"
ostream& operator<<(ostream& ostr, const Polynomial::Term& term)
{ if (term._exp == 0) return ostr << term._coef;
  if (term._coef == 1.0) ostr << "x";
  else if (term._coef == -1.0) ostr << "-x";
  else ostr << term._coef << "x";
  if (term._exp == 1) return ostr;
  else return ostr << "^" << term._exp;
}
Polynomial::Term::Term(double coef, unsigned exp)
  : _coef(coef), _exp(exp) {}
bool Polynomial::Term::operator==(const Term& t) const
{ return _exp == t._exp && _coef == t._coef;
}
bool Polynomial::Term::operator<(const Term& t) const
{ return _exp > t._exp;  // sort terms in decreasing order
}
ostream& operator<<(ostream& ostr, const Polynomial& p)
{ if (p == Polynomial::ZERO) return ostr << 0;
  Polynomial::CIt it=p._terms.begin();
```

```
      ostr << *it++;
    while (it != p._terms.end())
      ostr << " + " << *it++;
    return ostr;
  }
Polynomial operator*(const double x, const Polynomial& p1)
{ if (x == 0.0) return Polynomial::ZERO;
  Polynomial p(p1);
  for (Polynomial::It it=p._terms.begin(); it != p._terms.end(); it++)
    it->_coef *= x;
  return p;
}
Polynomial operator+(const Polynomial& p1, const Polynomial& p2)
{ Polynomial p;
  p._degree = max(p1._degree,p2._degree);
  p._terms = Polynomial::TermList(p1._terms.size()+p2._terms.size());
  merge(p1._terms.begin(),p1._terms.end(),
        p2._terms.begin(),p2._terms.end(),
        p._terms.begin());
  p.reduce();
  return p;
}
Polynomial::Polynomial(double coef, unsigned exp)
{ if (coef == 0.0)  // the "zero polynomial" has degree -1
  { _terms = TermList(0);
    _degree = -1;
  }
  else
  { _terms = TermList(1,Term(coef,exp));
    _degree = exp;
  }
}
bool Polynomial::operator==(const Polynomial& p) const
{ return _terms == p._terms;
}
double Polynomial::operator()(double x) const
{ CIt it=_terms.begin();
  if (it == _terms.end()) return 0.0;
  double y=it->_coef;
  unsigned e1=it->_exp;
  while (++it != _terms.end())
  { int e2=it->_exp;
    y *= pow(x,e1-e2);
    y += it->_coef;
    e1 = e2;
  }
  return y*pow(x,e1);
}
long Polynomial::degree() const
{ if (*this == ZERO) return -1;  // the zero polynomial
  return _degree;
}
```

```
unsigned Polynomial::terms() const
{ return _terms.size();
}
void Polynomial::reduce()
{ // collects terms and removes those with coefficient equal to 0.0
  if (*this == ZERO) return;
  Polynomial::It it1=_terms.begin(), it2=_terms.begin();
  while (it1 != _terms.end())
  { while (++it2 != _terms.end() && it2->_exp == it1->_exp)
      it1->_coef += it2->_coef;
    if (it1->_coef == 0.0) _terms.erase(it1,it2);
    else _terms.erase(++it1,it2);
    it1 = it2;
  }
  if (_terms.size() == 0) _degree = -1;
  else _degree = _terms.begin()->_exp;
}
  const Polynomial Polynomial::ZERO(0.0);    // the "zero polynomial"
```

The nested `Term` structure defines overloaded relational operators `==` and `<` for use by iterators on the `Polynomial` class. The `<` operator is defined so that one term will precede another when its exponent is greater than the other's. This is done because a `Polynomial` object's terms are stored as elements in the `_terms` list in decreasing order of their exponents. That is done to facilitate the implementation of the `Polynomial::operator()()` function.

The expression `<< *it++` in the `Polynomial::operator<<()` function calls the `Polynomial::Term::operator<<()` function on the `Term` object `*it` and then increments the iterator.

The `Polynomial::operator*()` function uses the characteristic iterator-controlled `for` loop to traverse the `p._terms` list, multiplying each term's coefficient by x.

The `Polynomial::operator+()` function uses the generic algorithm `merge()` to merge the `_terms` lists of the two given `Polynomial` objects. (See Example D.28.) The result is a list that contains a copy of each term from each of the two other lists. The function then calls the utility function `reduce()` to combine terms that have the same exponent and to remove zero terms (resulting from cancellations).

The `Polynomial` constructor handles the special case of the *zero polynomial* separately. Ordinary (non-zero) constant polynomials have degree 0. But, by definition, the polynomial $p(x) = 0$ has degree -1.

The `Polynomial::operator()()` function implements *Horner's Method* to evaluate the polynomial. This method minimizes the number of arithmetic operations by partially factoring the polynomial, like this: $2x^9 - 7x^4 + 6x + 5 = (((2)x^5 - 7)x^3 + 6)x + 5$. It uses the standard `pow()` function to compute powers like x^5.

The `Polynomial::reduce()` function uses a pair of nested loops to combine terms with equal exponents. The iterators `it1` and `it2` locate each segment of terms that have the same exponent. For example, suppose the polynomial includes the terms $9x^5 - 6x^5 - 3x^3 + 7x^2$, implemented like this:

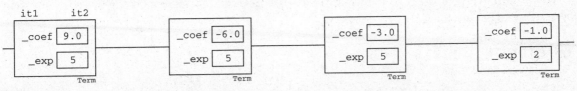

The inner loop advances the iterator `it2`, accumulating coefficients as it progresses, until it reaches either the end of the list or a term with a different exponent, as shown at the top of the next page.

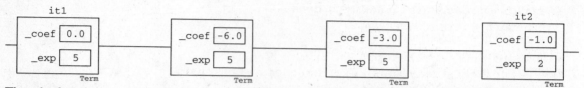

Then the function uses the list.erase() (see page 127) to remove those elements from the list whose coefficients have been accumulated. If the sum of the coefficients is 0.0, then all the terms with that exponent are removed; otherwise, all but the first of them is.

The ZERO polynomial is declared as a static constant in the class interface. It must then be defined in the class implementation, where it is initialized by the class constructor.

EXAMPLE 7.5 Testing the Polynomial Class

```
#include "Polynomial.h"
void print(string,Polynomial);

int main()
{ Polynomial p1;               print("p1",p1);    // p1(x) = 0
  p1 = Polynomial(1.0,2);      print("p1",p1);    // p1(x) = x^2
  p1 = 10*p1;                  print("p1",p1);    // p1(x) = 10x^2
  Polynomial p2(-1.0,2);       print("p2",p2);    // p2(x) = -x^2
  Polynomial p3 = p1 + p2;     print("p3",p3);    // p3(x) = 9x^2
  p3 = p1 + 10*p2;             print("p3",p3);    // p3(x) = 0
  Polynomial p4(4.0,7);        print("p4",p4);    // p4(x) = 4x^7
  p3 = p2 + p4;                print("p3",p3);    // p3(x) = 4x^7 - x^2
  p2 = Polynomial::ZERO;       print("p2",p2);    // p2(x) = 0
}

void print(string name, Polynomial p)
{ cout << name << "(x) = " << p;
  cout << "\tdegree=" << p.degree() << ", terms=" << p.terms()
       << ", " << name << "(2.0)=" << p(2.0) << '\n';
}
```

```
p1(x) = 0           degree=-1, terms=0, p1(2.0)=0
p1(x) = x^2         degree=2, terms=1, p1(2.0)=4
p1(x) = 10x^2       degree=2, terms=1, p1(2.0)=40
p2(x) = -x^2        degree=2, terms=1, p2(2.0)=-4
p3(x) = 9x^2        degree=2, terms=1, p3(2.0)=36
p3(x) = 0           degree=-1, terms=0, p3(2.0)=0
p4(x) = 4x^7        degree=7, terms=1, p4(2.0)=512
p3(x) = 4x^7 + -x^2     degree=7, terms=2, p3(2.0)=508
p2(x) = 0           degree=-1, terms=0, p2(2.0)=0
```

This test driver uses a print() function to test the degree(), terms(), operator()(), and operator<<() functions.

7.5 CIRCULAR LISTS

A *circular list* is a linked list whose last node is linked to its first node. Some problems are solved naturally by circular lists.

EXAMPLE 7.6 The Josephus Problem

This problem is based upon a report by the historian Joseph ben Matthias ("Josephus") on the outcome of a suicide pact among 40 soldiers and him who were besieged by superior Roman forces in 67 A.D. Josephus proposed that each man slay his neighbor and contrived to be the last among them. Thus he lived to tell the tale.

The *Josephus problem* simulates a slight generalization of this event. Let n be the number of men standing in a circle facing the center, let k be a "skip number" agreed upon in advance, and let A be the man who begins the process. On each iteration, x will kill the kth man on his left, where x begins with A and is reset to be the man on the left of the man killed each time. For example, if $n = 10$ (instead of 41) and $k = 3$ (instead of 1), then: A kills D, E kills H, I kills B, C kills G, etc.

```
class List
{ // circular list of chars
  protected:
    struct Node
    { Node(const char& ch=0) : _ch(ch) { }
      char _ch;
      Node* _next;
    };
    Node* _last;  // points to last node
    int _size;
  public:
    List(int=0);
    friend ostream& operator<<(ostream&, const List&);
    int size() const { return _size; }
    bool empty() const { return _size == 0; }
    char last() const { return _last->_ch; }
    char kill(int);
};
int main()
{ int n, skip;
  cout << "Enter number of soldiers: ";
  cin >> n;
  List list(n);
  cout << "\t\t" << list;
  cout << "Enter skip number: ";
  cin >> skip;
  while (list.size() > 1)
  { cout << '\t' << list.kill(skip) << " killed" << list;
  }
  cout << list.last() << " survived.\n";
}
```

```
List::List(int n) : _size(n)
{ _last = new Node('A'+n-1);
  Node* p = _last;
  for (int i=0; i<n-1; i++)
    p = p->_next = new Node('A'+i);
  p->_next = _last;
}
ostream& operator<<(ostream& ostr, const List& list)
{ ostr << "\tsize=" << list._size;
  if (list.empty()) cout << ":\t()\n";
  else
  { List::Node* p = list._last->_next;  // first node
    ostr << ": (" << p->_ch;
    for (p = p->_next; p != list._last->_next; p = p->_next)
      ostr << "," << p->_ch;
    ostr << ")\n";
  }
  return ostr;
}
char List::kill(int k)
{ static Node* p=_last;
  for (int i=0; i<k; i++)  // advance k nodes
    p = p->_next;
  Node* temp=p->_next;
  char killed = temp->_ch;
  p->_next = temp->_next;
  if (temp == _last) _last = p;  // reset _last, if deleted
  delete temp;
  --_size;
  return killed;
}
```

```
Enter number of men: 10
                        size=10:  (A,B,C,D,E,F,G,H,I,J)
Enter skip number: 3
        D killed        size=9:  (A,B,C,E,F,G,H,I,J)
        H killed        size=8:  (A,B,C,E,F,G,I,J)
        B killed        size=7:  (A,C,E,F,G,I,J)
        G killed        size=6:  (A,C,E,F,I,J)
        C killed        size=5:  (A,E,F,I,J)
        J killed        size=4:  (A,E,F,I)
        I killed        size=3:  (A,E,F)
        A killed        size=2:  (E,F)
        F killed        size=1:  (E)
E survived.
```

7.6 ORDERED LISTS

We can use inheritance to define a class for ordered lists.

EXAMPLE 7.7 An **OrderedList** Class

```
#include <iostream>
#include <list>
#include <string>
using namespace std;
template <class T>
class OrderedList : public list<T>
{ // elements are kept in nondecreasing order
  public:
    void add(const T&);
};
template <class T>
ostream& operator<<(ostream&, const list<T>&);
int main()
{ OrderedList<string> instruments;
  instruments.add(string("viola"));
  instruments.add(string("flute"));
  instruments.add(string("cello"));
  instruments.add(string("piano"));
  instruments.add(string("organ"));
  cout << instruments;
}
template <class T>
void OrderedList<T>::add(const T& t)
{ list<T>::iterator it=begin();
  while (it!=end() && *it<t)
    ++it;
  insert(it,t);
}
template <class T>
ostream& operator<<(ostream& ostr, const list<T>& l)
{ ostr << "size=" << l.size();
  if (l.empty()) cout << ":\t()\n";
  else
  { list<T>::const_iterator it=l.begin();
    ostr << ": (" << *it++;
    while (it!=l.end())
      ostr << "," << *it++;
    ostr << ")\n";
  }
  return ostr;
}
size=5: (cello,flute,organ,piano,viola)
```

7.7 AN UNBOUNDED **Integer** CLASS

One of the most useful applications of linked lists is the implementation of an integer class whose instances represent integers with size limited only by the memory of the computer, essentially unbounded. Some authors call this a BigInt class. We use the name Integer here.

EXAMPLE 7.8 An Integer Interface

```
class Integer
{ // instances represent arbitrarily large integers;
  // INVARIANTS: positive integers are stored in a list named _,
  //             with WIDTH digits per element;
  //             negative integers are stored as positive integers
  //             with _neg == true;
  public:
    friend ostream& operator<<(ostream&, const Integer&);
    friend Integer operator-(const Integer&);
    friend Integer operator+(const Integer&, const Integer&);
    friend Integer operator-(const Integer&, const Integer&);
    friend Integer operator*(const Integer&, const Integer&);
    friend Integer abs(const Integer&);
    friend int sign(const Integer&);  // -1, 0, or 1
    Integer(const int=0);
    Integer(const string&);
    bool operator==(const Integer&) const;
    bool operator<(const Integer&) const;
    string toString() const;
    static const Integer ZERO;
    static const Integer NAI;   // Not An Integer
    static const int WIDTH;     // number of digits per list element
    static const int RADIX;     // number of values per list element
  protected:
    static string pad(string);  // pad on left with 0s to len=9
    static Integer NotAnInteger();
    static int toInt(string);
    static string toString(int);
    static Integer toInteger(string);
    typedef list<int> List;
    typedef List::iterator It;
    typedef List::const_iterator CIt;
    typedef List::reverse_iterator RIt;
    typedef List::const_reverse_iterator CRIt;
    bool _neg;   // true iff this is negative
    List _;      // list of positive WIDTH-digit integers
};
```

The following code would construct an Integer object x that represents the integer value 10,203,040,506,070,809,000:

```
Integer x;
x = Integer(1020);
x = 10000*x + Integer(3040);
x = 10000*x + Integer(5060);
x = 10000*x + Integer(7080);
x = 10000*x + Integer(3040);
x = 10000*x + Integer(9000);
```

The resulting object x would look like this:

EXAMPLE 7.9 An Implementation of the Integer Class

```cpp
#include <cctype>    // defines isdigit() function
#include <sstream>   // defines ostringstream class
#include <numeric>   // defines inner_product() function
#include "Integer.h"
ostream& operator<<(ostream& ostr, const Integer& x)
{ return ostr << x.toString();
}
Integer operator-(const Integer& x)
{ Integer y(x);
  y._neg = !(x._neg);
  return y;
}
Integer operator+(const Integer& x, const Integer& y)
{ if (x==Integer::ZERO) return Integer(y);
  if (y==Integer::ZERO) return Integer(x);
  if (x._neg && !y._neg) return y - -x;
  if (!x._neg && y._neg) return x - -y;
  Integer z=Integer::NAI;
  const int R = Integer::RADIX;
  int sum=0;
  Integer::CIt itx=x._.begin(), ity=y._.begin();
  while (itx!=x._.end() && ity!=y._.end())
  { sum += *itx++ + *ity++;
    z._.push_back(sum%R);
    sum /= R;   // carry
  }
  while (itx!=x._.end())
  { sum += *itx++;
    z._.push_back(sum%R);
    sum /= R;   // carry
  }
  while (ity!=y._.end())
  { sum += *ity++;
    z._.push_back(sum%R);
    sum /= R;   // carry
  }
  return z;
}
Integer operator-(const Integer& x, const Integer& y)
{ if (x==y) return Integer::ZERO;
  if (x<y) return -(y - x);
  // x > y (so x._.size() >= y._.size()):
  if (x==Integer::ZERO) return -y;
  if (y==Integer::ZERO) return x;
  if (x._neg && !y._neg) return -(-x + y);
  if (!x._neg && y._neg) return x + -y;
  if (x._neg && y._neg) return -(x - y);
  // x > y > 0:
  Integer z=Integer::NAI;
  const int R = Integer::RADIX;
```

```
      Integer::CIt itx=x._.begin(), ity=y._.begin();
      int diff=0, borrow=0;
      while (ity!=y._.end())
      { diff = *itx++ - *ity++ - borrow;
        if (diff<0)
        { diff += R;
          borrow = 1;
        }
        z._.push_back(diff);
      }
      diff = *itx - borrow;
      if (diff>0) z._.push_back(diff);
      return z;
    }
    Integer operator*(const Integer& x, const Integer& y)
    { if (x==Integer::ZERO || y==Integer::ZERO) return Integer::ZERO;
      Integer z=Integer::NAI;
      if (x._neg && !y._neg || y._neg && !x._neg) z._neg = true;
      const int R = Integer::RADIX;
      unsigned u=0;
      Integer::CIt it1=x._.begin(), it2=x._.begin();
      Integer::CRIt rit=y._.rend();
      while (rit!=y._.rbegin())
      { u = inner_product(it1,++it2,--rit,u/R);
        z._.push_back(u%R);
      }
      while (it2!=x._.end())
      { u = inner_product(++it1,++it2,rit,u/R);
        z._.push_back(u%R);
      }
      while (it1!=x._.end())
      { u = inner_product(++it1,it2,rit,u/R);
        z._.push_back(u%R);
      }
      u /= R;   // carry
      while (u>0)
      { z._.push_back(u%R);
        u /= R;
      }
      return z;
    }
    Integer abs(const Integer& x)
    { Integer y(x);
      y._neg = false;
      return y;
    }
    int sign(const Integer& x)
    { if (x._neg) return -1;
      if (x==Integer::ZERO) return 0;
      return 1;
    }
```

```
Integer::Integer(int n) : _neg(n<0)
{ _.push_front(_neg?-n:n);
}
Integer::Integer(const string& s) : _neg(false)
{ *this = toInteger(s);
}
bool Integer::operator==(const Integer& x) const
{ return (_neg == x._neg && _ == x._);
}
bool Integer::operator<(const Integer& x) const
{ if (*this == x) return false;
  if (_neg && !x._neg) return true;
  if (!_neg && x._neg) return false;
  if (_neg && x._neg) return (abs(x) < abs(*this));
  if (_.size() < x._.size()) return true;
  if (_.size() > x._.size()) return false;
  Integer::CIt it=_.begin(), jt=x._.begin();
  while (it!=_.end())
    if (*it<*jt) return true;
    else if (*it++>*jt++) return false;
  return false;
}
string Integer::toString() const
{ if (_.empty()) return "NAI";
  string s=(_neg?"-":"");
  Integer::CRIt it=_.rbegin();  // last element of _ list
  s += Integer::toString(*it++);
  while ( it!=_.rend())
    s += Integer::pad(Integer::toString(*it++));
  return s;
}
string Integer::pad(string s)
{ if (s.length()>=WIDTH) return s;
  return string(WIDTH-s.length(),'0') + s;
}
Integer Integer::NotAnInteger()  // not an integer
{ Integer z;
  z._.clear();        // empty list
  return z;
}
int Integer::toInt(string s)
{ int len=s.length(), n=0, k;
  for (int i=0; i<len; i++)
    if (!isdigit(s[i])) return 0;
  for (k=0; k<len; k++)  // remove leading 0s
    if (s[k]!='0') break;
  s = s.substr(k);
  if (s.empty()) return 0;
  istringstream in(s);
  in >> n;
  return n;
}
```

```
string Integer::toString(int n)
{ ostringstream out;
  out << n;
  return out.str();
}
Integer Integer::toInteger(string s)
{ Integer x=NotAnInteger();
  if (s.empty() || s=="NAI") return x;
  if (s[0]=='-')
  { x._neg = true;
    s = s.substr(1);
  }
  for (int i=0; i<s.length(); i++)
    if (!isdigit(s[i])) return NotAnInteger();
  for (int len=s.length(); len>WIDTH; len -= WIDTH)
  { x._.push_back(Integer::toInt(s.substr(len-WIDTH)));
    s = s.substr(0,len-WIDTH);  // truncate last 4 digits
  }
  x._.push_back(Integer::toInt(s));
  return x;
}
const Integer Integer::ZERO(0);
const Integer Integer::NAI("NAI");          // "Not An Integer"
const int Integer::WIDTH=4;                 // 4 digits per list element
const int Integer::RADIX=pow(10,WIDTH);     // 10^4=10,000
```

7.8 IMPLEMENTION OF THE List CLASS

Finally, here is an implementation of the List class defined on page 127:

EXAMPLE 7.10 A Linked Implementation of the List Class

```
template <class T>
class List
{
  protected:
    class Node
    { public:
        Node(const T& data=T(), Node* prev=0, Node* next=0)
          : _data(data), _prev(prev), _next(next)
        { if (_prev == 0) _prev = this;
          if (_next == 0) _next = this;
        }
        T _data;
        Node* _prev, * _next;
    };
    Node* _;  // dummy node
    int _size;
  public:
    class Iterator
    {   friend class List;
```

```
      public:
        Iterator(Node* p) : _(p) { }
        T& operator*() {return _->_data; }
        void operator=(const Iterator& it) {_ = it._; }
        bool operator==(const Iterator& it) {return _ == it._; }
        bool operator!=(const Iterator& it) {return _ != it._; }
        Iterator operator++(int)  // postfix
        { Iterator it(_);
          _ = _->_next;
          return it;
        }
        Iterator& operator++() { _ = _->_next; return *this; }
        Iterator operator--(int)  // postfix
        { Iterator it(_);
          _ = _->_prev;
          return it;
        }
        Iterator& operator--() { _ = _->_prev; return *this; }
      protected:
        List<T>::Node* _;
    };
    List();
    List(const List&);
    List(int);
    List(int,const T&);
    List(Iterator&,Iterator&);
    ~List();
    int size() const;            // returns number of elements
    bool empty() const;          // returns true iff this is empty
    T& front() const;            // returns the first element
    T& back() const;             // returns the last element
    Iterator begin();            // points to first element
    Iterator end();              // points to dummy element
    void push_front(const T&);   // inserts given element in front
    void push_back(const T&);    // inserts given element in back
    void pop_front();            // removes element from front
    void pop_back();             // removes element from back
    Iterator insert(Iterator&,const T&);
    Iterator insert(Iterator&,int,const T&);
    void erase(Iterator&);
    void erase(Iterator&,Iterator&);
    void clear();
    void splice(Iterator,List&,Iterator);
};
template <class T>
List<T>::List() : _size(0)
{ _ = new Node();
}
template <class T>
List<T>::List(const List& l) : _size(l._size)
{ _ = new Node();   // dummy node
  Node* pp = _;
```

```
  for (Node* p=l._->_next; p != l._; p = p->_next, pp = pp->_next)
    pp->_next = pp->_next->_prev = new Node(p->_data,_,pp);
}
template <class T>
List<T>::List(int n) : _size(n)
{ _ = new Node();   // dummy node
  Node* p = _;
  for (int i=0; i<n; i++)
    p = p->_prev = new Node(T(),_,p);
  _->_next = p;
}
template <class T>
List<T>::List(int n, const T& t) : _size(n)
{ _ = new Node();   // dummy node
  Node* p = _;
  for (int i=0; i<n; i++)
    p = p->_prev = new Node(t,_,p);
  _->_next = p;
}
template <class T>
List<T>::List(Iterator& it1,Iterator& it2) : _size(0)
{ _ = new Node();   // dummy node
  Node* pp = _;
  for (Node* p=it1._; p != it2._; p = p->_next, pp = pp->_next)
  { pp->_next = new Node(p->_data,pp,_);
    ++_size;
  }
  _->_prev = pp;
}
template <class T>
List<T>::~List()
{ Node* p=_->_next;
  while (p != _)
  { Node* pp = p->_next;
    delete p;
    p = pp;
  }
  delete _;
}
template <class T>
int List<T>::size() const
{ return _size;
}
template <class T>
bool List<T>::empty() const
{ return _size == 0;
}
template <class T>
T& List<T>::front() const
{ return _->_next->_data;
}
```

```
template <class T>
T& List<T>::back() const
{ return _->_prev->_data;
}

template <class T>
List<T>::Iterator List<T>::begin()
{ return Iterator(_->_next);
}

template <class T>
List<T>::Iterator List<T>::end()
{ return Iterator(_);
}

template <class T>
void List<T>::push_front(const T& x)
{ _->_next = _->_next->_prev = new Node(x,_,_->_next);
  ++_size;
}

template <class T>
void List<T>::push_back(const T& x)
{ _->_prev = _->_prev->_next = new Node(x,_->_prev,_);
  ++_size;
}

template <class T>
void List<T>::pop_front()
{ Node* p = _->_next;
  _->_next = p->_next;
  p->_next->_prev = _;
  delete p;
  --_size;
}

template <class T>
void List<T>::pop_back()
{ Node* p = _->_prev;
  _->_prev = p->_prev;
  p->_prev->_next = _;
  delete p;
  --_size;
}

template <class T>
List<T>::Iterator List<T>::insert(Iterator& it, const T& x)
{ it._->_prev = it._->_prev->_next = new Node(x,it._->_prev,it._);
  it._ = it._->_prev;
  ++_size;
}
```

```
template <class T>
List<T>::Iterator List<T>::insert(Iterator& it, int n, const T& x)
{ Node* p=it._, * q = p->_prev;
  for (int i=0; i<n; i++)
    p = p->_prev = new Node(x,q,p);
  it._ = it._->_prev = q->_next = p;
  _size += n;
}
template <class T>
void List<T>::erase(Iterator& it)
{ if (_size == 0) return;
  Node* p = it._;
  p->_prev->_next = p->_next;
  p->_next->_prev = p->_prev;
  it._ = p->_next;
  delete p;
  --_size;
}
template <class T>
void List<T>::erase(Iterator& it1, Iterator& it2)
{ it1._->_prev->_next = it2._;
  it2._->_prev = it1._->_prev;
  Node* p=it1._->_next;
  while (it1._ != it2._)
  { delete it1._;
    it1._ = p;
    p = p->_next;
    --_size;
  }
}
template <class T>
void List<T>::clear()
{ Node* p=_, * q=p->_next;
  while (q != p)
  { p->_next = q->_next;
    q->_next->_prev = p;
    delete q;
    q = p->_next;
  }
  _size = 0;
}
template <class T>
void List<T>::splice(Iterator it1, List& l, Iterator it2)
{ Node* p=it1._, * pp=it1._->_prev, * q=it2._;
  p->_prev = pp->_next = q;
  q->_prev->_next = q->_next;
  q->_next->_prev = q->_prev;
  q->_prev = pp;
  q->_next = p;
  ++_size;
  --l._size;
}
```

Review Questions

7.1   How does a `list` object differ from a `vector` object?

7.2   Under what conditions should a `list` object be used instead of a `vector` object?

7.3   What is a self-organizing list?

Problems

7.1   Implement the following `friend` function for the `Polynomial::Term` structure (Example 7.3 on page 130):

```
friend Term operator-(const Term& t);
// returns the negative -t of the term t
```

7.2   Implement the following `friend` function for the `Polynomial` class (Example 7.3 on page 130):

```
friend Polynomial operator-(const Polynomial& p);
// returns the negative -p of the polynomial p
```

7.3   Implement the following `friend` function for the `Polynomial` class (Example 7.3 on page 130):

```
friend Polynomial operator-(const Polynomial& p,
                            const Polynomial& q);
// returns the difference p-q of the polynomials p and q
```

7.4   Implement the following `friend` function for the `Polynomial` class (Example 7.3 on page 130):

```
friend Polynomial operator*(const Polynomial& p,
                            const Polynomial& q);
// returns the product p*q of the polynomials p and q
```

7.5   Implement the following four member functions for the `Polynomial` class (Example 7.3 on page 130):

```
Polynomial& operator+=(const Polynomial& p);
// adds the polynomial p to this polynomial
Polynomial& operator-=(const Polynomial& p);
// subtracts the polynomial p from this polynomial
Polynomial& operator*=(const double x);
// multiplies this polynomial by the number x
Polynomial& operator*=(const Polynomial& p);
// multiplies this polynomial by the polynomial p
```

7.6   Implement the following member function for the `Polynomial::Term` structure (Example 7.3 on page 130):

```
bool operator!=(const Term& t) const;
// returns true iff this term is not equal to the term t
```

7.7   Implement the following member function for the `Polynomial` class (Example 7.3 on page 130):

```
bool operator!=(const Polynomial& p) const;
// returns true iff this is not equal to the polynomial p
```

7.8   Implement the following two `friend` functions for the `Polynomial::Term` structure (Example 7.3 on page 130):

```
friend Term derivative(const Term& t)
// returns the derivative of the term t; for example,
// if t represents 7x^5, then derivative(t) would represent 35x^4;
```

```
      friend Term antiderivative(const Term&);
      // returns the antiderivative of the term t; for example,
      // if t represents 8x^3, then derivative(t) would represent 2x^4;
```

7.9 Implement the following two `friend` functions for the `Polynomial` class (Example 7.3 on page 130):

```
      friend Polynomial derivative(const Polynomial& p);
      // returns the derivative of the polynomial p; for example,
      // if p represents 7x^5 + 9, then derivative(p) would
      // represent 35x^4;
      friend Polynomial antiderivative(const Polynomial& p);
      // returns the antiderivative of the polynomial p; for example,
      // if p represents 35x^4 + 8x^3, then derivative(p)
      // would represent 7x^5 + 2x^4;
```

7.10 Implement the following `static` declarations for the `Polynomial::Term` structure (Example 7.3 on page 130):

```
      static const Polynomial ONE;    // p(x) = 1
      static const Polynomial X;      // p(x) = x
```

7.11 Modify the `Polynomial` class (Example 7.3 on page 130) so that its output operator prints polynomials with negative terms like this:

```
      -19.6x^5 - 28.4x^4 - 72.6x^3 + 34.1x^2
```

instead of like this:

```
      -19.6x^5 + -28.4x^4 + -72.6x^3 + 34.1x^2
```

7.12 Solve the Josephus problem (Example 7.6 on page 135) using a standard C++ `list` object.

7.13 Use the `OrderedList` class (Example 7.7 on page 137) to implement the standard `sort` algorithm (Example D.60).

7.14 A *self-organizing list* is a list that moves each element to the front of the list whenever it is accessed. This modification improves the efficiency of the standard implementation if the list is used mostly for look-up. Use inheritance to define a `SelfOrganizingList` class template.

7.15 Implement the following `friend` function for the `Integer` class (Example 7.8 on page 138):

```
      friend istream& operator>>(istream& istr, Integer& x);
      // inputs x from the istr input stream
```

7.16 Implement the following `friend` function for the `Integer` class (Example 7.8 on page 138):

```
      friend Integer operator*(int n, const Integer& x);
      // returns the product n*x
```

7.17 Implement the following `friend` function for the `Integer` class (Problem 7.16):

```
      friend Integer operator*(const Integer& x, int n);
      // returns the product x*n
```

7.18 Implement the following four members of the `Integer` class (Example 7.8 on page 138):

```
      Integer& operator+=(const Integer& x);
      // adds the Integer x to this Integer
      Integer& operator-=(const Integer& x);
      // subtracts the Integer x from this Integer
      Integer& operator*=(int n);
      // multiplies this Integer by the int n
      Integer& operator*=(const Integer& x);
      // multiplies this Integer by the Integer x
```

7.19 Implement the following four members of the `Integer` class (Example 7.8 on page 138):

```
      bool operator!=(const Integer& x) const;
      // returns true iff this Integer is not equal to the Integer x
```

```
    bool operator<=(const Integer&) const;
    // returns true iff this Integer is not greater than the Integer x
    bool operator>(const Integer&) const;
    // returns true iff this Integer is greater than the Integer x
    bool operator>=(const Integer&) const;
    // returns true iff this Integer is not less than the Integer x
    Integer& operator-=(const Integer& x);
    // returns true iff this Integer is less than the Integer x
```

7.20 Implement the following member of the `Integer` class (Example 7.8 on page 138):

```
    int toInt() const;
    // returns an int that represents this Integer object
```

7.21 Implement the following member of the `Integer` class (Example 7.8 on page 138):

```
    double toDouble() const;
    // returns a double that represents this Integer object
```

Answers to Review Questions

7.1 A `list` object is implemented using links; a `vector` object is implemented using contiguous storage?

7.2 A `list` object should be used when frequent insertions and removals will be done at positions other than the end of the sequence. A `vector` object should be used when frequent data access (read and write) operations will be done.

7.3 A self-organizing list is a list in which each element is moved to the front of the list whenever it is accessed.

Solutions to Problems

7.1 Implementation of the `operator-(term)` function:

```
    Polynomial::Term operator-(const Polynomial::Term& term)
    { Polynomial::Term t(term);
      t._coef *= -1.0;
      return t;
    }
```

7.2 Implementation of the `operator-(polynomial)` function:

```
    Polynomial operator-(const Polynomial& p1)
    { Polynomial p(p1);
      for (Polynomial::It it=p._terms.begin();
           it != p._terms.end(); it++)
        it->_coef *= -1;
      return p;
    }
```

7.3 Implementation of the `operator-(polynomial,polynomial)` function:

```
    Polynomial operator-(const Polynomial& p1, const Polynomial& p2)
    { return p1 + -p2;
    }
```

7.4 Implementation of the `operator*(polynomial,polynomial)` function:

```
    Polynomial operator*(const Polynomial& p1, const Polynomial& p2)
    { Polynomial p;
      p._degree = p1._degree + p2._degree;
      for (Polynomial::CIt it1=p1._terms.begin();
           it1!=p1._terms.end(); it1++)
```

```
        for (Polynomial::CIt it2=p2._terms.begin();
             it2!=p2._terms.end(); it2++)
        { int exp = it1->_exp + it2->_exp;
          double coef = it1->_coef * it2->_coef;
          Polynomial::It it=p._terms.begin();
          for ( ; it != p._terms.end(); it++)
            if (it->_exp <= exp) break;
          if (it->_exp == exp) it->_coef += coef;
          else p._terms.insert(it,Polynomial::Term(coef,exp));
        }
    p.reduce();
    return p;
  }
```

7.5 Implementation of the overloaded arithmetic assignment operators for the `Polynomial` class:

```
Polynomial& Polynomial::operator+=(const Polynomial& p)
{ *this = *this + p;
  return *this;
}
Polynomial& Polynomial::operator-=(const Polynomial& p)
{ *this = *this - p;
  return *this;
}
Polynomial& Polynomial::operator*=(const double x)
{ *this = x * *this;
  return *this;
}
Polynomial& Polynomial::operator*=(const Polynomial& p)
{ *this = *this * p;
  return *this;
}
```

7.6 Implementation of the `operator!=(term)` function:

```
bool Polynomial::Term::operator!=(const Term& t) const
{ return _exp != t._exp || _coef != t._coef;
}
```

7.7 Implementation of the `operator!=(polynomial)` function:

```
bool Polynomial::operator!=(const Polynomial& p) const
{ return _terms != p._terms;
}
```

7.8 Implementation of the `derivative(term)` and `antiderivative(term)` functions:

```
Polynomial::Term derivative(const Polynomial::Term& t)
{ if (t._exp == 0) return Polynomial::Term(0.0,0);
  return Polynomial::Term(t._exp*t._coef,t._exp-1);
}
Polynomial::Term antiderivative(const Polynomial::Term& t)
{ if (t._coef == 0) return Polynomial::Term(1.0,0);
  return Polynomial::Term(t._coef/(t._exp+1),t._exp+1);
}
```

7.9 Implementation of the `derivative(polynomial)` and `antiderivative(polynomial)` functions:

```
Polynomial derivative(const Polynomial& p1)
{ if (p1._degree < 0) return Polynomial::ZERO;
  Polynomial p;
  p._degree = ( p1._degree>1 ? p1._degree - 1 : 0);
  for (Polynomial::CIt it=p1._terms.begin();
       it!=p1._terms.end(); it++)
    if (it->_exp>0) p._terms.push_back(derivative(*it));
```

```
            return p;
          }
          Polynomial antiderivative(const Polynomial& p1)
          { Polynomial p;
            p._degree = p1._degree + 1;
            for (Polynomial::CIt it=p1._terms.begin(); it!=p1._terms.end();
                it++)
              p._terms.push_back(antiderivative(*it));
            return p;
          }
```

7.10 Definitions of the `static` constants `Polynomial::ONE` and `Polynomial::X`:

```
          const Polynomial Polynomial::ONE(1.0,0);   // the monomial p(x) = 1
          const Polynomial Polynomial::X(1.0,1);     // the monomial p(x) = x
```

7.11 Modifications of the `Polynomial` class to improve output operator:

```
          Polynomial::Term abs(const Polynomial::Term& t)
          { Polynomial::Term term(t);
            if (term._coef < 0) term._coef *= -1.0;
            return term;
          }
          ostream& operator<<(ostream& ostr, const Polynomial& p)
          { if (p == Polynomial::ZERO) return ostr << 0;
            Polynomial::CIt it=p._terms.begin();
            ostr << *it++;
            while (it != p._terms.end())
              if (it->_coef < 0) ostr << " - " << abs(*it++);
              else ostr << " + " << *it++;
            return ostr;
          }
```

7.12 Solution to the Josephus problem using a standard `list` object:

```
          #include <iostream>
          #include <list>
          using namespace std;
          class List : public list<char>
          { // circular list of chars
            public:
              List(int);
              char kill(int);
          };
          ostream& operator<<(ostream&, const List&);
          int main()
          { int n, skip;
            cout << "Enter number of men: ";
            cin >> n;
            List list(n);
            cout << "\t\t" << list;
            cout << "Enter skip number: ";
            cin >> skip;
            while (list.size() > 1)
            { cout << '\t' << list.kill(skip) << " killed" << list;
            }
            cout << list.back() << " survived.\n";
          }
          List::List(int n)
          { for (int i=0; i<n; i++)
              push_back('A'+i);
          }
```

```
ostream& operator<<(ostream& ostr, const List& l)
{ ostr << "\tsize=" << l.size();
  if (l.empty()) cout << ":\t()\n";
  else
  { list<char>::const_iterator it=l.begin();
    ostr << ": (" << *it++;
    while (it!=l.end())
      ostr << "," << *it++;
    ostr << ")\n";
  }
  return ostr;
}
char List::kill(int k)
{ static list<char>::iterator it=begin();
  for (int i=0; i<k; i++)   // advance k elements
    it = ( ++it==end() ? begin() : it );   // circular wrap
  list<char>::iterator jt=it;
  it = ( ++it==end() ? begin() : it );
  char killed = *jt;
  erase(jt);
  return killed;
}
```

7.13 Using the `OrderedList` class to implement the standard `sort` algorithm:

```
#include "OrderedList.hpp"  // See Example 7.7 on page 137
template <class T, class It>
void sort(It it1, It it2);
int main()
{ char* p="GAJBHCHDIEFAGDHC";
  cout << p << '\n';
  sort(p,p+16);
  cout << p << '\n';
}
template <class T, class It>
void sort(It it1, It it2)
{ OrderedList<T> sorter;
  for (It it=it1; it!=it2; it++)
    sorter.add(*it);
  copy(sorter.begin(),sorter.end(),it1);
}
```

7.14 A subclass for self-organizing lists:

```
template <class T>
class SelfOrganizingList : public list<T>
{ public:
    bool contains(const T&);
};
template <class T>
bool SelfOrganizingList<T>::contains(const T& t)
{ list<T>::iterator it=find(begin(),end(),t);
  if (it == end()) return false;
  if (it != begin())
  { erase(it);
    push_front(t);
  }
  return true;
}
```

7.15 Implementation of the `operator>>(istr,x)` function:

```
istream& operator>>(istream& istr, Integer& x)
{ string s;
  istr >> s;
  x = Integer::toInteger(s);
  return istr;
}
```

7.16 Implementation of the `operator*(n,x)` function:

```
Integer operator*(int n, const Integer& x)
{ if (n==0 || x==Integer::ZERO) return Integer::ZERO;
  const int R = Integer::RADIX;
  Integer y=Integer::NAI;
  if (n<0) n = -n;
  if (n<0 && !x._neg) y._neg = true;
  if (n>0 &&  x._neg) y._neg = true;
  Integer::CIt it=x._.begin();
  int n0=n%R, n1=n/R;
  unsigned x0=*it++, x1;
  unsigned u=n0*x0;
  y._.push_back(u%R);
  u /= R;   // carry
  while (it!=x._.end())
  { x1 = *it++;
    u += n0*x1 + n1*x0;
    y._.push_back(u%R);
    u /= R;   // carry
    x0 = x1;
  }
  u += n1*x0;
  while (u>0)
  { y._.push_back(u%R);
    u /= R;
  }
  return y;
}
```

7.17 Implementation of the `operator*(x,n)` function:

```
Integer operator*(const Integer& x, int n)
{ return n*x;
}
```

7.18 Implementation of the four arithmetic assignment operators for the `Integer` class:

```
Integer& Integer::operator+=(const Integer& x)
{ *this = *this + x;
  return *this;
}
Integer& Integer::operator-=(const Integer& x)
{ *this = *this - x;
  return *this;
}
Integer& Integer::operator*=(int n)
{ *this = *this * n;
  return *this;
}
Integer& Integer::operator*=(const Integer& x)
{ *this = *this * x;
  return *this;
}
```

7.19 Implementation of the other four relational operators for the `Integer` class:

```
bool Integer::operator!=(const Integer& x) const
{ return !(*this == x);
}
bool Integer::operator<=(const Integer& x) const
{ return !(x < *this);
}
bool Integer::operator>(const Integer& x) const
{ return (x < *this);
}
bool Integer::operator>=(const Integer& x) const
{ return !(*this < x);
}
```

7.20 Implementation of the `toInt()` function:

```
int Integer::toInt() const
{ if (_.size()==0) return 0;
  int n=_.front();
  return (_neg?-n:n);
}
```

7.21 Implementation of the `toDouble()` function:

```
double Integer::toDouble() const
{ if (_.size()==0) return 0.0;
  Integer::CRIt it=_.rbegin();  // last element of _ list
  double t=double(*it++);
  while (t<DBL_MAX-RADIX && it!=_.rend())
    t = RADIX*t + double(*it++);
  if (it==_.rend()) return (_neg?-t:t);
  else return 0.0;
}
```

Chapter 8

Tables

A *table* (also called a *map*, a *lookup table*, an *associative array*, or a *dictionary*) is a container that allows direct access by any index type. It works like an array or vector except that the index variable need not be an integer. A good analogy is a dictionary; the index variable is the word being looked up, and the element that it indexes is its dictionary definition.

A table is a sequence of pairs. The first component of the pair is called the *key*. It serves as the index into the table, generalizing the subscript integer used in arrays. The second component is called the *value* of its key component. It contains the information being looked up. In the dictionary example, the key is the word being looked up, and the value is that word's definition (and everything else listed for that word).

A table is also called a map because we think of the keys being mapped into their values, like a mathematical function: $f(key) = value$. Tables are also called associative arrays because they can be implemented using two parallel arrays; the keys in one array and the values in the other.

8.1 THE STANDARD `pair` TYPE

The Standard C++ `map` container class template can be implemented as a sorted list of pairs, where each pair contains a key and its value. That implementation uses the `pair` type, implemented as a `struct` template with two template parameters.

EXAMPLE 8.1 The Standard `pair` Struct Template

Here is part of the definition of the Standard C++ `pair` structure template:

```
template <class T1, class T2>
class pair
{ T1 first;
  T2 second;
  pair() : first(T1()), second(T2()) { }
  pair(const T1& x, const T2& y) : first(x), second(y) { }
  // ...
};
```

It has two data members and two constructors. Since it is defined to be a `struct` instead of a `class`, all of its members are `public` by default. (That's really the only reason for using a `struct` instead of a `class`.) The first constructor is the default constructor; it creates a `pair` object, initializing its two components with the default values of their types. The second constructor is the copy constructor.

Pairs can be used like this:

```
pair<string,string> name("John","Smith");
cout << name.second << ", " << name.first << '\n';
```

Note that the `pair` class template has two template parameters. So any object declared to be a pair must specify in that declaration the types of its two components.

155

EXAMPLE 8.2 Using pair **as a Return Type**

```
#include <iostream>
#include <limits>  // defines the constant INT_MAX
using namespace std;
typedef pair<int,bool> Pair;
Pair factorial(int);

int main()
{ for (int n=-2; n<16; n++)
  { Pair p=factorial(n);
    if (p.second) cout << n << "!\t= " << p.first;
    else cout << "overflow for n = " << n;
    cout << '\n';
  }
}

Pair factorial(int n)
{ if (n<0) return Pair(0,false);
  if (n<2) return Pair(1,true);
  int f=2;
  for (int k=3; k<=n; k++)
    if (f > INT_MAX/k) return Pair(0,false);
    else f *= k;
  return Pair(f,true);
}
```

```
overflow for n = -2
overflow for n = -1
0!      = 1
1!      = 1
2!      = 2
3!      = 6
4!      = 24
5!      = 120
6!      = 720
7!      = 5040
8!      = 40320
9!      = 362880
10!     = 3628800
11!     = 39916800
12!     = 479001600
overflow for n = 13
overflow for n = 14
overflow for n = 15
```

We use a typedef to make the code more readable: objects of type Pair are pairs of variables, the first component an int and the second a bool.

The function factorial() returns an object of type Pair. If the second component is true, then the first component is the correct value for $n!$; otherwise, the second componenet signals overflow error.

Note that the default constructor is used in the function to return the pair by value, and the copy constructor is used to initalize the Pair object p in main().

The condition (f > INT_MAX/k) is equivalent to (k*f > INT_MAX) which means integer overflow. However, the latter condition will not work correctly because no int value can exceed INT_MAX.

8.2 APPLICATIONS USING THE `map` CLASS TEMPLATE

In addition to the standard vector functions, the Standard C++ `map` class template also includes the following member function:

```
    iterator find(const Key& key);
```
This returns an iterator that locates the pair whose first component is `key` if it exists in the table; otherwise, it returns the `end()` of the map.

The `map` class template requires that the keys have an *ordinal type* (*i.e.*, have the `<` operator defined) and that they be unique.

EXAMPLE 8.3 A German-English Dictionary

```cpp
#include <iostream>
#include <map>
using namespace std;
typedef map<string,string> Dictionary;

int main()
{ Dictionary d;
  d["Tag"] = "day";
  d["Hut"] = "hat";
  d["Tal"] = "valley";
  d["Hof"] = "court, courtyard, farm";
  d["Uhr"] = "clock";
  d["Mut"] = "courage";
  d["Tat"] = "action, act, deed";
  d["Rad"] = "wheel";
  d["Bau"] = "building";
  d["Ohr"] = "ear";
  d["Tor"] = "gate";
  d["Ehe"] = "marriage";
  d["Mal"] = "mark, sign, time";
  for (Dictionary::iterator it=d.begin(); it!=d.end(); it++)
    cout << it->first << " = " << it->second << '\n';
}
```

```
Bau = building
Ehe = marriage
Hof = court, courtyard, farm
Hut = hat
Mal = mark, sign, time
Mut = courage
Ohr = ear
Rad = wheel
Tag = day
Tal = valley
Tat = action, act, deed
Tor = gate
Uhr = clock
```

The typedefs are used to simplify the code.

The object d is a map of pairs of strings. The first component of each pair is a German word, and the second component its its English equivalent. The dictionary maps German word keys into English equivalent values.

Maps are implemented as lists of pairs, sorted by their key values. So the `for` loop that traverses the sequence prints the pairs with their key values in alphabetical order.

Each assignment statement in `main()` creates a new pair in the map object d:

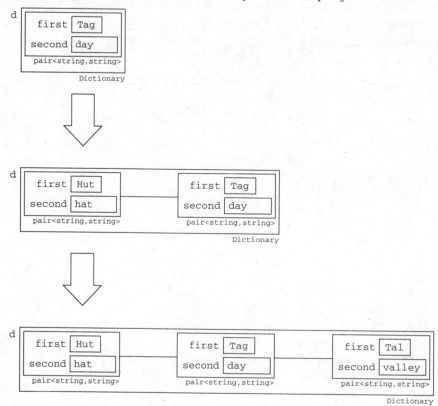

EXAMPLE 8.4 Interface for a Concordance Class

A *concordance* is a list of words that appear in a text document along with the numbers of the lines on which the words appear. It is just like an index of a book except that it lists line numbers instead of page numbers. Concordances are useful for analyzing documents to find word frequencies and associations that are not evident from reading the document directly.

Here is a class definition for concordances:

```
class Concordance
{ protected:
    typedef list<int> List;
    typedef map<string,List> Map;
    friend ifstream& operator>>(istream&, Concordance&);
    friend ostream& operator<<(ostream&, const Concordance&);
    friend ostream& operator<<(ostream& ostr, const List& l);
    Map _;
    bool extract(string&, string);
};
```

We use the Standard C++ `map` class template to implement a concordance. The data member named "_" is an ordered sequence of pairs. In each pair, the first component is a word and the second componenet is a list of line numbers for the word.

We overload the input and output operators for loading and displaying the concordance. The latter will need to print the line number lists, so we also overload the output operator for `List` objects. The `protected` function `extract()` is a utility function used by the overloaded input operator to extract individual words from the lines of text that it inputs.

Note that even though the overloaded operators are declared `protected`, they are still `public` because they are `friend` functions.

EXAMPLE 8.5 A Test Driver for the **Concordance** Class

```
int main()
{ ifstream fin("Shakespeare.txt");
  ofstream fout("Concordance.out");
  Concordance c;
  fin >> c;
  fout << c;
  cout << c;
}
```

Shakespeare.txt

```
Friends, Romans, countrymen, lend me your ears!
I come to bury Caesar, not to praise him.
The evil that men do lives after them,
The good is oft interred with their bones;
So let it be with Caesar.  The noble Brutus
Hath told you Caesar was ambitious;
If it were so, it was a grievous fault;
And grievously hath Caesar answer'd it.
Here, under leave of Brutus and the rest, --
For Brutus is an honourable man;
So are they all, all honourable men.
Come I to speak in Caesar's funeral.
He was my friend, faithful and just to me.
But Brutus says he was ambitious;
And Brutus is an honourable man.
He hath brought many captives home to Rome.
Whose ransoms did the general coffers fill:
Did this in Caesar seem ambitious?
When that the poor have cried, Caesar hath wept;
Ambition should be made of sterner stuff.
Yet Brutus says he was ambitious;
And Brutus is an honourable man.
You all did see that on the Lupercal
I thrice presented him with a kingly crown,
Which he did thrice refuse: was this ambition?
Yet Brutus says he was ambitious;
And, sure, is an honourable man.
I speak not to disprove what Brutus spoke,
But here I am to speak what I do know.
You all did love him once, not without cause.
What cause withholds you, then, to mourn for him?
O judgement! thou art fled to brutish beasts,
And men have lost their reason!
```

Concordance.out

```
A: 7, 24
AFTER: 3
ALL: 11, 23, 30
AM: 29
AMBITION: 20, 25
AMBITIOUS: 6, 14, 18, 21, 26
AN: 10, 15, 22, 27
AND: 8, 9, 13, 15, 22, 27, 33
ANSWER: 8
ARE: 11
ART: 32
BE: 5, 20
BEASTS: 32
BONES: 4
BROUGHT: 16
BRUTISH: 32
BRUTUS: 5, 9, 10, 14, 15, 21, 22, 26, 28
BURY: 2
BUT: 14, 29
CAESAR: 2, 5, 6, 8, 12, 18, 19
CAPTIVES: 16
CAUSE: 30, 31
COFFERS: 17
COME: 2, 12
COUNTRYMEN: 1
CRIED: 19
CROWN: 24
DID: 17, 18, 23, 25, 30
DISPROVE: 28
DO: 3, 29
EARS: 1
EVIL: 3
FAITHFUL: 13
```

This builds a concordance for the text shown above from Shakespeare's *Julius Caesar*. The first 33 lines of the resulting concordance are shown at its right. The output to the screen (cout) is the same. Note that the words are capitalized for simplicity.

A glance at this concordance reveals nine references to "Brutus" (more than to "Caesar") and the homonymous use of the word "brutish."

EXAMPLE 8.6 Implementation for the Concordance class

```
ifstream& operator>>(istream& istr, Concordance& c)
{ typedef Concordance::Map::iterator CMIt;
  string line, word;
  for (int n=1; getline(istr,line); n++)
    while (c.extract(word,line))
    { CMIt it=c._.find(word);
      if (it == c._.end())        // new word
      { Concordance::List list;   // new list
        list.push_back(n);
        c._[word] = list;   // inserts new (word,list) pair into c
      }
      else // word is already in concordance
      { Concordance::List& list = it->second;   // its list
        if (n > list.back()) list.push_back(n);
      }
    }
}

ostream& operator<<(ostream& ostr, const Concordance& c)
{ typedef Concordance::Map::const_iterator CMCIt;
  for (CMCIt it=c._.begin(); it!=c._.end(); it++)
    ostr << it->first << ": " << it->second << '\n';
  return ostr;
}

ostream& operator<<(ostream& ostr, const Concordance::List& l)
{ typedef Concordance::List::const_iterator CLCIt;
  if (l.empty()) return ostr;
  CLCIt it=l.begin();
  ostr << *it;
  while (++it!=l.end())
    ostr << ", " << *it;
  return ostr;
}

bool Concordance::extract(string& word, string line)
{ static int p=0;          // points to next character to be processed
  while (p<line.length() && !isalpha(line[p]))
    ++p;                            // look for beginning of next word
  if (p == line.length())    // there are no more words on this line
  { p = 0;         // begin at the beginning of next line on next call
    return false;            // this call found no word on this line
  }
```

```
   int start=p;                          // points to first letter of word
   while (isalpha(line[p]))                    // find end of word
     ++p;
   int len=p-start;                      // word = line[start:start+len]
   word = string(len,' ');          // allocate len characters to word
   for (int i=0; i<len; i++)              // extract word from line
     word[i] = toupper(line[start+i]);        // capitalize letters
   while (p<line.length() && !isspace(line[p]))
     ++p;                         // eat extraneous suffixes, such as "'s"
   return true;
 }
```

The input operator reads the text line by line. The `while` loop extracts one word at a time. It uses the `map::find()` function to determine whether the word is already in the concordance. That function returns a `map::iterator` that locates the element whose first component equals the argument passed to it. If the element is not found, then the `find()` function returns the `end()` iterator for the map. In that case, a new list object is created, the current line number is inserted into that list, and then the (word,list) pair is inserted into the concordance c by the assignment

```
   c._[word] = list;
```

If the word is already in the concordance, and if the current line number is greater than the last number in its list, then it is appended to the list.

8.3 HASH TABLES

A *hash table* is a table that uses a special function to compute the location of data values from their key values instead of storing the keys in the table. The special function is called the *hash function* for the table. Since the lookup time is independent of the size of the table, hash tables generally have faster access time.

EXAMPLE 8.7 Interface for HashTable Class Template

```
   template < class K, class T, class H=Hash<K> >
   class HashTable
   { protected:
       typedef pair<K,T> Pair;
       typedef vector<Pair> Vector;
       typedef Vector::iterator VIt;
       typedef Vector::const_iterator CVIt;
       static const float LOAD;                        // load factor
       static const CAP=109;               // default initial capacity
     public:
       HashTable(int cap=CAP, const H& h=H()) : _(cap), _hash(h) { }
       T& operator[](K);   // subscript op for insertions and updates
       bool insert(K,T);                       // inserts the given pair
       bool remove(K);                 // deletes the element with given key
       int size() const;               // number of elements in table
       int capacity() const { return _.size(); }  // number of lists
       void dump() const;              // displays the entire hash table
```

```
   protected:
     Vector _;                              // vector of lists of pairs
     H _hash;                                   // hash function object
     int hash(K);            // hash function built from _hash object
     void rebuild();    // rebuilds the hash table making it larger
};
```

EXAMPLE 8.8 Interface for Hash Function Template

```
template <class K>
struct Hash
{ int operator()(K s)
  { int h=0;
    for (int i=0; i<s.length(); i++)
      h += s[i];
    return h;
  }
};
```

EXAMPLE 8.9 Test Driver for HashTable Class Template

```
#include "HashTable.SC.hpp"
typedef HashTable<string,string> Table;
void print(const Table&);

int main()
{ Table t(5);
  t.insert("Ruf","cry");
  t.insert("Eis","ice");
  print(t);
  t.insert("Tor","gate");
  print(t);
  t.insert("Ast","branch");
  print(t);
  cout << "\nt[Ruf]=" << t["Ruf"] << "\n";
  t["Ruf"] = "shout";
  cout << "t[Ruf]=" << t["Ruf"] << "\n";
  t.remove("Ruf");
  print(t);
  t["Wal"] = "whale";
  t["Zug"] = "procession";
  t["Hof"] = "courtyard, farm";
  t["Rat"] = "advice, counsel";
  t["Lob"] = "praise";
  t["Mut"] = "courage";
  t["Tat"] = "action, deed";
  t["Ohr"] = "ear";
  t["Tor"] = "gate";
  t["Mal"] = "mark, sign";
  print(t);
}
```

```
void print(const Table& t)
{ cout << "\nsize=" << t.size()
       << "\tcapacity=" << t.capacity() << "\n";
  t.dump();
}
size=2  capacity=5
1: (Ruf: cry)
4: (Eis: ice)

size=3  capacity=5
0: (Tor: gate)
1: (Ruf: cry)
4: (Eis: ice)

size=4  capacity=23
2: (Ruf: cry)
10: (Tor: gate)
13: (Eis: ice)
20: (Ast: branch)

t[Ruf]=cry
t[Ruf]=shout
size=3  capacity=23
10: (Tor: gate)
13: (Eis: ice)
20: (Ast: branch)

size=12 capacity=23
6: (Mal: mark, sign)
9: (Hof: courtyard, farm)
10: (Tor: gate)
11: (Zug: procession)
12: (Lob: praise)
13: (Eis: ice)
14: (Mut: courage)
16: (Wal: whale)
19: (Rat: advice, counsel)
20: (Ast: branch)
21: (Tat: action, deed)
22: (Ohr: ear)
```

EXAMPLE 8.10 Implementation HashTable **Class Template**

```
template <class K, class T, class H>
const float HashTable<K,T,H>::LOAD=0.75;

template <class K, class T, class H>
T& HashTable<K,T,H>::operator[](K key)
{ const K ZERO_K=K();
  int k0=hash(key), k=k0;
  while (_[k].first != key && _[k].first != ZERO_K)
    k = (k+1)%_.size();
  if (_[k].first == key) return _[k].second;        // found
```

```
      if (size()+1 < LOAD*_.size())
      { _[k] = Pair(key,T());
        return _[k].second;
      }
      else
      { rebuild();
        return operator[](key);
      }
    }


    template <class K, class T, class H>
    bool HashTable<K,T,H>::insert(K key, T val)
    { const K ZERO_K=K();
      int k0=hash(key), k=k0;
      while (_[k].first != key && _[k].first != ZERO_K)
        k = (k+1)%_.size();
      if (_[k].first == key) return false;      // found: no insertion
      if (size()+1 < LOAD*_.size()) _[k] = Pair(key,val);
      else
      { rebuild();
        insert(key,val);
      }
      return true;                              // not found: insertion successful
    }


    template <class K, class T, class H>
    bool HashTable<K,T,H>::remove(K key)
    { int k0=hash(key), k=k0;
      while (_[k].first != key && _[k].first != key)
        k = (k+1)%_.size();
      if (_[k].first == key)                            // found: remove pair
      { _[k] = Pair(K(),T());
        return true;
      }
      return false;                                     // not found: no removal
    }


    template <class K, class T, class H>
    int HashTable<K,T,H>::size() const
    { int n=0;
      const K ZERO_K=K();
      for (int i=0; i<_.size(); i++)
        if (_[i].first != ZERO_K) ++n;   // accumulate the list sizes
      return n;
    }


    template <class K, class T, class H>
    void HashTable<K,T,H>::dump() const
    { const K ZERO_K=K();
```

```
      for (int i=0; i<_.size(); i++)
        if (_[i].first != ZERO_K)
          cout << i << ": ("
               << _[i].first << ": " << _[i].second << ")\n";
}

template <class K, class T, class H>
int HashTable<K,T,H>::hash(K key)
{ return _hash(key)%_.size();
}

template <class K, class T, class H>
void HashTable<K,T,H>::rebuild()
{ Vector old_(_);                           // copy current vector
  _ = Vector(4*_.size()+3);                 // create new larger table
  for (int i=0; i<old_.size(); i++)
    insert(old_[i].first,old_[i].second);   // rehash to new table
}
```

8.4 HASH FUNCTIONS

The hash function used in Example 8.8 on page 162 may be unsatisfactory for large data sets because it is invariant under permutation of characters: hash("ABC") = hash("CBA"). Good hash functions are those that are unlikely to return the same value for different keys.

EXAMPLE 8.11 Using Permutation-Insensitive Hash Function

```
      void print(const string&);
      const int SIZE=13;
      int a[SIZE]={0};
      int collisions=0;

      int main()
      { print("Ruf");
        print("Eis");
        print("Tor");
        print("Ast");
        print("Zug");
        print("Hof");
        print("Rat");
        print("Lob");
        print("Mut");
        print("Tat");
        print("Ohr");
        print("Mal");
        cout << "\n\t" << collisions << " collisions\n";
      }
```

```
void print(const string& s)
{ Hash<string> h;
  int n=h(s)%SIZE;
  cout << "h(" << s << ") = " << n << "\n";
  if (a[n]>0) ++collisions;
  ++a[n];
}
```

```
h(Ruf) = 2
h(Eis) = 3
h(Tor) = 10
h(Ast) = 10
h(Zug) = 11
h(Hof) = 12
h(Rat) = 9
h(Lob) = 12
h(Mut) = 11
h(Tat) = 11
h(Ohr) = 11
h(Mal) = 9
      6 collisions
```

EXAMPLE 8.12 Using Permutation-Sensitive Hash Function

```
template <class K>
struct Hash
{ // PRECONDITION: K == string
  int operator()(K s)
  { int h=0;
    for (int i=0; i<s.length(); i++)
      h += i*s[i];
    return h;
  }
};
```

```
h(Ruf) = 9
h(Eis) = 10
h(Tor) = 1
h(Ast) = 9
h(Zug) = 11
h(Hof) = 3
h(Rat) = 4
h(Lob) = 8
h(Mut) = 11
h(Tat) = 4
h(Ohr) = 7
h(Mal) = 1
       4 collisions
```

EXAMPLE 8.13 Using Compression Hash Function

```
template <class K>
struct Hash
{ // PRECONDITION: K == string
  int operator()(K s)
  { int h=0;
    for (string::const_iterator it=s.begin(); it!=s.end(); it++)
      h = (h<<1)^*it;
    return h;
  }
};
h(Ruf) = 10
h(Eis) = 8
h(Tor) = 1
h(Ast) = 3
h(Zug) = 4
h(Hof) = 5
h(Rat) = 3
h(Lob) = 6
h(Mut) = 10
h(Tat) = 5
h(Ohr) = 11
h(Mal) = 7
        3 collisions
```

8.5 SEPARATE CHAINING

EXAMPLE 8.14 Interface for `HashTable` Class Template

```
#include <iostream>
#include <list>
#include <vector>
#include "Hash1.hpp"
using namespace std;

template < class K, class T, class H=Hash<K> >
class HashTable
{ protected:
    typedef pair<K,T> Pair;
    typedef list<Pair> List;
    typedef vector<List> Vector;
    typedef List::iterator LIt;
    typedef Vector::iterator VIt;
    typedef Vector::const_iterator CVIt;
    static const float LOAD;                        // load factor
    static const CAP=109;                  // default initial capacity
  public:
    HashTable(int cap=CAP, const H& h=H()) : _(cap), _hash(h) { }
    T& operator[](K);  // subscript op for insertions and updates
```

```
       bool insert(K,T);                    // inserts the given pair
       bool remove(K);              // deletes the element with given key
       int size() const;                 // number of elements in table
       int capacity() const { return _.size(); }  // number of lists
       void dump() const;               // displays the entire hash table
    protected:
       Vector _;                        // vector of lists of pairs
       H _hash;                              // hash function object
       int hash(K);              // hash function built from _hash object
       void rebuild();    // rebuilds the hash table making it larger
    };
```

EXAMPLE 8.15 Interface for Hash Function Class Template

```
template <class K>
struct Hash
{ int operator()(K s)
  { int h=0;
    for (int i=0; i<s.length(); i++)
      h += s[i];
    return h;
  }
};
```

EXAMPLE 8.16 Test Driver for HashTable Class Template

Here is the output from the same test driver that we used for the open addressing implementation (Example 8.9 on page 162):

```
size=2  capacity=5
1: (Ruf: cry)
4: (Eis: ice)

size=3  capacity=5
1: (Ruf: cry)
4: (Tor: gate), (Eis: ice)

size=4  capacity=23
2: (Ruf: cry)
10: (Tor: gate)
13: (Eis: ice)
20: (Ast: branch)

t[Ruf]=cry
t[Ruf]=shout

size=3  capacity=23
10: (Tor: gate)
13: (Eis: ice)
20: (Ast: branch)

size=12 capacity=23
6: (Mal: mark, sign)
9: (Lob: praise), (Hof: courtyard, farm)
```

```
10: (Tor: gate)
11: (Mut: courage), (Zug: procession)
13: (Eis: ice)
16: (Wal: whale)
19: (Rat: advice, counsel)
20: (Ast: branch)
21: (Ohr: ear), (Tat: action, deed)
```

EXAMPLE 8.17 Implementation `HashTable` **Class Template**

```cpp
template <class K, class T, class H>
const float HashTable<K,T,H>::LOAD=0.75;

template <class K, class T, class H>
T& HashTable<K,T,H>::operator[](K key)
{ int k=hash(key);
  List& chain=_[k];
  for(LIt jt=chain.begin(); jt!=chain.end(); jt++)
    if (jt->first == key) return jt->second;        // found
  if (size()+1 < LOAD*_.size())
  { chain.push_front(Pair(key,T()));
    return chain.front().second;
  }
  else
  { rebuild();
    return operator[](key);
  }
}
template <class K, class T, class H>
bool HashTable<K,T,H>::insert(K key, T val)
{ int k=hash(key);
  List& chain=_[k];
  for(LIt jt=chain.begin(); jt!=chain.end(); jt++)
    if (jt->first == key) return false;     // found: no insertion
  if (size()+1 < LOAD*_.size()) chain.push_front(Pair(key,val));
  else
  { rebuild();
    insert(key,val);
  }
  return true;
}

template <class K, class T, class H>
bool HashTable<K,T,H>::remove(K key)
{ int k=hash(key);
  List& chain=_[k];
  for(LIt jt=chain.begin(); jt!=chain.end(); jt++)
    if (jt->first == key)                   // found: remove pair
    { chain.erase(jt);
      return true;
    }
```

```
      return false;                            // not found: no removal
    }

    template <class K, class T, class H>
    int HashTable<K,T,H>::size() const
    { int n=0;
      for (CVIt it=_.begin(); it!=_.end(); it++)
        n += it->size();                        // accumulate the list sizes
      return n;
    }

    template <class K, class T, class H>
    void HashTable<K,T,H>::dump() const
    { for (int i=0; i<_.size(); i++)
      { List chain=_[i];
        if (!chain.empty())
        { LIt jt=chain.begin();
          cout << i << ": ("
               << jt->first << ": " << jt->second << ")";
          while (++jt!=chain.end())
            cout << ", (" << jt->first << ": " << jt->second << ")";
          cout << "\n";
        }
      }
    }

    template <class K, class T, class H>
    int HashTable<K,T,H>::hash(K key)
    { return _hash(key)%_.size();
    }

    template <class K, class T, class H>
    void HashTable<K,T,H>::rebuild()
    { Vector old_(_);                            // copy current vector
      _ = Vector(4*_.size()+3);                  // create new larger table
      for (VIt it=old_.begin(); it!=old_.end(); it++)
        for(LIt jt=it->begin(); jt!=it->end(); jt++)
          insert(jt->first,jt->second);    // rehash to load new table
    }
```

Review Questions

8.1 What is the difference between a table and a vector?

8.2 Why is a table also called a "map"?

8.3 Why is a table also called an "associative array"?

8.4 Why is a table also called a "dictionary"?

8.5 What is a concordance?

8.6 What is a hash table?

Problems

8.1 Implement a function that returns both the minimum and the maximum values of an array.

8.2 Modify the Concordance class so that it filters out common words (pronouns, adverbs, *etc.*) whose listing would not contribute to new insights into the document. Store the common words in a separate file.

8.3 Implement a FrequencyTable class for producing a list of words together with their frequency of occurrence in a given text file.

8.4 Modify the HashTable class so that the load factor can be passed as a template parameter.

Answers to Review Questions

8.1 A vector provides direct access to its elements by means of its integer index. A table provides direct access to its elements by means of a key field which can be of any ordinal type: int, double, string, *etc.*

8.2 A table is also called a "map" because, like a mathematical function, it maps each key value into a unique element.

8.3 A table is also called an "associative array" because it acts like an array (see Answer 8.1 above) in which each key value is associated with its unique element; like a mathematical function, it maps each key value into a unique element.

8.4 A table is also called a "dictionary" because it is used the same way as an ordinary natural language dictionary: to look up elements, as one would look up words in a dictionary.

8.5 A *concordance* is a list of words that appear in a text document along with the numbers of the lines on which the words appear. (See page 158.)

8.6 A *hash table* is is a table that uses a special function to compute the location of data values from their key values instead of storing the keys in the table. (See page 161.)

Solutions to Problems

8.1 A function that returns both the minimum and the maximum values of an array:

```
#include <iostream>
using namespace std;
typedef pair<double,double> Pair;
Pair range(double*,int);

int main()
{ double a[] = {6.6,2.2,8.8,5.5,9.9,5.5,1.1,4.4,7.7};
  Pair p = range(a,9);
  cout << "min=" << p.first << ", max=" << p.second << "\n";
}

Pair range(double* a, int n)
{ if (n==0) return Pair(0.0,0.0);
  double min=a[0], max=a[0];
  for (int i=1; i<n; i++)
  if (a[i] < min) min = a[i];
  else if (a[i] > max) max = a[i];
  return Pair(min,max);
}
```

8.2   Modifications to the Concordance class for filtering common words:

```cpp
class Concordance
{ protected:
    typedef list<int> List;
    typedef map<string,List> Map;
    friend ifstream& operator>>(istream&, Concordance&);
    friend ostream& operator<<(ostream&, const Concordance&);
    friend ostream& operator<<(ostream& ostr, const List& l);
    Map _;
    bool extract(string&, string);
    bool isCommon(string& word);
    static const char* COMMONWORDS;   // name of file
};

ifstream& operator>>(istream& istr, Concordance& c)
{ typedef Concordance::Map::iterator CMIt;
  string line, word;
  for (int n=1; getline(istr,line); n++)
    while (c.extract(word,line))
      if (!(c.isCommon(word)))
      { CMIt it=c._.find(word);
        if (it == c._.end())  // new word
        { Concordance::List list;          // new list
          list.push_back(n);
          c._[word] = list;
        }
        else // word is already in concordance
        { Concordance::List& list = it->second;  // its list
          if (n > list.back()) list.push_back(n);
        }
      }
}
bool Concordance::isCommon(string& target)
{ ifstream in(COMMONWORDS);
  string word;
  while (in >> word)
    if (word == target) return true;
  return false;
}
const char* Concordance::COMMONWORDS="Common-
Words.dat";
```

The file named CommonWords.dat would look like this:

CommonWords.dat
A
AFTER
ALL
AM
AN
AND
ARE
BACK
BE
BROUGHT
BUT

8.3   A FrequencyList class:

```cpp
#include <fstream>
#include <iostream>
#include <list>
#include <map>
using namespace std;
class FrequencyList
{ protected:
    typedef map<string,int> Map;
    friend ifstream& operator>>(istream&, FrequencyList&);
    friend ostream& operator<<(ostream&, const FrequencyList&);
    Map _;
    bool extract(string&, string);
};
```

```
    int main()
    { ifstream fin("Shakespeare.txt");
      ofstream fout("FrequencyList.out");
      FrequencyList c;
      fin >> c;
      fout << c;
      cout << c;
    }
    ifstream& operator>>(istream& istr, FrequencyList& c)
    { typedef FrequencyList::Map::iterator CMIt;
      string line, word;
      for (int n=1; getline(istr,line); n++)
        while (c.extract(word,line))
          { CMIt it=c._.find(word);
            if (it == c._.end()) c._[word] = 1;   // insert it
            else ++(c._[word]);                    // count it
          }
    }
    ostream& operator<<(ostream& ostr, const FrequencyList& c)
    // same as in Example 8.6 on page 160
    bool FrequencyList::extract(string& word, string line)
    // same as in Example 8.6 on page 160
```

8.4   Adding the LOAD factor as a template parameter:

```
    template < class K, class T, float LOAD, class H=Hash<K> >
    class HashTable
    { protected:
        typedef pair<K,T> Pair;
        typedef vector<Pair> Vector;
        typedef Vector::iterator VIt;
        typedef Vector::const_iterator CVIt;
        static const CAP=109;                  // default initial capacity
      public:
        HashTable(int cap=CAP, const H& h=H()) : _(cap), _hash(h) { }
        T& operator[](K);   // subscript op for insertions and updates
        bool insert(K,T);                    // inserts the given pair
        bool remove(K);          // deletes the element with given key
        int size() const;             // number of elements in table
        int capacity() const { return _.size(); }  // number of lists
        void dump() const;           // displays the entire hash table
      protected:
        Vector _;                    // vector of lists of pairs
        H _hash;                     // hash function object
        int hash(K);         // hash function built from _hash object
        void rebuild();   // rebuilds the hash table making it larger
    };
```

Chapter 9

Trees

A *tree* is a nonlinear container that models a hierarchical relationship in which all but one element has a unique predecessor (parent) but may have many successors (children). The unique parentless element is called the *root* of the tree.

Computer file structures like the one shown on the right are trees. In this example, the root is named Desktop. It has eight children, including one named MAIL.

9.1 TREE TERMINOLOGY

The elements of a tree are called *nodes*. Every node has a unique path connecting it to the root of the tree. A *path* is a sequence of adjacent elements. The *length* of a path is the number of its adjacent connections, which is one less than the number of nodes that it connects. In the tree shown below, the path (M, H, C, A) connecting node M to the root node A has length 3.

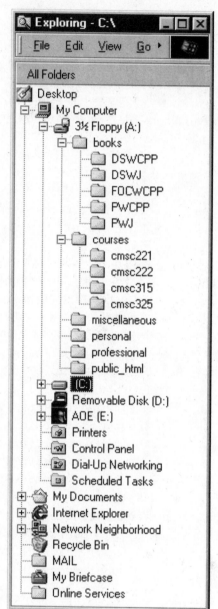

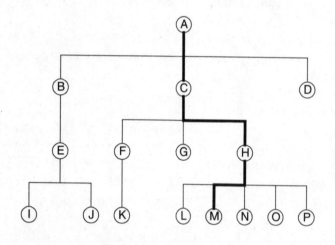

The *depth* of a node is the length of its path up to the root. In the tree shown above, node E has depth 2 and node M has depth 3. The root itself has depth 0. We also refer to the *level* of a tree, meaning all the nodes at a given depth. In the tree with root A shown above, level 2 consists of the set of nodes {E, F, G, H}.

The *height* of a tree is the greatest depth among all of its nodes. The tree shown above has height 3. The Windows directory tree shown on the right has height 4.

174

The tree whose root is its only node is called a *singleton* tree; its height is 0. The tree with 0 nodes is called the *empty tree*; its height is defined to be –1.

For each node x, let $\pi(x)$ denote the path from x to the root of the tree. For example in the tree shown here, $\pi(M) = (M, H, C, A)$. Except for x itself, the nodes in $\pi(x)$ are called the *ancestors* of x. For example, H, C, and A are the ancestors of M. Note that the root of a tree is the ancestor of all other nodes, and it is the only node that has no ancestors.

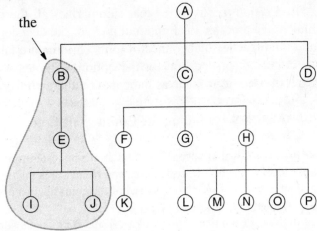

We say that x is a *descendant* of y if y is an ancestor of x. In this example, M is a descendant of C, so are F, G, H, K, L, N, O, and P. Note that all nodes except the root itself are descendants of the root node.

The adjacent ancestor of a node is called its *parent* node. The adjacent descendants of a node are called its *child* nodes. In the example above, C is the parent of H, and F, G, and H are the children of C. The root is the only node that has no parent. Nodes that have no children are called *leaf* nodes. In this example, D and M are leaf nodes. Nonleaf nodes are also called *internal* nodes. The 16-node tree shown here has 6 internal nodes (A, B, C, E, F, and H) and 10 leaf nodes.

For each node y in a tree, the set consisting of y and all its descendants form the *subtree* rooted at y. In the example above, the subtree rooted at B consists of B, E, I, and J. If T_2 is a subtree of T_1, then we say that T_1 is a *supertree* of T_2.

The *path length* of a tree is the sum of the lengths of all paths from its root. This is the same as the weighted sum, adding each level times the number of nodes on that level. The path length of the tree shown above is $1 \cdot 3 + 2 \cdot 4 + 3 \cdot 8 = 35$.

The *degree* of a node is the number of its children. In the example above, B has degree 1, D has degree 0, and H has degree 5. A tree is said to be *full* if all of its internal nodes have the same degree and all of its leaves are at the same level. The tree shown here is a full tree of degree 3. Note that it has a total of 40 nodes.

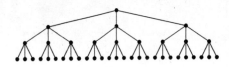

Theorem 9.1 The full tree of degree d and height h has $\dfrac{d^{h+1} - 1}{d - 1}$ nodes.

Corollary 9.1 The number of nodes in any tree of height h is at most $\dfrac{d^{h+1} - 1}{d - 1}$ where d is the maximum degree among its nodes.

Trees can also be defined recursively, as follows. A *tree* is either the empty set or a single node (its *root*) together with a sequence of zero or more disjoint trees (the subtrees of the root). If T_1 is a subtree of T_2, and if T_2 is a subtree of T_3, then T_1 is also a *subtree* of T_3. The *depth* of a subtree is the number of subtrees (counting itself) in its nesting sequence. An element is a *node* of a tree if it is the root of some subtree within it. The *depth* of the root is 0; the *depth* of any other node is the depth of the subtree of which it is the root. The other properties of trees are defined similarly.

9.2 DECISION TREES AND TRANSITION DIAGRAMS

A *decision tree* is a tree that summarizes all the different outcomes that could occur from a multistage process. Each internal node of the decision tree is labeled with a question (or option), and the branches that connect it to its children are labeled with the different possible answers to the question (or decision for the option). The leaves are labeled with the outcomes that result from the decisions made as indicated by the path from the root to the leaf.

EXAMPLE 9.1 Finding the Counterfeit Coin

Five coins which appear identical are to be tested to determine which one of them is counterfeit. The only feature that distinguishes the conterfeit coin is that it weighs less than the legitimate coins. The only available test is to weigh one subset of the coins against another. How should the subsets be chosen to find the counterfeit?

In the decision tree shown below, A and B represent subsets of the set $\{a, b, c, d, e\}$ of five coins. The boldface labels at the leaves indentify the counterfeit coin.

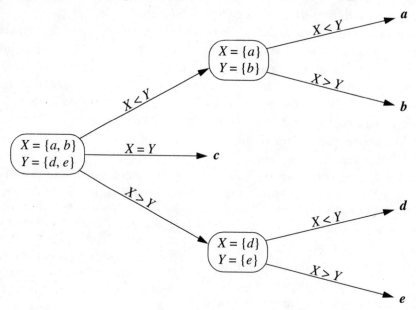

A *transition diagram* is a tree or graph (see Chapter 12) whose internal nodes represent different states (situations) that may be obtained during a multistage process. As in a decision tree, each leaf represents a different outcome from the process. Each branch is labeled with the (conditional) probability that the resulting child event will occur, given that the parent event has occurred.

EXAMPLE 9.2 The Game of Craps

The game of *craps* is a dice game played by two players, and X and Y. First X tosses the pair of dice. If the sum of the dice is 7 or 11, X wins the game. If the sum is 2, 3, or 12, Y wins. Otherwise, the sum is designated as the "point," to be matched by another toss. So if neither player has won on the first toss, then the dice are tossed repeatedly until either the point comes up or a 7 comes up. If a 7 comes up first, Y wins. Otherwise, X wins when the point comes up.

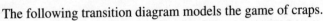

The following transition diagram models the game of craps.

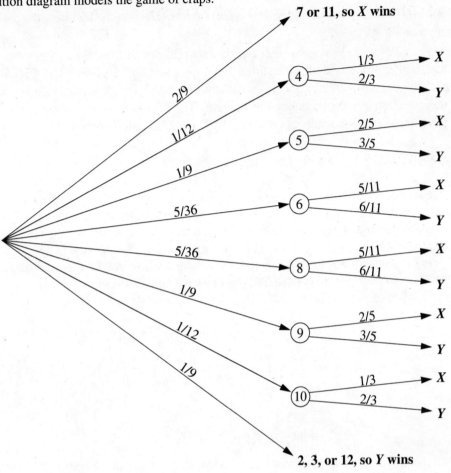

When a pair of dice is tossed, there are 36 different possible outcomes (6 outcomes on the first die, and 6 outcomes on the second for each outcome on the first). Of those 36 outcomes, 1 will produce a sum of 2 $(1 + 1)$, 2 will produce a sum of 3 $(1 + 2$ or $2 + 1)$, and 1 will produce a sum of 12 $(6 + 6)$. So there are a total of 4 chances out of 36 of the event "2, 3, or 12" happening. That's a probability of $4/36 = 1/9$. Similarly, there are 6 ways that a sum of 7 will occur and 2 ways that a sum of 11 will occur, so the probability of the event "7 or 11" is $8/36 = 2/9$. The other probabilities on the first level of the tree are computed similarly.

To see how the probabilities are computed for the second level of the tree, consider the case where the point is 4. If the next toss comes up 4, X wins. If it comes up 7, Y wins. Otherwise, that step is repeated. The transition diagram shown at the right summarizes those three possibilities. The probabilities 1/12, 1/6, and 3/4 are computed as follows:

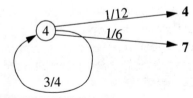

$P(4) = 3/36 = 1/12$
$P(7) = 6/36 = 1/3$
$P(2, 3, 5, 6, 8, 9, 10, 11,$ or $12) = 27/36 = 3/4$

So once the point 4 has been established on the first toss, X has a probability of 1/12 of winning on the second toss and a probability of 3/4 of getting to the third toss. So once the point 4 has been established on the first toss, X has a probability of $(3/4)(1/12)$ of winning on the third toss and a probability of $(3/4)(3/4)$ of getting to the fourth toss. Similarly, once the point 4 has been established on the first toss, X has a prob-

ability of (3/4)(1/12) + (3/4)(3/4)(1/12) of winning on the fourth toss, *etc.* Summing these partial probabilities, we find that once the point 4 has been established on the first toss, the probability that X wins on
<u>any</u> toss thereafter is

$$P_4 = \frac{1}{12} + \left(\frac{3}{4}\right)\frac{1}{12} + \left(\frac{3}{4}\right)^2\frac{1}{12} + \left(\frac{3}{4}\right)^3\frac{1}{12} + \left(\frac{3}{4}\right)^4\frac{1}{12} + \left(\frac{3}{4}\right)^5\frac{1}{12} + \cdots$$

$$= \frac{\frac{1}{12}}{1 - \frac{3}{4}}$$

$$= \frac{1/12}{1/4}$$

$$= \frac{1}{3}$$

This calculation applies the formula for geometric series. (See Section B.2 on page 282.)

If the probability 1/3 that X wins once the point 4 has been established on the first toss, the probability
that Y wins at that point must be 2/3. The other probabilities at the second level are computed similarly.

Now we can calculate the probability that X wins the game from the main transition diagram:

$$P = \frac{2}{9} + \frac{1}{12}(P_4) + \frac{1}{9}(P_5) + \frac{5}{36}(P_6) + \frac{5}{36}(P_8) + \frac{1}{9}(P_9) + \frac{1}{12}(P_{10})$$

$$= \frac{2}{9} + \frac{1}{12}\left(\frac{1}{3}\right) + \frac{1}{9}\left(\frac{2}{5}\right) + \frac{5}{36}\left(\frac{5}{11}\right) + \frac{5}{36}\left(\frac{5}{11}\right) + \frac{1}{9}\left(\frac{2}{5}\right) + \frac{1}{12}\left(\frac{1}{3}\right)$$

$$= \frac{244}{495}$$

$$= 0.4929$$

So the probability that X wins is 49.29% and the probability that Y wins is 50.71%.

A *stochastic process* is a process that can be analyzed by a transition diagram; *i.e.*, it can be
decomposed into sequences of events whose conditional probabilities can be computed. The
game of craps is actually an infinite stochastic process since there is no limit to the number of
events that could occur. As with the analysis in Example 9.2, most infinite stochastic processes
can be reformulated into an equivalent finite stochastic processs that is amenable to (finite)
computers.

Note that, unlike other tree models, decision trees and transition trees are usually drawn from
left to right to suggest the time-dependent movement from one node to the next.

9.3 TREE TRAVERSAL ALGORITHMS

A *traversal algorithm* is a method for processing a data structure that applies a given operation to each element of the structure. For example, if the operation is to print the contents of the
element, then the traversal would print every element in the structure. The process of applying
the operation to an element is called *visiting* the element. So executing the traversal algorithm
causes each element in the structure to be visited. The order in which the elements are visited
depends upon which traversal algorithm is used. There are three common algorithms for traversing a general tree.

The *level order traversal* algorithm visits the root, then visits each element on the first level, then visits each element on the second level, and so forth, each time visiting all the elements on one level before going down to the next level.

EXAMPLE 9.3 The Level Order Traversal

The level order traversal of the tree shown at right would visit the nodes in the following order: A, B, C, D, E, F, G, H, I, J, K, L, M.

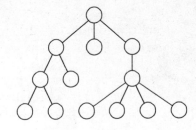

The *preorder traversal* algorithm visits the root first and then does a preorder traversal recursively to each subtree.

EXAMPLE 9.4 The Preorder Traversal

The preorder traversal of the tree shown in Example 9.3 would visit the nodes in the following order: A, B, E, H, I, F, C, D, G, J, K, L, M.

Note that the preorder traversal of a tree can be obtained by circumnavigating the tree, beginning at the root and visiting each node the first time it is encountered on the left:

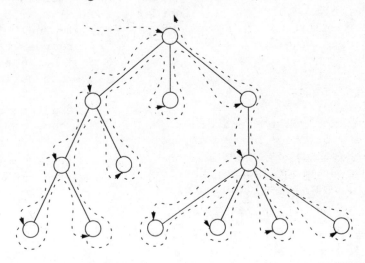

The *postorder traversal* algorithm does a postorder traversal recursively to each subtree before visiting the root.

EXAMPLE 9.5 The Postorder Traversal

The postorder traversal of the tree shown in Example 9.3 would visit the nodes in the following order: H, I, E, F, B, C, J, K, L, M, G, D, A.

Note that the level order and the preorder traversals always visit the root of each subtree first before visiting its other nodes. The postorder traversal always visits the root of each subtree last after visiting all of its other nodes. Also, the preorder always visits the right-most node last, while the postorder always visits the left-most node first.

The preorder and postorder traversals are recursive. They also can be implemented iteratively using a stack. The level order traversal is implemented iteratively using a queue.

9.4 A Tree CLASS INTERFACE

Here is part of an interface for a Tree container class:

```
class Tree
{    struct Node;
     typedef string Type;
     typedef list<Node*> List;
     typedef List::iterator LIt;
     List _nodes;                    // list of tree elements in preorder
  public:
     class Iterator;                           // Tree::Iterator class
     Tree();                                   // default constructor
     Tree(const Tree&);                          // copy constructor
     Tree(const Type&);                          // constructs singleton
     Tree(const Type&, const list<Tree*>&);        // definition
     ~Tree();                                   // destructs all nodes
     Tree& operator=(const Tree& t);             // Tree assignment
     void clear();                             // empties this tree
     Iterator begin();        // inorder traversal starts at root
     Iterator end();                          // ends with null iterator
     friend class Iterator                     // preorder traversal
     {    Tree* _tree;                    // the tree being traversed
          LIt _lit;                             // the current node
       public:
          Iterator();                        // default constructor
          Iterator(const Iterator&);           // copy constructor
          Iterator(Tree*,Node* =0);              // constructor
          Iterator(Tree*,LIt);                  // constructor
          void operator=(const Iterator& it);     // assignment
          bool operator==(const Iterator& it);      // equality
          bool operator!=(const Iterator& it);      // inequality
          Iterator& operator++();               // prefix increment
          Iterator operator++(int);            // postfix increment
          Type& operator*() const;              // current element
          bool operator!();                 // this iterator is null
          friend class Tree;
     };
};
```

The only data member of the Tree class is the _nodes list. This is a list of pointers to Node objects. The interface declares nine member functions and two inner structures: the Node structure and an Iterator class.

The Tree::Node structure is defined in the implementation file by

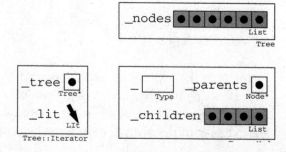

```
struct Tree::Node
{ Type _;
  List _children;
  Node* _parent;
  Node(Type =Type(), Node* =0);
};
```

This defines three data members: the actual element being stored in this node, a list of pointers to `this` node's child nodes, and a pointer to `this` node's parent node.

The nested `Iterator` class is `public`. It has two data members: a pointer to the tree upon which it iterates, and a `list` iterator that locates the current node indirectly through the tree's `_nodes` list. It has eleven member functions that are implemented in the `Tree` class implementation (Section 9.5).

We are using the following type definitions

```
typedef string Type;
typedef list<Node*> List;
typedef List::iterator LIt;
```

By using a type definition for `Type` instead of a class template, we can hide the entire implementation of the `Tree` class in the separate implementation file (`BinaryTree.cpp`).

EXAMPLE 9.6 The Implementation of a Tree

The tree shown below on the left would be implemented by the structure shown on the right:

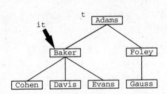

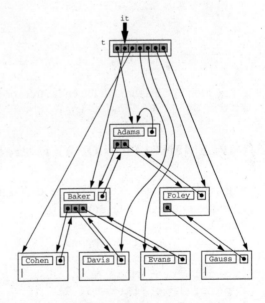

This shows a tree named `t` of size 7 and height 2, with root `Adams` and the four leaves `Cohen`, `Davis`, `Evans`, and `Gauss`. It also shows an iterator named `it` on the tree `t` which is locating the element `Baker`. Note that the `_parent` pointer of the root points to itself.

This interface defines four constructors for the `Tree` class. The fourth one is

```
Tree(const Type&, const list<Tree*>&);
```

This implements the recursive definition (page 175): a *tree* is either null or it consists of a root and a list of trees, its child subtrees. This allows the *bottom-up construction* of a binary tree.

EXAMPLE 9.7 The Bottom-Up Construction of a Binary Tree

The tree shown in Example 9.6 can be constructed like this:
```
int main()
{ TList tlist;
  tlist.push_back(new Tree("Cohen"));
  tlist.push_back(new Tree("Davis"));
  tlist.push_back(new Tree("Evans"));
  Tree t0("Baker",tlist);
  tlist.clear();
  tlist.push_back(new Tree("Gauss"));
  Tree t1("Foley",tlist);
  tlist.clear();
  tlist.push_back(&t0);
  tlist.push_back(&t1);
  Tree t("Adams",tlist);
  for (It it=t.begin(); it!=t.end(); it++)
    cout << *it << " ";
  cout << "\n";
}
```

The following pictures show the progress of the above code.

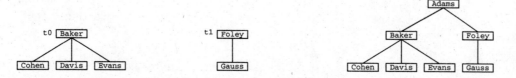

The `for` loop iterates through the entire tree, printing its data in a preorder traversal:
```
Adams Baker Cohen Davis Evans Foley Gauss
```

9.5 IMPLEMENTATION OF THE `Tree` CLASS

Along with some simplifying type definitions, this implementation uses a recursive local utility function named `clone()`:
```
#include "Tree.h"
typedef Tree::Type Type;
typedef Tree::List List;
typedef Tree::Node Node;
typedef Tree::Iterator It;
typedef Tree::List::iterator LIt;
typedef list<Tree*> TList;
typedef TList::const_iterator TLCIt;
Node* clone(Node*, List&, Node*);
```
The implementation of the constructor for the `Tree::Node` structure is
```
Node::Node(Type x, Node* p) : _(x), _parent(p)
{ if (!_parent) _parent = this;
}
```
The implementations of the default constructor and the copy constructor are:

```
    Tree::Tree()
    {
    }
    Tree::Tree(const Tree& t)
    { if (t._nodes.empty()) return;
      clone(t._nodes.front(),_nodes,0);
    }
```
The copy constructor uses the local `clone()` function to duplicate an existing tree:
```
    Tree::Tree(const Type& x)
    { _nodes.push_back(new Node(x));
    }
```
The fourth constructor implements the recursive definition of a tree:
```
    Tree::Tree(const Type& x, const list<Tree*>& list)
    { Node* root = new Node(x);
      _nodes.push_back(root);
      for(TLCIt it=list.begin(); it!=list.end(); it++)
        if (!((*it)->_nodes).empty())
        { Tree* tp = new Tree(**it);      // duplicate tree **it
          Node* p = tp->_nodes.front();   // points to root of t
          root->_children.push_back(p);      // connect to root
          p->_parent = root;
          LIt lit1=tp->_nodes.begin();
          LIt lit2=tp->_nodes.end();
          LIt lit3=_nodes.end();
          _nodes.insert(lit3,lit1,lit2);  // append *tp's nodes
        }
    }
```
First it constructs a root node for the given data value x and loads its pointer into the tree's _nodes list. Then it uses the copy constructor to duplicate each tree in the given list and add it to the root node's _children list. Finally, it uses the `list<T>::insert()` function to insert all the nodes of all the children trees into the new tree's _nodes list. This is accomplished by iterating through each child tree's _nodes list.

The Tree class destructor deletes each node by traversing the _nodes list:
```
    Tree::~Tree()
    { for (LIt lit=_nodes.begin(); lit!=_nodes.end(); lit++)
        delete *lit;
    }
```
The overloaded assignment operator uses the `clear()` function and the copy constructor:
```
    Tree& Tree::operator=(const Tree& t)
    { clear();                          // empty this tree
      Tree* p = new Tree(t);            // use copy constructor
      _nodes = p->_nodes;
      return *this;
    }
```
First it uses the `clear()` function to empty this tree. Then it uses the copy constructor to create an anonymous duplicate of the tree t. Then it copies the _nodes list of the tree t to the _nodes pointer of this tree. It returns *this so that assignments can be chained like this:
```
    t3 = t2 = t1 = t0;
```
The `clear()` function first traverses this tree's _nodes list to delete each node; then it uses the `list<T>::clear()` function to empty that list:

```
void Tree::clear()
{ for (LIt lit=_nodes.begin(); lit!=_nodes.end(); lit++)
    delete *lit;
  _nodes.clear();
}
```

Like the `clear()` function, the `begin()` function and the `end()` function are defined to conform to the C++ library standard for all container classes. The `begin()` function returns a `Tree` iterator that locates the root of the tree:

```
It Tree::begin()
{ return It(this,_nodes.begin());
}
```

The first pointer in the tree's `_nodes` list always points to the root of the tree. The `end()` function returns a `Tree` iterator that locates the null element that follows the last element of the tree:

```
It Tree::end()
{ return It(this,_nodes.end());
}
```

The `Tree::Iterator` class is an inner class, nested within the `Tree` class. This distinguishes `Tree` iterators from iterators of other types of containers (stacks, queues, lists, *etc.*). This implementation simply uses a `list<Node*>` iterator on the tree's `_nodes` list (see the picture on page 180) to iterate about the tree. Since the node pointers in the `_nodes` list are always in preorder, the resulting `Tree` iterator always follows a preorder traversal of the tree.

This iterator class defines eleven member functions: four constructors, an overloaded assignment operator, two overloaded boolean equality operators, two overloaded increment operators, an accessor function that overloads the `*` operator, and an overload of the `!` operator that tests whether the iterator's current element is valid:

```
It::Iterator()
{
}
It::Iterator(const It& it)
  : _tree(it._tree), _lit(it._lit)
{
}
It::Iterator(Tree* tree, Node* p) : _tree(tree)
{ List& nodes=_tree->_nodes;
  _lit = find(nodes.begin(),nodes.end(),p);
}
It::Iterator(Tree* tree, LIt lit) : _tree(tree), _lit(lit)
{
}
void It::operator=(const It& it)
{ _tree = it._tree;
  _lit = it._lit;
}
bool It::operator==(const It& it)
{ return _tree == it._tree && _lit == it._lit;
}
bool It::operator!=(const It& it)
{ return _tree != it._tree || _lit != it._lit;
}
```

```
It& It::operator++()              // prefix increment
{ ++_lit;
  return *this;
}
It It::operator++(int)        // postfix increment operator
{ It it(*this);                    // copy this iterator
  operator++();                 // increment this iterator
  return it;                         // return the copy
}
Type& It::operator*() const
{ return (*_lit)->_;
}
bool It::operator!()
{ return _lit == _tree->_nodes.end();
}
```

The overloaded prefix increment operator simply advances the corresponding `list<Node*>` iterator on the tree's _nodes list. The overloaded postfix increment operator calls the overloaded prefix increment operator, so both versions of the ++ operator will use the same traversal algorithm.

The local `clone()` function recursively duplicates the subtree rooted at `*p` and returns a pointer to the root of that duplicate. It also sets the _parent pointer of that new root to pp. It uses a preorder traversal to duplicates the nodes:

```
Node* clone(Node* p, List& nodes, Node* pp)
{ Node* cp = new Node(p->_,pp);
  nodes.push_back(cp);
  List& l=p->_children;
  List& cl=cp->_children;
  for (LIt lit=l.begin(); lit!=l.end(); lit++)
    cl.push_back(clone(*lit,nodes,cp));
  return cp;
}
```

Review Questions

9.1 True or false:
  a. Every leaf of a subtree is also a leaf of its supertree.
  b. The root of a subtree is also the root of its supertree.
  c. The number of ancestors of a node equals its depth.
  d. A node is a leaf if and only if it has degree 0.
  e. In any tree, the number of internal nodes must be less than the number of leaf nodes.
  f. A tree is full if and only if all of its leaves are at the same level.
  g. Every subtree of a full binary tree is full.
  h. Every subtree of a complete binary tree is complete.

9.2 For each of the five trees shown on the following page, list the leaf nodes, the children of node C, the depth of node F, all the nodes at level 3, the height of the tree, and the order of the tree.

a.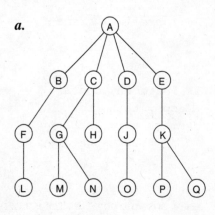

b.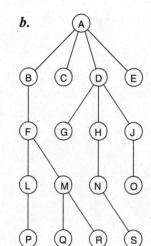

c.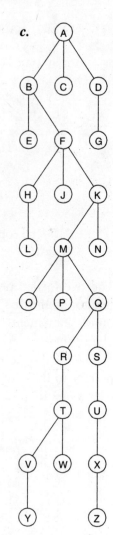

d.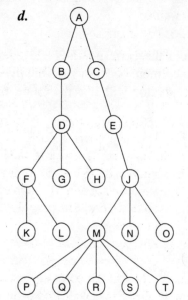

e.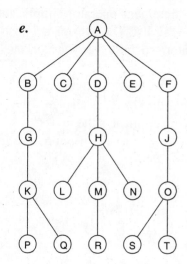

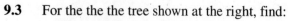

9.3 For the the the tree shown at the right, find:
a. all ancestors of node F;
b. all descendants of node F;
c. all nodes in the subtree rooted at F;
d. all leaf nodes.

9.4 How many nodes are in the full tree of:
a. degree 3 and height 4?
b. degree 4 and height 3?
c. degree 10 and height 4?
d. degree 4 and height 10?

9.5 Give the order of visitation of the tree shown
on page 174 using the:
a. level order traversal;
b. preorder traversal;
c. postorder traversal.

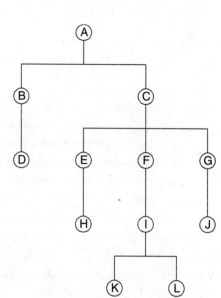

9.6 Which traversals always visit:
  a. the root first?
  b. the left-most node first?
  c. the root last?
  d. the right-most node last?

9.7 Which traversal algorithm is used in the call tree for Problem 4.31 on page 87?

Problems

9.1 Some people play the game of craps allowing 3 to be a possible point. In this version, player *Y* wins on the first toss only if it comes up 2 or 12. Use a transition diagram to analyze this version of the game and compute the probability that *X* wins.

9.2 Derive the formula for the path length of a full tree of degree *d* and height *h*.

9.3 The *St. Petersburg Paradox* is a betting strategy that seems to guarantee a win. It can be applied to any binomial game in which a win or lose are equally likely on each trial and in which the amount bet on each trial may vary. For example, in a coin-flipping game, the bettor may bet any number of dollars on each flip, and he will win what he bets if a head comes up, and he will lose what he bets if a tail comes up. The St. Petersburg strategy is to continue playing until a head comes up, and to double your bet each time it doesn't. For example, the the sequence of tosses is { , , , }, then the bettor will have bet $1 and lost, then $2 and lost, then $4 and lost, then $8 and won, ending up with a net win of –$1 + –$2 + –$4 + $8 = $1. Since a head has to come up eventually, the bettor is guaranteed to win $1, no matter how many coin flips it takes. Draw the transition diagram for this strategy showing the bettor's winnings at each stage of play. Then explain the flaw in this strategy.

9.4 Seven coins which appear identical are to be tested to determine which one of them is counterfeit. The only feature that distinguishes the conterfeit coin is that it weighs less than the legitimate coins. The only available test is to weigh one subset of the coins against another. How should the subsets be chosen to find the counterfeit? (See Example 9.1 on page 176.)

9.5 Implement the following `Tree` class member function:
```
bool empty() const;
// returns true iff this tree has no elements;
```

9.6 Implement the following `Tree` class member function:
```
int size() const;
// returns the number of elements in this tree;
```

9.7 Implement the following `Tree` class member function:
```
int leaves() const;
// returns the number of leaves in this tree;
```

9.8 Implement the following `Tree` class member function:
```
int height() const;
// returns the height of this tree;
```

9.9 Implement the following `Tree` class member function:
```
int level(Iterator it) const;
// returns the level of *it in this tree,
// or -1 if *it is not in this tree;
```

9.10 Implement the following `Tree` class member function:
```
int pathLength();
// returns the path length of this tree;
```

9.11   Implement the following static member function:

```
static bool isRoot(Iterator it);
// returns true iff *it has no parents;
```

9.12   Implement the following static member function:

```
static bool isLeaf(Iterator it);
// returns true iff *it has no children;
```

9.13   Implement the following Tree class member function:

```
Type& root() const;
// returns the data in the root of this tree;
```

9.14   Implement the following static nonmember function:

```
int generations(Iterator it, Iterator jt);
// returns the number of generation from *it down to *jt;
// for example, if *it is the grandparent of *jt, then
// level(it,jt) would return 2 and level(jt,it) would return -2;
// returns -1 if *it is neither ancestor nor descendant of *jt;
```

9.15   Implement the following static member function for the Tree class:

```
static Iterator parent(Iterator it);
// locates the parent of *it;
```

9.16   Implement the following static member function for the Tree class:

```
static int numChildren(Iterator it);
// returns the number of children of *it;
```

9.17   Implement the following static member function for the Tree class:

```
static bool isOldestChild(Iterator it);
// returns true iff *it is the oldest child of its parent;
```

9.18   Implement the following static member function for the Tree class:

```
static bool isYoungestChild(Iterator it);
// returns true iff *it is the youngest child of its parent;
```

9.19   Implement the following static member function for the Tree class:

```
static Iterator oldestChild(Iterator it);
// locates the oldest child of *it;
```

9.20   Implement the following static member function for the Tree class:

```
static Iterator youngestChild(Iterator it);
// locates the youngest child of *it;
```

9.21   Implement the following member function for the Tree class:

```
int width(int n);
// returns the total number of nodes at level n in this tree;
```

9.22   Implement the following member function for the Tree class:

```
int width();
// returns the maximum number of nodes at any level of this tree;
```

9.23   Implement the following member function for the Tree class:

```
void print(int n);
// prints all the elements that are at level n in this tree;
```

9.24   Implement the following member function for the Tree class:

```
void print();
// prints all the elements of this tree in level order;
```

9.25   Implement the following overloaded operator for the Tree class:

```
bool operator==(const Tree& t) const;
// returns true iff t has the same structure and elements as this
```

9.26   Implement the following overloaded operator for the Tree class:

```
bool operator!=(const Tree& t) const;
// returns false iff t has the same structure and elements as this
```

9.27 Implement the following member function for the `Tree` class:

```
void reflect();
// reverses the children list of each node in this tree;
```

9.28 Implement the following member function for the `Tree` class:

```
void defoliate();
// removes all the leaves from this tree;
```

9.29 Implement the following member function for the `Tree` class:

```
Iterator insert(Iterator it, const Type& x=Type());
// std lib
```

9.30 Implement the following member function for the `Tree` class:

```
void erase(Iterator it);
// std lib
```

9.31 Implement the following member function for the `Tree` class:

```
Iterator grow(Iterator it, const Type& x=Type());
// adds youngest child
```

9.32 Implement the following member function for the `Tree` class:

```
void prune(Iterator it);
// deletes youngest child of *it
```

9.33 Implement the following member function for the `Tree` class:

```
Iterator attach(Iterator it, Tree& tree);
// inserts in front of *it
```

9.34 Implement the following member function for the `Tree` class:

```
void detach(Iterator it, Tree& tree);
// removes subtree at *it
```

Answers to Review Questions

9.1   *a.* True.

     b. False.

     c. True.

     d. True.

     e. False.

     f. False.

     g. True.

     h. True.

9.2   *a.* The leaf nodes are , , , , , , ; the children of node are and ; node has depth 2; the nodes at 3 three are , , , , and ; the height of the tree is 3; the order of the tree is 4.

     b. The leaf nodes are , , , , , , and ; node has no children; node has depth 2; the nodes at level 3 are , , , and ; the height of the tree is 4; the order of the tree is 4.

     c. The leaf nodes are , , , , , , , , , and ; node has no children; node has depth 2; the nodes at level 3 are , , and ; the height of the tree is 9; the order of the tree is 3.

     d. The leaf nodes are , , , , , , , , , and ; the only child node has is node ; node F has depth 3; the nodes at level 3 are , , , and ; the height of the tree is 5; the order is 5.

     e. The leaf nodes are , , , , , , , and ; node has no children; node has depth 1; the nodes at level 3 are , , , , and ; the height of the tree is 4; the order of the tree is 5.

9.3   *a.* The ancestors of are and

     b. The descendants of are , , and .

     c. The nodes in the subtree rooted at are , , , and .

     d. The leaf nodes are , , , , and .

9.4 **a.** $(3^5 - 1)/2 = 121$ nodes
      b. $(4^4 - 1)/3 = 85$ nodes
      c. $(10^5 - 1)/9 = 11{,}111$ nodes
      d. $(4^{11} - 1)/3 = 1{,}398{,}101$ nodes

9.5 **a.** Level order: , ,   , , , , , , , , , , , , , , .
      b. Preorder: , , , , , ,   , , , , , , , , , , .
      c. Postorder: , , , , , , , , , , , , , , , , .

9.6 **a.** The level order and the preorder traversals always visit the root first.
      b. The postorder traversal always visit the left-most node first.
      c. The postorder traversal always visits the root last.
      d. The preorder traversal always visit the right-most node last.

9.7 The inorder traversal is used in Problem 4.31 on page 87.

Solutions to Problems

9.1 The version of Craps where 3 can be a point:

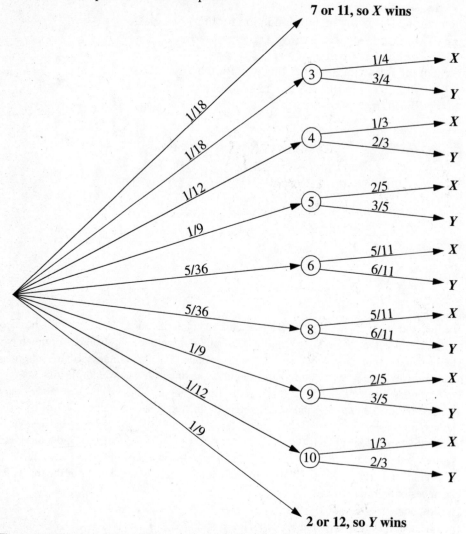

The probability that X wins this version is 0.5068 or 50.68%.

9.2   The path length of a full tree of degree d and height h is $\dfrac{d}{(d-1)^2}[hd^{h+1}-(h+1)d+1]$. For example, the path length of the full tree on page 175 is 102.

9.3   The tree diagram analysis of the St. Petersburg Paradox is shown below. The flaw in this strategy is that there is a distinct possibility (*i.e.*, a positive probability) that enough tail could come up in a row to make the required bet exceed the bettor's stake. After n successive tails, the bettor must bet $\$2^n$. For example, if 20 tails come up in a row, the next bet will have to be more than a million dollars!

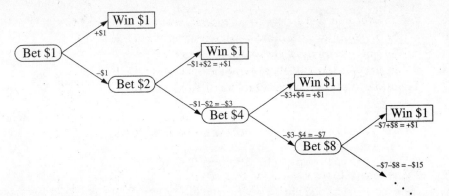

9.4   This decision tree shows all possible outcomes from the algorithm that solves the 7-coin problem:

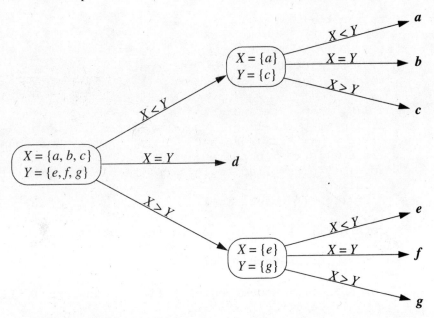

9.5
```
bool Tree::empty() const
{ return _nodes.empty();
}
```

9.6
```
int Tree::size() const
{ return _nodes.size();
}
```

9.7
```
int n(Node*);
int Tree::leaves() const
{ return n(_nodes.front());
}
```

```
      int n(Node* p)
      { if (!p) return 0;
        List& plist=p->_children;
        if (plist.empty()) return 1;   // *p is a leaf
        int n0=0;
        for (LIt plit=plist.begin(); plit!=plist.end(); plit++)
          n0 += n(*plit);
        return n0;
      }
```

9.8
```
      int h(Node*);
      int Tree::height() const
      { if (_nodes.empty()) return -1;
        else return h(_nodes.front());
      }
      int h(Node* p)
      { if (!p) return -1;   // the empty tree has height -1
        List& plist=p->_children;
        if (plist.empty()) return 0;
        int h0=0;
        for (LIt plit=plist.begin(); plit!=plist.end(); plit++)
        { int h1=h(*plit);
          if (h1>h0) h0 = h1;
        }
        return h0+1;
      }
```

9.9
```
      int l(Node*,Iterator);
      bool Tree::level(Iterator it) const
      { return l(_nodes.front(),it);
      }
      int l(Node* p, Iterator it)
      { if (!p) return -1;   // the empty tree has height -1
        if (p->_ == *it) return 0;            // *it was found
        List& plist=p->_children;
        for (LIt plit=plist.begin(); plit!=plist.end(); plit++)
        { int lc=l(*plit,it);
          if (lc>-1) return lc+1;
        }
        return -1;   // *it is not in this subtree
      }
```

9.10
```
      int Tree::pathLength()
      { int pl=0;
        for (LIt lit=_nodes.begin(); lit!=_nodes.end(); lit++)
          pl += level(It(this,*lit));
        return pl;
      }
```

9.11
```
      bool Tree::isRoot(Iterator it)
      { Node* p=*it._lit;
        return it._lit == (it._tree->_nodes).begin();;
      }
```

9.12
```
      bool Tree::isLeaf(Iterator it)
      { return (*it._lit)->_children.empty();
      }
```

9.13
```
      Type& Tree::root() const
      { return _nodes.front()->_;
      }
```

```
9.14    int Tree::generations(Iterator it, Iterator jt) const
        { if (!it || !jt) return -1;
          if (it == jt) return 0;
          int n=0;
          Node* p=(*jt._lit)->_parent;
          while (jt != it && p != *jt._lit)
          { Tree* tp=this;
            p=(*jt._lit)->_parent;
            jt = It(tp,p);
            ++n;
          }
          if (jt == it) return n;
          n = generations(jt,it);
          if (n != -1 && !!it && !!jt) return -n;
          return -1;
        }
9.15    Iterator Tree::parent(Iterator it)
        { Node* p=*it._lit;
          Tree* tree=it._tree;
          if (p->_parent == p) return It(tree,tree->_nodes.end());
          return It(tree,p->_parent);
        }
9.16    int Tree::numChildren(Iterator it)
        { return (*it._lit)->_children.size();
        }
9.17    bool Tree::isOldestChild(Iterator it)
        { Node* p=(*it._lit);
          if (p == p->_parent) return true;         // *p is the root
          return (p == p->_parent->_children.front());
        }
9.18    bool Tree::isYoungestChild(Iterator it)
        { Node* p=(*it._lit);
          if (p == p->_parent) return true;         // *p is the root
          return (p == p->_parent->_children.back());
        }
9.19    Iterator Tree::oldestChild(Iterator it)
        { if (!it) return 0;
          Node* p=*it._lit;
          if (!p) return 0;
          Tree* tree=it._tree;
          if (p->_children.empty()) return 0;
          return It(tree,(*it._lit)->_children.front());
        }
9.20    Iterator Tree::youngestChild(Iterator it)
        { if (!it) return 0;
          Node* p=*it._lit;
          if (!p) return 0;
          Tree* tree=it._tree;
          if (p->_children.empty()) return 0;
          return It(tree,(*it._lit)->_children.back());
        }
9.21    List level(int n);    // returns list of all nodes at level n
        int Tree::width(int n)
        { return level(n).size();
        }
```

```
        List Tree::level(int n)
        { List listn;
          if (empty()) return listn;
          queue<List*> q;
          Node* root=*(_nodes.begin());                  // points to root
          if (n==0) return List(1,root);
          q.push(&(root->_children));
          while (!q.empty())
          { List* p=q.front();
            List& list=*p;
            for (LIt lit=list.begin(); lit!=list.end(); lit++)
            { Node* p=*lit;
              It it(this,*lit);
              if (level(it)==n)
                listn.push_back(*lit);
              q.push(&((*lit)->_children));
            }
            q.pop();
          }
          return listn;
        }
```

9.22   ```
        int Tree::width()
        { if (_nodes.empty()) return 0;   // empty tree
          int w=1;
          for (int k=0; k<=height(); k++)
          { int w1=level(k).size();   // number of nodes at level k
            if (w1>w) w = w1;
          }
          return w;
        }
```

**9.23**   ```
        void Tree::print(int n)
        { List list=level(n);
          for (LIt it=list.begin(); it!=list.end(); it++)
            cout << (*it)->_ << " ";
          cout << "\n";
        }
```

9.24   ```
        void Tree::print()
        { int h=height();
          for (int level=0; level<=h; level++)
            print(level);
        }
```

**9.25**   ```
        bool Tree::operator==(const Tree& t) const
        { if (_nodes.size() != t._nodes.size()) return false;
          LCIt tlit=t._nodes.begin();
          for (LCIt lit=_nodes.begin(); lit!=_nodes.end(); lit++, tlit++)
            if ((*lit)->_ != (*tlit)->_) return false;
          return true;
        }
```

9.26   ```
        bool Tree::operator!=(const Tree& t) const
        { return !(*this == t);
        }
```

**9.27**   ```
        void Tree::reflect()
        { for (LIt lit=_nodes.begin(); lit!=_nodes.end(); lit++)
            (*lit)->_children.reverse();  // std lib function
        }
```

9.28   ```
void Tree::defoliate()
{ if (_nodes.size() < 2)
  { clear();
    return;
  }
  for (LIt lit=_nodes.begin(); lit!=_nodes.end(); lit++)
  { Node* p=*lit;
    if (p->_children.empty())
    { p->_parent->_children.clear();
      delete p;
      LIt tmp=lit;
      --lit;   // save location in _nodes list
      _nodes.erase(tmp);
    }
  }
}
```

**9.29**  The following four functions are used privately by later `Tree` class functions:

```
LIt Tree::litn(Node* p)
{ // returns the LIt for _nodes that locates p:
  if (p == 0) return LIt();
  return find(_nodes.begin(),_nodes.end(),p);
}
LIt Tree::litp(Node* p)
{ // returns the LIt for p->_parent that locates p:
  if (p == 0 || p == _nodes.front()) return LIt();
  List& pplist=p->_parent->_children;
  return find(pplist.begin(),pplist.end(),p);
}
LIt Tree::prevSibling(LIt lit)
{ // returns the LIt for _node that locates
  // the next older sibling of *lit
  if (_nodes.empty() || lit==_nodes.begin())
    return _nodes.end();
  if (lit==_nodes.end()) return _nodes.begin();
  Node* p1=*lit;
  LIt litp1=litp(p1);
  if (p1 == (p1->_parent->_children).front())
    return _nodes.end();
  return find(_nodes.begin(),--lit,*--litp1);
}
LIt Tree::nextSibling(LIt lit)
{ // returns the LIt for _node that locates
  // the next younger sibling of *lit
  if (lit==_nodes.begin() || lit==_nodes.end())
    return _nodes.end();
  Node* p2=*lit;
  LIt litp2=litp(p2);
  if (p2 == (p2->_parent->_children).back())
    return _nodes.end();
  return find(++lit,_nodes.begin(),*++litp2);
}

Iterator Tree::insert(Iterator it, const Type& x)
{ // new node is new parent of *it
  // _nodes maintains preorder traversal
  Node* np = new Node(x);
```
```

```
         if (!it)                 // insert at (preorder) end of tree
         { Node* pp = _nodes.back();
           pp->_children.push_back(np);
           _nodes.push_back(np);
         }
         else
         { Node* p=(*it._lit);
           Node* pp=p->_parent;
           np->_children.push_back(p);
           LIt lit = find(_nodes.begin(),_nodes.end(),p);
           _nodes.insert(lit,np);
           if (pp != p)                         // *p is not the root
           { List& list = pp->_children;
             lit = find(list.begin(),list.end(),p);
             *lit = np;                  // make *np the child of *pp
           }
         }
         return It(this,np);
       }
9.30   void Tree::erase(Iterator it)
       { if (!it) return;
         Node* p=(*it._lit);
         Node* pp=p->_parent;
         if (p->_children.empty())                   // *p is a leaf
         { LIt lit = find(_nodes.begin(),_nodes.end(),p);
           _nodes.erase(lit);
           if (pp != p)                         // *p is not the root
           { List& list = pp->_children;
             lit = find(list.begin(),list.end(),p);
             list.erase(lit);
           }
           delete p;
         }
         else                    // replace *p with oldest child
         { p->_ = p->_children.front()->_;
           erase(It(this,p->_children.front()));
         }
       }
9.31   Iterator Tree::grow(Iterator it, const Type& x)
       { LIt lit=it._lit;        // locates current node in _nodes
         Node* pp=*lit;
         Node* p=new Node(x,pp);
         pp->_children.push_back(p);
         Node* ppp=pp->_parent;
         List& ppplist=ppp->_children;
         if ( (ppp == pp)                        // *pp is the root
           || (pp == ppplist.back()) )    // or pp is the youngest
         { _nodes.push_back(p);
           lit=find(lit,_nodes.end(),p);
         }
         else                 // find next sibling of pp in _nodes:
         { LIt ppplit=find(ppplist.begin(),ppplist.end(),pp);
           ++ppplit;                     // locates next sibling of pp
           lit=find(lit,_nodes.end(),*ppplit);
           lit = _nodes.insert(lit,p);
         }
```

```
              return It(this,lit);
          }
9.32      void Tree::prune(Iterator it)
          { erase(youngestChild(it));
          }
9.33      Iterator Tree::attach(Iterator it, Tree& tree)
          { // PRECONDITION: it is an iterator on this tree;
            // if t is empty, it is replaced by t1;
            // if t1 is empty, there is no change;
            // otherwise, if (it == tree.begin()), the root of t1
            //    becomes the new root of t and the old root
            //    becomes its youngest child;
            // otherwise, if (it == tree.end()), the root of t1
            //    becomes the youngest child of the root of t;
            // otherwise, t1 is inserted in front of *it,
            //    becoming its next older sibling;
            // POSTCONDITIONS: t1 returns empty;
            //    it locates the root of the subtree that was t1;
            if (t1._nodes.empty()) return it;  // no change
            // move t1._nodes list into _nodes list:
            LIt lit1=t1._nodes.begin();
            LIt lit2=it._lit;
            Node* p1=*lit1;                          // points to root of t1
            _nodes.insert(lit2,lit1,t1._nodes.end());
            t1._nodes.clear();
```

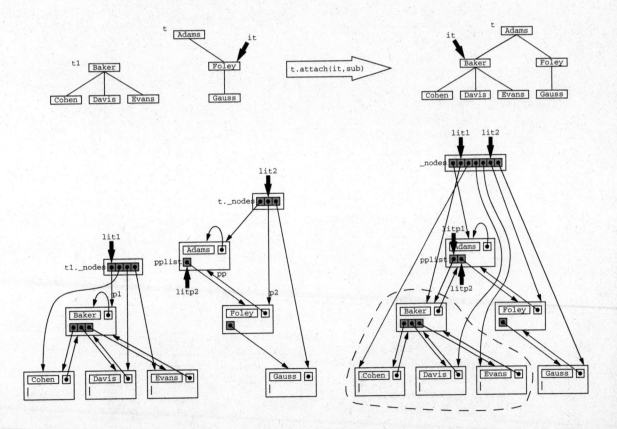

```
      // connect parent and children links:
      if (p1 == _nodes.front())           // *p1 is the new root:
        if (lit2 == _nodes.end()) ;          // tree was empty
        else    // make old root the youngest child of new root
        { Node* p2=*lit2;                    // points to *it node
          (p1->_children).push_back(p2);
          p2->_parent = p1;
        }
      else // root does not change
        if (lit2 == _nodes.end())   // t1 youngest child of root
        { Node* p2=_nodes.front();
          List& pplist=p2->_children;
          pplist.push_back(p1);
          p1->_parent = p2;
        }
        else
        { Node* p2=*lit2;                    // points to *it node
          List& pplist=p2->_parent->_children;
          LIt litp2=litp(p2);                // locates p2 in pplist
          pplist.insert(litp2,p1);
          p1->_parent = p2->_parent;
        }
      return It(this,lit1);
    }
9.34    void Tree::detach(Iterator it, Tree& tree)
    { // PRECONDITION: it is an iterator on this tree;
      // if t is empty or if (it == tree.end()),
      //    then t is left unchanged and t1 returns empty;
      // if (it == tree.begin()), then t1 is replaced by t
      //    and t returns empty;
      // POSTCONDITIONS: the previous contents of t1 are lost;
      //    t1 contains the nodes that were in the subtree of t
      //    rooted at it;
      t1._nodes.clear();
      if (_nodes.empty() || it == end()) return;     // t1 empty
      if (it == begin())
      { t1._nodes = _nodes;             // copy entire _nodes list
        _nodes.clear();                      // empty _nodes list
        return;
      }
      // move [lit1,lit2[ from _nodes to t1._nodes:
      LIt lit1=it._lit;
      LIt lit2=_nodes.end();
      for (Node* p=*lit1; lit2 == _nodes.end() && p != p->_parent;
           p = p->_parent)
        lit2=nextSibling(litn(p));
      t1._nodes.insert(t1._nodes.end(),lit1,lit2);
      _nodes.erase(lit1,lit2);
      // reset node pointers to disconnect subtree:
      Node* p1=*lit1;
      Node* pp=p1->_parent;
      List& pplist=pp->_children;
      LIt pplit1=litp(p1);              // p1's parent's pointer to *it
      pplist.erase(pplit1);
      p1->_parent = p1;        // *p1 is the root of the sub tree
```

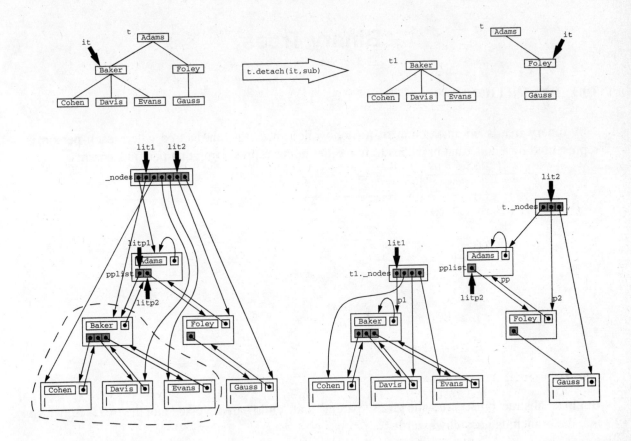

Binary Trees

10.1 DEFINITIONS

A binary tree is an abstraction of a (noncyclic) ancestral family tree where each person is represented by a node that branches to two other nodes representing that person's parents:

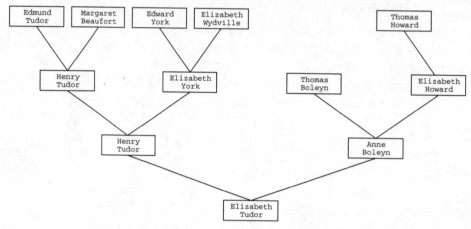

But in an abstract binary tree, the terms "parent" and "child" are reversed and the tree is drawn so that the branching goes downward:

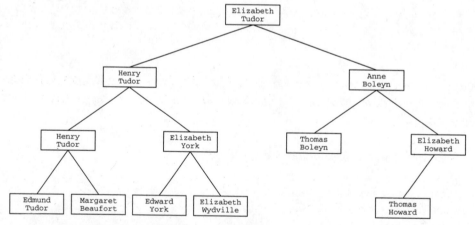

So in this example, the nodes containing Henry Tudor and Anne Boleyn would be considered the left and right children of the node containing Elizabeth Tudor.

A binary tree can be thought of as a tree of degree two. But that notion is not adequate for a precise definition because in a binary tree there are two different ways that a node can have only one child: either

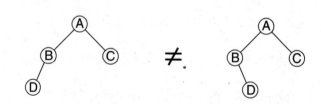

a left child or a right child. For example, the two four-node binary trees shown above are structurally different. As general trees of degree two, they would be the same.

One way to define binary trees is to attach an artificial null node for every missing child. Then we can define a *binary tree* to be a tree in which each nonnull node has exactly two children, named its *left child* and its *right child*. The null nodes would be considered the leaves if the tree were regarded as a general tree. But as nodes of a binary tree, we say that a node is a *leaf* if both of its children are null nodes. Thus the binary tree shown here has two leaves: node C and node D.

The other common definition for binary trees is recursive: a *binary tree* is either the empty set or a triplet (X, L, R) where X is an element and L and R are disjoint binary trees. The element X is called the *root* of the tree, and the trees L and R are called its *left subtree* and *right subtree*, respectively.

EXAMPLE 10.1 Verification of a Binary Tree

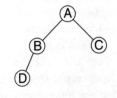

To verify the recursive definition for the tree shown here, we first verify that the leaves D and C are binary trees. Every leaf satisfies the recursive definition for binary trees because its left and right subtrees are both empty (and therefore binary trees). Next, it follows that the tree rooted at B is a binary tree because it is a triplet (X, L, R) where $X = B$, $L = D$, and $R = \varnothing$ (so L and R are binary trees). Finally, it follows that the entire tree satisfies the recursive definition because it is a triplet (X, L, R) where $X = A$, L is the binary tree that we just verified, and $R = C$, a singleton.

The definitions of the terms *size, path, length* of a path, *depth* of a node, *level, height, interior* node, *ancestor, descendant, subtree,* and *supertree* are the same for binary trees as for general trees. (See page 174.)

EXAMPLE 10.2 Characteristics of a Binary Tree

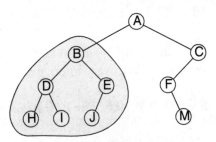

This is a binary tree of size 10 and height 3. Node A is its root. The path from node B to node H has length 2. B is at level 1, and H is at level 3. B is an ancestor of H, and H is a descendant of B. The part in the shaded region is a subtree of size 6 and height 2. Its root is node B.

10.2 COUNTING BINARY TREES

EXAMPLE 10.3 All the Binary Trees of Size 3

There are 5 different binary trees of size $n = 3$:
Four have height 2, and the other one has height 1.

EXAMPLE 10.4 All the Binary Trees of Size 4

There are 14 different binary trees of size $n = 4$:

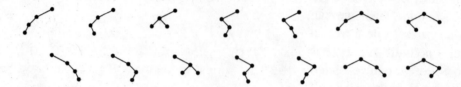

Ten have height 3, and the other four have height 2.

EXAMPLE 10.5 The Binary Trees of Size 5

To find all the binary trees of size 5, apply the recursive definition for binary trees. If t is a binary tree of size 5, then it must consist of a root node together with two subtrees the sum of whose sizes equals 4. There are 4 possibilities: the left subtree contains either 4, 3, 2, 1, or 0 nodes.

First count all the binary trees of size 5 whose left subtree has size 4. From Example 10.4, we see that there are 14 different possibilities for that left subtree. But for each of those 14 choices, there are no other options because the right subtree must be empty. Therefore, there are 14 different binary trees of size 5 whose left subtree has size 4.

Next, count all the binary trees of size 5 whose left subtree has size 3. From Example 10.3, we see that there are 5 different possibilities for that left subtree. But for each of those 5 choices, there are no other options because the right subtree must be a singleton. Therefore, there are 5 different binary trees of size 5 whose left subtree has size 3.

Next, count all the binary trees of size 5 whose left subtree has size 2. There are only 2 different possibilities for that left subtree. But for each of those 2 choices, we have the same 2 different possibilities for the right subtree because it also must have size 2. Therefore, there are $2 \times 2 = 4$ different binary trees of size 5 whose left subtree has size 2.

By similar reasoning, we find that there are 5 different binary trees of size 5 whose left subtree has size 1, and there are 14 different binary trees of size 5 whose left subtree has size 0. Therefore, the total number of different binary trees of size 5 is $14 + 5 + 4 + 5 + 14 = 42$.

10.3 FULL BINARY TREES

A binary tree is said to be *full* if all its leaves are at the same level and every interior node has two children.

EXAMPLE 10.6 The Full Binary Tree of Height 3

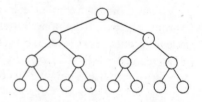

The tree shown at right is the full binary tree of height 3. Note that it has 15 nodes: 7 interior nodes and 8 leaves.

Theorem 10.1 The full binary tree of height h has $l = 2^h$ leaves and $m = 2^h - 1$ internal nodes.

Proof: The full binary tree of height $h = 0$ is a single leaf node; so it has $n = 1$ node, which is a leaf. Therefore, since $2^{h+1} - 1 = 2^{0+1} - 1 = 2^1 - 1 = 2 - 1 = 1$, $2^h - 1 = 2^0 - 1 = 1 - 1 = 0$, and $2^h = 2^0 = 1$, the formulas are correct for the case where $h = 0$. More generally, let $h > 0$ and assume (the inductive hypothesis) that the formulas are true for all full binary trees of height less than h.

Then consider a full binary tree of height h. Each of its subtrees has height $h-1$, so we apply the formulas to them: $l_L = l_R = 2^{h-1}$ and $m_L = m_R = 2^{h-1} - 1$. (These are the number of leaves in the left subtree, the number of leaves in the right subtree, the number of internal nodes in the left subtree, and the number of internal nodes in the right subtree, respectively.) Then

$$l = l_L + l_R = 2^{h-1} + 2^{h-1} = 2 \cdot 2^{h-1} = 2^h,$$

and

$$m = m_L + m_R + 1 = (2^{h-1} - 1) + (2^{h-1} - 1) + 1 = 2 \cdot 2^{h-1} - 1 = 2^I - 1.$$

Therefore, by the (Second) Principle of Mathematical Induction, the formulas must be true for full binary trees of any height $h \geq 0$.					**Q.E.D.**

By simply adding the formulas for m and l, we obtain the first corollary.

Corollary 10.1 The full binary tree of height h has a total of $n = 2^{h+1} - 1$ nodes.

By solving the formula $n = 2^{h+1} - 1$ for h, we obtain the following corollary.

Corollary 10.2 The full binary tree with n nodes has height $h = \lg(n+1) - 1$.

Note that the formula in Corollary 10.2 is correct even in the special case where $n = 0$: the *empty binary tree* has height $h = \lg(n+1) - 1 = \lg(0+1) - 1 = \lg(1) - 1 = 0 - 1 = -1$.

The next corollary applies Corollary 10.1 together with the fact that the full binary tree of height h has more nodes than any other binary tree of height h.

Corollary 10.3 In any binary tree of height h,

$$h + 1 \leq n \leq 2^{h+1} - 1 \text{ and } \lfloor \lg n \rfloor \leq h \leq n - 1$$

where n is the number of its nodes.

10.4 IDENTITY, EQUALITY, AND ISOMORPHISM

In a computer, two objects are *identical* if they occupy the same space in memory, so they have the same address. Their two names are synonyms; in C++, one or both names would be references:

```
int m=44;
int& n=m;   // m and n are identical
m = 55;     // changes both m and n
```
Two objects are *equal* if they have equal value. They need not be identical to be equal:

```
int m=44;
int n=44;   // m and n are equal but not identical
m = 55;     // changes m but not n
```
Equal objects can occupy different spaces in memory and thus can be independent.

Two objects are *isomorphic* if they have the same structure:

```
string s1="Tim";
string s2="Tom";   // s1 and s2 are isomorphic but not equal
s2 += "my";        // now s2 is not isomorphic to s1
```
Equal objects are isomorphic, but isomorphic objects need not be equal. Identical objects are equal, but equal objects need not be identical.

Scalar objects (*i.e.*, variables of fundamental type such as int, double, *etc.*) are isomorphic if they have the same type. Linear data structures (*i.e.*, sequences such as objects of type string, list, *etc.*) are isomorphic only if they have the same number of components and the corresponding components' types match. Nonlinear data types (*e.g.*, trees, graphs, networks, *etc.*) are isomorphic only if they have the same number of components, the corresponding components' types match, and the relationships between matching components are the same.

EXAMPLE 10.7 Isomorphic Trees

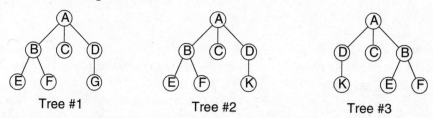

Tree #1   Tree #2   Tree #3

Tree #1 and Tree #2 are isomorphic but not equal. Tree #3 is not isomorphic (and therefore, not equal) to either of the other two trees because the first child of node A in Tree #3 has only one child.

Binary trees are different from general trees of degree 2. In a general tree, there is only one way that a node can have one child. But in a binary tree, there are two differenct ways that a node can have one child: having a left child but no right child is a different structure from having a right child but no left child.

EXAMPLE 10.8 Nonisomorphic Binary Trees

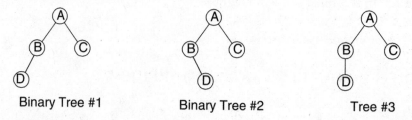

Binary Tree #1   Binary Tree #2   Tree #3

Binary tree #1 is _not_ isomorphic to binary tree #2 (and therefore they are not equal either). But as general (not binary) trees they would be isomorphic, both simply represented as Tree #3.

10.5 COMPLETE BINARY TREES

A *complete binary tree* is either a full binary tree or one that can be made into a full binary tree by adding leaves only in an uninterrupted segment of nodes in the right of the bottom level.

EXAMPLE 10.9 A Complete Binary Tree of Height 3

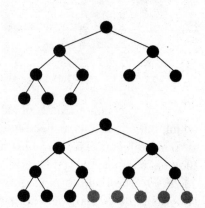

The tree shown at right is complete. The full binary tree below it was obtained by adding 5 leaves on the right at level 3.

Theorem 10.2 In a complete binary tree of height h,
$$h + 1 \leq n \leq 2^{h+1} - 1 \text{ and } h = \lfloor \lg n \rfloor$$
where n is the number of its nodes.

EXAMPLE 10.10 More Complete Binary Trees

Here are three more examples of complete binary trees:

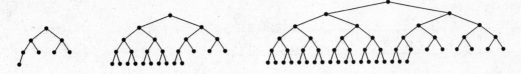

Complete binary trees are important because of the simple and natural way in which they can be stored as arrays. This is achieved by means of the *natural mapping* that assigns the array index numbers to the tree nodes by level, as shown in the picture below. The index 1 is assigned to the root; then for each node i, $2i$ is assigned to its left child and $2i + 1$ to its right child (if they exist). This assigns a unique positive integer to each node. The beauty of this natural mapping is the simple way that it allows the array indexes of the children and parent of a node to be computed from its index.

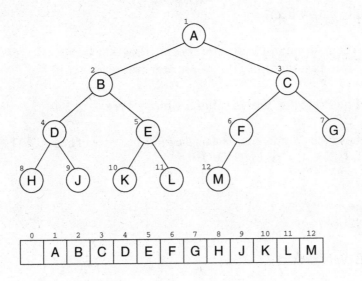

Algorithm 10.1 The Natural Mapping of a Complete Binary Tree into an Array

To navigate about a complete binary tree stored by its natural mapping in an array:
  1. The parent of the node stored at location i is stored at location $i/2$;
  2. The left child of the node stored at location i is stored at location $2i$;
  3. The right child of the node stored at location i is stored at location $2i + 1$.

For example, node E is stored at index $i = 5$ in the array; its parent node B is stored at index $i/2 = 5/2 = 2$; its left child node K is stored at location $2i = 2 \cdot 5 = 10$; and its right child node L is stored at index $2i + 1 = 2 \cdot 5 + 1 = 11$.

The use of the adjective "complete" should now be clear: The defining property for completeness is precisely the condition that guarantees that the natural mapping will store its nodes in an array with no gaps.

Warning: Some authors (notably [Cormen]) use "complete" to mean "full."

EXAMPLE 10.11 An Incomplete Binary Tree

Here is the binary tree from Example 10.2 on page 201:
It is not complete. The natural mapping of its nodes into an
array leaves gaps:

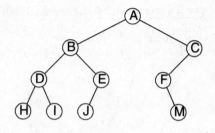

0	1	2	3	4	5	6	7	8	9	10	11	12
	A	B	C	D	E	F		H	J			M

10.6 TREE TRAVERSALS

The three traversal algorithms that are used for general trees (see Section 9.3 on page 178)
apply to binary trees as well: the preorder traversal, the postorder traversal, and the level order
traversal. In addition, binary trees support a fourth traversal algorithm: the inorder traversal.
These four traversal algorithms are given below.

Algorithm 10.2 The Preorder Traversal of a Binary Tree
To traverse a nonempty binary tree:
    1. Visit the root.
    2. If the left subtree is nonempty, do a preorder traversal on it.
    3. If the right subtree is nonempty, do a preorder traversal on it.

EXAMPLE 10.12 The Preorder Traversal of a Binary Tree

The picture below shows the preorder traversal on the full binary tree of height 3. The nodes are visited
in the order A, B, D, H, J, E, K, L, C, F, M, N, G, O, P.

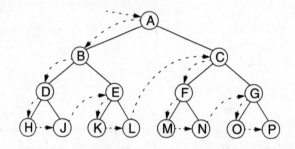

Note that the preorder traversal of a binary tree can be obtained by circumnavigating the tree,
beginning at the root and visiting each node the first time it is encountered on the left:

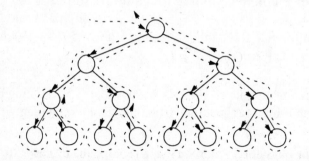

Algorithm 10.3 The Postorder Traversal of a Binary Tree

To traverse a nonempty binary tree:
1. If the left subtree is nonempty, do a postorder traversal on it.
2. If the right subtree is nonempty, do a postorder traversal on it.
3. Visit the root.

EXAMPLE 10.13 The Postorder Traversal of a Binary Tree

Here is how the preorder traversal looks on the full binary tree of height 3:

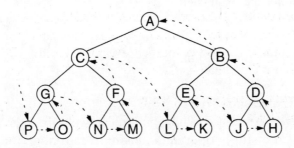

The nodes are visited in the order P, O, G, N, M, F, C, L, K, E, J, H, D, B, A.

The preorder traversal visits the root first and the postorder traversal visits the root last. This suggests a third alternative for binary trees: visit the root in between the traversals of the two subtrees. That is called the *inorder traversal*.

Algorithm 10.4 The Inorder Traversal of a Binary Tree

To traverse a nonempty binary tree:
1. If the left subtree is nonempty, do a preorder traversal on it.
2. Visit the root.
3. If the right subtree is nonempty, do a preorder traversal on it.

EXAMPLE 10.14 The Inorder Traversal of a Binary Tree

Here is how the preorder traversal looks on the full binary tree of height 3:

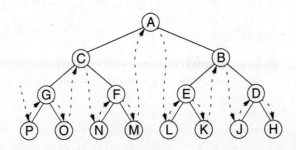

The nodes are visited in the order P, G, O, C, N, F, M, A, L, E, K, B, J, D, H.

10.7 EXPRESSION TREES

An *arithmetic expression* such as `(5 - x)*y + 6/(x + z)` is a combination of *arithmetic operators* (+, -, *, /, etc.), *operands* (5, x, y, 6, z, etc.), and parentheses to override the precedence of operations. Each expression can be represented by a unique binary tree whose structure is determined by the precedence of operations in the expression. Such a tree is called an *expression tree*.

EXAMPLE 10.15 An Expression Tree

Here is the expression tree for the expression
`(5 - x)*y + 6/(x + z)`:

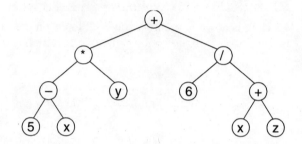

Here is a recursive algorithm for building
an expression tree:

Algorithm 10.5 Build an Expression Tree

The expression tree for a given expression can be built recursively from the following rules:
1. The expression tree for a single operand is a single root node that contains it.
2. If E_1 and E_2 are expressions represented by expression trees T_1 and T_2, and if *op* is an operator, then the expression tree for the expression E_1 *op* E_2 is the tree with the root node containing *op* and subtrees T_1 and T_2.

An expression has three representations, depending upon which traversal algorithms is used to traverse its tree. The preorder traversal produces the *prefix representation*, the inorder traversal produces the *infix representation*, and the postorder traversal produces the *postfix representation* of the expression. The postfix representation is also called *reverse Polish notation* or *RPN*.

EXAMPLE 10.16 The Three Representations of an Expression

The three representations for the expression in Example 10.15 are:

Prefix:	`+*-5xy/6+xz`
Infix:	`5-x*y+6/x+z`
Postfix (RPN):	`5x-y*6xz+/+`

Ordinary function syntax uses the prefix representation. The expression in Example 10.15 could be evaluated as

`sum(product(difference(5, x), y), quotient(6, sum(x, z)))`

Some scientific calculators use RPN, requiring both operands to be entered before the operator.

Expression are evaluated by applying the following algorithm to their postfix representation:

Algorithm 10.6 Evaluating an Expression from Its Postfix Representation

To evaluate an expression represented in postfix, scan the representation from left to right:

```
create a stack for operands;
while (not at end of representation)
{ read the next token x from the representation;
  if (op is an operand) push its value onto the stack;
  else
```

```
{ pop a from the stack;
  pop b from the stack;
  evaluate c = b op a;
  push c onto the stack;
}
the top element on the stack is the value of the expression;
}
```

EXAMPLE 10.17 Evaluating an Expression from Its Postfix Representation

Evaluate the expression in Example 10.16 using 2 for *x*, 3 for *y*, and 1 for *z*:

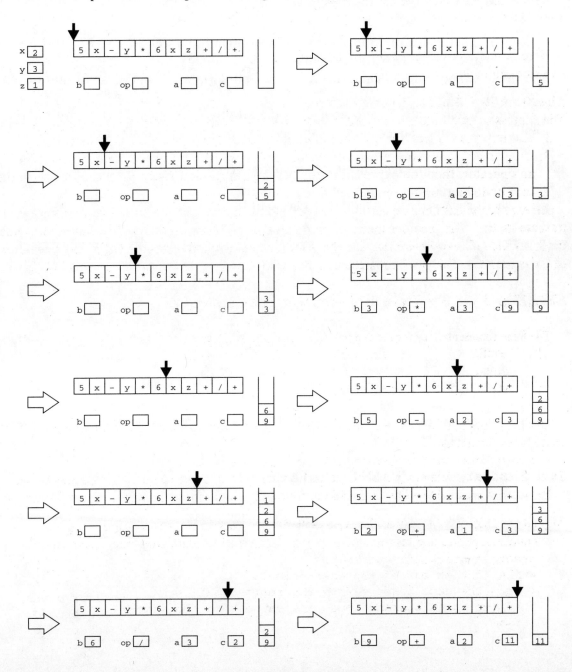

10.8 FORESTS

A *forest* is a list of trees.

EXAMPLE 10.18 A Forest

Here is a forest that consists of three trees:

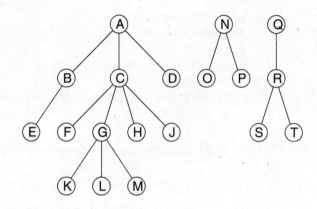

The following algorithm shows how a forest can be represented by a single binary tree.

Algorithm 10.7 The Natural Mapping of a Forest into a Binary Tree
1. Map the root of the first tree into the root of the binary tree.
2. If node X maps into X' and node Y is the first child of X, then map Y into the left child of X'.
3. If node X maps into X' and node Z is the sibling of X, then map Z into the right child of X'. The roots of the trees themselves are considered siblings.

EXAMPLE 10.19 Mapping a Forest into a Binary Tree

Here is the mapping of the forest shown in Example 10.18:

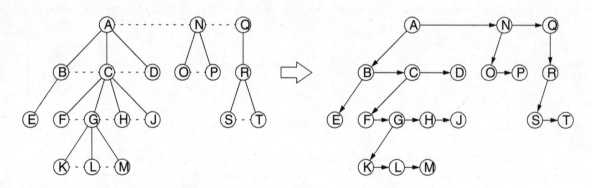

For example, in the original forest, C has oldest child F and next sibling D; so in the resulting binary tree, C has left child F and right child D.

10.9 A `BinaryTree` CLASS INTERFACE

Here is part of an interface for a `BinaryTree` container class:

```
class BinaryTree
{   struct Node;
    Node* _root;
  public:
    class Iterator;                    // BinaryTree::Iterator class
    BinaryTree();                      // default constructor
    BinaryTree(const BinaryTree&);         // copy constructor
```

```
      BinaryTree(const Type&);               // constructs singleton
      BinaryTree(const Type&, const BinaryTree&, const BinaryTree&);
      ~BinaryTree();                          // destructs all nodes
      BinaryTree& operator=(const BinaryTree& t);    // assignment
      void clear();                           // empties this tree
      Iterator begin();            // inorder traversal starts at root
      Iterator end();                    // ends with null iterator
      friend class Iterator              // preorder traversal
      {   BinaryTree* _tree;           // the tree being traversed
          Node* _p;                       // the current node
        public:
          Iterator();                      // default constructor
          Iterator(const Iterator&);        // copy constructor
          Iterator(BinaryTree*, Node* =0);    // constructor
          void operator=(const Iterator& it);    // assignment
          bool operator==(const Iterator& it);     // equality
          bool operator!=(const Iterator& it);     // inequality
          Iterator& operator++();             // prefix increment
          Iterator operator++(int);           // postfix increment
          Type& operator*() const;            // current element
          bool operator!();              // this iterator is null
          friend class BinaryTree;
      };
  };
```

The only data member of the `BinaryTree` class is the `_root` pointer. This interface declares nine member functions and two inner structures: a `Node` structure, and an `Iterator` class.

The `BinaryTree::Node` structure is defined by

```
    struct BinaryTree::Node
    { Type _;
      Node* _left;
      Node* _right;
      Node* _parent;
      Node(Type =Type(), Node* =0, Node* =0, Node* =0);
    };
```

This defines four data members: the actual element being stored in `this` node, pointers to the roots of `this` node's left and right subtrees, and a pointer to `this` node's parent node. This `struct` definition is placed in the separate implementation file (`BinaryTree.cpp`).

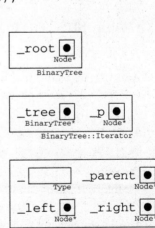

The nested `Iterator` class is `public`. It has two data members: a pointer to the binary tree upon which it iterates, and a pointer to the current node of that tree. It has 10 member functions that are implemented in the `BinaryTree` class implementation (Section 10.10).

We use the following type definition

```
    typedef string Type;
```

instead of a class template. This allows the entire implementation of the `BinaryTree` class to be placed in the separate implementation file (`BinaryTree.cpp`).

EXAMPLE 10.20 The Implementation of a Binary Tree

The binary tree shown below on the left would be implemented by the structure shown on the right:

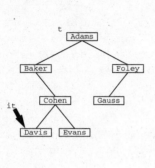 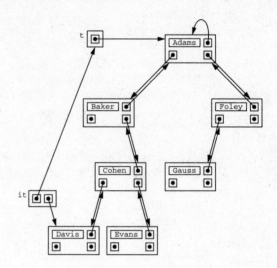

This shows a binary tree named t of size 7 and height 3, with root Adams and the three leaves Davis, Evans, and Gauss. Note that the left child of Baker and the right child of Foley are null. It also shows an iterator named it on the tree t which is locating the element Davis. Note that the _parent pointer of the root points to itself.

This interface defines four constructors for the BinaryTree class. The fourth one is

```
BinaryTree(const Type&, const BinaryTree&, const BinaryTree&);
```

This implements the recursive definition (page 201) of binary trees: a *binary tree* is either null or it consists of a root element and two binary trees, its left and right subtrees. This allows the *bottom-up construction* of a binary tree.

EXAMPLE 10.21 The Bottom-Up Construction of a Binary Tree

The tree shown in Example 10.20 could be constructed like this:

```
BinaryTree left("Davis");               // third constructor
BinaryTree right("Evans");              // third constructor
BinaryTree sub("Cohen",left,right);     // fourth constructor
left = BinaryTree("Gauss");             // third constructor
BinaryTree null;                        // default constructor
right = BinaryTree("Foley",left,null);  // fourth constructor
left = BinaryTree("Baker",null,sub);    // fourth constructor
BinaryTree t("Adams",left,right);       // fourth constructor
```

The following pictures show the progress of the above code.

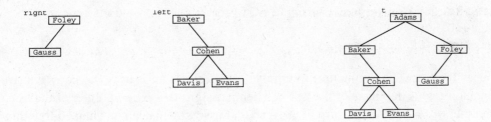

10.10 IMPLEMENTATION OF THE `BinaryTree` CLASS

Along with some simplifying type definitions, this implementation uses three local utility functions, named `destroy()`, `preorderSuccessor()`, and `clone()`:

```
#include "BinaryTree.h"
typedef BinaryTree::Node Node;
typedef BinaryTree::Iterator It;
void destroy(Node*);     // postorder deletion for destructor
Node* preorderSuccessor(Node*);
Node* clone(Node*,Node*);
```

The implementation of the constructor for the `BinaryTree::Node` structure is

```
BinaryTree::Node::Node(Type x, Node* left, Node* right,
                       Node* parent)
 : _(x), _left(left), _right(right), _parent(parent)
{ if (!_parent) _parent = this;  // the root
}
```

The implementations of the four constructors for the `BinaryTree` class are:

```
BinaryTree::BinaryTree() : _root(0)
{
}
BinaryTree::BinaryTree(const BinaryTree& t)
{ _root = clone(t._root,0);
}
BinaryTree::BinaryTree(const Type& x)
{ _root = new Node(x);
}
BinaryTree::BinaryTree(const Type& x, const BinaryTree& lTree,
                       const BinaryTree& rTree)
{ _root = new Node(x);
  _root->_left = clone(lTree._root,_root);
  _root->_right = clone(rTree._root,_root);
}
```

Two of these use the recursive `clone()` function to duplicate an existing tree.

The destructor uses the recursive `destroy()` function to delete each node separately:

```
BinaryTree::~BinaryTree()
{ destroy(_root);
}
```

The overloaded assignment operator uses the `clear()` function and the copy constructor:

```
BinaryTree& BinaryTree::operator=(const BinaryTree& t)
{ clear();                            // empty this tree
```

```
BinaryTree* p = new BinaryTree(t); // use copy constructor
_root = p->_root;
return *this;
}
```

First it uses the `clear()` function to empty `this` tree. Then it uses the copy constructor to create an anonymous duplicate of the tree `t`. Then it assigns the _root pointer of the tree `t` to the _root pointer of `this` tree. It returns `*this` so that assignments can be chained like this:

```
t3 = t2 = t1 = t0;
```

The `clear()` function uses the recursive `destroy()` function to remove every element from the `this` tree:

```
void BinaryTree::clear()
{ destroy(_root);
}
```

Like the `clear()` function, the `begin()` function and the `end()` function are defined to conform to the C++ library standard for all container classes. The `begin()` function returns a `BinaryTree` iterator that locates the root of the tree:

```
It BinaryTree::begin()
{ return It(this,_root);
}
```

The `end()` function returns a `BinaryTree` iterator that locates the null element that follows the last element of the tree:

```
It BinaryTree::end()
{ return It(this,0);
}
```

The `BinaryTree::Iterator` class is an inner class, nested within the `BinaryTree` class. This distinguishes `BinaryTree` iterators from iterators of other types of containers (stacks, queues, lists, trees, *etc.*). This iterator class defines ten member functions: three constructors, an overloaded assignment operator, two overloaded boolean equality operators, two overloaded increment operators, an accessor function that overloads the * operator, and an overload of the ! operator that tests whether the iterator's current element is valid:

```
It::Iterator()
{
}
It::Iterator(const It& it) : _tree(it._tree), _p(it._p)
{
}
It::Iterator(BinaryTree* tree, Node* p) : _tree(tree), _p(p)
{
}
void It::operator=(const It& it)
{ _tree = it._tree;
  _p = it._p;
}
bool It::operator==(const It& it)
{ return _tree == it._tree && _p == it._p;
}
bool It::operator!=(const It& it)
{ return _tree != it._tree || _p != it._p;
}
```

```
It& It::operator++()                    // prefix increment
{ _p = preorderSuccessor(_p);
  return *this;
}
It It::operator++(int)        // postfix increment operator
{ It it(*this);                         // copy this iterator
  operator++();                    // increment this iterator
  return it;                             // return the copy
}
Type& It::operator*() const
{ return _p->_;
}
bool It::operator!()
{ return _p == 0;
}
```

The overloaded prefix increment operator uses the local recursive `preorderSuccessor()` function to traverse the tree. This could be replaced by an `inorderSuccessor()` function, a `postorderSuccessor()` function, or a `levelorderSuccessor()` function. The overloaded postfix increment operator calls the overloaded prefix increment operator, so both versions of the ++ operator will use the same traversal algorithm.

The local `destroy()` function performs a recursive postorder traversal, deleting each node in the subtree rooted at `*p`:

```
void destroy(Node* p)
{ if (!p) return;
  destroy(p->_left);
  destroy(p->_right);
  delete p;
}
```

The local `preorderSuccessor()` function returns a pointer to the node that follows `*p` in a preorder traversal of the tree.

```
Node* preorderSuccessor(Node* p)
{ if (p->_left) return p->_left;
  if (p->_right) return p->_right;
  // move up tree until p is the root or p has a younger sibling:
  while (p->_parent != p
         && (p->_parent->_right==p || p->_parent->_right==0))
    p = p->_parent;
  if (p->_parent==p) return 0;   // p is the root
  return p->_parent->_right;   // younger sibling is successor
}
```

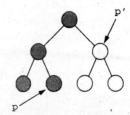

If `*p` has a left child, then that node is its preorder successor. Otherwise, if `*p` has a right child, then that node is its preorder successor. Otherwise, `*p` is a leaf node, so its preorder successor has to be found by navigating back up the tree until a node with a younger sibling is found. This navigation is accomplished by means of the nodes' `_parent` pointers. The `while` loop continues moving p back up the tree until either `p->_parent == p` or `p->_parent->_right` locates an unvisited node. At that point, if `p->_parent == p`, then `*p` is the root and it has no right child,

so there are no more preorder successors and the traversal is finished. Otherwise,
p->_parent->_right locates the next node in the preorder traversal.

The local clone() function recursively duplicates the subtree rooted at *p and returns a
pointer to the root of that duplicate. It also sets the _parent pointer of that new root to pp. It
uses a preorder traversal to duplicate the nodes:

```
Node* clone(Node* p, Node* pp)
{ if (!p) return 0;                       // basis of the recursion
  Node* cp = new Node(p->_,0,0,pp);       // duplicate the current node
  cp->_left = clone(p->_left,cp);         // duplicate the left subtree
  cp->_right = clone(p->_right,cp);       // duplicate the right subtree
  return cp;
}
```

Review Questions

10.1   How many leaf nodes does the full binary tree of height $h = 3$ have?
10.2   How many internal nodes does the full binary tree of height $h = 3$ have?
10.3   How many nodes does the full binary tree of height $h = 3$ have?
10.4   How many leaf nodes does a full binary tree of height $h = 9$ have?
10.5   How many internal nodes does a full binary tree of height $h = 9$ have?
10.6   How many nodes does a full binary tree of height $h = 9$ have?
10.7   What is the range of possible heights of a binary tree with $n = 100$ nodes?
10.8   Why is there no inorder traversal for general trees?

Problems

10.1   Give the order of visitation of the binary tree shown at the
           right using
           a. the level order traversal;
           b. the preorder traversal;
           c. the inorder traversal;
           d. the postorder traversal.

10.2   Give the order of visitation of the binary tree of size 10
           shown in Example 10.2 on page 201 using
           a. the level order traversal;
           b. the preorder traversal;
           c. the inorder traversal;
           d. the postorder traversal.

10.3   Give the order of visitation of the
           binary tree shown at the right using
           a. the level order traversal;
           b. the preorder traversal;
           c. the inorder traversal;
           d. the postorder traversal.

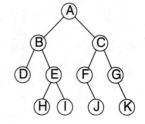

10.4   Show the array that is obtained by
           using the natural mapping (page 205) to store the binary tree shown in Problem 10.1 above.

10.5   Show the array that is obtained by using the natural mapping to store the binary tree shown in Example 10.2 on page 201.

10.6   Show the array that is obtained by using the natural mapping to store the binary tree shown in Problem 10.3 above.

10.7   If the nodes of a binary tree are numbered according to their natural mapping, and the visit operation prints the node's number, which traversal algorithm will print the numbers in order?

10.8   Write the expression tree for the expression $a * (b + c) * (d * e + f)$.

10.9   Write the prefix and the postfix representations for the expressions in Problem 10.8.

10.10   What are the bounds on the number n of nodes in a binary tree of height 4?

10.11   What are the bounds on the height h of a binary tree with 7 nodes?

10.12   What form does the highest binary tree have for a given number of nodes?

10.13   What form does the lowest binary tree (*i.e.*, the least height) have for a given number of nodes?

10.14   Verify the recursive definition of binary trees (page 201) for the binary tree shown at the right.

10.15   Draw all 42 binary trees of size $n = 5$.

10.16   How many different binary trees of size $n = 6$ are there?

10.17   Derive a recurrence relation for the number $f(n)$ of binary trees of size n.

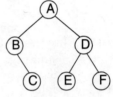

10.18   Show that, for all $n \leq 8$, the function $f(n)$ derived in Problem 10.17 produces the same sequence as the following explicit formula

$$f(n) = \frac{\binom{2n}{n}}{n+1} = \frac{(2n)!}{n!(n+1)!} = \frac{(2n)(2n-1)(2n-2)\cdots(2n+3)(2n+2)}{(n)(n-1)(n-2)(n-3)\cdots(2)(1)}$$

For example,

$$f(4) = \frac{\binom{8}{4}}{5} = \frac{8!}{4!5!} = \frac{(8)(7)(6)}{(4)(3)(2)(1)} = \frac{(8)(7)}{4} = 14$$

10.19   Prove Corollary 10.3 on page 203.

10.20   Prove Theorem 10.2 on page 204.

10.21   Prove that every subtree of a complete binary tree is complete.

10.22   Draw the forest that is represented by the binary tree shown on the right.

10.23   Derive an explicit formula for the number $f(h)$ of complete binary trees of height h.

10.24   Derive an explicit formula for the number $f(h)$ of full binary trees of height h.

10.25   Implement the following member function for the `BinaryTree` class:

```
bool empty() const;
// returns true iff this tree is empty
```

10.26   Implement the following member function for the `BinaryTree` class:

```
int size() const;
// returns the number of elements in this tree
```

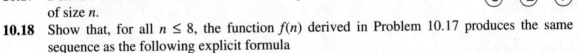

10.27   Implement the following member function for the `BinaryTree` class:

```
int leaves() const;
// returns the number of leaves in this tree
```

10.28   Implement the following member function for the `BinaryTree` class:

```
int height() const;
// returns the height of this tree
```

10.29   Implement the following member function for the `BinaryTree` class:

```
int level(Iterator it);
// returns the level of the element *it in this tree
```

10.30   Implement the following member function for the `BinaryTree` class:

```
void reflect();
// swaps the two children of each node in this tree
```

10.31   Implement the following member function for the `BinaryTree` class:

```
void defoliate();
// removes all the leaves from this tree
```

10.32   Implement the following member function for the `BinaryTree` class:

```
Type& root() const;
// provides read-write access to this tree's root element
```

10.33   Implement the following `static` member function for the `BinaryTree` class:

```
static bool isRoot(Iterator it);
// true iff *it has no parents
```

10.34   Implement the following `static` member function for the `BinaryTree` class:

```
static bool isLeaf(Iterator it);
// true iff *it has no children
```

10.35   Implement the following `static` member function for the `BinaryTree` class:

```
static Iterator parent(Iterator it);
// returns location of parent of *it
```

10.36   Implement the following `static` member function for the `BinaryTree` class:

```
static Iterator leftChild(Iterator);
// returns location of left child of *it
```

10.37   Implement the `static` member function for the `BinaryTree` class:

```
static Iterator rightChild(Iterator);
// returns location of right child of *it
```

10.38   Implement the following member function for the `BinaryTree` class:

```
Iterator find(Iterator begin, Iterator end, const Type& x);
// returns location of x in [begin,end[
```

Answers to Review Questions

10.1   The full binary tree of height 3 has $l = 2^3 = 8$ leaves.

10.2   The full binary tree of height 3 has $m = 2^3 - 1 = 7$ internal nodes.

10.3   The full binary tree of height 3 has $n = 2^{3+1} - 1 = 2^4 - 1 = 16 - 1 = 15$ nodes.

10.4   The full binary tree of height 9 has $l = 2^9 = 512$ leaves.

10.5   The full binary tree of height 9 has $m = 2^9 - 1 = 512 - 1 = 511$ internal nodes.

10.6   The full binary tree of height 9 has $n = 2^{9+1} - 1 = 2^{10} - 1 = 1024 - 1 = 1023$ nodes.

10.7   By Corollary 10.3, in any binary tree: $\lfloor \lg n \rfloor \le h \le n-1$. Thus in a binary tree with 100 nodes $\lfloor \lg 100 \rfloor \le h \le 100 - 1 = 99$. Since $\lfloor \lg 100 \rfloor = \lfloor (\log 100)/(\log 2) \rfloor = \lfloor 6.6 \rfloor = 6$, it follows that the height must be between 6 and 99, inclusive: $6 \le h \le 99$.

10.8   The inorder traversal algorithm for binary trees recursively visits the root in between traversing the left and right subtrees. This presumes the existence of exactly two (possibly empty) subtrees at every (nonempty) node. In general trees, a node may have any number of subtrees, so there is no simple algorithmic way to generalize the inorder traversal.

Solutions to Problems

10.1　*a.* Level order: A, B, C, D, E, F, G, H, I, J, K.
　　　　b. Preorder: A, B, D, E, H, I, C, F, J, G, K.
　　　　c. Inorder: D, B, H, E, I, A, F, J, C, G, K.
　　　　d. Postorder: D, H, I, E, B, J, F, K, G, C, A.

10.2　*a.* Level order traversal: A, B, C, D, E, F, H, I, J, M.
　　　　b. Preorder traversal: A, B, D, H, I, E, J, C, F, M.
　　　　b. Inorder traversal: H, D, I, B, J, E, A, F, M, C.
　　　　c. Postorder traversal: H, I, D, J, E, B, M, F, C, A.

10.3　*a.* Level order traversal: A, B, C, D, E, F, G, H, J, K, L, M, N, O.
　　　　b. Preorder traversal: A, B, D, G, M, H, C, E, J, N, F, K, O, L.
　　　　b. Inorder traversal: G, M, D, H, B, A, N, J, E, C, K, O, F, L.
　　　　c. Postorder traversal: M, G, H, D, B, N, J, E, O, K, L, F, C, A.

10.4　The picture below shows the natural mapping of the given binary tree.

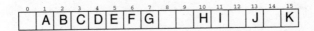

10.5　The picture below shows the natural mapping of the binary tree shown in Example 10.2 on page 201.

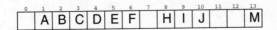

10.6　The picture below shows the natural mapping of the given binary tree.

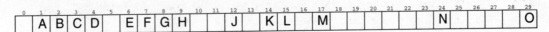

10.7　The level order traversal will print the numbers from the natural mapping in order.

10.8　The expression tree for $a * (b + c) * (d * e + f)$
　　　　is shown at right.

10.9　The prefix representation is $*a*+bc+*def$ and
　　　　the postfix representation is $abc+de*f+**$.

10.10　In a binary tree of height $h = 4$, $5 \le n \le 31$.

10.11　In a binary tree with $n = 7$ nodes, $2 \le h \le 6$.

10.12　For a given number of nodes, the highest binary
　　　　tree is a linear sequence.

10.13　For a given number of nodes, the lowest binary
　　　　tree is a complete binary tree.

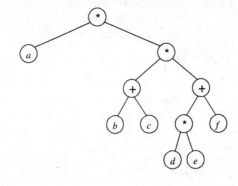

10.14　To verify the recursive definition for the given
　　　　tree, we first note that the leaves D, E, and F are
　　　　binary trees because every singleton satisfies
　　　　the recursive definition for binary trees because
　　　　its left and right subtrees are both empty (and
　　　　therefore binary trees). Next, it follows that the subtree rooted at B is a binary tree because it is a triplet
(X, L, R) where $X = $ B, $L = \varnothing$, and $R = $ C. Similarly, it follows that the subtree rooted at D is a binary
tree because it is a triplet (X, L, R) where $X = $ D, $L = $ E, and $R = $ F. Finally, it follows that the entire tree
satisfies the recursive definition because it is a triplet (X, L, R) where $X = $ A, L is the binary tree rooted
at B, and L is the binary tree rooted at D.

10.15   Here are the 42 different binary trees of size $n = 5$:

10.16   There are 132 different binary trees of size 6: $1 \cdot 42 + 1 \cdot 14 + 2 \cdot 5 + 5 \cdot 2 + 14 \cdot 1 + 42 \cdot 1 = 132$.

10.17   A nonempty binary tree consists of a root X, a left subtree L, and a right subtree R. Let n be the size of the binary tree, let $n_L = |L| =$ the size of L, and $n_R = |R| =$ the size of R. Then $n = 1 + n_L + n_R$. So there are only n different possible values for the pair (n_L, n_L): $(0, n-1)$, $(1, n-2)$, ..., $(n-1, 0)$. For example, if $n = 6$ (as in Problem 10.16), the only possibilities are $(0, 5)$, $(1, 4)$, $(2, 3)$, $(3, 2)$, $(4, 1)$, or $(5, 0)$. In the $(0, n-1)$ case, L is empty and $|R| = n-1$; there are $f(0) \cdot f(n-1)$ different binary trees in that case. In the $(1, n-2)$ case, L is a singleton and $|R| = n-2$; there are $f(1) \cdot f(n-2)$ different binary trees in that case. The same principle applies to each case. Therefore the total number of different binary trees of size n is

$$f(n) = 1 \cdot f(n-1) + 1 \cdot f(n-2) + 2 \cdot f(n-3) + 5 \cdot f(n-4) + \cdots + f(i-1) \cdot f(n-i) + \cdots + f(n-1) \cdot 1$$

In closed form, the formula is

$$f(n) = \sum_{i=1}^{n} f(i-1) \cdot f(n-i)$$

10.18 These are called the *Catalan numbers*:

n	$\binom{2n}{n}$	$n+1$	$\dfrac{\binom{2n}{n}}{(n+1)}$	$\sum f(i-1)\cdot f(n-i)$
0	1	1	1	1
1	2	2	1	$1\cdot1=1$
2	6	3	2	$1\cdot1+1\cdot1=2$
3	20	4	5	$1\cdot2+1\cdot1+2\cdot1=5$
4	70	5	14	$1\cdot5+1\cdot2+2\cdot1+5\cdot1=14$
5	252	6	42	$1\cdot14+1\cdot5+2\cdot2+5\cdot1+14\cdot1=42$
6	924	7	132	$1\cdot42+1\cdot14+2\cdot5+5\cdot2+14\cdot1+42\cdot1=132$
7	3432	8	429	$1\cdot132+1\cdot42+2\cdot14+5\cdot5+14\cdot2+42\cdot1+132\cdot1=429$
8	12,870	9	1430	$1\cdot429+1\cdot132+2\cdot42+5\cdot14+14\cdot5+42\cdot2+132\cdot1+429\cdot1=1430$

10.19 For a given height $h > 0$, the binary tree with the most nodes is the full binary tree. Corollary 10.2 on page 203 states that that number is $n = 2^{h+1} - 1$. Therefore, in any binary tree of height h, the number n of nodes must satisfy $n \le 2^{h+1} - 1$. The binary tree with the fewest nodes for a given height h is the one in which every internal node has only one child; that linear tree has $n = h + 1$ nodes because every node except the single leaf has exactly one child. Therefore, in any binary tree of height h, the number n of nodes must satisfy $n \ge h + 1$. The second pair of inequalities follows from the first by solving for h.

10.20 Let T be a complete tree of height h and size n. Let T_1 be the full subtree obtained by removing the bottom level of leaves from T, and let T_2 be the full supertree obtained by filling in the rest of the bottom level of leaves in T. Then T_1 has height $h - 1$ and T_2 has height h. Then, by Corollary 10.1 on page 203, $n_1 = |T_1| = 2^h - 1$ and $n_2 = |T_2| = 2^{h+1} - 1$. Now $n_1 < n \le n_2$, so $2^h - 1 = n_1 < n \le n_2 = 2^{h+1} - 1$, and so $2^h = n_1 + 1 \le n \le n_2 < n_2 + 1 = 2^{h+1}$. Thus $h \le \lg n < h + 1$, so $h = \lfloor \lg n \rfloor$. **Q.E.D.**

10.21 **Theorem.** Every subtree of a complete binary tree is complete.

Proof: Let T be a complete binary tree, and let S be a subtree of T. By definition then, S consists of some node of T together with all of its descendants in T. Therefore the leaves of S are also leaves of T. But all the leaves of T are at two adjacent levels because T is complete. Therefore, all the leaves of S are at two adjacent levels. Similarly, if there are any missing leaves at the bottom level of S, then the corresponding leaves are missing from T; so they must be to the right of all the existing leaves of T at that bottom level, and thus they must also be to the right of all the existing leaves of S at that bottom level. Therefore S is complete. **Q.E.D.**

10.22 By definition, T is a complete binary tree with the heap property. Therefore by the theorem of Problem 10.21 on page 221, S is also a complete binary tree. Let x be the root of S, and let p be any root-to-leaf path in S. Then x is an element of T since S is a subtree of T, and there is a unique path q in T from x to the root of T. Also, p is a path in T that connects x to a leaf of T since S is a subtree of T. Let q^{-1} represent the reverse of the path q, and let $q^{-1}p$ represent the concatenation of q^{-1} with p in T. Then $q^{-1}p$ is a root-to-leaf path in T. Hence the elements along $q^{-1}p$ must be nonincreasing because T has the heap property. Therefore the elements along p are nonincreasing. Thus S also has the heap property. **Q.E.D.**

10.23 The forest that produced the given binary tree is obtained by reversing the natural map:

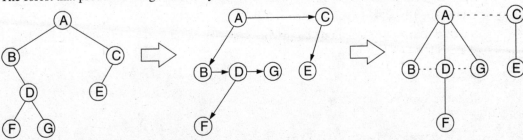

10.24 $f(h) = 1$

10.25 $f(h) = h$

10.26
```
bool BinaryTree::empty() const
{ return _root == 0;
}
```

10.27
```
int s(Node*);
int BinaryTree::size() const
{ return s(_root);;
}
int s(Node* p)
{ if (!p) return 0;
  int nl=s(p->_left);
  int nr=s(p->_right);
  return 1 + nl + nr;
}
```

10.28
```
int n(Node*);
int BinaryTree::leaves() const
{ return n(_root);;
}
int n(Node* p)
{ if (!p) return 0;
  if (p->_left == 0 && p->_right == 0) return 1;
  return n(p->_left) + n(p->_right);
}
```

10.29
```
int h(Node*);
int BinaryTree::height() const
{ return h(_root);
}
int h(Node* p)
{ if (!p) return -1;
  int hl=h(p->_left);
  int hr=h(p->_right);
  return 1 + max(hl,hr);
}
```

10.30
```
int l(Node*,It);
int BinaryTree::level(It it)
{ return l(_root,it);
}
int l(Node* p, It it)
{ if (!p) return -1;
  if (p->_ == *it) return 0;
  int ll=l(p->_left,it);
  if (ll > -1) return 1 + ll;
  int lr=l(p->_right,it);
  if (lr > -1) return 1 + lr;
  return -1;
}
```

10.31
```
void r(Node*,It);
void BinaryTree::reflect()
{ return r(_root,it);
}
void r(Node* p)
{ if (!p) return;
  r(p->_left);
  r(p->_right);
  swap(p->_left,p->_right);
}
```

10.32
```
       void d(Node*,It);
       void BinaryTree::defoliate()
       { if (!_root) return;
         if (_root->_left || _root->_right) d(_root);
         else clear();
       }
       void d(Node* p)
       { // precondition: *p is not a leaf
         Node* lc=p->_left;
         if (lc && (lc->_left || lc->_right)) d(lc);
         else  // *lc is a leaf
         { delete lc;
           p->_left = 0;
         }
         Node* rc=p->_right;
         if (rc && (rc->_left || rc->_right)) d(rc);
         else  // *rc is a leaf
         { delete rc;
           p->_right = 0;
         }
       }
```

10.33
```
       Type& BinaryTree::root() const
       { return _root->_;
       }
```

10.34
```
       bool BinaryTree::isRoot(It it)
       { return bool(_p == _tree._root);
       }
```

10.35
```
       bool BinaryTree::isLeaf(It it)
       { Node* p=it._p;
         if (!p || p->_left || p->_right) return false;
         return true;
       }
```

10.36
```
       It BinaryTree::parent(It it)
       { if (isRoot(it)) return It(it._tree,0);
         return It(it._tree,(it._p)->_parent);
       }
```

10.37
```
       It BinaryTree::leftChild(It it)
       { Node* p=it._p;
         if (!p || p->_left) return It(it._tree,p->_left);
         return It(it._tree,0);
       }
```

10.38
```
       It BinaryTree::rightChild(It it)
       { Node* p=it._p;
         if (!p || p->_right) return It(it._tree,p->_right);
         return It(it._tree,0);
       }
```

10.39
```
       It BinaryTree::find(It begin, It end, const Type& x)
       { BinaryTree* tree=begin._tree;
         Node* p=begin._p;
         while (p != end._p)
           if (p->_ == x) return It(tree,p);
           else p = preorderSuccessor(p);
         return It(this,0);  // not found
       }
```

Chapter 11

Search Trees

Tree structures are used to store data because their organization renders more efficient access to the data. A *search tree* is a tree that maintains its data in some sorted order.

11.1 BINARY SEARCH TREES

A *binary search tree* is a binary tree whose elements include a *key field* of some ordinal type and which has the following property: if k is the key value at any node, then $k \geq x$ for every key x in the node's left subtree and $k \leq y$ for every key y in the node's right subtree. This property, called the *BST property*, guarantees that an inorder traversal of the binary search tree will produce the elements in increasing order.

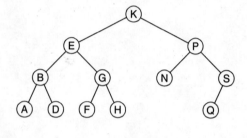

The BST property is applied for each insertion into the tree:

Algorithm 11.1 Inserting into a Binary Search Tree
To insert an element with key value k into a binary search tree:
1. If the tree is empty, insert the new element at the root. Then return.
2. Let p locate the root.
3. If k is less than the key stored at p and if the node at p has no left child, insert the new element as the left child of p. Then return.
4. If k is less than the key stored at p and if the node at p has a left child, let p locate that left child of p. Then go back to Step 3.
5. If the node at p has no right child, insert the new element as the right child of p. Then return.
6. Let p locate the right child of p. Then go back to Step 3.

EXAMPLE 11.1 Inserting into a Binary Search Tree

Apply Algorithm 11.1 to insert an element with key M into the binary search tree shown above.

Step 1 starts the iterator p at the root K. Since M is greater than K (*i.e.*, it follows it lexicographically) and node K has a right child, the algorithm proceeds to Step 6, resetting the iterator p to node P, and then goes back to Step 3. Next, since M is less than P (*i.e.*, it precedes it lexicographically) and node P has a left child, the algorithm proceeds to Step 4, resetting the iterator p to node N, and then goes back to Step 3. Next, since M is also less than N but node N has no left child, the algorithm proceeds to Step 5, inserts the new element as the left child of node N and then returns.

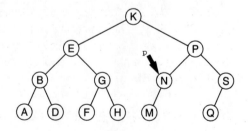

EXAMPLE 11.2 Building a Binary Tree

The following sequence of pictures shows the binary search tree that is built by inserting the input sequence 44, 77, 55, 22, 99, 33, 88:

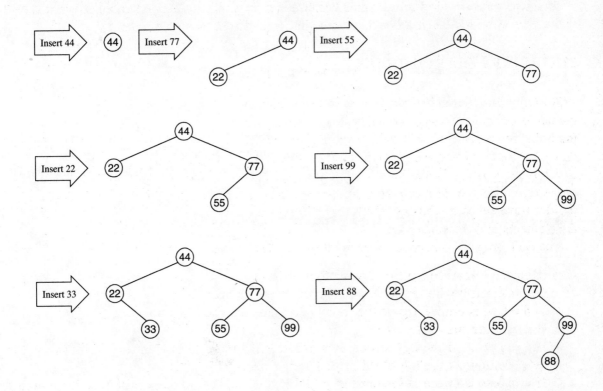

If a binary search tree is balanced, it allows for very efficient searching. As with the Binary Search, it takes $O(\lg n)$ steps to find an element in a balanced binary search tree. But without further restrictions, a binary search tree may grow to be very unbalanced. The worst case is when the elements are inserted in sorted order. In that case the tree degrades to a linear list, thereby making the search algorithm an $O(n)$ sequential search.

EXAMPLE 11.3 An Unbalanced Binary Search Tree

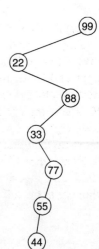

This is the same input data as in Example 11.2, but in a different order: 99, 22, 88, 33, 77, 55, 44. The resulting binary search tree is shown at right.

This shows that the same input in different order produces a different tree. But more important, it shows that it is not unlikely for the binary search tree to be linear, or nearly linear.

11.2 IMPLEMENTATION OF BINARY SEARCH TREES

EXAMPLE 11.4 Interface for a `BinarySearchTree` Class

Here is a simple little class for binary search trees:

```
class BinarySearchTree
{    struct Node;
     Node* _root;
   public:
    .BinarySearchTree();
     void insert(const Type);
     void print() const;
     Type search(const Type) const;
   protected:
     void insert(Node*&, const Type);
     void print(Node*) const;
     Type search(Node*, const Type) const;
};
```

This assumes that the key values are the elements themselves, having type Type. It defines the default constructor, and insert() function, a print() function, and a search() function. These last three member functions each work by calling a corresponding protected recursive function that will traverse the tree.

EXAMPLE 11.5 Testing the **BinarySearchTree** Class

Here is a test driver:

```
int main()
{ BinarySearchTree t;
  t.insert("oats");
  t.insert("corn");
  t.insert("peas");
  t.insert("tuna");
  t.insert("beer");
  t.insert("pork");
  t.insert("eggs");
  t.insert("wine");
  t.print();
  cout << "Searching for okra: " << t.search("okra") << "\n";
  t.insert("okra");
  t.print();
  cout << "Searching for okra: " << t.search("okra") << "\n";
}
```

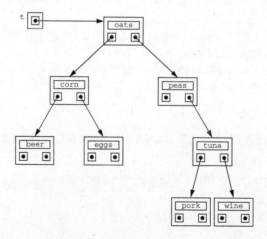

```
beer corn eggs oats peas pork tuna wine
Searching for okra:
beer corn eggs oats okra peas pork tuna wine
Searching for okra: okra
```

The resulting tree looks like the picture on the previous page after the first 8 elements are inserted. Then the first call to search() fails because "okra" is not in the tree. Then, after it is inserted, the second call to search() finds it.

EXAMPLE 11.6 Implementation of the **BinarySearchTree** Class

```
struct BinarySearchTree::Node
{ Type _;
  Node* _left;
  Node* _right;
  Node(Type =Type(), Node* =0, Node* =0);
};
BinarySearchTree::Node::Node(Type x, Node* left, Node* right)
 : _(x), _left(left), _right(right)
{
}
BinarySearchTree::BinarySearchTree() : _root(0)
{
}
void BinarySearchTree::insert(const Type x)
{ insert(_root,x);
}
void BinarySearchTree::print() const
{ print(_root);
  cout << "\n";
}
Type BinarySearchTree::search(const Type x) const
{ return search(_root,x);
}
void BinarySearchTree::insert(Node*& p, const Type x)
{ if (!p) p = new Node(x);
  else if (x == p->_) return;
  else if (x < p->_) return insert(p->_left,x);
  else insert(p->_right,x);
}
void BinarySearchTree::print(Node* p) const
{ if (!p) return;
  print(p->_left);
  cout << p->_ << " ";
  print(p->_right);
}
Type BinarySearchTree::search(Node* p, const Type x) const
{ if (p == 0) return Type();
  else if (x == p->_) return p->_;
  else if (x < p->_) return search(p->_left,x);
  else return search(p->_right,x);
}
```

The `BinarySearchTree::Node` structure is a standard tree node object without any parent pointers. Its constructor and the `BinarySearchTree` default constructor do the usual.

The `insert()` function calls its recursive version to traverse the tree. This code is a direct implementation of Algorithm 11.1 on page 224. Note that the node pointer p must be passed by reference.

The `print()` function calls its recursive version to traverse the tree.

The `search()` function calls its recursive version to traverse the tree. If it is invoked on a null node, it returns the default (null) value for the `Type` type by calling its default constructor. For the `string` class, that is the empty string. Otherwise, the function returns x when it finds it.

11.3 PERFORMANCE CHARACTERISTICS OF BINARY SEARCH TREES

Both the `insert()` and the `search()` functions begin at the root of the tree and proceed down toward the leaves, making one comparison at each level of the tree. Therefore the time required to execute either algorithm is proportional to $h + 1$, where h is the height of the tree. The `search()` function may terminate before reaching a leaf, but $h + 1$ is still an upper bound on the number of comparisons that it can make.

Theorem 11.1 In a binary search tree of size n, the `insert()` and the `search()` functions each require $O(\lg n)$ comparisons in the best case.

Proof: In the best case, the binary tree is completely balanced and nearly full, so by Corollary 10.2 on page 203, $h + 1 \approx \lg(n + 1) = O(\lg n)$.

Theorem 11.2 In a binary search tree of size n, the `insert()` and the `search()` functions each require $O(n)$ comparisons in the worst case.

Proof: In the worst case the tree is linear so $h + 1 = n = O(n)$.

Theorem 11.3 In a binary search tree of size n, the `insert()` and the `search()` functions each require $O(2 \ln n) \approx O(1.39 \lg n)$ comparisons in the average case.

The proof of this result is beyond the scope of this outline.

11.4 AVL TREES

The imbalance problem illustrated in Example 11.3 can be avoided by imposing balance constraints on the nodes of the binary search tree. An *AVL tree* is a binary search tree in which the difference between the heights of the two subtrees is no more than 1 at every element in the tree. The name comes from the two inventors of this method: G. M. Adel'son-Velskii and Y. M. Landis.

The insertion algorithm for AVL trees maintains a balance number at each node, defined to be the height of the node's right subtree minus the height of its left subtree. For the tree to remain balanced, each balance number must be 1, 0, or –1. If an insertion changes a balance number to 2 or to –2, then the insertion algorithm performs a subtree rotation to restore the balance. The following example illustrates the algorithm.

EXAMPLE 11.7 AVL Tree Insertions

This example illustrates the various kinds of rotations that the AVL insertion algorithm uses to keep the tree balanced. The data being inserted are strings holding the names of the U.S. presidents, inserted in chronological order.

The first picture shows the insertion of the seventh president, Andrew Jackson, into the tree where the first six presidents have already been inserted. The balance number for each node is shown directly beneath it. Before `Jackson` is inserted, the node containing `Adams, J.` has balance number 1, and the other 5 nodes have balance number 0. The string `Jackson` is lexicographically less than `Jefferson`, greater than `Adams, J.`, and greater than `Adams, J.Q.`, so the pointer moves left, right, and right down the tree from the root. This leads `Jackson` to become the right child of `Adams, J.Q.` That changes the balance number of each of the three nodes along the insertion path. The balance number for `Jefferson` decreases by 1 because the new node is to its left. The balance numbers for `Adams, J.`, and `Adams, J.Q.`, increase by 1 because the new node is to their right. The resulting changes create an imbalance (a balance number of 2) at `Adams, J.`:

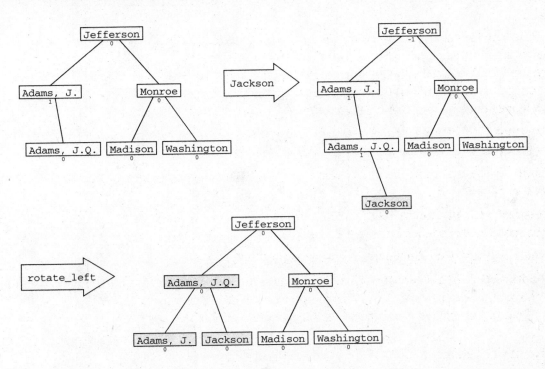

The node that has the illegal balance number (in this case, `Adams, J.`) is called the *pivot* for the required rotation. Since the pivot's balance number is +2, a `rotate_left` operation is performed. (A balance number of −2 would require the symmetrically opposite `rotate_right` operation.) The pivot becomes the left child of its own right child (`Adams, J.Q.`), which is moved up to take the place of the pivot. This reduces the pivot's balance number by 2 (making it 0) and it reduces the balance number of the node that replaces the pivot by 1 (making it 0 in this case). The net effect is that the balance is restored, while preserving the binary search tree property.

The picture on the next page illustrates a double rotation. The eleventh president `Polk` is inserted as the left child of `Tyler`. This causes an imbalance three levels higher, at `Monroe`, which is therefore the pivot element for the rotation. But the balance number of the pivot (2) has the opposite sign from the balance number (−1) of its child (`Van Buren`) on the insertion path. The opposite signs indicate that a double rotation is necessary to restore balance. So first, a single rotation right about the child of the pivot is performed, and then a rotation left about the pivot is performed.

Although a bit complicated, the insertion algorithm for AVL trees is very efficient, requiring the changing of only several pointers. The result is a balanced binary search tree that provides very efficient access.

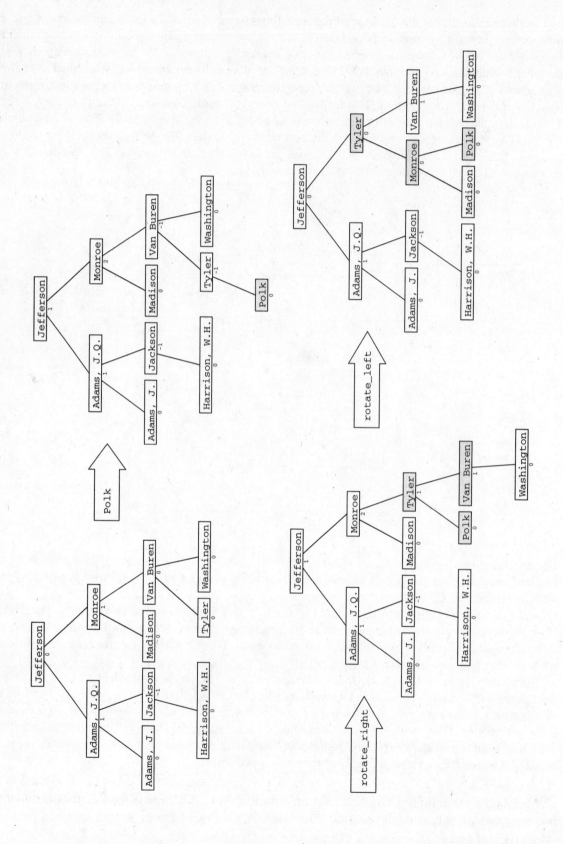

Review Questions

11.1   What are the advantages and disadvantages of using a Binary Search tree?

11.2   What are the advantages and disadvantages of using an AVL tree?

11.3   Which traversal algorithm does the `BinarySearchTree::print()` function (page 227) make?

11.4   Which traversal algorithm does the `BinarySearchTree::search()` function (page 227) make?

11.5   What would the `BinarySearchTree::search()` function (page 227) do if it were invoked on a binary tree that does not satisfy the BST property? Why can't that happen?

Problems

11.1   Determine which of the following binary trees is a binary search tree:

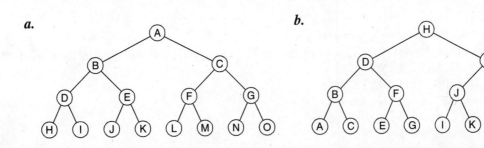

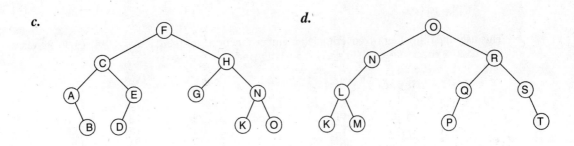

11.2   Find two other orderings of the 13 keys in Problem 11.2 that will produce the same binary search tree.

11.3   Write the following function that uses a binary search tree to sort an array a of n elements:

```
void sort(Type* a, int n);
```

Then explain the complexity of the algorithm.

11.4   Encapsulate Problem 11.3.

11.5   Here are the U.S. Postal abbreviations of the first 10 states, in the order that they ratified the U.S. Constitution: DE, PA, NJ, GA, CT, MA, MD, SC, NH, VA. Show the AVL tree after the insertion of each of these strings.

11.6   Prove that every subtree of a binary tree is also a binary tree.

Answers to Review Questions

11.1   The disadvantage of a binary search tree is that it may become very unbalanced, in which case searching degenerates into an $O(n)$ algorithm. The advantage is the efficiency that a binary tree enjoys for insertions and deletions.

11.2   The advantage of an AVL tree is that it is always balanced, guaranteeing the $O(\lg n)$ speed of the Binary Search algorithm. The disadvantages are the complex rotations used by the insertion and removal algorithms needed to maintain the tree's balance.

11.3   The `BinarySearchTree::print()` function does an inorder traversal of the tree.

11.4   The `BinarySearchTree::search()` function does a preorder traversal of the tree.

11.5   If the `BinarySearchTree::search()` function were invoked on a binary tree that does not satisfy the BST property, it would return the default (null) value generated by `Type()` if it were searching for a value which was in the wrong place in the tree. But that can't happen since the only way an element can be inserted into the tree is by the `insert()` function which enforces the BST Property.

Solutions to Problems

11.1   All except *a* are binary search trees.

11.2   Two other orderings of the 7 keys in Example 11.2 on page 225 that will produce the same BST:
a. 44, 22, 33, 77, 55, 99, 88;
b. 44, 22, 77, 33, 55, 99, 88.

11.3   Here is the `sort()` function:

```
void sort(Type* a, int n)
{ BinarySearchTree t;
  for (int i=0; i < n; i++)
    t.insert(a[i]);
  t.load(a);
}
```

This uses the following two overloaded member functions for the `BinarySearchTree` class:

```
void BinarySearchTree::load(Type* a) const
{ int i=0;
  load(_root,a,i);
}
void BinarySearchTree::load(Node* p, Type* a, int& i) const
{ if (!p) return;
  load(p->_left,a,i);
  a[i++] = p->_;
  load(p->_right,a,i);
}
```

The first `load()` function is called once to reload the array from the tree. It calls the recursive `load()` function that performs an inorder traversal of the tree, copying one element from the tree to the array on each call. This requires n calls. The preceding `for` loop makes *n* iterations, each time doing an $O(\lg n)$ search, so the entire sorting process has complexity $O(n \lg n)$. This algorithm is called the *Binary Tree* Sort.

11.4   This class uses a binary search tree to sort an array:

```
class BSTSorter : public BinarySearchTree
{ public:
    void load(Type*) const;
    void load(Node*, Type*, int&) const;
};
```

```
void BSTSorter::load(Type* a) const
{ int i=0;
  load(_root,a,i);
}

void BSTSorter::load(Node* p, Type* a, int& i) const
{ if (!p) return;
  load(p->_left,a,i);
  a[i++] = p->_;
  load(p->_right,a,i);
}
```

11.5   The solution is shown in the diagrams below.

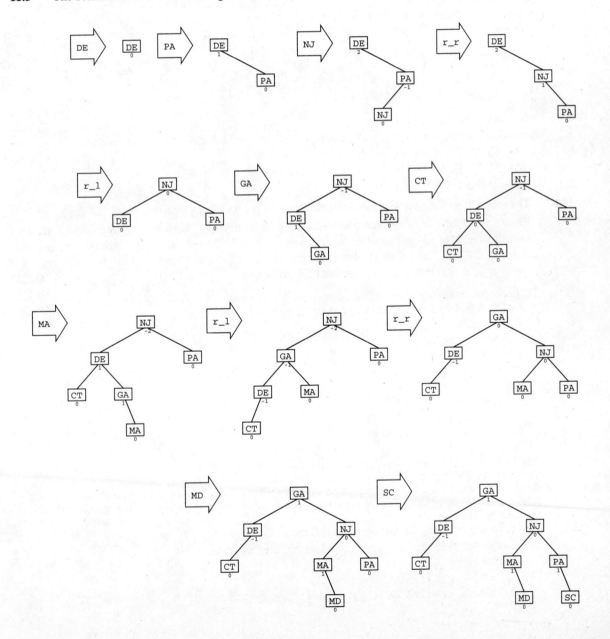

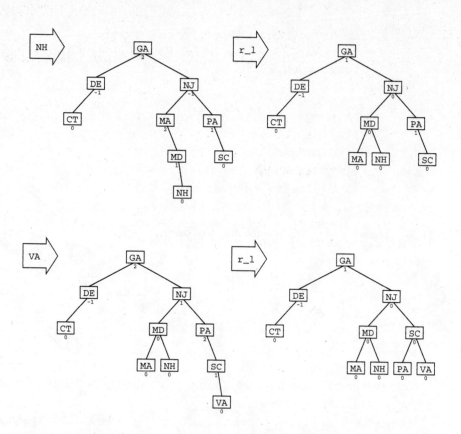

11.6   Theorem. Every subtree of a binary search tree is a binary search tree.

Proof: Let T be a binary search tree, and let S be a subtree of T. Let x be any element in S and let L and R be the left and right subtrees, respectively, of x in S. Then since S is a subtree of T, x is also an element of T, and L and R are the left and right subtrees of x in T. Therefore $y \leq x \leq z$ for every $y \in L$ and every $z \in R$. Therefore S too has the BST property.   **Q.E.D.**

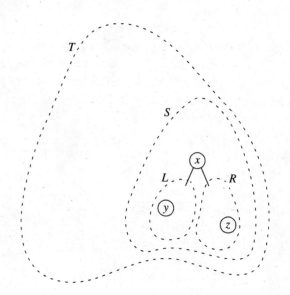

Heaps and Priority Queues

12.1 HEAPS

A *heap* is a complete binary tree whose elements have keys that satisfy the following *heap property*: the keys along any path from root to leaf are nonincreasing. For example, the tree shown here is a heap because it is a complete binary tree and the elements along each of its root-to-leaf paths are nonincreasing:

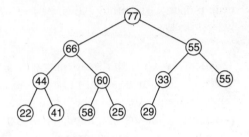

$$77 \geq 66 \geq 44 \geq 22;$$
$$77 \geq 66 \geq 44 \geq 41;$$
$$77 \geq 66 \geq 60 \geq 58;$$
$$77 \geq 66 \geq 60 \geq 25;$$
$$77 \geq 55 \geq 33 \geq 29;$$
$$77 \geq 55 \geq 55.$$

Note that heaps could represent family descendant trees because the heap property means that every parent is older than his/her children.

Heaps are used to implement priority queues (Section 12.5 on page 238) and the Heap Sort algorithm (Section 13.8 on page 257).

12.2 THE NATURAL MAPPING

Every complete binary tree has a natural mapping into an array. (See page 205.) For example, the heap shown above maps into the array shown here. The

0	1	2	3	4	5	6	7	8	9	10	11	12
	77	66	55	44	60	33	55	22	41	58	25	29

natural mapping is obtained from a level order traversal of the tree. In the resulting array, the parent of the element at index i is at index $i/2$ and the children of that element are at indexes $2i$ and $2i+1$. For example, element 60 is at index $i = 5$, its parent is element 66 at index $i/2 = 2$, and its children are elements 58 and 25 at indexes $2i = 10$ and $2i + 1 = 11$.

The natural mapping between a complete binary tree and an array is a two-way correspondence. To map the array elements back into a complete binary tree, simply number the tree nodes consecutively in a level order traversal beginning with number 1 at the root. Then copy the array element at index i into the tree node numbered i. If the resulting tree has the heap property, then we also say that the array has the *heap property*.

235

EXAMPLE 12.1 Determining Whether an Array has the Heap Property

To determine whether this array has the heap property, we first map it into a binary tree. Then check each root-to-leaf path.

The path { 88, 66, 44, 51 } is *not* nonincreasing because 44 < 51. Hence, the tree does not have the heap property. Therefore, the array does not have the heap property.

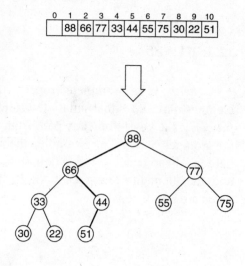

An array with the heap property is *partially ordered*. That means that most of the larger keys come before most of the smaller keys. More precisely, it means that every heap-path subarray is sorted in nonincreasing order, where a *heap-path subarray* is a subsequence of array elements in which each index number is half that of its successor. For example, the subarray { a[1], a[2], a[5], a[11], a[22], a[45], a[90], a[180] } would be a heap-path subarray of an array a[] of 200 elements. The Heap Sort algorithm (Section 13.8 on page 257) exploits this fact to obtain a fast and efficient method for sorting arrays.

12.3 INSERTION INTO A HEAP

Elements are inserted into a heap next to its right-most leaf at the bottom level. Then the heap property is restored by percolating the new element up the tree until it is no longer "older" (*i.e.*, its key is greater) than its parent. On each iteration, the child is swapped with its parent.

EXAMPLE 12.2 Inserting into a Heap

Here is how the key 75 would be inserted into the heap shown above:

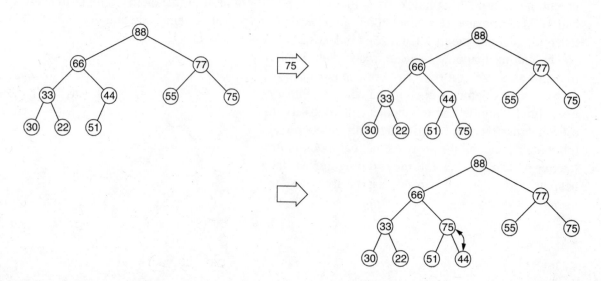

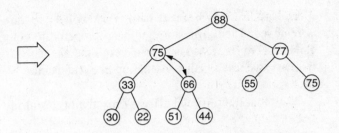

The element 75 is added to the tree as a new last leaf. Then it is swapped with its parent element 44 because 75 > 44. Then it is swapped with its parent element 66 because 75 > 66. Now the heap property has been restored because the new element 75 is less than its parent and greater than its children.

Note that the insertion affects only the nodes along a single root-to-leaf path.

12.4 REMOVAL FROM A HEAP

The heap removal algorithm always removes the root element from the tree. This is done by moving the last leaf element into the root element and then restoring the heap property by percolating the new root element down the tree until it is no longer "younger" (*i.e.*, its key is less) than its children. On each iteration, the parent is swapped with the older of its two children.

EXAMPLE 12.3 Removing from a Heap

Here is how the root element (key 88) would be removed from a heap:

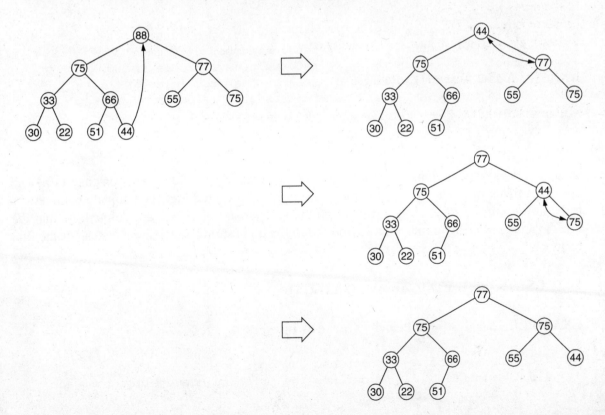

The last leaf (key 44) is removed and copied into the root, replacing the previous root (key 88) which is removed. Then, to restore the heap property, the element 44 is swapped with the larger of its two children (77). That step is repeated until the element 44 is no longer smaller than any of its children. In this case, the result is that 44 ends up as a leaf again.

Note that the removal affects only the nodes along a single root-to-leaf path.

12.5 PRIORITY QUEUES

A *stack* is a "LIFO" container: the last one in comes out first. A *queue* is a "FIFO" container: the first one in comes out first. A *priority queue* is a "BIFO" container: the best one in comes out first. That means that each element is assigned a priority number, and the element with the highest priority comes out first.

Priority queues are widely used in computer systems. For example, if a printer is shared by several computers on a local area network, the print jobs that are queued to it would normally be held temporarily in a priority queue wherein smaller jobs are given priority over larger jobs.

Priority queues are usually implemented as heaps since the heap data structure always keeps the element with the largest key at the root and its insertion and removal operations are so efficient.

Here is part of the interface for the Standard C++ `priority_queue` container class template:

```
template <class T>
class priority_queue
{ public:
    priority_queue();
    priority_queue(const priority_queue&);
    ~priority_queue();
    priority_queue& operator=(const priority_queue&);
    int size() const;        // returns number of elements
    bool empty() const;      // returns true iff this is empty
    const T& top() const;    // returns the front element
    void push(const T&);     // inserts given element at back
    void pop();              // removes element from front
  private:
    //...
};
```

These are the same functions as for the `queue` class template. (See Section 6.1 on page 110.) The only significant difference is that the `priority_queue` class requires the template parameter T to be an *ordinal type* (*i.e.*, a type for which the comparison operators are defined) so that the `pop()` and `top()` functions remove and return the highest priority element instead of the first element.

12.6 USING `priority_queue` OBJECTS

EXAMPLE 12.4 Testing a Priority Queue of Integers

```
#include <iostream>  // defines the cout object
#include <queue>     // defines the priority_queue class template
using namespace std;
```

```
typedef priority_queue<int> PriorityQueue;
void print(PriorityQueue);  // prints a copy of given queue

int main()
{ PriorityQueue pq;    print(pq);
  pq.push(44);         print(pq);
  pq.push(66);         print(pq);
  pq.push(22);         print(pq);
  pq.push(55);         print(pq);
  pq.push(33);         print(pq);
}

void print(PriorityQueue q)
{ cout << "size=" << q.size();
  if (q.size()>0)
  { cout << ", top=" << q.top() << ": (" << q.top();
    q.pop();
    while (!q.empty())
    { cout << "," << q.top();
      q.pop();
    }
    cout << ")";
  }
  cout << "\n";
}
```

```
size=0
size=1, top=44: (44)
size=2, top=66: (66,44)
size=3, top=66: (66,44,22)
size=4, top=66: (66,55,44,22)
size=5, top=66: (66,55,44,33,22)
```

The print() function suggests that the elements are stored in the priority queue in descending order. But that is probably not true. The function uses the priority_queue::pop() function to access the elements, and that member function is required to remove the elements in order of their priority. But there is no obligation on the priority_queue itself to store the elements in any particular order. Indeed, most implementations keep the elements only *partially* ordered. (See page 236.)

12.7 USING A HEAP TO IMPLEMENT A PriorityQueue CLASS TEMPLATE

This implementation uses a vector to store the heap elements:

```
template <class T>
class PriorityQueue
{ public:
    PriorityQueue();
    PriorityQueue(const PriorityQueue&);
    ~PriorityQueue();
    PriorityQueue& operator=(const PriorityQueue&);
    int size() const;           // returns number of elements
    bool empty() const;         // returns true iff this is empty
    const T& top() const;       // returns the front element
    void push(const T&);        // inserts given element at back
```

```
   void pop();                        // removes element from front
 protected:
   vector<T> _;                       // dynamic array for queue elements
   void heapifyDown();                // restores the heap property
   void heapifyUp();                  // restores the heap property
};
```

This implementation is similar to the vector implementation of the Stack class template
(Problem 5.13 on page 105). Most of the required member functions for the PriorityQueue
class template call the corresponding member function for the vector class template.

```
template <class T>
PriorityQueue<T>::PriorityQueue()
{
}

template <class T>
PriorityQueue<T>::PriorityQueue(const PriorityQueue& q) : _(q._)
{
}

template <class T>
PriorityQueue<T>::~PriorityQueue()
{
}

template <class T>
PriorityQueue<T>& PriorityQueue<T>::operator=(const PriorityQueue& q)
{ _ = q._;
}

template <class T>
int PriorityQueue<T>::size() const
{ return _.size();
}

template <class T>
bool PriorityQueue<T>::empty() const
{ return _.empty();
}

template <class T>
const T& PriorityQueue<T>::top() const
{ return _.front();
}

template <class T>
void PriorityQueue<T>::pop()
{ _.front() = _.back();   // delete the front element
  _.pop_back();           // move the back element to the front
  heapifyDown();          // restore the heap property
}
```

```
template <class T>
void PriorityQueue<T>::push(const T& x)
{ _.push_back(x);          // insert the new element at the back
  heapifyUp();             // restore the heap property
}
```

The `heapifyDown()` function percolates the root element down toward the leaf level in order to restore the heap property. It does that by swapping each parent along the root-to-leaf path with its older child. Since the loop control variable `i` is doubled on each iteration, the entire process requires no more than lg n iterations.

```
template <class T>
void PriorityQueue<T>::heapifyDown()
{ int n=_.size(), j;
  for (int i=0; i<n/2; i=j)
  { j=2*i+1;                 // _[j] and _[j+1] are the children of _[i]
    if (j<n && _[j]<_[j+1]) ++j;
    if (_[i] >= _[j]) break;
    swap(_[i],_[j]);
  }
}
```

The `heapifyUp()` function percolates the last leaf element up toward the root in order to restore the heap property. It does that by swapping each child along the root-to-leaf path with its younger parent. Since the loop control variable `j` is halved on each iteration, the entire process requires no more than lg n iterations.

```
template <class T>
void PriorityQueue<T>::heapifyUp()
{ int n=_.size(), i;
  for (int j=n-1; j>0; j=i)
  { i=(j-1)/2;               // _[i] is the parent of _[j]
    if (_[j] <= _[i]) break;
    swap(_[j],_[i]);
  }
}
```

The implementation of a priority queue as a heap data structure is very efficient. Both the `push()` and the `pop()` functions run in O(lg n) time.

12.8 APPLICATIONS OF PRIORITY QUEUES

Queues are widely used in simulations. In any situation where the rate at which users' demands for services can exceed the rate at which those services can be supplied, queues are normally used.

The following example could be modified to simulate customers waiting in line at a bank, computer print jobs waiting in printer A queue, or Internet message packets waiting to be routed.

EXAMPLE 12.5 The Toll Plaza Simulation Again

This program simulates the process of cars waiting in line and being served at a highway toll plaza. We assume there are 4 toll booths and one line of cars that feed into them. Time is measured in "ticks" that represent tenths of a second so that time variables can be declared as ints that can be incremented and decremented. The time between car arrivals and the time that it takes for a car to be served at a toll booth are exponentially distributed random variables. In this simulation we set the average time between arrivals to be 2 seconds (20 ticks) and the average service time to be 16 seconds (160 ticks). The program uses three classes: the Exp class whose objects generate exponentially distributed random numbers, the Car class whose objects represent cars in the simulation, and the TollBooth class whose objects represent the four toll booths.

```cpp
const int BOOTHS=4;      // 4 toll booths
const int TICKS=600;     // 60 seconds = 1 minute
const float IAT=20;      // average arrival every 2 seconds
const float ST=80;       // average 8 seconds per service

class Exp : public Random
{ public:
    Exp(float mean) : _mean(mean) {}
    float time() { return -_mean*log(1.0-real()); }
  private:
    float _mean;
};

class Car
{    friend class TollBooth;
     friend ostream& operator<<(ostream& ostr, const Car& car)
     { ostr << "#" << car._id << "(" << car._arrive
            << "," << car._service << "," << car._server
            << "," << car._exit << ")";
       return ostr;
     }
     static int _count;
   public:
     Car(int time=0) : _id(_count++), _arrive(time),
       _service(0), _remaining(0.0), _exit(0) {}
     int id() { return _id; }
     bool finished() { return _remaining <= 0.0; }
   protected:
     int _id;
     int _arrive;
     int _service;
     float _remaining;
     int _exit;
     char _server;
};

class TollBooth
{    static Exp _service;  // generates random service times
   public:
     TollBooth() : _serving(false), _p(0) {}
```

```
      void setId(char ch) { _id = ch; }
      bool isServing() { return _serving; }
      Car& car() { return *_p; }
      void enter(Car* p, int time)
      { _serving = true;
        _p = p;
        p->_service = time;
        p->_remaining = _service.time();
        p->_server = _id;
      }
      void serviceCar() { _p->_remaining -= 1.0; }
      void vacate(int time)
      { _serving = false;
        _p->_exit = time;
      }
   private:
      char _id;
      bool _serving;
      Car* _p;
};

int Car::_count = 0;           // initializes Car counter
Exp TollBooth::_service(ST);   // initializes _service generator

int main()
{ vector<TollBooth> booth(BOOTHS);
  for (int i=0; i<BOOTHS; i++)
    booth[i].setId('A'+i);   // name booths as 'A', 'B', 'C', etc.
  queue<Car*> line;
  Exp arrival(IAT);          // generates random arrival intervals
  float timeToNextArrival=0.0;
  for (int t=0; t<TICKS; t++, timeToNextArrival -= 1.0)
  { if (timeToNextArrival <= 0.0)  // a car has arrived
    { Car* p = new Car(t);         // construct new Car object
      line.push(p);                // move car to back of line
      timeToNextArrival = arrival.time();
    }
    for (int i=0; i<BOOTHS; i++)
      if (booth[i].isServing())
      { Car& car=booth[i].car();
        booth[i].serviceCar();
        if (car.finished())
        { booth[i].vacate(t);      // move car out of booth
          cout << car << "\n";
        }
      }
      else if (!line.empty())      // move front car to booth
      { Car* p=line.front();
        booth[i].enter(p,t);
        line.pop();
      }
  }
```

The `Exp` class is defined to be a subclass of the `Random` class (see Section E.20 in Appendix E). The `Random::real()` function returns numbers x that are uniformly distributed in the interval $0 \le x < 1$. The `Exp::time()` function uses that function to generate numbers t that are exponentially distributed with mean value `_mean`. The exponential density function is shown at right. The value c is the reciprocal of the mean. This distribution is the standard mathematical model used to simulate events that occur at random times.

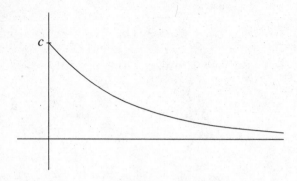

The `Car` class produces objects that represent cars at the toll booth plaza. Each Car object stores an identification number `_id`, the time `_arrive` (in ticks) when it arrived at the plaza, the time `_service` when it arrived at a toll booth, the time `_exit` when it left the toll booth, the character `_server` that identifies the toll booth that served the car, and an integer `_remaining` that is used to count down the time ticks until the toll booth has finished serving the car. The class uses a static counter `_count` to generate identification numbers for the cars (car #1, car #2, *etc.*).

The `TollBooth` class instantiates objects that represent the toll booths. The main program uses a vector of four `TollBooth` objects. Each object stores an identification letter `_id` (booth A, booth B, *etc.*), a flag `_serving` to determine whether the booth is currently serving a customer, and a pointer `_p` to the car that it is serving. The class has three mutator functions: `enter()` which is called when a car arrives at the toll booth, `serviceCar()` which is called once at each tick during which the booth is serving its car, and `vacate()` which is called when its car leaves the toll booth.

The main program first initializes the vector `booth` of four `TollBooth` objects, the queue `line` of Car pointers, the `Exp` random number generator `arrival` that will generate interarrival times for the cars, and the integer `timeToNextArrival` that records how long before the next car arrives. Then it begins the main timing loop which iterates once for each 0.1-second click of the clock. If it is time for a new car to arrive, it constructs one and inserts it at the back of the `line` queue. Then it checks each of the four toll booths. If it is serving a car, then it calls that booth's `serviceCar()` function to update the car's data members and then check whether it is time for the car to leave the booth. If it is not serving a car and if there are cars waiting in the `line` queue, then it moves the front car to that booth.

The output consists of one line for each car that leaves a toll booth. It shows the car's identification number, the time the car arrived at the toll plaza, the time that it entered a toll booth, the name of that toll booth, and the time that it left the toll booth. The rows are printed in the order in which the cars left their toll booths:

```
#3(38,38,C,123)
#2(24,24,B,143)
#1(0,0,A,195)
#5(73,124,C,247)
#4(48,48,D,254)
#6(88,144,B,262)
#7(102,196,A,824)
```

Review Questions

12.1   What are the two main applications of heaps?

12.2   What is the difference between a queue and a priority queue?

12.3   Why are heaps used to implement priority queues?

Problems

12.1 Determine which of the following binary trees is a heap.

a.

```
        (88)
       /    \
     (66)   (44)
     /  \   /  \
   (33)(55)(77)(33)
```

b.

```
        (88)
       /    \
     (77)   (66)
     /  \   /  \
   (55)(44)(33)(22)
```

c.

```
        (55)
       /    \
     (33)   (77)
     /  \   /  \
   (22)(44)(66)(88)
```

d.

```
        (88)
       /    \
     (77)   (66)
     /      /  \
   (44)   (55)(33)
```

e.

```
        (88)
       /    \
     (77)   (66)
     /  \   /
   (44)(33)(55)
```

f.

```
        (99)
      / |  \
   (88)(77)(66)
   /  \   /  \
 (55)(44)(33)(22)
```

12.2 Determine which of the following arrays have the heap property.

a.

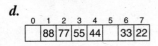

b.

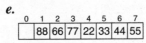

c.

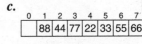

d.

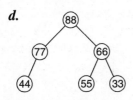

e.

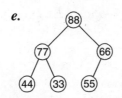

f.

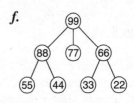

12.3 Show the heap after inserting each of these keys in this order: 44, 66, 33, 88, 77, 55, 22.

12.4 Show the array obtained from the natural map of each of the heaps obtained in Problem 12.3.

12.5 Prove that every subtree of a heap is a heap.

Answers to Review Questions

12.1 Heaps are used to implement priority queues and to implement the Heap Sort (see Section 13.8 on page 257).

12.2 Elements are removed from a queue in the same order in which they are inserted: first-in–first-out. Elements in a priority queue must have an ordinal key field which determines the priority order in which they are to be removed.

12.3 Heaps are used to implement priority queues because they allow $O(\lg n)$ insertions and removals. This is because both the `push()` and the `pop()` functions are implemented by traversing a root-to-leaf path through the heap. Such paths are no longer than the height of the tree which is at most $\lg n$.

Solutions to Problems

12.1 *a.* This is *not* a heap because the root-to-leaf path { 88, 44, 77 } is *not* nonincreasing (44 < 77).

b. This is a heap.

c. This is *not* a heap because the root-to-leaf path { 55, 33, 44 } is *not* nonincreasing (33 < 44) and the root-to-leaf path { 55, 77, 88 } is *not* nonincreasing (55 < 77 < 88).

d. This is *not* a heap because the binary tree is *not* complete.

e. This is a heap.

f. This is *not* a heap because the tree is *not* binary.

12.2   **a.** This array does *not* have the heap property because the root-to-leaf path { a[1], a[3], a[6] } = { 88, 44, 77 } is *not* nonincreasing (44 < 77).

  b. This array does have the heap property.

  c. This array does have the heap property.

  d. This array does *not* have the heap property because its data elements are *not* contiguous: it does *not* represent a complete binary tree.

  e. This array does have the heap property.

  f. This array does *not* have the heap property because the root-to-leaf path { a[1], a[3], a[6] } = { 88, 22, 55 } is *not* nonincreasing (22 < 55) and the root-to-leaf path { a[1], a[3], a[7] } = { 88, 22, 66 } is *not* nonincreasing (22 < 66).

12.3   Inserting the keys 44, 66, 33, 88, 77, 55, 22 into a heap:

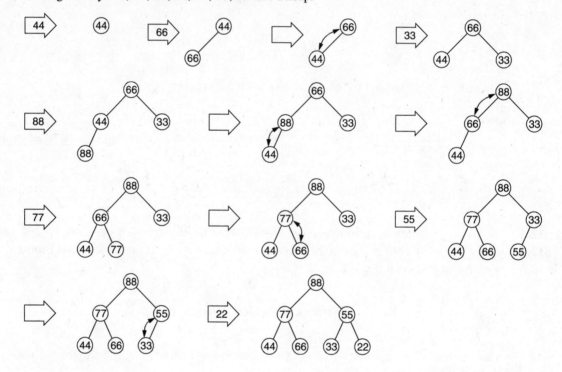

12.4   The arrays for the heaps in Problem 12.3:

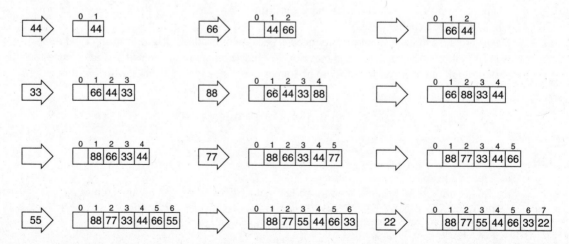

12.5 **Theorem.** Every subtree of a heap is also a heap.

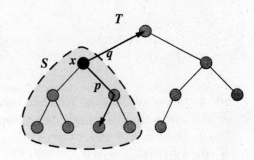

Proof: Let T be a heap, and let S be a subtree of T. By definition, T is a complete binary tree with the heap property. Therefore by the theorem of Problem 10.21 on page 221, S is also a complete binary tree. Let x be the root of S, and let p be any root-to-leaf path in S. Then x is an element of T since S is a subtree of T, and there is a unique path q in T from x to the root of T. Also, p is a path in T that connects x to a leaf of T since S is a subtree of T. Let q^{-1} represent the reverse of the path q, and let $q^{-1}p$ represent the concatenation of q^{-1} with p in T. Then $q^{-1}p$ is a root-to-leaf path in T. Hence the elements along $q^{-1}p$ must be nonincreasing because T has the heap property. Therefore the elements along p are nonincreasing. Thus S also has the heap property.   **Q.E.D.**

Chapter 13

Sorting

Sorting is one of the most common types of algorithms implemented on computers. Its importance is due mainly to the fact that searching a list is much faster if the list is sorted.

13.1 PRELIMINARIES

Each sorting algorithm presented here is defined as a C++ function template on an array `a` of n elements of type `T`, where `T` is the template parameter. The function prototype is:

```
template<class T> void sort(T* a, int n);
// Precondition: a has at least n elements.
// Postcondition: a[0] <= a[1] <= a[2] <= ... <= a[n-1].
```

Each sorting function can be tested with the same test driver:

```
int main()
{ int a[] = { 77, 44, 99, 66, 33, 55, 88, 22, 44 };
  print(a, 9);
  sort(a, 9);
  print(a, 9);
}
```

This uses the following `print()` function template:

```
template<class T> void print(T* a, int n)
{ cout << a[0];
  for (int i=1; i < n; i++)
    cout << ", " << a[i];
  cout << endl;
}
```

The output will be

```
77, 44, 99, 66, 33, 55, 88, 22, 44
22, 33, 44, 44, 55, 66, 77, 88, 99
```

13.2 THE BUBBLE SORT

The Bubble Sort is probably the simplest of the sorting algorithms. Its name comes from the idea that the larger elements "bubble up" to the top (the high end) of the array like the bubbles in a carbonated beverage.

Algorithm 13.1 The Bubble Sort

```
template<class T> void sort(T* a, int n)
{ for (int i=1; i < n; i++)
    for (int j=1; j <= n-i; j++)
      if (a[j-1] > a[j]) swap(a[j-1], a[j]);
    // Invariant: the i largest elements are in the correct locations.
}
```

EXAMPLE 13.1 Tracing the Bubble Sort

Here is a trace of the Bubble Sort on the array of 9 integers listed above:

a[0]	a[1]	a[2]	a[3]	a[4]	a[5]	a[6]	a[7]	a[8]
77	44	99	66	33	55	88	22	44
44	77							
		66	99					
			33	99				
				55	99			
					88	99		
						22	99	
							44	99
	66	77						
		33	77					
			55	77				
					22	88		
						44	88	
	33	66						
		55	66					
				22	77			
					44	77		
33	44							
			22	66				
				44	66			
		22	55					
			44	55				
	22	44						
22	33							

On each iteration of the outside i loop, the next largest element "bubbles up" to the right. On the first iteration, 99 bubbles up, bouncing off of 11, 33, 55, 88, 22, and 66. On the second iteration, 88 bubbles up, bouncing off of 66. Also notice that 77 bubbles up to a[4] on the second iteration.

Theorem 13.1 The Bubble Sort is correct.

Proof: The loop invariant can be used to prove that the Bubble Sort does indeed sort the array. After the first iteration of the main i loop, the largest element must have moved to the last position. Wherever it began, it had to be moved step-by-step all the way to the right, because on each comparison the larger element is moved right. For the same reason, the second largest element must have been moved to the second-from-last position in the second iteration of the main i loop. So the 2 largest elements are in the correct locations. This reasoning verifies that the loop invariant is true at the end of every iteration of the main i loop. But then, after the last iteration, the n-1 largest elements must be in their correct locations. That forces the nth largest (*i.e.*, the smallest) element also to be in its correct location, so the array must be sorted. **Q.E.D.**

Theorem 13.2 The complexity of the Bubble Sort is $O(n^2)$.

Proof: The complexity function $O(n^2)$ means that, for large values of n, the number of loop iterations tends to be proportional to n^2. That means that, if one large array is twice the size of another, it should take about four times as long to sort. The inner j loop iterates $n-1$ times on the first iteration of the outside i loop, $n-2$ times on the second iteration of the i loop, $n-3$ times on the third iteration of the i loop, *etc.* For example, when $n=7$, there are 6 comparisons made on the first iteration of the i loop, 5 comparisons made on the second iteration of the i loop, 4 comparisons made on the third iteration of the i loop, *etc.*, so the total number of comparisons is $6+5+4+3+2+1=21$. In general, the total number of comparisons will be $(n-1)$ $+(n-2)+(n-3)+\cdots+3+2+1$. This sum is $n(n-1)/2$. (See Theorem B.8 on page 278.) For large values of n, that expression is nearly $n^2/2$ which is proportional to n^2.   **Q.E.D.**

13.3 THE SELECTION SORT

The Selection Sort works like the Bubble Sort: on each iteration of the main i loop, the next largest element is moved into its correct position. But instead of "bubbling" these elements into position, the Selection Sort finds the element to be moved without first moving any elements. Then it is put into place with a single swap. This is more efficient than the Bubble Sort.

This implementation of the Selection Sort puts the next smallest element (instead of the next largest element) in place on each iteration of the main i loop. Both versions work equally well.

Algorithm 13.2 The Selection Sort

```
template<class T> void sort(T* a, int n)
{ for (int i=0; i < n-1; i++)
  { int min=i;
    for (int j=i+1; j < n; j++)
      if (a[j] < a[min]) min = j;
    // Invariant: a[min] <= a[j] for i <= j < n.
    swap(a[min], a[i]);
    // Invariant: the subarray a[0:i] is sorted.
  }
}
```

EXAMPLE 13.2 Tracing the Selection Sort

Here is a trace of the Selection Sort on the same array of 9 integers:

a[0]	a[1]	a[2]	a[3]	a[4]	a[5]	a[6]	a[7]	a[8]
77	44	99	66	33	55	88	22	44
22							88	
	33			44				
		44		99				
			44					66
				55	99			
					66			99
						77	88	

Theorem 13.3 The Selection Sort is correct.

Proof: This proof is similar to that for the corresponding theorem for the Bubble Sort. The first loop invariant is true because each time an element a[j] was found to be less than a[min], the value of min was changed to j. That was done for all j in the range from i up to n-1. The second loop invariant follows from the first, because the `swap()` puts the `i`th smallest element into position `a[i]`. On the last iteration of the outer loop, `i == n-2`. So after that, elements `a[0]` up to `a[n-2]` must be in their correct positions. That forces the `n`th element, `a[n-1]` also to be in its correct position.　　　　　　　　　　　　　　　　　　　　**Q.E.D.**

Theorem 13.4 The complexity of the Selection Sort is $O(n^2)$.

Proof: Again, the proof is essentially the same as that for the corresponding theorem for the Bubble Sort. On the first iteration of the outer `i` loop, the inner `j` loop iterates $n-1$ times. On the second, it iterates $n-2$ times. This progression continues, giving a total of

$$(n-1) + (n-2) + \cdots + 2 + 1 = n(n-1)/2$$

　　　　　　　　　　　　　　　　　　　　　　　　　　　　　　　Q.E.D.

13.4 THE INSERTION SORT

The Insertion Sort is so named because on each iteration of its main loop it inserts the next element in its correct position relative to the subarray that has already been processed. This is the common method people use to sort playing cards dealt to them in card games. Unlike the Bubble Sort and the Quick Sort, the Insertion Sort does not use the `swap()` function. Instead, it shifts elements over to make room for each new element inserted. In the `i`th iteration of the main loop, all the elements on the left of `a[i]` that are less than `a[i]` are shifted one position to the right, making room for the insertion of `a[i]` into its correct position relative to the previously processed `i-1` elements.

Algorithm 13.3 The Insertion Sort

```
template<class T> void sort(T* a, int n)
{ for (int i=1; i < n; i++)
  { T temp = a[i];
    for (int j=i; j > 0 && a[j-1] > temp; j--)
      a[j] = a[j-1];
    a[j] = temp;
    // Invariant: a[0] <= a[1] <= ... <= a[i].
  }
}
```

EXAMPLE 13.3 Tracing the Insertion Sort

Here is a trace of the Insertion Sort on the same array of 9 integers:

a[0]	a[1]	a[2]	a[3]	a[4]	a[5]	a[6]	a[7]	a[8]
77	44	99	66	33	55	88	22	44
44	77							
	66	77	99					
33	44	66	77	99				
		55	66	77	99			
					88	99		
22	33	44	55	66	77	88	99	
			44	55	66	77	88	99

Theorem 13.5 The Insertion Sort is correct.

Proof: As with the previous two correctness theorems, this too will be proved as soon as the algorithm's loop invariant is verified. On the first iteration of the main `i` loop, `a[1]` is compared with `a[0]` and interchanged if necessary. So `a[0] <= a[1]` after the first iteration. If we assume that the loop invariant is true prior to some `k`th iteration, then it must also be true after that iteration has finished, because during it `a[k+1]` is inserted between the elements that are less than or equal to it and those that are greater. It follows from the Principle of Mathematical Induction then that the loop invariant is true for all `k`.   **Q.E.D.**

Theorem 13.6 The complexity of the Insertion Sort is O(n^2).

Proof: The proof is similar to that for the corresponding theorems for the Bubble Sort and the Selection Sort. On the first iteration of the outer `i` loop, the inner `j` loop iterates once. On the second, it iterates once or twice, depending upon whether `a[1] > a[2]`. On the third iteration, the inner `j` loop iterates at most three times, again depending upon how many of the elements on the left of `a[3]` are greater than `a[3]`. This pattern continues, so that on the `k`th iteration of the outer loop, the inner loop iterates at most `k` times. Therefore, the total number of iterations is:

$$1 + 2 + 3 + \cdots + (n-2) + (n-1) = n(n-1)/2$$ **Q.E.D.**

Theorem 13.7 If the array is already sorted, the Insertion Sort has complexity O(n).

Proof: In this case, the inner loop will iterate only once for each iteration of the outer loop. So the total number of iterations of the inner loop is:

$$1 + 1 + 1 + \cdots + 1 + 1 = n-1$$ **Q.E.D.**

An algorithm that has complexity function O(n) is said to be *linear*, or to "run in linear time." The term "linear' is used because the graph of the equation $y = x$ is a straight line. Similarly, an algorithm that has complexity function O(n^2) is said to be *quadratic* because $y = x^2$ is a quadratic equation. We can summarize the last two theorems by saying that the Insertion Sort is a quadratic algorithm whose "best case" performance is linear.

At first glance, Theorem 13.7 seems silly: why would anyone re-sort an array that is already sorted? Of course, one wouldn't. But one might often need to sort an array that is already *nearly* sorted. In those cases, Theorem 13.7 suggests that the Insertion Sort will be almost linear. It certainly will be faster than the Bubble Sort or the Selection Sort.

13.5 THE MERGE SORT

The Merge Sort is a recursive algorithm. It works by splitting the array into sorted 2-element subarrays, merging them pairwise into sorted 4-element subarrays, merging them into sorted 8-element subarrays, *etc.*, until there are only two sorted subarrays to be merged. After that last merge, a single sorted "subarray" remains.

The C++ code exploits the fact that an array name is actually a pointer that supports pointer arithmetic. For example, `a+4` is the subarray of `a` that begins with element `a[4]`. So the call

```
sort(a+4, m);
```

applies the `sort()` function to the subarray { `a[4]`, `a[5]`, `...`, `a[4+m-1]` } containing `m` elements.

The Merge Sort is noticeably more complicated than any of the three previous algorithms. It is recursive and it uses an auxiliary function that has four separate loops. But these complicating factors produce an algorithm that is much faster than the others.

Algorithm 13.4 The Merge Sort

```
template<class T> void merge(T* a, int n1, int n2)
{ T* temp = new T[n1+n2];
  int i=0, j1=0, j2=0;
    while (j1 < n1 && j2 < n2)
      temp[i++] = ( a[j1] <= a[n1+j2] ? a[j1++] : a[n1+j2++] );
    while (j1 < n1)
      temp[i++] = a[j1++];
    while (j2 < n2)
      temp[i++] = (a+n1)[j2++];
    for (i=0; i < n1+n2; i++)
      a[i] = temp[i];
    delete [] temp;
}

template<class T> void sort(T* a, int n)
{ if (n > 1)
    { int n1 = n/2;
      int n2 = n - n1;
      sort(a, n1);
      sort(a+n1, n2);
      merge(a, n1, n2);
    }
}
```

Here is a trace of the Merge Sort on the same array of 9 integers:

a[0]	a[1]	a[2]	a[3]	a[4]	a[5]	a[6]	a[7]	a[8]
77	44	99	66	33	55	88	22	44
44	77							
		66	99					
	66	77						
						22	44	88
				22	33	44	55	
22	33	44	44	55	66	77	88	99

The calling tree for this example is shown on the next page.

The Merge Sort is correct, but its proof is beyond the scope of this outline.

Theorem 13.8 The complexity of the Merge Sort is $O(n \lg n)$.

Proof: In general, the Merge Sort works by repeatedly dividing the array in half until the pieces are singletons, and then it merges the pieces pairwise until a single piece remains. The number of iterations in the first part equals the number of times n can be halved: that is $\lg n$, the binary logarithm of n. In terms of the number and sizes of the pieces, the second part of the process reverses the first; merging two pieces reverses halving them. So the second part also has $\lg n$

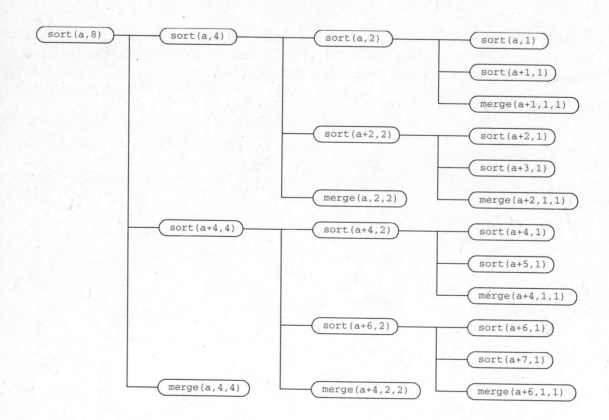

steps. So the entire algorithm has $2\lg n$ steps. Each step compares all n elements. So the total number of comparisons is $2n\lg n$, which is proportional to $n\lg n$.   **Q.E.D.**

This analysis can be visualized as shown in the diagram below.

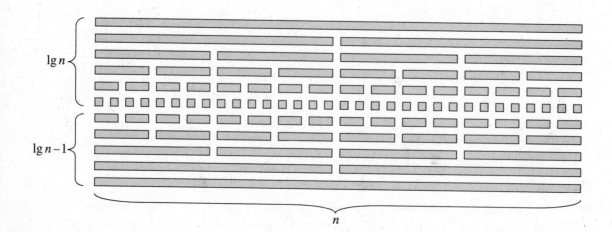

13.6 THE QUICK SORT

The Quick Sort is like the Merge Sort: it is recursive, it requires an auxiliary function with several loops, and it has $O(n \lg n)$ complexity. But in most cases, it is quicker than the Merge Sort; hence its name.

The Quick Sort works by partitioning the array into two pieces separated by a single element that is greater than all the elements in the left piece and smaller than all the elements in the right piece. This guarantees that that single element, called the *pivot* element, is in its correct position. Then the algorithm proceeds, applying the same method to the two pieces separately. This is naturally recursive, and very quick.

Algorithm 13.5 The Quick Sort
```
template<class T> void quicksort(T* a, int lo, int hi)
{ if (lo >= hi) return;
  T pivot = a[hi];
  int i = lo - 1;
  int j = hi;
  while (i < j)
  { while (a[++i] < pivot) ;
    while (j >= 0 && a[--j] > pivot) ;
    if (i < j) swap(a[i], a[j]);
  }
  swap(a[i], a[hi]);
  // Invariant: a[j] <= a[i] <= a[k] for lo <= j < i < k <= hi
  quicksort(a, lo, i-1);
  quicksort(a, i+1, hi);
}

template<class T> void sort(T* a, int n)
{ quicksort(a, 0, n-1);
}
```

EXAMPLE 13.4 Tracing the Quick Sort

Here is a trace of the Quick Sort on the same array of 9 integers:

a[0]	a[1]	a[2]	a[3]	a[4]	a[5]	a[6]	a[7]	a[8]
77	44	99	66	33	55	88	22	44
22							77	
		33		99				
			44					66
	33	44						
				55	99			
					66			99
							88	
						77	88	

Warning: Some authors write the Quick Sort algorithm so that the pivot element is chosen each time to be the first element of the subarray instead of the last element. Other authors choose the middle element. These versions work equally well.

The Quick Sort is correct, but its proof is beyond the scope of this outline.

Theorem 13.9 The complexity of the Quick Sort is $O(n \lg n)$.

The proof of the general statement in this theorem is beyond the scope of this outline. However, the analysis of the "best case" is not.

The Quick Sort proceeds through a series of steps. At each step, each piece of the array is split in two pieces. In the best case, each pivot element will be the median value among those in its piece. So the partition of each piece will result in it being split into two pieces of equal length. Thus, on each step, each piece is halved, like this:

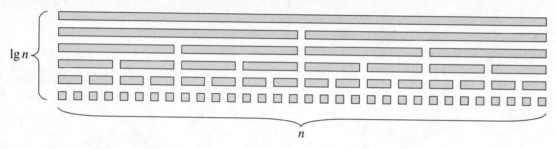

$\lg n$

n

With the splitting balanced this way, the number of steps is $\lg n$. Since each step compares all n elements, the entire process takes $n \lg n$ comparisons.

13.7 HEAPS

A binary tree is said to have the *heap property* if the elements along any path from root to leaf are nonincreasing. A *heap* is a complete binary tree that has the heap property.

EXAMPLE 13.5 A Heap

This binary tree shown here has the heap property. It has six root-to-leaf paths, one for each leaf: 88-66-55-33, 88-66-55-55, 88-66-66-11, 88-66-66-33, 88-77-55-22, and 88-77-44. Each one is nonincreasing (*i.e.*, $x \geq y$ if y follows x in the sequence).

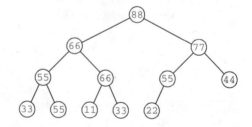

Note that the heap property is consistent with ordinary family trees of people: each child is younger than his/her parent.

Theorem 13.10 In a heap, every element is the maximum value of all the elements in its subtree.

Proof: Every element y in the subtree rooted at a given element x is in a path from x to a leaf. That path can be extended back up to the root of the whole tree. In that path, y follows x. So by the heap property, $x \geq y$.   **Q.E.D.**

Corollary 13.1 In a heap, the largest element is at the root, and the smallest element is at some leaf.

Warning: Some authors define a heap by the opposite condition: the elements along any path from root to leaf are nondecreasing. The two versions are equally useful. In this version, the root of every subtree contains the minimum value in the subtree.

Warning: The word "heap" is also frequently used to describe the collection of unallocated bytes in memory. Other authors refer to this as the *free store*.

By definition, a heap is a complete binary tree. This means that a heap can be stored naturally in an array.

EXAMPLE 13.6 A Heap Stored as an Array

Here is the heap from Example 13.5, stored in an array of 13 elements: Note that the heap property is

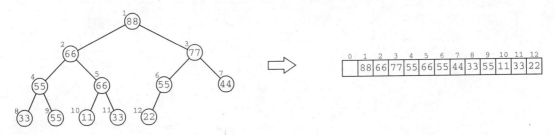

easy to see in the tree structure, but not clear at all in the linearized array.

13.8 THE HEAP SORT

A heap is, by definition, partially sorted, because each linear string from root to leaf is sorted. This leads to an efficient general sorting algorithm called the Heap Sort. As with all sorting algorithms, it applies to an array (or `vector`). But the underlying heap structure which the array represents is used to define this algorithm.

Like the Merge Sort and the Quick Sort, the Heap Sort uses an auxiliary function which is called from the `sort()` function. And also like the Merge Sort and the Quick Sort, the Heap Sort has complexity function $O(n \lg n)$. But unlike the Merge Sort and the Quick Sort, the Heap Sort is not recursive.

The natural mapping (Algorithm 10.1 on page 205) of a complete binary tree into an array maps the n elements of the tree into array elements `a[1]` through `a[n]`. But to be consistent with all our other sorting algorithms, the n elements should be stored in positions `a[0:n-1]` in the array. So for this reason, we modify the natural mapping so that the correspondence looks like this:

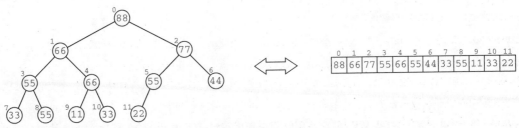

The only consequences of this modification are that now:
- the children of element k are elements $2k + 1$ and $2k + 2$;
- the parent of element k is element $(k - 1)/2$;

These recurrence relations are used in the algorithm to traverse paths back and forth between root and leaves.

Algorithm 13.6 The Heap Sort

```
template<class T> void heapify(T* a, int k, int n)
{ T t = a[k];
  while (k < n/2)
  { int j = 2*k + 1;                      // make j the oldest child of k
    if (j+1 < n && a[j] < a[j+1]) ++j;
    if (t > a[j]) break;
    a[k] = a[j];
    k = j;
  }
  a[k] = t;
}
template<class T> void sort(T* a, int n)
{ for (int i= n/2 - 1; i >= 0; i--)
    heapify(a, i, n);
  for (int i = n-1; i > 0; i--)
  { swap(a[0], a[i]);
    // Invariant: the elements a[i:n-1] are in the correct positions.
    heapify(a, 0, i);
    // Invariant: the subarray a[0:i-1] has the heap property.
  }
}
```

The `sort()` function first converts the array so that its underlying complete binary tree is transformed into a heap. This is done by applying the `heapify()` function to each nontrivial subtree. The nontrivial subtrees (*i.e.*, those having more than one element) are the subtrees that are rooted above the leaf level. In the array, the leaves are stored at positions `a[n/2]` through `a[n]`. So the first `for` loop in the `sort()` function applies the `heapify()` function to elements `a[n/2-1]` back through `a[0]` (which is the root of the underlying tree). The result is an array whose corresponding tree has the heap property:

Now the main (second) `for` loop progresses through `n-1` iterations. Each iteration does two things: it swaps the root element with element `a[i]`, and then it applies the `heapify()` function to the subtree of elements `a[0:i-1]`. That subtree consists of the part of the array that is still unsorted. Before the `swap()` executes on each iteration, the subarray `a[0:i]` has the heap property, so by Corollary 13.1 `a[i]` is the largest element in that subarray. That means that the `swap()` puts element `a[i]` in its correct position.

The first seven iterations of the main `for` loop have the effect shown by the seven pictures on the next two pages. The array (and its corresponding imaginary binary tree) is partitioned into two parts: the first part is the subarray `a[0:i-1]` that has the heap property, and the second part is the remaining `a[i:n-1]` whose elements are in their correct positions. The second part is shaded in each of the seven pictures below. Each iteration of the main `for` loop decrements the size of the first part and increments the size of the second part. So when the loop has finished, the first part is empty and the second (sorted) part constitutes the entire array. This analysis verifies that the Heap Sort works:

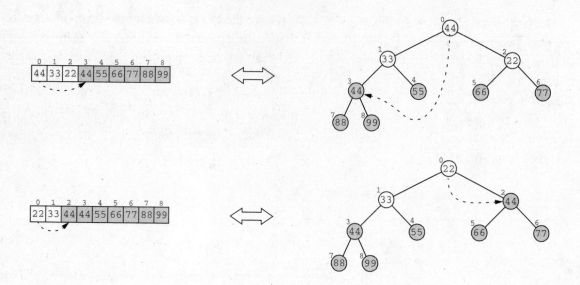

EXAMPLE 13.7 Tracing the Heap Sort

Here is the trace of the Heap Sort on this array:

a[0]	a[1]	a[2]	a[3]	a[4]	a[5]	a[6]	a[7]	a[8]
77	44	99	66	33	55	88	22	44
	66		33					
99		88				77		
44								99
88		77	44			44		
22							88	
77		55			22			
44						77		
66	44							
22					66			
55		22						
33				55				
44			33					
33			44					
44	33							
22		44						
33	22							
22	33							

Notice that, like the Bubble Sort, the Heap Sort does not detect when it is sorted. The last two swaps are made after the array is sorted.

Theorem 13.11 The complexity of the Heap Sort is $O(n \lg n)$.

Each call to the `heapify()` function takes at most $\lg n$ steps because it iterates only along a path from the current element down to a leaf. The longest such path for a complete binary tree of n elements is $\lg n$. The `heapify()` function is called $n/2$ times in the first `for` loop, and $n-1$ times in the second `for` loop. That comes to less than $(3n/2) \lg n$, which is proportional to $n \lg n$.

If we regard a sorting algorithm as a stream process wherein elements stream into an array in random order and then stream out in sorted order, then the Heap Sort can be regarded as an efficient mean between the extremes of the Selection Sort and the Insertion Sort. The Selection Sort does all its sorting during the removal stage of the process, having stored the elements in the unsorted order in which they arrived. The Insertion Sort does all its sorting during the insertion stage of the process, so that the elements can stream out of the array in the sorted order in which they were stored. But the Heap Sort does a partial sorting by inserting the elements into a heap and then finishes the sorting as the elements are removed from the heap. The payoff from this mean between the extremes is greater efficiency: $O(n \lg n)$ instead of $O(n^2)$.

13.9 THE SHELL SORT

The Shell Sort preprocesses the given array by applying the Insertion Sort to skip-arrays embedded within it. A *skip-array* is the array of elements {a[j], a[j+d], a[j+2*d], . . .} selected from a larger array a. The parameter d is called the *increment* of the skip-array. There are d such skip-arrays, one for each starting index j for 0 <= j < d. For example, the array

{ 34, 35, 36, 37, 38, 39, 40, 41, 42, 43, 44, 45, 46, 47, 48, 49, 50, 51, 52, 53, 54, 55 }

has the following four skip-arrays of increment 4:

{ 34, 38, 42, 46, 50, 54 }

{ 35, 39, 43, 47, 51, 55 }

{ 36, 40, 44, 48, 52 }

{ 37, 41, 45, 49, 53 }

Sorting the array's skip-arrays first renders the given array nearly sorted. And for nearly sorted arrays, the Insertion Sort runs in nearly linear time. Consequently, the Shell sort accelerates the Insertion Sort substantially.

Algorithm 13.7 The Shell Sort

```
template<class T> void sort(T* a, int n)
template<class T> void sort(T* a, int n)
{ int d=1,j;
  while (d<n/9)
    d = 3*d + 1;
  while (d>0)
  { for (int i=d; i<n; i++)
    { T t = a[i];
      j=i;
      while (j>=d && a[j-d]>t)
      { a[j] = a[j-d];
        j -= d;
      }
      a[j] = t;
    }
    // Invariant: a[j] <= a[j+d] <= a[j+2d] <= a[j+3d] <= ...
    //    for each j in the range 0 <= j < d.
    d /= 3;
  }
}
```

This implementation uses the increment sequence 1, 4, 13, 40, 121, 364, ... For example, on an array of 5000 elements, it first applies the Insertion Sort to each of the 364 skip-arrays with increment 364. Then it applies the Insertion Sort to each of the 121 skip-arrays with increment 121. Then it applies the Insertion Sort to each of the 40 skip-arrays with increment 40. This continues until it finally applies the Insertion Sort to the 1 skip-array with increment 1, *i.e.*, the full array. After the initial pass that sorts the skip-arrays with increment 364, each successive application of the Insertion Sort runs in nearly linear time because the successive skip-arrays are already nearly sorted.

The complxity of the Shell Sort remains unknown. Current estimates are about $O(n\sqrt{n})$.

13.10 THE SPEED LIMIT FOR EXCHANGE SORTS

Theorem 13.12 No sorting algorithm that rearranges the array by comparing its elements can have a worst-case complexity function better than $O(n \lg n)$.

Proof: Consider the decision tree that covers all possible outcomes of the algorithm on an array of size n. Since the algorithm rearranges the array by comparing its elements, each node in the decision tree represents a condition of the form `(a[i] < a[j])`. Each such condition has two possible outcomes (`true` or `false`), so the decision tree is a binary tree. And since the tree must cover all possible arrangements, it must have at least $n!$ leaves. Therefore, by Corollary 10.3 on page 203, the height of the decision tree must be at least $\lg(n!)$. In the worst case, the number of comparisons that the algorithm makes is the same as the height of the decision tree. Therefore, the algorithm's worst-case complexity function must be $O(\lg(n!))$.

Now by Stirling's Formula (Theorem B.11 on page 281),

$$n! \approx \sqrt{2n\pi}\left(\frac{n}{e}\right)^n$$

so

$$\log(n!) \approx \log\left(\sqrt{2n\pi}\left(\frac{n}{e}\right)^n\right) \approx \log(n^n) = n\log n$$

(Here, "log" means the binary logarithm $\lg = \log_2$.) Therefore, the algorithm's worst-case complexity function must be $O(n \lg n)$.   **Q.E.D.**

Review Questions

13.1   Why is the Bubble Sort so slow?

13.2   The proof to Theorem 13.2 concludes that the Bubble Sort makes $n(n-1)/2$ comparisons. How does it follow that its complexity function is $O(n^2)$?

Problems

13.1   If an $O(n^2)$ algorithm (*e.g.*, the Bubble Sort, the Selection Sort, or the Insertion Sort) takes 3.1 milliseconds to run on an array of 200 elements, how long would you expect it to take to run on a similar array of:
a. 400 elements?

b. 40,000 elements?

13.2   If an O($n \lg n$) algorithm (*e.g.*, the Merge Sort, the Quick Sort, or the Heap Sort) takes 3.1 milliseconds to run on an array of 200 elements, how long would you expect it to take to run on a similar array of 40,000 elements?

13.3   The Insertion Sort runs in linear time on an array that is already sorted. How does it do on an array that is sorted in reverse order?

13.4   How does the Bubble Sort perform on:
a. an array that is already sorted?
b. an array that is sorted in reverse order?

13.5   How does the Selection Sort perform on:
a. an array that is already sorted?
b. an array that is sorted in reverse order?

13.6   How does the Merge Sort perform on:
a. an array that is already sorted?
b. an array that is sorted in reverse order?

13.7   How does the Quick Sort perform on:
a. an array that is already sorted?
b. an array that is sorted in reverse order?

13.8   How does the Heap Sort perform on:
a. an array that is already sorted?
b. an array that is sorted in reverse order?

13.9   The Bubble Sort, the Selection Sort, and the Insertion Sort are all O(n^2) algorithms. Which is the fastest, and which is the slowest among them?

13.10 The Merge Sort, the Quick Sort, and the Heap Sort are all O($n \lg n$) algorithms. Which is the fastest, and which is the slowest among them?

13.11 Improve the Bubble Sort by making it smart enough to stop when the array is sorted.

13.12 The Merge Sort applies the general method, known as *divide and conquer*, to sort an array. It divides the array into pieces and applies itself recursively to each piece. What other sorting algorithm(s) use this method?

13.13 The Merge Sort is *parallelizable*. That means that parts of it can be performed simultaneously, independent of each other, provided that the computer has multiple processors that can run in parallel. This works for the Merge Sort because several different parts of the array can be subdivided or merged independently of other parts. Which of the other sorting algorithms described in this chapter are parallelizable.

13.14 A sorting algorithm is said to be *stable* if it preserves the order of equal elements. Which of the sorting algorithms are stable?

13.15 Trace by hand the execution of each of the first six sorting algorithms on the array:
```
int a[] = { 44, 77, 55, 99, 66, 33, 22, 88, 77 }
```

Answers to Review Questions

13.1   The Bubble Sort is so slow because it operates only locally. Each element moves only one position at a time. For example, the element 99 in Example 13.1 is moved by six separate calls to the swap() function to be put into its correct position at a[8].

13.2   The jump from $n(n-1)/2$ to O(n^2) is justified as follows:
a. For large values of n (*e.g.*, $n > 1000$), $n(n-1)/2$ is nearly the same as $n^2/2$.

b. A complexity function is used only for comparisons. For example, how much longer will it take to sort an array that is twice as large? For that analysis, proportional functions are equivalent. And since $n^2/2$ is proportional to n^2, we can drop the (1/2) factor and simplify our conclusion with $O(n^2)$.

Soultions to Problems

13.1 The $O(n^2)$ algorithm should take:

a. 12.4 milliseconds (4 times as long) to run on the 400-element array;

b. 124 seconds (40,000 times as long) to run on the 40,000-element array. That's about 2 minutes. This answer can be computed algebraically as follows. The running time t is proportional to n^2, so there is some constant c for which $t = c \cdot n^2$. If it takes $t = 3.1$ milliseconds to sort $n = 200$ elements, then (3.1 milliseconds) $= c \cdot (200$ elements$)^2$, so $c = (3.1$ milliseconds$)/(200$ elements$)^2 = 0.0000775$ milliseconds/element^2. Then, for $n = 40,000$, $t = c \cdot n^2 = (0.0000775$ milliseconds/element$^2) \cdot (40,000$ elements$)^2 = 124,000$ milliseconds $= 124$ seconds.

13.2 The $O(n \lg n)$ algorithm should take 1.24 seconds (400 times as long) to run on the 40,000-element array. This answer can be computed algebraically. The running time t is proportional to $n \lg n$, so there is some constant c for which $t = c \cdot n \lg n$. If it takes $t = 3.1$ milliseconds to sort $n = 200$ elements, then $(3.1) = c \cdot (200) \lg(200)$, so $c = (3.1$ milliseconds$)/(200 \cdot \lg(200)) = 0.0155/\lg(200)$. Then, for $n = 40,000$, $t = c \cdot n \lg n = (0.0155/\lg(200))(40,000 \cdot \lg(40,000)) = 620 \cdot (\lg(40,000)/\lg(200))$. Now $40,000 = 200^2$, so $\lg(40,000) = \lg(200^2) = 2 \cdot \lg 200$. Thus, $\lg(40,000)/\lg(200) = 2$, so $t = 620 \cdot 2$ milliseconds $= 1240$ milliseconds $= 1.24$ s.

13.3 The Insertion Sort has its worst performance on an array that is sorted in reverse order, because each new element inserted requires all of the elements on its left to be shifted one position to the right.

13.4 The Bubble Sort, as implemented in Algorithm 13.1, is *insensitive to input*. That means that it will execute the same number $n(n-1)/2$ of comparisons regardless of the original order of the elements in the array. So it doesn't matter whether the array is already sorted or whether it is sorted in reverse order; it is still very slow.

13.5 The Selection Sort is also insensitive to input: it takes about the same amount of time to sort arrays of the same size, regardless of their initial order.

13.6 The Merge Sort is also insensitive to input: it takes about the same amount of time to sort arrays of the same size, regardless of their initial order.

13.7 The Quick Sort is quite sensitive to input. As implemented in Algorithm 13.5, the Quick Sort will degrade into an $O(n^2)$ algorithm in the special cases where the array is initially sorted in either order. That is because the pivot element will always be an extreme value within its subarray, so the partitioning splits the subarray very unevenly, thereby requiring n steps instead of $\lg n$.

13.8 The Heap Sort is a little sensitive to input, but not much. The `heapify()` function may require fewer than $\lg n$ iterations.

13.9 The Bubble Sort is slower than the Selection Sort, and the Insertion Sort (in most cases) is a little faster.

13.10 The Merge Sort is slower than the Heap Sort, and the Quick Sort (in most cases) is faster.

13.11
```
template<class T>
void sort(T* a, int n)
{ bool sorted=false;
  for (int i=1; i < n && !sorted; i++)
    for (int j=1; j <= n-i; j++)
    { sorted = true;
      if (a[j-1] > a[j])
      { swap(a[j-1], a[j]);
        sorted = false;
      }
    }.
}
```

13.12 Among the six sorting algorithms presented here, only the Merge Sort and the Quick Sort apply the method of *divide and conquer*. Like the Merge Sort, the Quick Sort divides the array into pieces and then applies itself recursively to each piece.

13.13 Besides the Merge Sort, the only other sorting algorithm among the first six described here that is parallelizable is the Quick Sort. The partitioning process in the `quicksort()` function could be performed simultaneously on several separate sections of the array.

13.14 The Quick Sort and the Shell Sort are unstable. All the other exchange sorts discussed in this chapter are stable.

13.15 *a.* Trace of the Bubble Sort:

a[0]	a[1]	a[2]	a[3]	a[4]	a[5]	a[6]	a[7]	a[8]
44	77	55	99	66	33	22	88	77
	55	77						
			66	99				
			33	99				
				22	99			
					88	99		
						77	99	
		66	77					
			33	77				
				22	77			
						77	88	
		33	66					
			22	66				
	33	55						
		22	55					
33	44							
	22	44						
22	33							

b. Trace of the Selection Sort:

a[0]	a[1]	a[2]	a[3]	a[4]	a[5]	a[6]	a[7]	a[8]
44	77	55	99	66	33	22	88	77
22						44		
	33				77			
		44				55		
			55			99		
						77		99

c. Trace of the Insertion Sort:

a[0]	a[1]	a[2]	a[3]	a[4]	a[5]	a[6]	a[7]	a[8]
44	77	55	99	66	33	22	88	77
	55	77						
		66	77	99				
33	44	55	66	77	99			
22	33	44	55	66	77	99		
						88	99	
						77	88	99

d. Trace of the Merge Sort:

a[0]	a[1]	a[2]	a[3]	a[4]	a[5]	a[6]	a[7]	a[8]
44	77	55	99	66	33	22	88	77
44	55	77	99					
				33	66			
							77	88
				22	33	66	77	88
22	33	44	55	66	77	77	88	99

e. Trace of the Quick Sort:

a[0]	a[1]	a[2]	a[3]	a[4]	a[5]	a[6]	a[7]	a[8]
44	77	55	99	66	33	22	88	77
			22			99		
						77		99
22			44					
	33				77			
		44	55					

f. Trace of the Heap Sort:

a[0]	a[1]	a[2]	a[3]	a[4]	a[5]	a[6]	a[7]	a[8]
44	77	55	99	66	33	22	88	77
	99		77					
			88				77	
99	44							
	88		44					
			77				44	
77								99
88	77							
44							88	
77	44							
	77		44					
22						77		
77	22							
	66			22				
33					77			
66	33							

a[0]	a[1]	a[2]	a[3]	a[4]	a[5]	a[6]	a[7]	a[8]
	44		33					
22				66				
55		22						
		33	22					
22			55					
44	22							
33		44						
22	33							

Appendix A

References

Publishers:

Addison-Wesley Publishing Company, Reading, MA, `http://www.awl.com`
CRC Press, Boca Raton, FL, `http://www.crcpress.com`
Harcourt/Academic Press, Orlando, FL, `http://www.apnet.com`
John Wiler & Sons, New York, NY, `http://www.wiley.com`
Jones and Bartlett Publishers, Sudbury, MA, `http://www.jbpub.com`
Macmillan, New York, NY, `http://www.macmillan.com`
McGraw-Hill, New York, NY, `http://www.mhhe.com`
Morgan Kaufmann Publishers, San Francisco, CA, `http://www.mkp.com`
Oxford University Press, New York, NY, `http://www.oup-usa.com`
Perseus Books, Reading, MA, `http://www.perseusbooksgroup.com`
Prentice Hall, Englewood Cliffs, NJ, `http://www.prenhall.com`
PWS Publishing Company, Boston, MA, `http://www.brookscole.com`
Springer-Verlag, New York, NY, `http://link.springer.de`
W. H. Freeman and Co., Berlin, `http://www.macmillan-press.co.uk/science`
WCB/McGraw-Hill, New York, NY, `http://www.mcgraw-hill.com`

[Adams]

C++ An Introduction to Computing, by Joel Adams, Sanford Leestma, and Larry Nyhoff.
Prentice Hall, Englewood Cliffs, NJ, 1995, 0-02-369402-5.

[Aho1]

Data Structures and Algorithms, by Alfred V. Aho, John E. Hopcroft, and Jeffrey D. Ullman.
Addison-Wesley Publishing Company, Reading, MA, 1983, 0-201-00023-7.

[Aho2]

Foundations of Computer Science, by Alfred V. Aho, and Jeffrey D. Ullman.
W. H. Freeman and Co., New York, NY, 1995, 0-7167-8284-7.

[Baeza-Yates]

Handbook of Algorithms and Data Structures, by R. Baeza-Yates and G. H. Gonnet.
Addison-Wesley Publishing Company, Reading, MA, 1994.

[Barton]

Scientific and Engineering C++, by John J. Barton and Lee R. Nackman.
Addison-Wesley Publishing Company, Reading, MA, 1994, 0-201-53393-6.

[Bergin]

Data Abstraction, the Object-Oriented Approach Using C++, by Joseph Bergin.
McGraw-Hill, Inc., New York, NY, 1994, 0-07-911691-4.

[Berman1]

Data Structures via C++, by A. Michael Berman.
Oxford University Press, 1997, 0-19-510843-4.

[Berman2]

Introduction to Combinatorics, by Gerald Berman and K. D. Fryer.
Academic Press, New York, NY, 1972, 0-07-911691-4.

[Budd1]

An Introduction to Object-Oriented Programming, Second Edition, by Timothy A. Budd.
Addison-Wesley Publishing Company, Reading, MA, 1994, 0-201-82419-1.

[Budd2]

Data Structures in C++ Using the Standard Template Library, by Timothy A. Budd.
Addison-Wesley Publishing Company, Reading, MA, 1998, 0-201-30879-7.

[Buzzi-Ferraris]

Scientific C++, by G. Buzzi-Ferraris.
Addison-Wesley Publishing Company, Reading, MA, 1994, 0-201-63192-X.

[Capper]

Introducing C++ for Scientists, Engineers and Mathematicians, by D. M. Capper.
Springer-Verlag, London, 1994, 3-540-19847-4.

[Cargill]

C++ Programming Style, by Tom Cargill.
Addison-Wesley Publishing Company, Reading, MA, 1992, 0-201-56365-7.

[Carroll]

Designing and Coding Reusable C++, by Martin D. Carroll and Margaret A. Ellis.
Addison-Wesley Publishing Company, Reading, MA, 1995, 0-201-51284-X.

[Cline]

C++ FAQs, Second Edition, by Marshall P. Cline, Greg A. Lomow, and Mike Girou.
Addison-Wesley Publishing Company, Reading, MA, 1999, 0-201-30983-1.

[Collins]

Data Structures: An Object-Oriented Approach, by William J. Collins.
Addison-Wesley Publishing Company, Reading, MA, 1992, 0-201-56953-1.

[Coplien]

Advanced C++, Programming Styles and Idioms, by James O. Coplien.
Addison-Wesley Publishing Company, Reading, MA, 1992, 0-201-54855-0.

[Cormen]

Introduction to Algorithms, by T. H. Cormen, C. E. Leierson, and R. L. Rivest.
MIT Press/McGraw-Hill, Cambridge, MA, 1990.

[Dale1]

Abstract Data Types, by Nell Dale and Henry M. Walker.
D. C. Heath and Company, Lexington, MA, 1996, 0-669-35444-9.

[Dale2]

C++ Plus Data Structures, by Nell Dale.
Jones & Bartlett, Sudbury, MA, 1999, 0-7637-0621-3.

[Decker]

Working Classes, Data Structures and Algorithms Using C++, by Rick Decker and Stuart Hirshfield.
PWS Publishing Company, Boston, MA, 1996, 0-534-94566-X.

[Deitel]

C++ How to Program, Second Edition, by H. M. Deitel and P. J. Deitel.
Prentice Hall, Englewood Cliffs, NJ, 1998, 0-13-528910-6.

[Dorfman]

C++ by Example: Object-Oriented Analysis, Design, & Programming, by L. Dorfman.
McGraw-Hill, New York, NY, 1995, 0-07-911954-9.

[Drozdek]

Data Structures and Algorithms in C++, by Adam Drozdek.
PWS Publishing Company, Boston, MA, 1996, 0-534-94974-6.

[Ellis]

The Annotated C++ Reference Manual, by Margaret A. Ellis and Bjarne Stroustrup.
Addison-Wesley Publishing Company, Reading, MA, 1992, 0-201-51459-1.

[Flamig]

Practical C++ Algorithms and Data Structures, by B. Flamig.
John Wiley & Sons, Inc, New York, NY, 1993, 0-471-55863-X.

[Ford]

Data Structures with C++, by William Ford and William Topp.
Prentice-Hall, Englewood Cliffs, NJ, 1996, 0-02-420971-6.

[Gersting]

Mathematical Structures for Computer Science, Fourth Edition, by Judith L. Gersting.
W. H. Freeman and Company, New York, NY, 1999, 0-7167-8306-1.

[Gorlen]

Data Abstraction and Object-Oriented Programming in C++, by K.E. Gorlen, *et al.*
John Wiley & Sons, New York, NY, 1993, 0-471-55863-X.

[Graham]

Concrete Mathematics, by R. L. Graham, D. E. Knuth, and O. Patashnik.
Addison-Wesley Publishing Company, Reading, MA, 1988.

[Harary]

Graph Theory, by Frank Harary.
Perseus Books, Reading, MA, 1969, 0-201-41033-8.

[Hausner]

Discrete Mathematics, by Melvin Hausner.
Saunders College Publishing, Orlando, FL, 1992, 0-03-003278-4.

[Headington]

Data Abstraction and Structures Using C++, by Mark R. Headington and David D. Riley.
Jones and Bartlett Publishers, Sudbury, MA, 1997, 0-7637-0295-1.

[Henderson]

Object-Oriented Specification and Design with C++, by Peter Henderson.
McGraw-Hill Book Company, London, UK, 1993, 0-07-707585-4.

[Horowitz]

Fundamentals of Data Structures in C++, by Ellis Horowitz, Sartaj Sahni, and Dinesh Mehta.
W. H. Freeman and Company, New York, NY, 1995, 0-7167-8292-8.

[Horstmann]

Mastering Object Oriented Design in C++, by Cay S. Horstmann.
John Wiley & Sons, New York, NY, 1994, 0-471-59484-9.

[Hubbard1]

Programming with C++, Second Edition, by John R. Hubbard.
McGraw-Hill, New York, NY, 1999, 0-07-030837-3.

[Hubbard2]

Fundamentals of Computing with C++, by John R. Hubbard.
McGraw-Hill, New York, NY, 1996, 0-07-030868-3.

[Ince]

Object-Oriented Software Engineering with C++, by D. Ince.
McGraw-Hill, New York, NY, 1991, 0-07-707402-5.

[Johnsonbaugh1]

Discrete Mathematics, Third Edition, by Richard Johnsonbaugh.
Macmillan, 1993, 0-02-360721-1.

[Johnsonbaugh2]

Object-Oriented Programming in C++, by Richard Johnsonbaugh and Martin Kalin.
Prentice Hall, Englewood Cliffs, NJ, 1995, 0-02-360682-7.

[Josuttis]

The C++ Standard Library: A Tutorial and Reference, by Nicolai M. Josuttis.
Addison-Wesley Publishing Company, Reading, MA, 1999, 0-201-37926-0.

[Knuth1]

The Art of Computer Programming, Vol. 1: Fundamental Algorithms, Third Edition, by Donald E. Knuth.
Addison-Wesley Publishing Company, Reading, MA, 1997, 0-201-89683-4.

[Knuth2]

The Art of Computer Programming, Vol. 2: Seminumerical Algorithms, Third Edition, by D. E. Knuth.
Addison-Wesley Publishing Company, Reading, MA, 1998, 0-201-89684-2.

[Knuth3]

The Art of Computer Programming, Vol. 3: Sorting and Searching, Second Edition, by Donald E. Knuth.
Addison-Wesley Publishing Company, Reading, MA, 1998, 0-201-89685-0.

[Kolman]

Discrete Mathematical Structures, Third Edition, by Bernard Kolman, R. C. Busby, and S. Ross.
Prentice Hall, Englewood Cliffs, NJ, 1996, 0-13-320912-1.

[Kreher]

Combinatorial Algorithms, by Donald L. Kreher and Douglas R. Stinson.
CRC Press, Boca Raton, FL, 1999, 0-8493-3988-X.

[Ladd]

C++ Templates and Tools, by Scott Robert Ladd.
M&T Books, New York, NY, 1995, 0-55851-437-6.

[Langsam]

Data Structures Using C and C++, Second Edition, by Y. Langsam, M. Augenstein, and A. Tenenbaum.
Prentice Hall, Englewood Cliffs, NJ, 1996, 0-13-036997-7.

[Lipschutz1]

Schaum's Outline of Discrete Mathematics, Seymour Lipschutz.
McGraw-Hill, Inc., New York, NY, 1976, 0-07-037981-5.

[Lipschutz2]

Schaum's Outline of Essential Computer Mathematics, Seymour Lipschutz.
McGraw-Hill, Inc., New York, NY, 1982, 0-07-037990-3.

[Lipschutz3]

Schaum's Outline of Data Structures, Seymour Lipschutz.
McGraw-Hill, Inc., New York, NY, 1986, 0-07-038001-5.

[Main]

Data Structures & Other Objects, by Michael Main and Walter Savitch.
Addison-Wesley Publishing Company, Reading, MA, 1997, 0-8053-7470-1.

[Meyers1]

Effective C++, by Scott Meyers.
Addison-Wesley Publishing Company, Reading, MA, 1992.

[Meyers2]

More Effective C++, by Scott Meyers.
Addison-Wesley Publishing Company, Reading, MA, 1992, 0-201-63371-X.

[Model]

Data Structures, Data Abstraction: A Contemporary Introduction Using C++, by M. L. Model.
Prentice Hall, Englewood Cliffs, NJ, 1994, 0-13-088782-X.

[Murray]

C++ Strategies and Tactics, by Robert B. Murray.
Addison-Wesley Publishing Company, Reading, MA, 1993, 0-201-56382-7.

[Nelson]

C++ Programmers Guide to the Standard Template Library, by Mark Nelson.
IDG Books Worldwide, Inc., Foster City, CA, 1995, 0-56884-314-3.

[Parker]

Algorithms and Data Structures in C++, by A. Parker.
CRC Press, Boca Raton, FL, 1993, 0-8493-7171-6.

[Perry]

An Introduction to Object-Oriented Design in C++, by Jo Ellen Perry and Harold D. Levin.
Addison-Wesley Publishing Company, Reading, MA, 1996, 0-201-76564-0.

[Plauger1]

The Standard C Library, by P. J. Plauger.
Prentice Hall, Englewood Cliffs, NJ, 1992, 0-13-131509-9.

[Plauger2]

The Draft Standard C++ Library, by P. J. Plauger.
Prentice Hall, Englewood Cliffs, NJ, 1995, 0-13-117003-1.

[Preiss]

Data Structures and Algorithms with Object-Oriented Design Patterns in C++, by Bruno R. Preiss.
John Wiley & Sons, New York, NY, 1999, 0-471-24134-2.

[Riordan]

Introduction to Combinatorial Analysis, by John Riordan.
John Wiley & Sons, New York, NY, 1958.

[Rudd]

Mastering C++, by Anthony Rudd.
John Wiley & Sons, New York, NY, 1995, 0-471-06565-X.

[Sahni]

Data Structures, Algorithms, and Applications in C++, by Sartaj Sahni.
ACB/McGraw-Hill, New York, NY, 1998, 0-07-109219-6.

[Savitch]

Problem Solving with C++, by Walter Savitch.
Addison-Wesley Publishing Company, Reading, MA, 1996, 0-8053-7440-X.

[Schildt1]

C++ from the Ground Up, by Herbert Schildt.
Osborne/McGraw-Hill, New York, NY, 1994, 0-07-881969-5.

[Schildt2]

C++: The Complete Reference, Third Edition, by Herbert Schildt.
Osborne/McGraw-Hill, New York, NY, 1995, 0-07-882123-1.

[Schildt3]

STL Programming from the Ground Up, by Herbert. Schildt.
Osborne/McGraw-Hill, New York, NY, 1999, 0-07-882507-5.

[Sedgewick]

Algorithms in C++, Third Edition, by Robert Sedgewick.
Addison-Wesley Publishing Company, Reading, MA, 1998, 0-201-35088-2.

[Sengupta]

C++ Object-Oriented Data Structures, by Saumyendra Sengupta and Carl Phillip Korobkin.
Springer-Verlag, New York, NY, 1994, 0-387-94194-0

[Sessions]

Object-Oriented Data Structures   by Roger Sessions.
Prentice Hall, Englewood Cliffs,   , 0-13-630104-5.

[Standish]

Data Structures, Algorithms, and Software Principles, by T. A. Standish.
Addison-Wesley Publishing Company, Reading, MA, 1995.

[Stepanov]

"The Standard Template Library," *Technical Report HPL-94-34*, by A. A. Stepanov and M. Lee.
Hewlett-Packard Laboratories, April 1994.

[Stroustrup1]

The Design and Evolution of C++, by Bjarne Stroustrup.
Addison-Wesley Publishing Company, Reading, MA, 1994, 0-201-54330-3.

[Stroustrup2]

The C++ Programming Language, Third Edition, by Bjarne Stroustrup.
Addison-Wesley Publishing Company, Reading, MA, 1997, 0-201-88954-4.

[Teale]

C++ IOStreams, by Steve Teale.
Addison-Wesley Publishing Company, Reading, MA, 1993, 0-201-59641-5.

[Wang]

C++ with Object-Oriented Programming, by Paul S. Wang.
PWS Publishing Company, Boston, MA, 1994, 0-534-19644-6.

[Weiss1]

Algorithms, Data Structures, and Problem Solving with C++, by Mark Allen Weiss.
Addison-Wesley Publishing Company, Reading, MA, 1996, 0-8053-1666-3.

[Weiss2]

Data Structures & Algorithm Analysis in C++, Second Edition, by Mark Allen Weiss.
Addison-Wesley Publishing Company, Reading, MA, 1999, 0-201-36122-1.

[Wirth]

Algorithms + Data Structures = Programs, by Nicklaus Wirth.
Prentice-Hall, Inc., Englewood Cliffs, NJ, 1976, 0-13-022418-9.

Appendix B

Essential Mathematics

B.1 THE FLOOR AND CEILING FUNCTIONS

The *floor* of a real number x, denoted by $\lfloor x \rfloor$, is the greatest integer that is not greater than x. The *ceiling* of x, denoted by $\lceil x \rceil$, is the least integer that is not less than x.

Theorem B.1 The Floor and Ceiling Functions
If $m = \lfloor x \rfloor$ and $n = \lceil x \rceil$, then
$$m \le x < m + 1$$
$$n - 1 < x \le n$$
$$m \le x \le n$$
Moreover, if x is an integer then $x = m = n$; otherwise, $m < x < n$.

B.2 LOGARITHMS

The *logarithm* of a number x is the exponential power of the given base that produces the value x. For example, the base 10 logarithm of 1000 is 3 ($\log_{10} 1000 = 3$) because 3 is the exponential power of 10 that produces the value 1000: $10^3 = 1000$.

Social scientists usually use base 10 and write $\log x$ for $\log_{10} x$; this is called the *common logarithm* or the *Briggsian logarithm*. Physical scientists and mathematicians usually use base e ($= 2.718281828459$) and write $\ln x$ for $\log_e x$; this is called the *natural logarithm* or the *Naperian logarithm*. Computer scientists usually use base 2 and write $\lg x$ for $\log_2 x$; this is called the *binary logarithm* or just the *binary log*.

As mathematical functions, logarithms are the inverses of exponential functions:
$$y = \log_b x \Leftrightarrow b^y = x$$
For example, $\log_2 256 = 8$ because $2^8 = 256$. This equivalence may be taken as the definition of logarithms. The following properties of logarithms follow from this definition.

Theorem B.2 The Laws of Logarithms
$$\log_b(b^y) = y$$
$$b^{(\log_b x)} = x$$
$$\log_b x = \frac{\log_c x}{\log_c b}$$
$$\log_b uv = \log_b u + \log_b v$$
$$\log_b u/v = \log_b u - \log_b v$$
$$\log_b u^v = v \log_b u$$

EXAMPLE B.1 Applying the Laws of Logarithms

$$\log_2 256 = \log_2(2^8) = 8$$

$$\log_2 1000 = \frac{\log_{10} 1000}{\log_{10} 2} = \frac{3}{0.30103} = 9.966$$

$$\log_2 1,000,000,000,000 = \log_2 1000^4 = 4(\log_2 1000) = 4(9.966) = 39.86$$

The *integral binary logarithm* of a number n is $\lfloor \log_2 n \rfloor$. This integer is essentially the number of times that n can be divided by 2 before reaching 1. For example, the integral binary logarithm of 1000 is 9 because 1000 can be divided by 2 10 times: 500, 250, 125, 62, 31, 15, 7, 3, 1.

B.3 THE FIRST PRINCIPLE OF MATHEMATICAL INDUCTION

The First Principle of Mathematical Induction, also called "weak induction," is often used to prove formulas about the natural numbers.

Theorem B.3 (The First Principle of Mathematical Induction)
If $\{P(1), P(2), P(3), P(4), \dots\}$ is a sequence of statements with the following two properties, then all of the statements are true:
1. $P(1)$ is true.
2. Any one of the statements can be deduced from its predecessor.

EXAMPLE B.2 Using Weak Induction

Prove the inequality $2^n \le (n+1)!$ for all $n \ge 1$
The formula asserts the following sequence of statements:

$P(1)$: $\quad 2^1 \le 2!$
$P(2)$: $\quad 2^2 \le 3!$
$P(3)$: $\quad 2^3 \le 4!$
$P(4)$: $\quad 2^4 \le 5!$
etc.

These first four statements are obviously true, because:

$2^1 = 2 \le 2 = 2!$
$2^2 = 4 \le 6 = 3!$
$2^3 = 8 \le 24 = 4!$
$2^4 = 16 \le 120 = 5!$

Any one of the other formulas could also be verified directly this way. But they can't all be verified this way because there are infinitely many of them.

Part 1 of Theorem B.3 requires that $P(1)$ be verified. This was done in the preceding paragraph. Part 2 of the theorem requires the deduction of $P(n)$ from $P(n-1)$. So assume that $P(n-1)$ is true for some $n > 1$. That means we are assuming that $2^{n-1} \le n!$ is true for some n. Then to deduce $P(n)$ from that assumption, look for some relationship between $P(n-1)$ and $P(n)$; that is, try to relate the two formulas:

$P(n-1)$: $\quad 2^{n-1} \le n!$
$P(n)$: $\quad 2^n \le (n+1)!$

The statement $P(n)$ can be rewritten as:

$P(n)$: $\quad (2)(2^{n-1}) \le (n+1)(n!)$

Now the progress from $P(n-1)$ to $P(n)$ is apparent: the left side of the inequality increases by a factor of 2 while the right side increases by a factor of $n+1$. So as long as $n+1 > 2$, the increase on the left is less than the increase on the right. And we know that $n+1 > 2$ because $n > 1$. Thus we have the implication:

$2^{n-1} \le n! \quad \Rightarrow \quad 2^n \le (n+1)!$
i.e., $\quad P(n-1) \quad \Rightarrow \quad P(n)$

This is the requirement of part 2 of Theorem B.3. Thus we can conclude that $P(n)$ is true for all $n \geq 1$.

Q.E.D.

Part 1 of Theorem B.3 is called the *basis* of the proof and part 2 is called the *inductive step*. The assumption in part 2 that $P(n)$ is true for some n is called the *inductive hypothesis*.

B.4 THE SECOND PRINCIPLE OF MATHEMATICAL INDUCTION

The Second Principle of Mathematical Induction, also called "strong induction," is nearly the same as the First Principle. The only difference is in the inductive step (part 2).

Theorem B.4 The Second Principle of Mathematical Induction
If $\{P(1), P(2), P(3), P(4), \dots \}$ is a sequence of statements with the following two properties, then all of the statements are true:
1. $P(1)$ is true.
2. Any one of the statements can be deduced from <u>all</u> of its predecessors.

The inductive step (part 2) means that $P(n)$ can be deduced from the assumption that all of its preceding statements $\{P(1), P(2), P(3), \dots, P(n-1)\}$ are true.

EXAMPLE B.3 Proof of the Fundamental Theorem of Arithmetic

Theorem B.5 The Fundamental Theorem of Arithmetic
Every positive integer has a unique representation as a product of powers of prime numbers:

$$p_1^{n_1} \cdot p_2^{n_2} \cdot p_3^{n_3} \cdot \cdot \cdot p_k^{n_k}$$

where $p_1, p_2, p_3, \dots$ are the prime numbers: $p_1 = 2, p_2 = 3, p_3 = 5$, *etc.*, and each n_j is a nonnegative integer.

For example, the positive integer 23,115,456 has the unique representation $2^6 3^4 5^0 7^3 11^0 13^1$.

The proof applies the Second Principle of Mathematical Induction to the sequence of statements:

$P(1)$ = "1 has a unique representation as a product of prime numbers."
$P(2)$ = "2 has a unique representation as a product of prime numbers."
$P(3)$ = "3 has a unique representation as a product of prime numbers."
$P(4)$ = "4 has a unique representation as a product of prime numbers."
etc.

These first four statements are true because:

$1 = 2^0$
$2 = 2^1$
$3 = 3^1$
$4 = 2^2$

The first of these statements verifies the basis of the induction. To verify the inductive step, we assume that all the statements $\{P(1), P(2), P(3), \dots, P(n-1)\}$ are true for some $n > 1$.

If n has a prime factor, call it p and let $m = n/p$. Then m is a positive integer that is less than n, so by the inductive hypothesis, $P(m)$ must be true; *i.e.*, m has a unique representation as a product of prime powers. But then so does n, because $n = p \cdot m$. Thus $P(n)$ is true in this case.

If n has no prime factors, then it must be a prime number itself, so it certainly does have a unique representation as a product of prime powers: $n = n^1$. Thus $P(n)$ is true in this case.

The proof is complete because we have deduced $P(n)$ by assuming that $\{P(1), P(2), P(3), ..., P(n-1)\}$ are true.   **Q.E.D.**

B.5 GEOMETRIC SERIES

A *geometric series* is a sum in which each term is the same multiple of its previous term. For example, $10 + 30 + 90 + 270 + 810 + 2430 + \cdots$ is a geometric series because each term is 3 times the size of its predecessor. The multiplier 3 is called the *common ratio* of the series.

Theorem B.6 Sum of a Finite Geometric Series

$$a + ar + ar^2 + ar^3 + \cdots + ar^{n-1} = \frac{a(1 - r^n)}{1 - r}$$

Here, a is the first term of the series, r is the common ratio, and n is the number of terms in the sum.

EXAMPLE B.4 Finding the Sum of a Finite Geometric Series

$10 + 30 + 90 + 270 + 810 + 2{,}430 = 10(1 - 3^6)/(1 - 3) = 10(1 - 729)/(-2) = 10(-728)/(-2) = 3{,}640$

Theorem B.7 The Sum of an Infinite Geometric Series

$$+ ar + ar^2 + ar^3 + \cdots = \frac{a}{1 - r}$$

This formula is valid only for $-1 < r < 1$.

EXAMPLE B.5 Finding the Sum of an Infinite Geometric Series

$6 + 3 + 3/2 + 3/4 + 3/8 + \cdots = 6/(1 - 1/2) = 6/(1/2) = 12$

B.6 SUMMATION FORMULAS

Theorem B.8 Sum of the First n Positive Integers

$$+ 2 + 3 + \cdots + n = \frac{n(n + 1)}{2}$$

Note that the parameter n equals the number of terms in the sum.

EXAMPLE B.6 Finding the Sum of an Arithmetic Sequence

$1 + 2 + 3 + 4 + 5 + 6 + 7 + 8 = 8(9)/2 = 36$

Theorem B.9 Sum of the First n Squares

$$2 + 2^2 + 3^2 + \cdots + n^2 = \frac{n(n + 1)(2n + 1)}{6}$$

Note that the sum is an integer even though the right-hand side appears to be a fraction.

EXAMPLE B.7 Finding a Sum of Squares

$1 + 4 + 9 + 16 + 25 + 36 + 49 = 7(8)(15)/6 = 140$

B.7 ASYMPTOTIC COMPLEXITY CLASSES

In computer science, algorithms are classified by their complexity functions. These are functions that describe the algorithms' running times relative to the sizes of the problems that they solve. For example, the Bubble Sort (page 249) has complexity $O(n^2)$ because if you use it to sort an array that is twice as long, it will take 4 times as long to run: $(2n)^2 = 4n^2$. The symbol $O()$ stands for "order" and $O(n^2)$ is pronounced "order n-squared."

The "big Oh" notation can be defined precisely in terms of limits. If f and g are nondecreasing functions on the set positive integers, let $L(f, g)$ denote the limit

$$L(f, g) = \lim_{n \to \infty} \frac{f(n)}{g(n)}$$

This constant could be 0, any positive number, or infinite. For example, if $f(n) = n^2$ and $g(n) = \sqrt{n}$, then $L(f, g) = \infty$ because $n^2/\sqrt{n} = n^{3/2} \to \infty$. With this notation, we can define all three standard complexity classes:

$$O(g) = \{ f \mid 0 \le L(f, g) < \infty \}$$
$$\Theta(g) = \{ f \mid 0 < L(f, g) < \infty \}$$
$$\Omega(g) = \{ f \mid 0 < L(f, g) \le \infty \}$$

Although these classes are sets of functions, it is traditional to write $f(n) = O(g(n))$ instead of the more mathematically precise $f \in O(g)$ (and $f(n) \ne O(g(n))$ instead of $f \notin O(g)$).

Note that

$$\Theta(g) = O(g) \cap \Omega(g)$$

EXAMPLE B.8 Complexity Classes

$n \lg n = O(n^2)$ but $n \lg n \ne \Theta(n^2)$ because $(n \lg n)/(n^2) = (\lg n)/n \to 0$;

$n \lg n = \Theta(n \lg n)$ because $(n \lg n)/(n \log n) = (\log_2 n)/(\log_{10} n) = \log_{10} 2$, which is a positive constant;

$n \lg n = \Omega(\sqrt{n})$ but $n \lg n \ne O(\sqrt{n})$ because $(n \lg n)/(\sqrt{n}) = \sqrt{n} \lg n \to \infty$

B.8 HARMONIC NUMBERS

The *harmonic numbers* are defined by the formula:

$$H_n = \sum_{k=1}^{n} \frac{1}{k} = 1 + \frac{1}{2} + \frac{1}{3} + \frac{1}{4} + \frac{1}{5} + \cdots + \frac{1}{n}$$

n	H_n
1	1.000000
2	1.500000
3	1.833333
4	2.083333
5	2.283333
6	2.450000

The first 6 harmonic numbers are shown in the table on the right.

The harmonic sequence grows very slowly. But as the next theorem and its corollary show, the sequence does continue to grow without bound.

Theorem B.10 The Harmonic Sequence is Asymptotically Logarithmic
The limit $\lim_{n \to \infty} (H_n - \ln n)$ is a positive constant.

Corollary B.1 $H_n = \Theta(\ln n)$

The following example provides impirical evidence that Theorem B.10 is true.

EXAMPLE B.9   Euler's Constant

```cpp
int main()
{ cout.setf(ios::right,ios::adjustfield);
  cout << setiosflags(ios::fixed) << setprecision(10);
  cout << "       n           H(n)           ln(n)        H(n)-ln(n)\n";
  cout << "   ---------  -------------  -------------  ------------\n";
  double h=0.0;          // harmonic numbers
  int pow2=1;            // powers of  2
  for (int n=1; n<1e9; n++)
  { h += 1.0/n;          // add reciprocals
    if (n==pow2)         // print only for powers of 2:
    { double ln=log(n);  // natural logarithm (base e)
      cout << setw(11) << n << setw(15) << h << setw(15) << ln
           << setw(14) << h-ln << endl;
      pow2 *= 2;
    }
  }
  cout << "   ---------  -------------  -------------  ------------\n";
}
```

n	H(n)	ln(n)	H(n)-ln(n)
1	1.0000000000	0.0000000000	1.0000000000
2	1.5000000000	0.6931471806	0.8068528194
4	2.0833333333	1.3862943611	0.6970389722
8	2.7178571429	2.0794415417	0.6384156012
16	3.3807289932	2.7725887222	0.6081402710
32	4.0584951954	3.4657359028	0.5927592926
64	4.7438909037	4.1588830834	0.5850078203
128	5.4331470926	4.8520302639	0.5811168287
256	6.1243449628	5.5451774445	0.5791675183
512	6.8165165346	6.2383246250	0.5781919095
1024	7.5091756723	6.9314718056	0.5777038667
2048	8.2020787718	7.6246189862	0.5774597857
4096	8.8951038970	8.3177661667	0.5773377302
8192	9.5881900461	9.0109133473	0.5772766988
16384	10.2813067100	9.7040605278	0.5772461822
32768	10.9744386320	10.3972077084	0.5772309236
65536	11.6675781832	11.0903548890	0.5772232943
131072	12.3607215491	11.7835020695	0.5772194796
262144	13.0538668223	12.4766492501	0.5772175722
524288	13.7470130492	13.1697964306	0.5772166186
1048576	14.4401597529	13.8629436112	0.5772161417
2097152	15.1333066951	14.5560907918	0.5772159033
4194304	15.8264537564	15.2492379723	0.5772157841
8388608	16.5196008774	15.9423851529	0.5772157245
16777216	17.2127480281	16.6355323334	0.5772156947
33554432	17.9058951938	17.3286795140	0.5772156798
67108864	18.5990423669	18.0218266946	0.5772156724
134217728	19.2921895437	18.7149738751	0.5772156686
268435456	19.9853367224	19.4081210557	0.5772156668
536870912	20.6784839021	20.1012682362	0.5772156658

As n increases, the difference $H_n - \ln n$ approaches the constant 0.5772156665. This number is known as *Euler's constant* and is usually denoted by the Greek letter gamma:

$$\gamma = \lim_{n \to \infty} (H_n - \ln n) = 0.5772156665 \cdots$$

It remains unknown whether γ is a rational number.

B.9 STIRLING'S FORMULA

The factorial function occurs frequently in computer science analysis. In that context, the analysis concerns the magnitude of expressions involving $n!$ as n grows large. But these values are difficult to obtain directly because they are so large. For example, $70! > 10^{100}$. *Stirling's formula* provides a convenient method for approximating large factorials:

Theorem B.11 Stirling's Formula

$$< \frac{n!}{\sqrt{2n\pi}} \left(\frac{e}{\pi}\right)^n < 1 + \frac{1}{2n}$$

Here, e and π are the mathematical constants $e = 2.71828$ and $\pi = 3.14159$.

Corollary B.2 Stirling's Approximation

$$! = \Theta\!\left(\sqrt{2n\pi}\left(\frac{n}{e}\right)^n\right)$$

Stirling's formula provides a convenient method for approximating large factorials. As the following table shows, the approximation is quite good.

n	$\dfrac{n}{e}$	$\left(\dfrac{n}{e}\right)^n$	$\sqrt{2n\pi}\left(\dfrac{n}{e}\right)^n$	$n!$
10	3.68	4.540×10^5	3.599×10^6	3.629×10^6
20	7.36	2.161×10^{17}	2.423×10^{18}	2.433×10^{18}
30	11.04	1.927×10^{31}	2.645×10^{32}	2.653×10^{32}
40	14.72	5.136×10^{46}	8.142×10^{47}	8.159×10^{47}
50	18.39	1.713×10^{63}	3.036×10^{64}	3.041×10^{64}
60	22.07	4.280×10^{80}	8.309×10^{81}	8.321×10^{81}
70	25.75	5.705×10^{98}	1.196×10^{100}	1.198×10^{100}
80	29.43	3.189×10^{117}	7.149×10^{118}	7.157×10^{118}
90	33.11	6.242×10^{136}	1.484×10^{138}	1.486×10^{138}
100	36.79	3.720×10^{156}	9.325×10^{157}	9.333×10^{157}

Note that Stirling's approximation is accurate to within 1%, and that this relative accuracy improves as n increases.

B.10 FIBONACCI NUMBERS

The *Fibonacci numbers* are defined recursively by:

$$F_n = \begin{cases} 0, & \text{if } n = 0 \\ 1, & \text{if } n = 1 \\ F_{n-1} + F_{n-2}, & \text{if } n > 1 \end{cases}$$

The first 6 Fibonacci numbers are shown in the table on the right.

n	F_n
0	0
1	1
2	1
3	2
4	3
5	5

EXAMPLE B.10 Implementation of the Fibonacci Function

```
long f(int n)
{ if (n < 2) return n;
  return f(n-1) + f(n-2);
}
```

B.11 THE GOLDEN MEAN

The *golden mean* is the mathematical constant

$$\phi = \frac{1 + \sqrt{5}}{2} \approx 1.618$$

It originates as the solution to the following ancient Greek problem: determine the point C on a line segment AB so that $AB/AC = AC/CB$. This intermediate point was called the *golden section*, the *golden ratio*, or the golden mean.

Theorem B.12 The Golden Mean
If C is the golden mean of AB, then AB/AC = ϕ.

Proof: If $r = AC/CB$, then $r = AC/CB = AB/AC = (AC + CB)/AC = 1 + CB/AC = 1 + 1/r$, so $r^2 = r + 1$. Completing the square produces $(r - 1/2)^2 = r^2 - r + 1/4 = (r + 1) - r + 1/4 = 5/4$, so $r - 1/2 = \pm\sqrt{5/4}$ and $r = (1 \pm \sqrt{5})/2$. The decimal forms of these two roots are

$$r_1 = (1 + \sqrt{5})/2 = \phi = 1.6180339887498948482045868343656 \cdots$$

$$r_2 = (1 - \sqrt{5})/2 = \psi = -0.6180339887498948482045868343656 \cdots$$

Since the golden mean ϕ is the only positive solution, it must be the correct ratio.   **Q.E.D.**

The negative root $r_2 = (1 - \sqrt{5})/2 = \psi$ that appears in the proof above is called the *conjugate golden mean*. It and ϕ have some unusual properties:

Theorem B.13 Some Properties of the Golden Mean
If $\phi = (1 + \sqrt{5})/2$ and $\psi = (1 - \sqrt{5})/2$, then

$$\phi^2 = \phi + 1$$
$$\psi^2 = \psi + 1$$
$$1/\phi = \phi - 1$$
$$1/\psi = \psi - 1$$
$$\phi + \psi = 1$$
$$\phi - \psi = \sqrt{5}$$

The golden mean is tied to the Fibonacci numbers, and thus to computer science, by the following result.

Theorem B.14 The Explicit Formula for the Fibonacci Numbers

$$F_n = \frac{\phi^n - \psi^n}{\sqrt{5}}$$

Proof:

$$F_0 = \frac{\phi^0 - \psi^0}{\sqrt{5}} = \frac{1-1}{\sqrt{5}} = \frac{0}{\sqrt{5}} = 0$$

$$F_1 = \frac{\phi^1 - \psi^1}{\sqrt{5}} = \frac{\phi - \psi}{\sqrt{5}} = \frac{\sqrt{5}}{\sqrt{5}} = 1$$

$$F_{n+1} = \frac{\phi^{n+1} - \psi^{n+1}}{\sqrt{5}} = \frac{(\phi^n + \phi^{n-1}) - (\psi^n + \psi^{n-1})}{\sqrt{5}}$$

$$= \frac{\phi^n + \psi^n}{\sqrt{5}} + \frac{\phi^{n-1} + \psi^{n-1}}{\sqrt{5}}$$

$$= F_n + F_{n-1}, \text{ by the inductive hypotheis}$$

Q.E.D.

The formula in Theorem B.14 is remarkable because, although ϕ, ψ, and $\sqrt{5}$ are all irrational numbers, the Fibonacci numbers are positive integers.

Corollary B.3
The Fibonacci Function is Asymptotically Exponential: $F_n = \Theta(\phi^n)$.

Proof: Since $-1 < \psi < 0$, high powers of ψ are negligible; therefore, $F_n = k\phi^n$, where k is the constant $1/\sqrt{5}$.

B.12 THE EUCLIDEAN ALGORITHM

The *Euclidean Algorithm* computes the greatest common multiple of two positive integers. For example, the gcd of 494 and 130 is 26 because the divisors of 494 are {1, 2, 13, 19, **26**, 38, 247, 494} and the divisors of 130 are {1, 2, 5, 10, 13, **26**, 130}.

Algorithm B.1 The Euclidean Algorithm[1]
The iterative version is:
```
long gcd(long a, long b)
{ while (b>0)
  { long r=a%b;
    a = b;
    b = r;
    // INVARIANT: gcd(a,b) is constant
  }
  return a;
}
```
The recursive version is:
```
long gcd(long a, long b)
{ if (b==0) return a;
  // INVARIANT: gcd(a,b) is constant
  return gcd(b,a%b);
}
```

1. This algorithm appears in *The Elements of Mathematics* (Book VII, Proposition 2), written by the Greek mathematician Euclid around 300 B.C. Before his appointment as head of the mathematics department of the university at Alexandria, he had been the tutor of Alexander the Great.

For example, this trace shows why `gcd(494,130)` returns `26`:

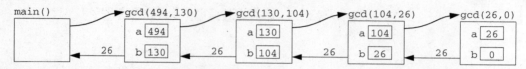

Lemma. If $a > b > 0$ and $r = a\%b$ and $d \mid b$, then $d \mid a \Leftrightarrow d \mid r$.

Corollary 1. $(d \mid a) \wedge (d \mid b) \Leftrightarrow (d \mid b) \wedge (d \mid r)$.

Corollary 2. $\gcd(a, b) = \gcd(b, r)$.

For example, $\gcd(494,130) = \gcd(130,104) = \gcd(104,26) = \gcd(26,0) = 26$.

Theorem 1. The Euclidean Algorithm is correct.

The loop invariant is Q_k: $\text{gdc}(a_k, b_k) = \text{gdc}(a,b)$, where a_k and b_k are the values of a and b on the kth iteration.

Theorem 2. The complexity of the Euclidean Algorithm is logarithmic.

Lemma. The Euclidean Algorithm executes at most $\log_\varphi a$ divisions, where ϕ is the golden mean.

Proof. On the kth iteration, $a_k = q_k b_k + r_k$, where $q_k = a_k/b_k \geq 1$ and $r_k = a_k \% b_k$. Thus $a_k \geq b_k + r_k$. But $b_k = a_{k+1}$ and $r_k = b_{k+1} = a_{k+2}$. Thus $a_k \geq a_{k+1} + a_{k+2}$. Now consider the reverse sequence $\{x_i\}$ where $x_0 = a_m$ and $x_i = a_{m-i}$: $x_0 \geq 1$, $x_1 \geq 1$, and $x_i \geq x_{i-1} + x_{i-2}$ for all i, so $x_2 \geq x_1 + x_0 \geq 1 + 1 = 2$, $x_3 \geq x_2 + x_1 \geq 2 + 1 = 3$, *etc.* Thus $x_i \geq F_{i+1}$ (the Fibonacci numbers). Thus $a = x_m \geq F_{m+1} \geq \varphi^m$, so $\log_\varphi a \geq m$.

Corollary. The Euclidean Algorithm has complexity $O(\lg n)$, where $n = \max\{a, b\}$.

Appendix C

Standard Container Classes

This appendix summarizes the standard C++ container class templates and their most widely used member functions. This is the part of standard C++ that used to be called the Standard Template Library (STL).

C.1 THE vector CLASS TEMPLATE

A vector object acts like an array with index range checking (using its at() member function). As an object, it has the additional advantages over an array of being able to be assigned, passed by value, and returned by value. The vector class template is defined in the <vector> header. See Example C.1 on page 287.

```
vector();
// default constructor: creates an empty vector;

vector(const vector& v);
// copy constructor: creates a copy of the vector v;
// postcondition: *this == v;

vector(unsigned n, const T& x=T());
// constructor: creates a vector containing n copies of the element x;
// precondition: n >= 0;
// postcondition: size() == n;

~vector();
// destructor: destroys this vector;

vector& operator=(const vector& v);
// assignment operator: assigns v to this vector, making it a duplicate;
// postcondition: *this == v;

unsigned size() const;
// returns the number of elements in this vector;

unsigned capacity() const;
// returns the maximum number of elements that this vector can have
// without being reallocated;

void reserve(unsigned n);
// reallocates this vector to a capacity of n elements;
// precondition: capacity() <= n;
// postcondition: capacity() == n;
```

```
bool empty() const;
// returns true iff size() == 0;

void assign(unsigned n, const T& x=T());
// clears this vector and then inserts n copies of the element x;
// precondition: n >= 0;
// postcondition: size() == n;

T& operator[](unsigned i);
// returns element number i;
// precondition: 0 <= i < size();
// result is unpredictable if precondition is false;

T& at(unsigned i);
// returns element number i;
// precondition: 0 <= i < size();
// exception is thrown if precondition is false;

T& front();
// returns the first element of this vector;

T& back();
// returns the last element of this vector;

iterator begin();
// returns an iterator pointing to the first element of this vector;

iterator end();
// returns an iterator pointing to the dummy element that follows
// the last element of this vector;

iterator rbegin();
// returns a reverse iterator pointing to the last element of this vector;

iterator rend();
// returns a reverse iterator pointing to the dummy element that precedes
// the first element of this vector;

void push_back(const T& x);
// appends a copy of the element x to the back of this vector;
// postcondition: back() == x;
// postcondition: size() has been incremented;

void pop_back();
// removes the last element of this vector;
// precondition: size() > 0;
// postcondition: size() has been decremented;

iterator insert(iterator p, const T& x);
// inserts a copy of the element x at position p; returns p;
// precondition: begin() <= p <= end();
// postcondition: size() has been incremented;
```

```
iterator erase(iterator p);
// removes the element at position p; returns p
// precondition: begin() <= p <= end();
// postcondition: size() has been decremented;

iterator erase(iterator p1, iterator p2);
// removes the elements from position p1 to the position before p2;
// returns p1;
// precondition: begin() <= p1 <= p2 <= end();
// postcondition: size() has been decreased by int(p2-p1);

void clear();
// removes all the elements from this vector;
// postcondition: size() == 0;
```

EXAMPLE C.1 Using an Iterator on a **vector** Object

```
#include <iostream>
#include <vector>
using namespace std;
typedef vector<int>::reverse_iterator It;

int main()
{ vector<int> v(4);
  for (int i=0; i<4; i++)
    v[i] = 222*i + 333;
  cout << "Using the iterator it in a for loop:\n";
  for (It it=v.begin(); it!=v.end(); it++)
    cout << "\t*it=" << *it << "\n";
  cout << "Using the iterator p in a while loop:\n";
  It p=v.begin();
  while(p!=v.end())
    cout << "\t*p++=" << *p++ << "\n";
}
```

```
Using the iterator it in a for loop:
        *it=333
        *it=555
        *it=777
        *it=999
Using the iterator p in a while loop:
        *p++=333
        *p++=555
        *p++=777
        *p++=999
```

The vector v has 4 elements: 333, 555, 777, and 999. The second for loop uses the iterator it to traverse the vector v from beginning to end, accessing each of its elements with *it. The while loop has the same effect using *p.

EXAMPLE C.2 Using a Reverse Iterator on a **vector** Object

```
#include <iostream>
#include <vector>
using namespace std;
typedef vector<int>::reverse_iterator RIt;
```

```
int main()
{ vector<int> v(4);
  for (int i=0; i<4; i++)
    v[i] = 222*i + 333;
  cout << "Using the reverse iterator rit in a for loop:\n";
  for (RIt rit=v.rbegin(); rit!=v.rend(); rit++)
    cout << "\t*rit=" << *rit << "\n";
  cout << "Using the reverse iterator rp in a while loop:\n";
  RIt rp=v.rbegin();
  while(rp!=v.rend())
    cout << "\t*rp++=" << *rp++ << "\n";
}
```
```
Using the reverse iterator rit in a for loop:
        *rit=999
        *rit=777
        *rit=555
        *rit=333
Using the reverse iterator rp in a while loop:
        *rp++=999
        *rp++=777
        *rp++=555
        *rp++=333
```

The vector v has 4 elements: 333, 555, 777, and 999 (the same as in Example C.1). The second for loop uses the reverse iterator rit to traverse the vector v backwards, accessing each of its elements with *rit. The while loop has the same effect using *rp.

EXAMPLE C.3 Using the `insert()` Function on a `vector` Object

```
#include <iostream>
#include <vector>
using namespace std;
typedef vector<int> Vector;
typedef Vector::iterator It;
void print(const Vector&);

int main()
{ Vector v(4);
  for (int i=0; i<4; i++)
    v[i] = 222*i + 333;
  print(v);
  It it = v.insert(v.begin()+2,666);
  print(v);
  cout << "*it=" << *it << "\n";
}

void print(const Vector& v)
{ cout << "size=" << v.size() << ": (" << v[0];
  for (int i=1; i<v.size(); i++)
    cout << "," << v[i];
  cout << ")\n";
}
```
```
size=4: (333,555,777,999)
size=5: (333,555,666,777,999)
*it=666
```

The vector v has 4 elements: 333, 555, 777, and 999 (the same as in Example C.1). The second for loop uses the reverse iterator rit to traverse the vector v backwards, accessing each of its elements with *rit. The while loop has the same effect using *rp.

EXAMPLE C.4 Using Some Generic Algorithms on a **vector** Object

```cpp
#include <iostream>
#include <vector>
using namespace std;
typedef vector<int> Vector;
typedef Vector::iterator It;
void print(const Vector&);

int main()
{ Vector v(9);
  for (int i=0; i<9; i++)
    v[i] = 111*i + 111;
  print(v);
  It it=v.begin();
  fill(it+2,it+5,400);   // replaces v[2:5] with 400
  print(v);
  reverse(it+4,it+7);    //
  print(v);
  iter_swap(it+6,it+8);
  print(v);
  sort(it+4,it+9);
  print(v);
}

void print(const Vector& v)
{ cout << "size=" << v.size() << ": (" << v[0];
  for (int i=1; i<v.size(); i++)
    cout << "," << v[i];
  cout << ")\n";
}
size=9: (111,222,333,444,555,666,777,888,999)
size=9: (111,222,400,400,400,666,777,888,999)
size=9: (111,222,400,400,777,666,400,888,999)
size=9: (111,222,400,400,777,666,999,888,400)
size=9: (111,222,400,400,400,666,777,888,999)
```

EXAMPLE C.5 Using Some More Generic Algorithms on a **vector** Object

```cpp
#include <iostream>
#include <vector>
using namespace std;
typedef vector<int> Vector;
typedef Vector::iterator It;
void print(const Vector&);

int main()
{ Vector v1(9);
  for (int i=0; i<9; i++)
    v1[i] = 111*i + 111;
  print(v1);
  Vector v2(9);
```

```
      print(v2);
      It p1=v1.begin(), p2=v2.begin();
      copy(p1+3,p1+8,p2+3);
      print(v2);
      It p = min_element(p1+4,p1+8);
      cout << "*p=" << *p << "\n";
      p = max_element(p1+4,p1+8);
      cout << "*p=" << *p << "\n";
      p = find(p1,p1+9,444);
      if (p != p1+9) cout << "*p=" << *p << "\n";
   }

   void print(const Vector& v)
   { cout << "size=" << v.size() << ": (" << v[0];
     for (int i=1; i<v.size(); i++)
        cout << "," << v[i];
     cout << ")\n";
   }
```

```
size=9:  (111,222,333,444,555,666,777,888,999)
size=9:  (0,0,0,0,0,0,0,0,0)
size=9:  (0,0,0,444,555,666,777,888,0)
*p=555
*p=888
*p=444
```

C.2 THE deque CLASS TEMPLATE

A deque (pronounced "deck") object is a double-ended queue, intended to provide efficient insertion and deletion at both its beginning and its end. It has the following two member functions in addition to all the member functions that a vector class has except the capacity() and reserve() functions. The deque class template is defined in the <deque> header.

```
void push_front(const T& x);
// inserts a copy of the element x at the front of this deque;
// postcondition: front() == x;
// postcondition: size() has been incremented;
```

```
void pop_front();
// removes the first element of this vector;
// precondition: size() > 0;
// postcondition: size() has been decremented;
```

C.3 THE stack CLASS TEMPLATE

A stack object is a sequential container that allows insertions and deletions only at one end, called its *top*. In the standard C++ library, the stack class template is adapted from the deque class template. This means that stack member functions are implemented with deque member functions, as shown below. The stack class template is defined in the <stack> header.

```
template <class T> class stack
{ public:
     unsigned size() const { return _d.size(); }
     bool empty() const    { return _d.empty(); }
     T& top()              { return _d.back(); }
     void push(const T& x) { _d.push_back(x); }
     void pop()            { _d.pop_back(); }
  protected:
     deque<T> _d;
};
```

C.4 THE queue CLASS TEMPLATE

A queue object is a sequential container that allows insertions only at one end and deletions only at the other end. Like the stack class template, the queue class template is adapted from the deque class template in the standard C++ library. This means that queue member functions are implemented with deque member functions, as shown below.   The queue class template is defined in the <queue> header.

```
template <class T> class stack
{ public:
     unsigned size() const { return _d.size(); }
     bool empty() const    { return _d.empty(); }
     T& front()            { return _d.front(); }
     T& back()             { return _d.back(); }
     void push(const T& x) { _d.push_back(x); }
     void pop()            { _d.pop_front(); }
  protected:
     deque<T> _d;
};
```

C.5 THE priority_queue CLASS TEMPLATE

A priority_queue object is a container that acts like a queue except that the order in which the elements are popped is determined by their priorities. This means that the operator<() function must be defined for the element type T. The priority_queue class template is defined in the <queue> header. See Example C.6 on page 291.

```
vector();
// constructs an empty vector;
```

```
vector(const vector& v);
// constructs a copy of the vector v;
// postcondition: *this == v;
```

EXAMPLE C.6 Using a priority_queue Object

```
#include <iostream>
#include <queue>
using namespace std;
```

```
int main()
{ priority_queue<string> pq;
  pq.push("Japan");
  pq.push("Japan");
  pq.push("Korea");
  pq.push("China");
  pq.push("India");
  pq.push("Nepal");
  pq.push("Qatar");
  pq.push("Yemen");
  pq.push("Egypt");
  pq.push("Zaire");
  pq.push("Libya");
  pq.push("Italy");
  pq.push("Spain");
  pq.push("Chile");
  while (!pq.empty())
  { cout << pq.top() << "\n";
    pq.pop();
  }
}
```

```
Zaire
Yemen
Spain
Qatar
Nepal
Libya
Korea
Japan
Japan
Italy
India
Egypt
China
Chile
```

The priority queue always maintains its highest priority element at the top (*i.e.*, the front) of the queue. Using the standard lexicographic ordering (*i.e.*, the dictionary ordering) of strings, that results in the names being accessed in reverse alphabetical order.

Note that `priority_queue` objects store duplicate elements.

C.6 THE list CLASS TEMPLATE

A `list` object is a sequential container that allows efficient insertion and deletion at any position in the sequence. It has the following member functions in addition to all the member functions that the `deque` class has (except the `operator[]()` and `at()` functions). The `list` class template is defined in the `<list>` header. See Example C.7 on page 293.

```
void splice(iterator p, list& l, iterator p1);
// moves the element from l at position p1 to this list at position p;
// precondition: p is a valid iterator on this list;
// precondition: p1 is a valid iterator on list l;
```

```
void splice(iterator p, list& l, iterator p1, iterator p2);
// moves the elements from l at positions [p1:p2-1] to this list
// beginning at position p;
// precondition: p is a valid iterator on this list;
// precondition: p1 and p2 are valid iterators on list l;
// precondition p1 < p2;
```

```
void remove(const T& x);
// removes from this list all elements that are equal to x;
// invariant: the order of all elements that are not removed;
// invariant: all iterators pointing to elements that are not removed;
```

```
void unique();
// removes from this list all duplicate elements;
// invariant: the order of all elements that are not removed;
// invariant: all iterators pointing to elements that are not removed;
```

```
void merge(list& l);
// merges all elements of list l into this list;
// precondition: both list l and this list are sorted;
// postcondition: size() is increased by l.size();
// postcondition: l.size() == 0;
// complexity: O(n);
```

```
void reverse();
// reverses the order of the elements of this list;
// invariant: size();
// complexity: O(n);
```

```
void sort();
// sorts the elements of this list;
// postcondition: this list is sorted;
// invariant: size();
// complexity: O(n*log(n));
```

EXAMPLE C.7 Sorting and Reversing a list Object

```
#include <iostream>
#include <list>
using namespace std;
typedef list<string> List;
typedef List::iterator It;
void print(List&);

int main()
{ List l;
  l.push_back("Kenya");
  l.push_back("Sudan");
  l.push_back("Egypt");
  l.push_back("Zaire");
  l.push_back("Libya");
  l.push_back("Congo");
  l.push_back("Ghana");
  print(l);
  l.sort();
```

```
      print(l);
      l.reverse();
      print(l);
  }

  void print(List& l)
  { cout << "\n";
    for (It it=l.begin(); it != l.end(); it++)
      cout << *it << "\n";
  }
```

```
Kenya
Sudan
Egypt
Zaire
Libya
Congo
Ghana

Congo
Egypt
Ghana
Kenya
Libya
Sudan
Zaire

Zaire
Sudan
Libya
Kenya
Ghana
Egypt
Congo
```

C.7 THE map CLASS TEMPLATE

A map object (also called a *dictionary*, a *table*, or an *associative array*) acts like an array whose index can be any type that implements the < operator. A map is like a mathematical function that gives a unique y-value for each x-value. The x-value, called the *key* value, is the index. The y-value is the stored object that the key identifies.

An English language dictionary is an example of a map object. The key value is the word, and its associated object is the dictionary's definition of the word.

Another standard example would be a database table of student records. The key value is the student identification number (*e.g.*, Social Security number), and its associated object is the data record for that student.

The map class template is defined in the <map> header. It has the same member functions as the vector class template.

EXAMPLE C.8 Using a map Object

```
  #include <iostream>
  #include <map.h>
```

```
using namespace std;

struct Country
{ friend ostream& operator<<(ostream&, const Country&);
  Country();
  Country(string, string, string, int, int);
  string abbr, capital, language;
  int population, area;
};

typedef map<string,Country> Map;
typedef Map::iterator It;
typedef pair<const string,Country> Pair;
void load(Map&);
void print(Map&);
void find(Map&, const string&);

int main()
{ Map map;
  load(map);
  print(map);
  find(map,"Cuba");
  find(map,"Iran");
  find(map,"Oman");
}

ostream& operator<<(ostream& ostr, const Country& c)
{ return ostr << c.abbr << ", " << c.capital << ", " << c.language
            << ", pop=" << c.population << ", area=" << c.area;
}

Country::Country()
  : abbr(""), capital(""), language(""), population(0), area(0) { }

Country::Country(string ab, string c, string l, int p, int ar)
  : abbr(ab), capital(c), language(l), population(p), area(ar) { }

void load(Map& m)
{ m["Iran"] = Country("IR","Tehran","Persian",68959931,632457);
  m["Iran"] = Country("IR","Tehran","Farsi",68959931,632457);
  m["Peru"] = Country("PE","Lima","Spanish",26111110,496223);
  m["Iraq"] = Country("IQ","Baghdad","Arabic",21722287,167975);
  m.insert(Pair("Togo",Country("TG","Lome","French",4905824,21927)));
  m.insert(Pair("Fiji",Country("FJ","Suva","English",802611,7054)));
  m.insert(Pair("Fiji",Country("FJ","Suva","Fijian",802611,7054)));
}

void print(Map& m)
{ for (It it=m.begin(); it != m.end(); it++)
    cout << it->first << ":\t" << it->second << "\n";
  cout << "size=" << m.size() << "\n";
}

void find(Map& m, const string& s)
{ cout << s;
  It it = m.find(s);
```

```
    if (it == m.end()) cout << " was not found.\n";
    else cout << ":\t" << it->second << "\n";
}
Fiji:    FJ, Suva, English, pop=802611, area=7054
Iran:    IR, Tehran, Farsi, pop=68959931, area=632457
Iraq:    IQ, Baghdad, Arabic, pop=21722287, area=167975
Peru:    PE, Lima, Spanish, pop=26111110, area=496223
Togo:    TG, Lome, French, pop=4905824, area=21927
size=5
Cuba was not found.
Iran:    IR, Tehran, Farsi, pop=68959931, area=632457
Oman was not found.
```

The program creates a map whose keys are four-letter names of countries and whose mapped values are Country objects, where Country is a class defined to have five fields: abbr, capital, language, population, and area. It uses a separate function to load the data into the map.

The load() function illustrates two different ways to insert a pair element into a map. The first four lines use the subscript operator and the last three lines use the insert() function. The subscript operator works the same way on a map container as with other container classes: just like an array, except that with a map the index need not be an integer. In this example it is a string.

The insert() function takes a single pair argument, where the two component types must be the same as for the map itself, except that the first component (the *key field*) must be const.

The map class does not allow duplicate keys. Note that the subscript operator replaces existing elements when a duplicate key is inserted, so that the last pair inserted is the one that remains. But the insert() function does not replace existing elements when a duplicate key is inserted, so the first pair inserted is the one that remains.

The print() function uses the iterator it to traverse the map. On each iteration of the for loop, it points to a pair object whose first component is the key value and whose second component is the data object. These two components are accessed by the expressions it->first and it->second. The first component is a string, the four-letter name of the country. The second component is a Country object which can be passed to the output operator since it is overloaded in the Country class definition. Note that the pairs are sorted automatically by their key values.

The find() function uses the find member function of the map class. The call m.find(s) returns an iterator that points to the map element whose first component equals s. If no such element is found, then the returned pointer points to m.end(), which is the dummy element that follows the last element of the map container.

C.8 THE set CLASS TEMPLATE

A set object acts like a map object with only the keys stored.

The set class template is defined in the <set> header.

EXAMPLE C.9 Using set Functions

The program defines overloaded operators +, *, and – to perform set-theoretic union, intersection, and relative complement operations. These are implemented using the insert() and erase() member functions and the set_intersection() and set_difference() generic algorithms (nonmember functions). This example illustrates the distinctions between the set generic algorithms (set_union(), set_difference(), and set_difference()) and the corresponding set-theoretic operations (union, intersection, and complement).

```cpp
#include <iostream>
#include <set>
#include <string>
using namespace std;
typedef set<string> Set;
typedef set<string>::iterator It;

void print(Set);
Set operator+(Set&,Set&);   // union
Set operator*(Set&,Set&);   // intersection
Set operator-(Set&,Set&);   // relative complement

int main()
{ string str1[] = { "A", "B", "C", "D", "E", "F", "G" };
  string str2[] = { "A", "E", "I", "O", "U" };
  Set s1(str1,str1+7);
  Set s2(str2,str2+5);
  print(s1);
  print(s2);
  print(s1+s2);
  print(s1*s2);
  print(s1-s2);
}

Set operator+(Set& s1, Set& s2)
{ Set s(s1);
  s.insert(s2.begin(),s2.end());
  return s;
}

Set operator*(Set& s1, Set& s2)
{ Set s(s1);
  It it = set_intersection(s1.begin(),s1.end(),
                           s2.begin(),s2.end(),s.begin());
  s.erase(it,s.end());
  return s;
}
Set operator-(Set& s1, Set& s2)
{ Set s(s1);
  It it = set_difference(s1.begin(),s1.end(),
                         s2.begin(),s2.end(),s.begin());
  s.erase(it,s.end());
  return s;
}

void print(Set s)
{ cout << "size=" << s.size() << ": {";
  for (It it=s.begin(); it != s.end(); it++)
    if (it == s.begin()) cout << *it;
    else cout << "," << *it;
  cout << "}\n";
}
size=7: {A,B,C,D,E,F,G}
size=5: {A,E,I,O,U}
size=10: {A,B,C,D,E,F,G,I,O,U}
size=2: {A,E}
size=5: {B,C,D,F,G}
```

The set objects `s1` and `s2` are constructed from the string arrays `str1` and `str2` using the expressions `str1`, `str1+7`, `str2`, and `str2+7` as iterators.

The elements of a `set` object are always stored in sorted order. That allows the union function (`operator+()`) to be implemented with the `set::insert()` function.

The main reason why the `set` generic algorithms do not produce directly the expected set-theoretic operations is that they leave the size of the target set unchanged. Thus we use the `erase()` member function together with the `set_intersection()` and `set_difference()` generic algorithms to implement the `operator*()` and `operator-()` functions.

Generic Algorithms

The *generic algorithms* in standard C++ are the 70 nonmember function templates that apply to container objects. There are 66 listed here alphabetically. We use the symbol [p,q[to represent the segment of elements from *p to *(q-1) (*i.e.*, including the element *p but excluding the element *q). The parameters are

```
iterator p, q;    // used to describe the segment [p,q[
iterator r;       // p <= r <= q
unsigned n;       // used as a counter
T& x, y;          // values of the sequence's element type
class p;          // a predicate class, with boolean operator()()
```

The parameter list (p,q,pp) is used frequently; it means that the elements from the segment [p,q[are to be copied into the segment [pp,pp+n[where n is the number of elements in [p,q[, namely, q-p.

For simplicity, we use arrays instead of general container objects. In that context, pointers serve as iterators. Recall that if a is an array and k is an int, then a+k represents the subarray that starts with a[k], and *(a+k) = a[k]. Also, if l is the length of the array, then a+l points to the (imaginary) element that follows the last element of the array.

The following print() function is used to display the n elements, a[0],...,a[n-1] of an array a:

```
void print(int* a, int n)
{ cout << "n=" << n << ": {" << a[0];
  for (int i=1; i<n; i++)
    cout << "," << a[i];
  cout << "}\n";
}
```

The 66 algorithms listed here naturally fall into 8 groups, summarized in the following tables:

Searching and Sorting Algorithms in `<algorithm>`

binary_search()	Determines whether a given value is an element in the segment.
inplace_merge()	Merges two adjacent sorted segments into one sorted segment.
lower_bound()	Finds the first element in the segment that has a given value.
merge()	Merges two sorted segments into a third sorted segment.
nth_element()	Finds the first occurrence of a given value.
partial_sort()	Sorts the first *n* elements of the segment.
partial_sort_copy()	Copies the smallest *n* elements of the segment into another sorted segment.
partition()	Partitions the segment so that $P(x)$ is true for the elements in the first part.
sort()	Sorts the segment.
upper_bound()	Finds the last element in the segment that has a given value.

Nonmodifying Algorithms on Sequences in `<algorithm>`

`adjacent_find()`	Finds the first adjacent pair in the segment.
`count()`	Counts the number of elements that have a given value.
`count_if()`	Counts the number of elements that satisfy a given predicate.
`equal()`	Determines whether two segments have the same value in the same order.
`find()`	Finds the first element that has a given value.
`find_end()`	Finds the location of the last occurrence of a given substring.
`find_first_of()`	Finds the location of the first occurrence of any element of a given segment.
`find_if()`	Finds the first element that satisfies a given predicate.
`for_each()`	Applies a given function to each element.
`mismatch()`	Finds the first position where two segments do not match.
`search()`	Searches for a given subsequence.
`search_n()`	Searches for a subsequence of n consecutive elements that have a given value.

Modifying Algorithms on Sequences in `<algorithm>`

`copy()`	Copies the segment to a new location.
`copy_backward()`	Copies the segment to a new location.
`fill()`	Replaces each element in the segment with a given value.
`fill_n()`	Replaces n elements in the segment with a given value.
`generate()`	Assigns the output from successive calls to $f(x)$ to elements of the segment.
`generate_n()`	Assigns the output from n successive calls to $f(x)$ to elements of the segment.
`iter_swap()`	Swaps the elements at the positions of the given iterators.
`random_shuffle()`	Shuffles the elements in the segment.
`remove()`	Shifts to the left all elements that do not have a given value.
`remove_copy()`	Copies all elements into another segment that do not have a given value.
`remove_copy_if()`	Copies all elements into another segment for which $P(x)$ is false.
`remove_if()`	Shifts to the left all elements for which $P(x)$ is false.
`replace()`	Changes the value of each element in the segment from x to y.
`replace_copy()`	Copies each element to another segment changing each x to y.
`replace_copy_if()`	Copies each element to another segment changing x to y where $P(x)$ is true.
`replace_if()`	Changes those elements in the segment from x to y where $P(x)$ is true.
`reverse()`	Reverses the elements in the segment.
`reverse_copy()`	Copies the elements to a new segment in reverse order.
`rotate()`	Shifts the elements to the left, wrapping around the end of the segment.
`rotate_copy()`	Copies elements to another segment, shifting to the left and wrapping.
`swap()`	Swaps the two given elements.
`transform()`	Applies $f(x)$ to each element, storing the results in another segment.
`unique()`	Shifts one of each occurring value to the left.
`unique_copy()`	Copies the nonduplicate elements to another segment.

Comparison Algorithms in `<algorithm>`

`lexicographical_compare()`	Returns true iff first segment is lexicographically less than second.
`max()`	Returns the largest element in the segment.
`max_element()`	Returns the position of largest element in the segment.
`min()`	Returns the smallest element in the segment.
`min_element()`	Returns the position of smallest element in the segment.

Algorithms on Sets in `<algorithm>`

`includes()`	Returns true iff every element of the second segment is in the first.
`set_difference()`	Copies to a third segment the relative complement of two sets.
`set_intersection()`	Copies to a third segment the intersection of two sets.
`set_symmetric_difference()`	Copies to a third segment the symmetric difference of two sets.
`set_union()`	Copies to a third segment the union of two sets.

Algorithms on Heaps in `<algorithm>`

`make_heap()`	Rearranges the elements of the segment into a heap.
`pop_heap()`	Moves first element to end and then `make_heap()` on rest.
`push_heap()`	Shifts last element to left to make segment a heap.
`sort_heap()`	Applies `pop_heap()` *n* times to sort the segment.

Permutation Algorithms in `<algorithm>`

`next_permutation()`	Permutes the segment; *n*! calls produce *n*! distinct permutations.
`prev_permutation()`	Permutes the segment; *n*! calls produce *n*! distinct permutations.

Numeric Algorithms on Sequences in `<numeric>`

`accumulate()`	Adds the elements of the segment; returns $x + sum$.
`adjacent_difference()`	Loads second segment with the differences of adjacent elements.
`inner_product()`	Returns x + inner product of two segments.
`partial_sum()`	Loads second segment with the partial sums from first.

Algorithms that search for an element always return an iterator that locates it or one that locates the dummy end element that follows the last element of the sequence.

Algorithms that use predicates are illustrated with the following predicate class:

```
class Odd
{ public:
    bool operator()(int n) { return n%2 ? true : false; }
};
```

This class is passed as a function, like this: `Odd()`. (See Example D.8 on page 304.)

Note that the modifying algorithms do not change the length of the segment `[p,q[`. Instead, they return an iterator that points to the element that follows the modified part.

```
accumulate(p,q,x);
// returns x plus the sum of the elements in the segment [p,q[;
// invariant: [p,q[ is left unchanged;
```

EXAMPLE D.1 Testing the `accumulate()` Algorithm

```
    int main()
    { int a[] = {0,1,1,2,3,5,8,13,21,34};
      int sum = accumulate(a,a+10,1000);
      cout << "sum=" << sum << '\n';
    }
    sum=1088
```

```
adjacent_difference(p,q,pp);
// loads the segment a[pp,pp+p-q[ with b[i] = a[i]-a[i-1];
// invariant: [p,q[ is left unchanged;
```

EXAMPLE D.2 Testing the `adjacent_difference()` Algorithm

```
    int main()
    { int a[] = {0,1,1,2,3,5,8,13,21,34};
      print(a,10);
      int b[10];
      adjacent_difference(a,a+10,b);
      print(b,10);
    }
    n=10: {0,1,1,2,3,5,8,13,21,34}
    n=10: {0,1,0,1,1,2,3,5,8,13}
```

The `adjacent_difference()` algorithm is the inverse of the `partial_sum()` algorithm (Example D.36 on page 314).

```
adjacent_find(p,q);
// returns the location of the first element in the segment a[p,q[
// that has the same value as its successor;
// invariant: [p,q[ is left unchanged;
```

EXAMPLE D.3 Testing the `adjacent_find()` Algorithm

```
    int main()
    { int a[] = {0,1,0,1,1,1,0,1,1,0};
      print(a,10);
      int* r = adjacent_find(a,a+10);
      cout << "*r=" << *r << '\n';      // this is the element a[i]
      cout << "r-a=" << r-a << '\n';    // this is the index i
    }
    n=10: {0,1,0,1,1,1,0,1,1,0}
    *r=1
    r-a=3
```

```
binary_search(p,q,x);
// returns true iff x is in the segment [p,q[;
// precondition: the segment [p,q[ must be sorted;
// invariant: [p,q[ is left unchanged;
```

EXAMPLE D.4 Testing the `binary_search()` Algorithm

```
int main()
{ int a[] = {0,1,1,2,3,5,8,13,21,34};
  print(a,10);
  bool found = binary_search(a,a+10,21);
  cout << "found=" << found << '\n';
  found = binary_search(a+2,a+7,21);
  cout << "found=" << found << '\n';
}
n=10: {0,1,1,2,3,5,8,13,21,34}
found=1
found=0
```

```
copy(p,q,pp);
// copies the segment [p,q[ to [pp,pp+n[ where n=q-p;
// invariant: [p,q[ is left unchanged;
```

EXAMPLE D.5 Testing the `copy()` Algorithm

```
int main()
{ int a[] = {100,111,122,133,144,155,166,177,188,199};
  print(a,10);
  copy(a+7,a+10,a+2);
  print(a,10);
  int b[3];
  copy(a+7,a+10,b);
  print(b,3);
}
n=10: {100,111,122,133,144,155,166,177,188,199}
n=10: {100,111,177,188,199,155,166,177,188,199}
n=3: {177,188,199}
```

```
copy_backward(p,q,pp);
// copies the segment [p,q[ to [qq-n,qq[ where n=q-p;
// invariant: [p,q[ is left unchanged;
```

EXAMPLE D.6 Testing the `copy_backward()` Algorithm

```
int main()
{ int a[] = {100,111,122,133,144,155,166,177,188,199};
  print(a,10);
  copy_backward(a+7,a+10,a+5);
  print(a,10);
  int b[3];
```

```
        copy_backward(a+7,a+10,b+3);
        print(b,3);
    }
    n=10: {100,111,122,133,144,155,166,177,188,199}
    n=10: {100,111,177,188,199,155,166,177,188,199}
    n=3: {177,188,199}
```

count(p,q,x);
// returns the number of occurrences of x in the segment [p,q[;
// invariant: [p,q[is left unchanged;

EXAMPLE D.7 Testing the count() Algorithm

```
    int main()
    { int a[] = {0,1,0,1,1,1,0,1,1,0};
      print(a,10);
      int n = count(a,a+10,1);
      cout << "n=" << n << '\n';
    }
    n=10: {0,1,0,1,1,1,0,1,1,0}
    n=6
```

count_if(p,q,P());
// returns the number of occurrences where P(x) in the segment [p,q[;
// invariant: [p,q[is left unchanged;

EXAMPLE D.8 Testing the count_if() Algorithm

```
    int main()
    { int a[] = {0,1,0,1,1,1,0,1,1,0};
      print(a,10);
      int n = count_if(a,a+10,Odd());
      cout << "n=" << n << '\n';
    }
    n=10: {0,1,0,1,1,1,0,1,1,0}
    n=6
```

equal(p,q,pp);
// returns true iff the segment [p,q[matches [pp,pp+n[, where n = q-p;
// invariant: [p,q[and [pp,qq+n[are left unchanged;

EXAMPLE D.9 Testing the equal() Algorithm

```
    int main()
    int main()
    { int a[] = {0,1,0,1,1,1,0,1,1,0};
      int b[] = {0,1,0,0,1,1,0,1,0,0};
      print(a,10);
      print(b,10);
```

```
      cout << "equal(a,a+10,b)=" << equal(a,a+10,b) << '\n';
      cout << "equal(a+1,a+4,a+5)=" << equal(a+1,a+4,a+5) << '\n';
    }
    n=10: {0,1,0,1,1,1,0,1,1,0}
    n=10: {0,1,0,0,1,1,0,1,0,0}
    equal(a,a+10,b)=0
    equal(a+1,a+4,a+5)=1
```

fill(p,q,x);
// replaces each element in the segment [p,q[with x;

EXAMPLE D.10 Testing the **fill()** Algorithm

```
    int main()
    { int a[] = {0,1,1,2,3,5,8,13,21,34};
      print(a,10);
      fill(a+6,a+9,0);
      print(a,10);
    }
    n=10: {0,1,1,2,3,5,8,13,21,34}
    n=10: {0,1,1,2,3,5,0,0,0,34}
```

fill_n(p,n,x);
// replaces each element in the segment [p,p+n[with x;

EXAMPLE D.11 Testing the **fill_n()** Algorithm

```
    int main()
    { int a[] = {0,1,1,2,3,5,8,13,21,34};
      print(a,10);
      fill_n(a+6,3,0);
      print(a,10);
    }
    n=10: {0,1,1,2,3,5,8,13,21,34}
    n=10: {0,1,1,2,3,5,0,0,0,34}
```

find(p,q,x);
// returns the first location of x in the segment [p,q[;
// invariant: [p,q[is left unchanged;

EXAMPLE D.12 Testing the **find()** Algorithm

```
    int main()
    { int a[] = {0,1,1,2,3,5,8,13,21,34};
      print(a,10);
      int* r = find(a,a+10,13);
      cout << "*r=" << *r << '\n';     // this is the element a[i]
      cout << "r-a=" << r-a << '\n';   // this is the index i
      r = find(a,a+6,13);
```

```
        cout << "*r=" << *r << '\n';     // this is the element a[i]
        cout << "r-a=" << r-a << '\n';    // this is the index i
    }
n=10: {0,1,1,2,3,5,8,13,21,34}
*r=13
r-a=7
*r=8
```

find_end(p,q,pp,qq);
// returns the location of the last occurrence of the segment [pp,qq[
// within the segment [p,q[;
// invariant: [p,q[and [pp,qq[are left unchanged;

EXAMPLE D.13 Testing the find_end() Algorithm

```
    int main()
    { int a[] = {0,1,0,1,1,1,0,1,1,0};
      int b[] = {1,0,1,1,1};
      int* r = find_end(a,a+10,b,b+5);   // search for 10111 in a
      cout << "*r=" << *r << '\n';        // this is the element a[i]
      cout << "r-a=" << r-a << '\n';      // this is the index i
      r = find_end(a,a+10,b,b+4);         // search for 1011 in a
      cout << "*r=" << *r << '\n';
      cout << "r-a=" << r-a << '\n';
    }
*r=1
r-a=1
*r=1
r-a=5
```

find_first_of(p,q,pp,qq);
// returns the position in [p,q[of the first element found that is also in
// [pp,qq[;
// invariant: [p,q[and [pp,qq[are left unchanged;

EXAMPLE D.14 Testing the find_first_of() Algorithm

```
    int main()
    { int a[] = {0,1,1,2,3,5,8,13,21,34};
      int b[] = {6,7,8,9,10,11,12,13,14,15};
      int* r = find_first_of(a,a+10,b,b+10);
      cout << "*r=" << *r << '\n';     // this is the element a[i]
      cout << "r-a=" << r-a << '\n';   // this is the index i
    }
*r=8
r-a=6
```

find_if(p,q,P());
// returns the first location of where P(x) is in the segment [p,q[;
// invariant: [p,q[is left unchanged;

EXAMPLE D.15 Testing the `find_if()` Algorithm

```
int main()
{ int a[] = {2,4,8,16,32,64,128,256,333,512};
  int* r = find_if(a,a+10,Odd());
  cout << "*r=" << *r << '\n';    // this is the element a[i]
  cout << "r-a=" << r-a << '\n';  // this is the index i
  r = find_if(a,a+5,Odd());
  cout << "*r=" << *r << '\n';    // this is the element a[i]
  cout << "r-a=" << r-a << '\n';  // this is the index i
}
*r=333
r-a=8
*r=64
```

`for_each(p,q,f);`
`// applies the function f(x) to each x in the segment [p,q[;`

EXAMPLE D.16 Testing the `for_each()` Algorithm

```
void print(int);

int main()
{ int a[] = {0,1,1,2,3,5,8,13,21,34};
  for_each(a,a+10,print);
}

void print(int x)
{ cout << x << " ";
}
0 1 1 2 3 5 8 13 21 34
```

`generate(p,q,f);`
`// assigns to [p,q[ the outputs of successive calls to f(x);`

EXAMPLE D.17 Testing the `generate()` Algorithm

```
long fibonacci();

int main()
{ int a[10]={0};
  generate(a,a+10,fibonacci);
  print(a,10);
}

long fibonacci()
{ static int f1=0, f2=1;
  int f0=f1;
  f1 = f2;
```

```
      f2 += f0;
      return f0;
   }
   n=10: {0,1,1,2,3,5,8,13,21,34}
```

generate_n(p,n,f);
// assigns the outputs of successive calls f(x) to each x in [p,p+n[;

EXAMPLE D.18 Testing the **generate_n()** Algorithm

```
   long fibonacci();

   int main()
   { int a[10]={0};
     generate_n(a,10,fibonacci);
     print(a,10);
   }

   long fibonacci()
   { static int f1=0, f2=1;
     int f0=f1;
     f1 = f2;
     f2 += f0;
     return f0;
   }
   n=10: {0,1,1,2,3,5,8,13,21,34}
```

includes(p,q,pp,qq);
// returns true iff every element of [pp,qq[is found in [p,q[;
// precondition: both segments must be sorted;
// invariant: [p,q[and [pp,qq[are left unchanged;

EXAMPLE D.19 Testing the **includes()** Algorithm

```
   int main()
   { int a[] = {0,1,1,2,3,5,8,13,21,34};
     int b[] = {0,1,2,3,4};
     bool found = includes(a,a+10,b,b+5);
     cout << "found=" << found << '\n';
     found = includes(a,a+10,b,b+4);
     cout << "found=" << found << '\n';
   }
   found=0
   found=1
```

inner_product(p,q,pp,x)
// returns the sum of x and the inner product of [p,q[with [pp,pp+n[,
// where n = q-p;
// invariant: [p,q[and [pp,qq[are left unchanged;

EXAMPLE D.20 Testing the `inner_product()` Algorithm

```
int main()
{ int a[] = {1,3,5,7,9};
  int b[] = {4,3,2,1,0};
  int dot = inner_product(a,a+4,b,1000);
  cout << "dot=" << dot << '\n';
}
sum=1030
```

inplace_merge(p,r,q);
```
// merges the segments [p,r[ and [r,q[;
// precondition: the two segments must be contiguous and sorted;
// postcondition: the segment [p,r[ is sorted;
```

EXAMPLE D.21 Testing the `inplace_merge()` Algorithm

```
int main()
{ int a[] = {22,55,66,88,11,33,44,77,99};
  print(a,9);
  inplace_merge(a,a+4,a+9);
  print(a,9);
}
n=9: {22,55,66,88,11,33,44,77,99}
n=9: {11,22,33,44,55,66,77,88,99}
```

iter_swap(p,q);
```
// swaps the elements *p and *q;
```

EXAMPLE D.22 Testing the `iter_swap()` Algorithm

```
int main()
{ int a[] = {11,22,33,44,55,66,77,88,99};
  int b[] = {10,20,30,40,50,60,70,80,90};
  print(a,9);
  print(b,9);
  iter_swap(a+4,b+7);
  print(a,9);
  print(b,9);
}
n=9: {11,22,33,44,55,66,77,88,99}
n=9: {10,20,30,40,50,60,70,80,90}
n=9: {11,22,33,44,80,66,77,88,99}
n=9: {10,20,30,40,50,60,70,55,90}
```

lexicographical_compare(p,q,pp,qq);
```
// compares the two segments [pp,qq[ and [p,q[ lexicographically;
// returns true iff the first precedes the second;
// invariant: [p,q[ and [pp,qq[ are left unchanged;
```

EXAMPLE D.23 Testing the `lexicographical_compare()` Algorithm

```
void test(char*,int,char*,int);

int main()
{ char* s1="COMPUTER";
  char* s2="COMPUTABLE";
  char* s3="COMPUTE";
  test(s1,3,s2,3);
  test(s1,8,s2,10);
  test(s1,8,s3,7);
  test(s2,10,s3,7);
  test(s1,7,s3,7);
}

char* sub(char*,int);

void test(char* s1, int n1, char* s2, int n2)
{ bool lt=lexicographical_compare(s1,s1+n1,s2,s2+n2);
  bool gt=lexicographical_compare(s2,s2+n2,s1,s1+n1);
  if (lt) cout << sub(s1,n1) << " < " << sub(s2,n2) << "\n";
  else if (gt) cout << sub(s1,n1) << " > " << sub(s2,n2) << "\n";
  else cout << sub(s1,n1) << " == " << sub(s2,n2) << "\n";
}

char* sub(char* s, int n)
{ char* buffer = new char(n+1);
  strncpy(buffer,s,n);
  buffer[n] = 0;
  return buffer;
}
```
```
COM == COM
COMPUTER > COMPUTABLE
COMPUTER > COMPUTE
COMPUTABLE < COMPUTE
COMPUTE == COMPUTE
```

```
lower_bound(p,q,x);
// returns the position of the first occurrence of x in [p,q[;
// precondition: the segment must be sorted;
// invariant: [p,q[ is left unchanged;
```

EXAMPLE D.24 Testing the `lower_bound()` Algorithm

```
int main()
{ int a[] = {11,22,22,33,44,44,44,55,66};
  int* p = lower_bound(a,a+9,44);
  cout << "*p=" << *p << '\n';
  cout << "p-a=" << p-a << '\n';
}
```
```
*p=44
p-a=4
```

```
make_heap(p,q);
// rearranges the elements of [p,q[ into a heap;
// postcondition: [p,q[ is a heap;
```

EXAMPLE D.25 Testing the `make_heap()` Algorithm

```
int main()
{ int a[] = {44,88,33,77,11,99,66,22,55};
  print(a,9);
  make_heap(a,a+9);
  print(a,9);
}
n=9: {44,88,33,77,11,99,66,22,55}
n=9: {99,88,66,77,11,33,44,22,55}
```

```
max(x,y);
// returns the maximum of x and y;
```

EXAMPLE D.26 Testing the `max()` Algorithm

```
int main()
{ cout << "max(48,84)=" << max(48,84) << '\n';
}
max(48,84)=84
```

```
max_element(p,q);
// returns the position of the maximum element in the segment [pp,qq[;
// invariant: [p,q[ is left unchanged;
```

EXAMPLE D.27 Testing the `max_element()` Algorithm

```
int main()
{ int a[] = {77,22,99,55,11,88,44,33,66};
  const int* p = max_element(a,a+9);
  cout << "*p=" << *p << '\n';
  cout << "p-a=" << p-a << '\n';
}
*p=99
p-a=2
```

```
merge(p,q,pp,qq,ppp);
// merges the segments [p,q[ and [pp,qq[ into [ppp,ppp+n[,
// where n = q - p + qq - pp;
// precondition: [p,q[ and [pp,qq[ must be sorted;
// postcondition: the segment [ppp,ppp+n[ is sorted;
// invariant: [p,q[ and [pp,qq[ are left unchanged;
```

EXAMPLE D.28 Testing the `merge()` Algorithm

```
int main()
{ int a[] = {22,55,66,88};
  int b[] = {11,33,44,77,99};
  int c[9];
  merge(a,a+4,b,b+5,c);
  print(c,9);
}
n=9: {11,22,33,44,55,66,77,88,99}
```

`min(x,y);`
```
// returns the minimum of x and y;
```

EXAMPLE D.29 Testing the `min()` Algorithm

```
int main()
{ cout << "min(48,84)=" << min(48,84) << '\n';
}
min(48,84)=48
```

`min_element(p,q);`
```
// returns the position of the minimum element in the segment [p,q[;
// invariant: [p,q[ is left unchanged;
```

EXAMPLE D.30 Testing the `min_element()` Algorithm

```
int main()
{ int a[] = {77,22,99,55,11,88,44,33,66};
  const int* p = min_element(a,a+9);
  cout << "*p=" << *p << '\n';
  cout << "p-a=" << p-a << '\n';
}
*p=11
p-a=4
```

`mismatch(p,q,pp);`
```
// returns a pair of iterators giving the positions in [p,q[ and
// in [pp,qq[ where the first mismatch of elements occurs;
// if the two segments match entirely, then their ends are returned;
// invariant: [p,q[ and [pp,qq[ are left unchanged;
```

EXAMPLE D.31 Testing the `mismatch()` Algorithm

```
int main()
{ char* s1="Aphrodite, Apollo, Ares, Artemis, Athena";
  char* s2="Aphrodite, Apallo, Ares, Artimis, Athens";
  int n=strlen(s1);
  cout << "n=" << n << '\n';
  pair<char*,char*> x = mismatch(s1,s1+n,s2);
```

```
      char* p1 = x.first;
      char* p2 = x.second;
      cout << "*p1=" << *p1 << ", *p2=" << *p2 << '\n';
      cout << "p1-s1=" << p1-s1 << '\n';
   }
n=40
*p1=o, *p2=a
p1-s1=13
```

next_permutation(p,q);
```
// permutes the elements of [p,q[; n! calls will cycle through all n!
// permutations of the n elements, where n = q-p;
```

EXAMPLE D.32 Testing the **next_permutation()** Algorithm

```
int main()
{ char* s="ABCD";
  for (int i=0; i<24; i++)
  { next_permutation(s,s+4);
    cout << (i%8?'\t':'\n') << s;
  }
}
```

ABDC	ACBD	ACDB	ADBC	ADCB	BACD	BADC	BCAD
BCDA	BDAC	BDCA	CABD	CADB	CBAD	CBDA	CDAB
CDBA	DABC	DACB	DBAC	DBCA	DCAB	DCBA	ABCD

The next_permutation() algorithm is the inverse of the prev_permutation() algorithm (Example D.39 on page 315).

nth_element(p,r,q);
```
// rearranges the elements of [p,q[ so that *r partitions it into the two
// subsegments [p,r1[ and [r1+2,q], where r1 is the new location of *r,
// all the elements of [p,r1] are <= to *r, and all the elements of
// [r1+2,q] are >= to *r; *r is called the pivot element;
```

EXAMPLE D.33 Testing the **nth_element()** Algorithm

```
int main()
{ int a[] = {77,22,99,55,44,88,11,33,66};
  print(a,9);
  nth_element(a,a+3,a+9);
  print(a,9);
}
n=9: {77,22,99,55,44,88,11,33,66}
n=9: {11,22,33,44,55,88,66,99,77}
```

partial_sort(p,r,q);
```
// sorts the first r-p elements of [p,q[, placing them in [p,r[ and
// shifting the remaining q-r elements down to [r,q[;
```

EXAMPLE D.34 Testing the `partial_sort()` Algorithm

```
int main()
{ int a[] = {77,22,99,55,44,88,11,33,66};
  print(a,9);
  partial_sort(a,a+3,a+9);
  print(a,9);
}
n=9: {77,22,99,55,44,88,11,33,66}
n=9: {11,22,33,99,77,88,55,44,66}
```

`partial_sort_copy(p,q,pp,qq);`
```
// copies the qq-pp smallest elements of [p,q[ into [pp,qq[ in sorted
// order; then copies the remaining n elements into [qq,qq+n[,
// where n = q-p+pp-qq;
// invariant: [p,q[ is left unchanged;
```

EXAMPLE D.35 Testing the `partial_sort_copy()` Algorithm

```
int main()
{ int a[] = {77,22,99,55,44,88,11,33,66};
  print(a,9);
  int b[3];
  partial_sort_copy(a,a+9,b,b+3);
  print(a,9);
  print(b,3);
}
n=9: {77,22,99,55,44,88,11,33,66}
n=9: {77,22,99,55,44,88,11,33,66}
n=3: {11,22,33}
```

`partial_sum(p,q,pp);`
```
// invariant: a[p,q[ is left unchanged;
// postcondition b[i] == a[0]+...+a[i] for each b[i] in [pp,pp+q-p[;
```

EXAMPLE D.36 Testing the `partial_sum()` Algorithm

```
int main()
{ int a[] = {0,1,1,2,3,5,8,13,21,34};
  int b[10];
  partial_sum(a,a+10,b);
  print(a,10);
  print(b,10);
}
n=10: {0,1,1,2,3,5,8,13,21,34}
n=10: {0,1,2,4,7,12,20,33,54,88}
```

The `partial_sum()` algorithm is the inverse of the `adjacent_difference()` algorithm (Example D.2 on page 302).

```
partition(p,q,P());
// partitions [p,q[ into [p,r[ and [r,q[ so that
// x is in [p,r[ iff P(x) is true;
```

EXAMPLE D.37 Testing the `partition()` Algorithm

```
int main()
{ int a[] = {0,1,1,2,3,5,8,13,21,34};
  print(a,10);
  partition(a,a+10,Odd());
  print(a,10);
}
n=10: {0,1,1,2,3,5,8,13,21,34}
n=10: {21,1,1,13,3,5,8,2,0,34}
```

```
pop_heap(p,q);
// moves *p into temp, then shifts elements to the left so that the
// remaining elements in [p,q-1[ form a heap, then copies temp into *(q-1);
// precondition: [p,q[ must be a heap;
// postcondition: [p,q-1[ is a heap;
```

EXAMPLE D.38 Testing the `pop_heap()` Algorithm

```
int main()
{ int a[] = {44,88,33,77,11,99,66,22,55};
  print(a,9);
  make_heap(a,a+9);
  print(a,9);
  pop_heap(a,a+9);
  print(a,9);
  print(a,8);
}
n=9: {44,88,33,77,11,99,66,22,55}
n=9: {99,88,66,77,11,33,44,22,55}
n=9: {88,77,66,55,11,33,44,22,99}
n=8: {88,77,66,55,11,33,44,22}
```
See Example D.25 on page 311.

```
prev_permutation(p,q);
// permutes the elements of [p,q[; n! calls will cycle backward through
// all n! permutations of the n elements, where n = q-p;
```

EXAMPLE D.39 Testing the `prev_permutation()` Algorithm

```
int main()
{ char* s="ABCD";
  for (int i=0; i<24; i++)
  { prev_permutation(s,s+4);
    cout << (i%8?'\t':'\n') << s;
  }
}
```

DCBA	DCAB	DBCA	DBAC	DACB	DABC	CDBA	CDAB
CBDA	CBAD	CADB	CABD	BDCA	BDAC	BCDA	BCAD
BADC	BACD	ADCB	ADBC	ACDB	ACBD	ABDC	ABCD

The `prev_permutation()` algorithm is the inverse of the `next_permutation()` algorithm (Example D.32 on page 313).

push_heap(p,q);
```
// adds the element at *(q-1) to those in [p,q-1[ so that [p,q[ is a heap;
// precondition: [p,q-1[ must be a heap;
// postcondition: [p,q[ is a heap;
```

EXAMPLE D.40 Testing the `push_heap()` Algorithm

```
int main()
{ int a[] = {66,44,88,33,55,11,99,22,77};
  print(a,8);
  make_heap(a,a+8);
  print(a,8);
  print(a,9);
  push_heap(a,a+9);
  print(a,9);
}
n=8: {66,44,88,33,55,11,99,22}
n=8: {99,55,88,33,44,11,66,22}
n=9: {99,55,88,33,44,11,66,22,77}
n=9: {99,77,88,55,44,11,66,22,33}
```

The `push_heap()` algorithm reverses the effect of `pop_heap()` (Example D.38 on page 315.)

random_shuffle(p,q);
```
// performs a random (but deterministic) shuffle on [pp,qq[
```

EXAMPLE D.41 Testing the `random_shuffle()` Algorithm

```
int main()
{ char* s="ABCDEFGHIJ";
  cout << s << '\n';
  for (int i=0; i<4; i++)
  { random_shuffle(s,s+10);
    cout << s << '\n';
  }
}
ABCDEFGHIJ
CIJDBEAHGF
CFBDEIGAHJ
IDJABEFGHC
```

remove(p,q,x);
// removes all occurrences of x from [p,q[, shifting (copying) the
// remaining elements to the left;
// invariant: the length of the segment remains unchanged;

EXAMPLE D.42 Testing the **remove()** Algorithm

```
int main()
{ char* s="All is flux, nothing is stationary.";   // Heraclitus
  int l = strlen(s);
  int n = count(s,s+l,' ');
  cout << "l=" << l << '\n';
  cout << "n=" << n << '\n';
  remove(s,s+l,' ');
  cout << s << '\n';
  s[l-n] = 0;   // truncate s
  cout << s << '\n';
}
l=35
n=5
Allisflux,nothingisstationaryonary.
Allisflux,nothingisstationary.
```

Since 5 blanks were removed, the last 5 letters remain after their copies were shifted left.

remove_copy(p,q,pp,x);
// copies all elements of [p,q[that do not match x to [pp,pp+n[,
// where n is the number of nonmatching elements;
// returns pp+n;
// invariant: [p,q[remains unchanged;

EXAMPLE D.43 Testing the **remove_copy()** Algorithm

```
int main()
{ char* s="All is flux, nothing is stationary.";   // Heraclitus
  char buffer[80];
  int l = strlen(s);
  int n = count(s,s+l,' ');
  cout << "l=" << l << '\n';
  cout << "n=" << n << '\n';
  char* ss = remove_copy(s,s+l,buffer,' ');
  *ss = 0;   // truncate buffer
  cout << s << '\n';
  cout << buffer << '\n';
  cout << ss-buffer << '\n';
}
l=35
n=5
All is flux, nothing is stationary.
Allisflux,nothingisstationary.
29
```

```
remove_copy_if(p,q,pp,P());
// copies all elements x of [p,q[ for which !P(x) to [pp,pp+n[,
// where n is the number of nonmatching elements;
// returns pp+n;
// invariant: [p,q[ remains unchanged;
```

EXAMPLE D.44 Testing the `remove_copy_if()` Algorithm

```
class Blank
{ public:
    bool operator()(char c) { return c == ' '; }
};

int main()
{ char* s="All is flux, nothing is stationary.";   // Heraclitus
  char buffer[80];
  int l = strlen(s);
  int n = count(s,s+1,' ');
  cout << "l=" << l << '\n';
  cout << "n=" << n << '\n';
  char* ss = remove_copy_if(s,s+1,buffer,Blank());
  *ss = 0;   // truncate buffer
  cout << s << '\n';
  cout << buffer << '\n';
  cout << ss-buffer << '\n';
}
l=35
n=5
All is flux, nothing is stationary.
Allisflux,nothingisstationary.
29
```

This is the same as Example D.43 on page 317 except that a predicate is used.

```
remove_if(p,q,P());
// removes all x from [p,q[ for which !P(x), shifting (copying) the
// remaining elements to the left;
```

EXAMPLE D.45 Testing the `remove_if()` Algorithm

```
class Blank
{ public:
    bool operator()(char c) { return c == ' '; }
};

int main()
{ char* s="All is flux, nothing is stationary.";   // Heraclitus
  int l = strlen(s);
  int n = count(s,s+1,' ');
  cout << "l=" << l << '\n';
  cout << "n=" << n << '\n';
  remove_if(s,s+1,Blank());
```

```
      cout << s << '\n';
      s[l-n] = 0;
      cout << s << '\n';
   }
   l=35
   n=5
   Allisflux,nothingisstationaryonary.
   Allisflux,nothingisstationary.
```

This is the same as Example D.42 on page 317 except that a predicate is used.

replace(p,q,x,y);
```
// replaces all occurrences of x with y in [p,q[;
// invariant: the length of the segment remains unchanged;
```

EXAMPLE D.46 Testing the replace() Algorithm

```
   int main()
   { char* s="All is flux, nothing is stationary.";   // Heraclitus
     int l = strlen(s);
     cout << s << '\n';
     replace(s,s+1,' ','!');
     cout << s << '\n';
   }
   All is flux, nothing is stationary.
   All!is!flux, !nothing!is!stationary.
```

replace_copy(p,q,pp,x,y);
```
// copies all elements of [p,q[ to [pp,pp+n[, replacing each occurrence
// of x with y, where n = q-p;
// returns pp+n;
// invariant: [p,q[ remains unchanged;
```

EXAMPLE D.47 Testing the replace_copy() Algorithm

```
   int main()
   { char* s="All is flux, nothing is stationary.";   // Heraclitus
     cout << s << '\n';
     int l = strlen(s);
     char buffer[80];
     char* ss = replace_copy(s,s+1,buffer,'n','N');
     *ss = 0;   // truncate buffer for printing
     cout << s << '\n';
     cout << buffer << '\n';
   }
   All is flux, nothing is stationary.
   All is flux, nothing is stationary.
   All is flux, NothiNg is statioNary.
```

```
replace_copy_if(p,q,pp,P(),y);
// copies all elements of [p,q[ to [pp,pp+n[, replacing each x for
// which P(x) is true with y, where n = q-p;
// returns pp+n;
// invariant: [p,q[ remains unchanged;
```

EXAMPLE D.48 Testing the `replace_copy_if()` Algorithm

```
class Blank
{ public:
    bool operator()(char c) { return c == ' '; }
};

int main()
{ char* s="All is flux, nothing is stationary.";  // Heraclitus
  int l = strlen(s);
  char buffer[80];
  cout << s << '\n';
  char* ss = replace_copy_if(s,s+l,buffer,Blank(),'!');
  *ss = 0;  // truncate buffer
  cout << s << '\n';
  cout << buffer << '\n';
}
All is flux, nothing is stationary.
All is flux, nothing is stationary.
All!is!flux, !nothing!is!stationary.
```

This is the same as Example D.47 on page 319 except that a predicate is used.

```
replace_if(p,q,P(),y);
// replaces each x for which P(x) with y in [p,q[;
```

EXAMPLE D.49 Testing the `replace_if()` Algorithm

```
class Blank
{ public:
    bool operator()(char c) { return c == ' '; }
};

int main()
{ char* s="All is flux, nothing is stationary.";  // Heraclitus
  int l = strlen(s);
  cout << s << '\n';
  replace_if(s,s+l,Blank(),'!');
  cout << s << '\n';
}
All is flux, nothing is stationary.
All!is!flux, !nothing!is!stationary.
```

This is the same as Example D.46 on page 319 except that a predicate is used.

```
reverse(p,q);
// reverses the segment [p,q[;
```

EXAMPLE D.50 Testing the `reverse()` Algorithm

```
    int main()
    { char* s="ABCDEFGHIJKLMNOpQRSTUVWXYZ";
      cout << s << '\n';
      reverse(s,s+26);
      cout << s << '\n';
    }
    ABCDEFGHIJKLMNOpQRSTUVWXYZ
    ZYXWVUTSRQpONMLKJIHGFEDCBA
```

```
reverse_copy(p,q,pp);
// copies the segment [p,q[ into [pp,pp+n[ in reverse order,
// where n = q-p;
// returns pp+n
// invariant: [p,q[ remains unchanged;
```

EXAMPLE D.51 Testing the `reverse_copy()` Algorithm

```
    int main()
    { char* s="ABCDEFGHIJKLMNOpQRSTUVWXYZ";
      cout << s << '\n';
      char buffer[80];
      char* ss = reverse_copy(s,s+26,buffer);
      *ss = 0;  // truncate buffer for printing
      cout << s << '\n';
      cout << buffer << '\n';
    }
    ABCDEFGHIJKLMNOpQRSTUVWXYZ
    ABCDEFGHIJKLMNOpQRSTUVWXYZ
    ZYXWVUTSRQpONMLKJIHGFEDCBA
```

```
rotate(p,r,q);
// shifts [r,q[ to the left by r positions into [p,p+q-r[,
// and wraps [p,r[ around to the right end into [p+q-r,q[;
```

EXAMPLE D.52 Testing the `rotate()` Algorithm

```
    int main()
    { char* s="ABCDEFGHIJKLMNOpQRSTUVWXYZ";
      cout << s << '\n';
      rotate(s,s+4,s+26);
      cout << s << '\n';
    }
    ABCDEFGHIJKLMNOpQRSTUVWXYZ
    EFGHIJKLMNOpQRSTUVWXYZABCD
```

```
rotate_copy(p,r,q,pp);
// copies the segment [r,q[ into [pp,pp+m[, where m = q-r,
// and copies the segment [p,r[ into [pp+m,pp+n[, where n = q-p;
// returns pp+m+n;
// invariant: [p,q[ remains unchanged;
```

EXAMPLE D.53 Testing the `rotate_copy()` Algorithm

```
int main()
{ char* s="ABCDEFGHIJKLMNOpQRSTUVWXYZ";
  cout << s << '\n';
  char buffer[80];
  char* ss = rotate_copy(s,s+4,s+26,buffer);
  *ss = 0;  // truncate buffer for printing
  cout << s << '\n';
  cout << buffer << '\n';
}
ABCDEFGHIJKLMNOpQRSTUVWXYZ
ABCDEFGHIJKLMNOpQRSTUVWXYZ
EFGHIJKLMNOpQRSTUVWXYZABCD
```

```
search(p,q,pp,qq);
// searches for the subsequence [pp,qq[ in [p,q[;
// if found, the position r of its first occurrence is returned;
// otherwise, q is returned;
// postcondition: either r = q or [r,r+n[ = [pp,qq[, where n = qq-pp;
// invariant: [p,q[ is left unchanged;
```

EXAMPLE D.54 Testing the `search()` Algorithm

```
int main()
{ char* p="ABCDEFGHIJKLABCDEFGHIJKL";
  char* pp="HIJK";
  char* r = search(p,p+24,pp,pp+4);
  int n = r-p;  // number of characters before pp in p
  cout << "n=r-p=" << n << '\n';
  cout << "*r=" << *r << '\n';
  cout << p << '\n';
  cout << string(n,'-') << pp << string(20-n,'-') << '\n';
  pp = "LMNOp";
  r = search(p,p+24,pp,pp+5);
  n = r-p;
  cout << "n=r-p=" << n << '\n';
  cout << p << '\n';
  cout << string(n,'-') << '\n';
}
n=r-p=7
*r=H
ABCDEFGHIJKLABCDEFGHIJKL
-------HIJK-------------
n=r-p=24
ABCDEFGHIJKLABCDEFGHIJKL
------------------------
```

```
search_n(p,q,n,x);
// searches for the subsequence of n consecutive copies of x in [p,q[;
// if found, the position r of its first occurrence is returned;
// otherwise, q is returned;
// postcondition: either r = q or [r,r+n[ = [pp,qq[, where n = qq-pp;
// invariant: [p,q[ is left unchanged;
```

EXAMPLE D.55 Testing the `search_n()` Algorithm

```
    int main()
    { char* p="0010111001111110";
      char* r = search_n(p,p+16,3,'1');
      int m = r-p;   // number of characters before the substring in p
      cout << "m=r-p=" << m << '\n';
      cout << p << '\n';
      cout << string(m,'-') << string(3,'1') << string(13-m,'-') << '\n';
      r = search_n(p,p+16,4,'1');
      m = r-p;   // number of characters before substring in p
      cout << "m=r-p=" << m << '\n';
      cout << p << '\n';
      cout << string(m,'-') << string(4,'1') << string(12-m,'-') << '\n';
    }
```
```
m=r-p=4
0010111001111110
----111---------
m=r-p=9
0010111001111110
---------1111---
```

```
set_difference(p,q,pp,qq,ppp);
// copies into [ppp,ppp+n[ the elements in [p,q[ that are not in [pp,qq[;
// returns ppp+n, where n is the number of elements copied;
// invariant: [p,q[ and [pp,qq[ are left unchanged;
```

EXAMPLE D.56 Testing the `set_difference()` Algorithm

```
    int main()
    { char* p="ABCDEFGHIJ";
      char* pp="AEIOUXYZ";
      char ppp[16];
      char* qqq = set_difference(p,p+10,pp,pp+8,ppp);
      cout << p << '\n';
      cout << pp << '\n';
      *qqq = 0;   // terminates the ppp string
      cout << ppp << '\n';
    }
```
```
ABCDEFGHIJ
AEIOUXYZ
BCDFGHJ
```

```
set_intersection(p,q,pp,qq,ppp);
// copies into [ppp,ppp+n[ the elements in [p,q[ that are also in [pp,qq[;
// returns ppp+n, where n is the number of elements copied;
// invariant: [p,q[ and [pp,qq[ are left unchanged;
```

EXAMPLE D.57 Testing the `set_intersection()` Algorithm

```
    int main()
    { char* p="ABCDEFGHIJ";
      char* pp="AEIOUXYZ";
      char ppp[16];
      char* r = set_intersection(p,p+10,pp,pp+8,ppp);
      cout << p << '\n';
      cout << pp << '\n';
      *r = 0;   // terminates the ppp string
      cout << ppp << '\n';
    }
    ABCDEFGHIJ
    AEIOUXYZ
    AEI
```

```
set_symmetric_difference(p,q,pp,qq,ppp);
// copies into [ppp,ppp+n[ the elements in [p,q[ that are not in [pp,qq[
// and those that are in [pp,qq[ but not in [p,q[;
// returns ppp+n, where n is the number of elements copied;
// invariant: [p,q[ and [pp,qq[ are left unchanged;
```

EXAMPLE D.58 Testing the `set_symmetric_difference()` Algorithm

```
    int main()
    { char* p="ABCDEFGHIJ";
      char* pp="AEIOUXYZ";
      char ppp[16];
      char* qqq = set_symmetric_difference(p,p+10,pp,pp+8,ppp);
      cout << p << '\n';
      cout << pp << '\n';
      *qqq = 0;   // terminates the ppp string
      cout << ppp << '\n';
    }
    ABCDEFGHIJ
    AEIOUXYZ
    BCDFGHJOUXYZ
```

```
set_union(p,q,pp,qq,ppp);
// copies into [ppp,ppp+n[ all the elements in [p,q[ and all the elements
// in [pp,qq[ without duplicates;
// returns ppp+n, where n is the number of elements copied;
// invariant: [p,q[ and [pp,qq[ are left unchanged;
```

EXAMPLE D.59 Testing the `set_union()` Algorithm

```
int main()
{ char* p="ABCDEFGHIJ";
  char* pp="AEIOUXYZ";
  char ppp[16];
  char* r = set_union(p,p+10,pp,pp+8,ppp);
  cout << p << '\n';
  cout << pp << '\n';
  *r = 0;   // terminates the ppp string
  cout << ppp << '\n';
}
ABCDEFGHIJ
AEIOUXYZ
ABCDEFGHIJOUXYZ
```

```
sort(p,q);
```
```
// sorts [p,q[;
```

EXAMPLE D.60 Testing the `sort()` Algorithm

```
int main()
{ char* p="GAJBHCHDIEFAGDHC";
  cout << p << '\n';
  sort(p,p+16);
  cout << p << '\n';
}
GAJBHCHDIEFAGDHC
AABCCDDEFGGHHHIJ
```

```
sort_heap(p,q);
```
```
// sorts [p,q[;
```

EXAMPLE D.61 Testing the `sort_heap()` Algorithm

```
int main()
{ int a[] = {66,88,44,77,33,55,11,99,22};
  print(a,9);
  make_heap(a,a+9);
  print(a,9);
  sort_heap(a,a+9);
  print(a,9);
}
n=9: {66,88,44,77,33,55,11,99,22}
n=9: {99,88,55,77,33,44,11,66,22}
n=9: {11,22,33,44,55,66,77,88,99}
```

```
swap(x,y);
// swaps the two elements x and y;
```

EXAMPLE D.62 Testing the `swap()` Algorithm

```
    int main()
    { char* p="ABCDEFGHIJ";
      cout << p << '\n';
      swap(p[2],p[8]);
      cout << p << '\n';
    }
```
```
ABCDEFGHIJ
ABIDEFGHCJ
```

```
transform(p,q,pp,f);
// applies the function f(x) to each x in [p,q[ and copies the result
// into [pp,pp+n[, where n = q-p;
// invariant: [p,q[ remains unchanged;
```

EXAMPLE D.63 Testing the `transform()` Algorithm

```
    char capital(char);

    int main()
    { char* s="All is flux, nothing is stationary.";   // Heraclitus
      int len = strlen(s);
      char buffer[80];
      char* ss = transform(s,s+len,buffer,capital);
      *ss = 0;   // truncate buffer
      cout << s << '\n';
      cout << buffer << '\n';
    }

    char capital(char c)
    { return (isalpha(c) ? toupper(c) : c);
    }
```
```
All is flux, nothing is stationary.
ALL IS FLUX, NOTHING IS STATIONARY.
```

```
unique(p,q);
// removes all adjacent duplicates in [p,q[ shifting their suffixes left;
// returns the position that follows the last shifted element;
```

EXAMPLE D.64 Testing the `unique()` Algorithm

```
    int main()
    { char* s="All is flux, nothing is stationary.";   // Heraclitus
      int len = strlen(s);
      cout << s << '\n';
      sort(s,s+len);
      cout << s << '\n';
      char* ss = unique(s,s+len);
      cout << s << '\n';
```

```
      *ss = 0;   // truncate buffer
      cout << s <<· '\n';
    }
All is flux, nothing is stationary.
       ,.Aaafghiiiilllnnnoorsssttttuxy
  ,.Aafghilnorstuxyllnnnoorsssttttuxy
  ,.Aafghilnorstuxy
```

unique_copy(p,q,pp);
// copies the nonduplicate elements of [p,q[into [pp,pp+n[,
// where n is the number of unique elements in [p,q[;;
// returns pp+n;
// invariant: [p,q[is left unchanged;

EXAMPLE D.65 Testing the unique_copy() Algorithm

```
    int main()
    { char* s="All is flux, nothing is stationary.";   // Heraclitus
      int len = strlen(s);
      cout << s << '\n';
      sort(s,s+len);
      cout << s << '\n';
      char buffer[80];
      char* ss = unique_copy(s,s+len,buffer);
      *ss = 0;   // truncate buffer for printing
      cout << s << '\n';
      cout << buffer << '\n';
    }
All is flux, nothing is stationary.
       ,.Aaafghiiiilllnnnoorsssttttuxy
       ,.Aaafghiiiilllnnnoorsssttttuxy
  ,.Aafghilnorstuxy
```

upper_bound(p,q,x);
// returns the position that immediately follows the last occurrence
// of x in [pp,qq[;
// precondition: [p,q[must be sorted;
// invariant: [p,q[is left unchanged;

EXAMPLE D.66 Testing the upper_bound() Algorithm

```
    int main()
    { int a[] = {11,22,22,33,44,44,44,55,66};
      int* p = upper_bound(a,a+9,44);
      cout << "*p=" << *p << '\n';
      cout << "p-a=" << p-a << '\n';
    }
*p=55
p-a=7
```

Appendix E

Example Classes

This appendix contains the C++ source code for the interface and the implementation of the nonstandard class and class template used in this book. The following headers are used:

```
#include <cmath>        // defines the atan() and sqrt() functions
#include <ctype.h>      // defines atoi(), atof(), and toupper() functions
#include <iostream>     // defines the cin and cout objects
#include <list>         // defines the list class template
#include <map>          // defines the map class template
#include <sstream>      // defines ostringstream class
using namespace std;    // obviates the prefix std::
```

All this source code is available in the Classes folder. Each class interface is saved in its own .h header file. Each class implementation is saved in its own .cpp source code file. Each class template (interface and implementation together) is saved in its own .hpp source code file. Each class and class template also has a test driver program in its own test_Xxxx.cpp file.

E.1 A `BinaryTree` CLASS

```
class BinaryTree
{   struct Node;
    Node* _root;
  public:
    class Iterator;                      // BinaryTree::Iterator class
    BinaryTree();                                // default constructor
    BinaryTree(const BinaryTree&);               // copy constructor
    BinaryTree(const Type&);                     // constructs singleton
    BinaryTree(const Type&, const BinaryTree&, const BinaryTree&);
    ~BinaryTree();                               // destructs all nodes
    BinaryTree& operator=(const BinaryTree& t);  // assignment
    void clear();                                // empties this tree
    bool empty() const;                  // true iff this tree is empty
    int size() const;            // number of elements in this tree
    int leaves() const;          // number of elements in this tree
    int height() const;                  // height of this tree
    int level(Iterator) const;                   // current level
    void reflect();            // swaps all left and right children
    void defoliate();                    // removes all the leaves
    Type& root() const;        // read-write access to root element
    static bool isRoot(Iterator);                // has no parents
    static bool isLeaf(Iterator);                // has no children
    static Iterator parent(Iterator);
    static Iterator leftChild(Iterator);
    static Iterator rightChild(Iterator);
```

328

```
        Iterator begin();          // inorder traversal starts at root
        Iterator end();                    // ends with null iterator
        Iterator find(Iterator, Iterator, const Type&);
        friend class Iterator              // preorder traversal
        {   BinaryTree* _tree;       // the tree being traversed
            Node* _p;                      // the current node
          public:
            Iterator();                    // default constructor
            Iterator(const Iterator&);     // copy constructor
            Iterator(BinaryTree*, Node* =0);   // constructor
            void operator=(const Iterator& it);   // assignment
            bool operator==(const Iterator& it);   // equality
            bool operator!=(const Iterator& it);   // inequality
            Iterator& operator++();        // prefix increment
            Iterator operator++(int);      // postfix increment
            Type& operator*() const;       // current element
            bool operator!();              // this iterator is null
            friend class BinaryTree;
        };
};

typedef BinaryTree::Node Node;
typedef BinaryTree::Iterator It;
void destroy(Node*);     // postorder deletion for destructor
int s(Node*);
int n(Node*);
int h(Node*);
int l(Node*,It);
void r(Node*);
void d(Node*);
Node* preorderSuccessor(Node*);
Node* clone(Node*,Node*);


//////////////////////////////////////////////////////////
// definition of protected BinaryTree::Node struct:

struct BinaryTree::Node
{ Type _;
  Node* _left;
  Node* _right;
  Node* _parent;
  Node(Type =Type(), Node* =0, Node* =0, Node* =0);
};

BinaryTree::Node::Node(Type x, Node* left, Node* right,
                       Node* parent)
 : _(x), _left(left), _right(right), _parent(parent)
{ if (!_parent) _parent = this;  // the root
 }
```

```
/////////////////////////////////////////////////////////
// public member functions of the BinaryTree class:

BinaryTree::BinaryTree() : _root(0)
{
}

BinaryTree::BinaryTree(const BinaryTree& t)
{ _root = clone(t._root,0);
}

BinaryTree::BinaryTree(const Type& x)
{ _root = new Node(x);
}

BinaryTree::BinaryTree(const Type& x, const BinaryTree& lTree,
                       const BinaryTree& rTree)
{ _root = new Node(x);
  _root->_left = clone(lTree._root,_root);
  _root->_right = clone(rTree._root,_root);
}

BinaryTree::~BinaryTree()
{ destroy(_root);
}

BinaryTree& BinaryTree::operator=(const BinaryTree& t)
{ clear();                               // empty this tree
  BinaryTree* p = new BinaryTree(t); // use copy constructor
  _root = p->_root;
  return *this;
}

void BinaryTree::clear()
{ destroy(_root);
}

bool BinaryTree::empty() const
{ return _root == 0;
}

int BinaryTree::size() const
{ return s(_root);
}

int BinaryTree::leaves() const
{ return n(_root);
}
```

```
int BinaryTree::height() const
{ return h(_root);
}

int BinaryTree::level(It it) const
{ return l(_root,it);
}

void BinaryTree::reflect()
{ r(_root);
}

void BinaryTree::defoliate()
{ if (!_root) return;
  if (_root->_left || _root->_right) d(_root);
  else clear();
}

Type& BinaryTree::root() const
{ return _root->_;
}

bool BinaryTree::isRoot(It it)
{ return it._p == it._tree->_root;
}

bool BinaryTree::isLeaf(It it)
{ Node* p=it._p;
  if (!p || p->_left || p->_right) return false;
  return true;
}

It BinaryTree::parent(It it)
{ if (isRoot(it)) return It(it._tree,0);
  return It(it._tree,(it._p)->_parent);
}

It BinaryTree::leftChild(It it)
{ Node* p=it._p;
  if (!p || p->_left) return It(it._tree,p->_left);
  return It(it._tree,0);
}

It BinaryTree::rightChild(It it)
{ Node* p=it._p;
  if (!p || p->_right) return It(it._tree,p->_right);
  return It(it._tree,0);
}
```

```
It BinaryTree::begin()
{ return It(this,_root);
}


It BinaryTree::end()
{ return It(this,0);
}


It BinaryTree::find(It begin, It end, const Type& x)
{ BinaryTree* tree=begin._tree;
  Node* p=begin._p;
  while (p != end._p)
    if (p->_ == x) return It(tree,p);
    else p = preorderSuccessor(p);
  return It(this,0);   // not found
}


/////////////////////////////////////////////////////////////
//  public member functions of the BinaryTree::Iterator class:

It::Iterator()
{
}


It::Iterator(const It& it) : _tree(it._tree), _p(it._p)
{
}


It::Iterator(BinaryTree* tree, Node* p) : _tree(tree), _p(p)
{
}


void It::operator=(const It& it)
{ _tree = it._tree;
  _p = it._p;
}


bool It::operator==(const It& it)
{ return _tree == it._tree && _p == it._p;
}


bool It::operator!=(const It& it)
{ return _tree != it._tree || _p != it._p;
}


It& It::operator++()                          // prefix increment
{ _p = preorderSuccessor(_p);
  return *this;
}
```

```
It It::operator++(int)        // postfix increment operator
{ It it(*this);                        // copy this iterator
  operator++();               // increment this iterator
  return it;                            // return the copy
}

Type& It::operator*() const
{ return _p->_;
}

bool It::operator!()
{ return _p == 0;
}

/////////////////////////////////////////////////////////////
//  local recursive utility functions:

void destroy(Node* p)
{ if (!p) return;
  destroy(p->_left);
  destroy(p->_right);
  delete p;
}

int s(Node* p)
{ if (!p) return 0;
  int nl=s(p->_left);
  int nr=s(p->_right);
  return 1 + nl + nr;
}

int n(Node* p)
{ if (!p) return 0;
  if (p->_left == 0 && p->_right == 0) return 1;
  return n(p->_left) + n(p->_right);
}

int h(Node* p)
{ if (!p) return -1;
  int hl=h(p->_left);
  int hr=h(p->_right);
  return 1 + max(hl,hr);
}

int l(Node* p, It it)
{ if (!p) return -1;
  if (p->_ == *it) return 0;
  int ll=l(p->_left,it);
  if (ll > -1) return 1 + ll;
  int lr=l(p->_right,it);
```

```
    if (lr > -1) return 1 + lr;
    return -1;
}


void r(Node* p)
{ if (!p) return;
  r(p->_left);
  r(p->_right);
  swap(p->_left,p->_right);
}


void d(Node* p)
{ // precondition: *p is not a leaf
  Node* lc=p->_left;
  if (lc && (lc->_left || lc->_right)) d(lc);
  else  // *lc is a leaf
  { delete lc;
    p->_left = 0;
  }
  Node* rc=p->_right;
  if (rc && (rc->_left || rc->_right)) d(rc);
  else  // *rc is a leaf
  { delete rc;
    p->_right = 0;
  }
}


Node* preorderSuccessor(Node* p)
{ if (p->_left) return p->_left;
  if (p->_right) return p->_right;
  // move up tree until p is the root or p has a younger sibling
  while (p->_parent!=p
         && (p->_parent->_right==p || p->_parent->_right==0))
    p = p->_parent;
  if (p->_parent==p) return 0;  // p is the root
  return p->_parent->_right;  // younger sibling is successor
}


Node* clone(Node* p,Node* pp)
{ // recursive preorder traversal;
  // returns a duplicate of Node *p,
  // including the duplication of all its descendants
  if (!p) return 0;                      // basis of the recursion
  Node* cp = new Node(p->_,0,0,pp);  // duplicate the current node
  cp->_left = clone(p->_left,cp);    // duplicate the left subtree
  cp->_right = clone(p->_right,cp);  // duplicate the right subtree
  return cp;
}
```

E.2 A `BinarySearchTree` CLASS

```
class BinarySearchTree
{    struct Node;
     Node* _root;
  public:
     BinarySearchTree();
     void insert(const Type);
     void print() const;
     Type search(const Type) const;
  protected:
     void insert(Node*&, const Type);
     void print(Node*) const;
     Type search(Node*, const Type) const;
};

struct BinarySearchTree::Node
{ Type _;
  Node* _left;
  Node* _right;
  Node(Type =Type(), Node* =0, Node* =0);
};

BinarySearchTree::Node::Node(Type x, Node* left, Node* right)
 : _(x), _left(left), _right(right)
{
}

BinarySearchTree::BinarySearchTree() : _root(0)
{
}

void BinarySearchTree::insert(const Type x)
{ insert(_root,x);
}

void BinarySearchTree::print() const
{ print(_root);
  cout << "\n";
}

Type BinarySearchTree::search(const Type x) const
{ return search(_root,x);
}

void BinarySearchTree::insert(Node*& p, const Type x)
{ if (!p) p = new Node(x);
  else if (x == p->_) return;
  else if (x < p->_) return insert(p->_left,x);
```

```
      else insert(p->_right,x);
}

void BinarySearchTree::print(Node* p) const
{ if (!p) return;
  print(p->_left);
  cout << p->_ << " ";
  print(p->_right);
}

Type BinarySearchTree::search(Node* p, const Type x) const
{ if (p == 0) return Type();
  else if (x == p->_) return p->_;
  else if (x < p->_) return search(p->_left,x);
  else return search(p->_right,x);
}
```

E.3 A Card CLASS

```
class Card
{ //  instances represent playing cards
    friend ostream& operator<<(ostream&, const Card&);
  public:
    enum Rank { TWO, THREE, FOUR, FIVE, SIX, SEVEN, EIGHT, NINE,
                TEN, JACK, QUEEN, KING, ACE };
    enum Suit { CLUB, DIAMOND, HEART, SPADE };
    Card(Rank=ACE,Suit=SPADE);       // default constructor
    Card(int,int);                   // constructor
    Card(const Card&);               // copy constructor
    ~Card();                         // destructor
    Rank rank() const;
    Suit suit() const;
    bool isFaceCard() const;
    int count() const;
    string toString() const;
    string abbr() const;
    bool operator<(const Card&) const;
    bool operator>(const Card&) const;
    bool operator<=(const Card&) const;
    bool operator>=(const Card&) const;
    bool operator==(const Card&) const;
    bool operator!=(const Card&) const;
  private:
    Rank _rank;
    Suit _suit;
    static int _count[13][4];
};
```

```cpp
ostream& operator<<(ostream& ostr, const Card& card)
{ return ostr << card.toString();
}


Card::Card(Rank rank, Suit suit) : _rank(rank), _suit(suit)
{ ++_count[_rank][_suit];
}


Card::Card(int r, int s) : _rank(Rank(r)), _suit(Suit(s))
{ ++_count[_rank][_suit];
}


Card::Card(const Card& card) : _rank(card._rank), _suit(card._suit)
{ ++_count[_rank][_suit];
}


Card::~Card()
{ --_count[_rank][_suit];
}


Card::Rank Card::rank() const
{ return _rank;
}


Card::Suit Card::suit() const
{ return _suit;
}


bool Card::isFaceCard() const
{ return (_rank > NINE);
}


int Card::count() const
{ return _count[_rank][_suit];
}


string Card::toString() const
{ string str;
  switch (_rank)
  { case TWO:   str = "two of ";    break;
    case THREE: str = "three of ";    break;
    case FOUR:  str = "four of ";    break;
    case FIVE:  str = "five of ";    break;
    case SIX:   str = "six of ";    break;
    case SEVEN: str = "seven of ";   break;
    case EIGHT: str = "eight of ";   break;
    case NINE:  str = "nine of ";    break;
    case TEN:   str = "ten of ";    break;
    case JACK:  str = "jack of ";    break;
    case QUEEN: str = "queen of ";   break;
```

```
    case KING:   str = "king of ";    break;
    default:     str = "ace of ";
  }
  switch (_suit)
  { case CLUB:    str += "clubs";      break;
    case DIAMOND: str += "diamonds";   break;
    case HEART:   str += "hearts";     break;
    default:      str += "spades";
  }
  return str;
}

string Card::abbr() const
{ string str;
  switch (_rank)
  { case TWO:    str = "2";  break;
    case THREE:  str = "3";  break;
    case FOUR:   str = "4";  break;
    case FIVE:   str = "5";  break;
    case SIX:    str = "6";  break;
    case SEVEN:  str = "7";  break;
    case EIGHT:  str = "8";  break;
    case NINE:   str = "9";  break;
    case TEN:    str = "T";  break;
    case JACK:   str = "J";  break;
    case QUEEN:  str = "Q";  break;
    case KING:   str = "K";  break;
    default:     str = "A";
  }
  switch (_suit)
  { case CLUB:    str += "C";  break;
    case DIAMOND: str += "D";  break;
    case HEART:   str += "H";  break;
    default:      str += "S";
  }
  return str;
}

bool Card::operator<(const Card& card) const
{ return _rank < card._rank || _rank == card._rank && _suit < card._suit;
}

bool Card::operator>(const Card& card) const
{ return _rank > card._rank || _rank == card._rank && _suit > card._suit;
}

bool Card::operator<=(const Card& card) const
{ return _rank <= card._rank || _rank == card._rank && _suit <= card._suit;
}
```

```cpp
bool Card::operator>=(const Card& card) const
{ return _rank >= card._rank || _rank == card._rank && _suit >= card._suit;
}


bool Card::operator==(const Card& card) const
{ return _rank == card._rank && _suit == card._suit;
}


bool Card::operator!=(const Card& card) const
{ return _rank != card._rank || _suit != card._suit;
}


int Card::_count[13][4]={{0}};
```

E.4 A Concordance CLASS

```cpp
class Concordance
{ protected:
    typedef list<int> List;
    typedef map<string,List> Map;
    friend ifstream& operator>>(istream&, Concordance&);
    friend ostream& operator<<(ostream&, const Concordance&);
    friend ostream& operator<<(ostream& ostr, const List& l);
    Map _;
    bool extract(string&, string);
};


ifstream& operator>>(istream& istr, Concordance& c)
{ typedef Concordance::Map::iterator CMIt;
  int n=0;
  string line, word;
  for (int n=1; getline(istr,line); n++)
    while (c.extract(word,line))
    { CMIt it=c._.find(word);
      if (it == c._.end())   // new word
      { Concordance::List list;         // new list
        list.push_back(n);
        c._[word] = list;
      }
      else // word is already in concordance
      { Concordance::List& list = it->second;  // its list
        if (n > list.back()) list.push_back(n);
      }
    }
}
```

```
ostream& operator<<(ostream& ostr, const Concordance& c)
{ typedef Concordance::Map::const_iterator CMCIt;
  for (CMCIt it=c._.begin(); it!=c._.end(); it++)
    ostr << it->first << ": " << it->second << '\n';
  return ostr;
}


ostream& operator<<(ostream& ostr, const Concordance::List& l)
{ typedef Concordance::List::const_iterator CLCIt;
  if (l.empty()) return ostr;
  CLCIt it=l.begin();
  ostr << *it;
  while (++it!=l.end())
    ostr << ", " << *it;
  return ostr;
}


bool Concordance::extract(string& word, string line)
{ static int p=0;          // points to next character to be processed
  while (p<line.length() && !isalpha(line[p]))
    ++p;                             // look for beginning of next word
  if (p == line.length())   // there are no more words on this line
  { p = 0;       // begin at the beginning of next line on next call
    return false;           // this call found no word on this line
  }
  int start=p;                     // points to first letter of word
  while (isalpha(line[p]))                      // find end of word
    ++p;
  int len=p-start;                 // word = line[start:start+len]
  word = string(len,' ');      // allocate len characters to word
  for (int i=0; i<len; i++)            // extract word from line
    word[i] = toupper(line[start+i]);      // capitalize letters
  while (p<line.length() && !isspace(line[p]))
    ++p;                      // eat extraneous suffixes, such as "'s"
  return true;
}
```

E.5 A Date CLASS

```
class Date
{ // instances represent calendar dates
    friend ostream& operator<<(ostream&, const Date&);
    friend istream& operator>>(istream&, Date&);
    friend int operator-(const Date&, const Date&);
    friend Date operator+(const Date&, const int);
    friend Date operator-(const Date&, const int);
```

```
  public:
    Date(int=0);
    Date(int, int, int);
    Date(string);
    int day() const;
    int year() const;
    int month() const;
    int dayOfMonth() const;
    int dayOfYear() const;
    string dayOfWeek() const;
    string toString() const;
    static const Date Y2K;
    static Date today();
    Date& operator++();   // pre-increment
    Date& operator--();   // pre-decrement
    Date operator++(int);   // post-increment
    Date operator--(int);   // post-decrement
    Date& operator+=(const int);
    Date& operator-=(const int);
    bool operator<(const Date&) const;
    bool operator>(const Date&) const;
    bool operator<=(const Date&) const;
    bool operator>=(const Date&) const;
    bool operator==(const Date&) const;
    bool operator!=(const Date&) const;
  private:
    int _day;   // 0 = Dec 31 1600, 1 = Jan 1 1601
    static bool isLeap(const int);
    static int monthNumber(string);
    static string monthName(const int);
    static int daysInMonth(const int, const int);
    int yearNum() const;
    int quadyearNum() const;
    int centuryNum() const;
    int quadcenturyNum() const;
    void validate();   // CONSTRAINT: 0.0 <= _day
    static const int LY;   // = 365
    static const int LQY;   // = 1461
    static const int LC;   // = 36524
    static const int LQC;   // = 146097
    static const int BASE_YEAR;   // = 1601
};


ostream& operator<<(ostream& ostr, const Date& date)
{ return ostr << date.toString();
}
```

```
istream& operator>>(istream& istr, Date& date)
{ string str;
  istr >> str;
  date = Date(str);
  return istr;
}

int operator-(const Date& date1, const Date& date2)
{ return date1._day - date2._day;
}

Date operator+(const Date& date1, const int days)
{ return Date(date1._day + days);
}

Date operator-(const Date& date1, const int days)
{ return Date(date1._day - days);
}

Date::Date(int day) : _day(day)
{ validate();
}

Date::Date(int year, int month, int day)
{ int y = year - BASE_YEAR;  // number of years in current era
  int nqc = y/400;  // number of quadcenturies in current era
  int nc  = y%400/100;  // number of centuries in current quadcentury
  int nqy = y%100/4;  // number of quadyears in current century
  int ny  = y%4;  // number of years in current quadyear
  _day = LQC*nqc + LC*nc + LQY*nqy + LY*ny;
  for (int m=1; m<month; m++)
    _day += daysInMonth(m,year);
  _day += day;
  validate();
}

Date::Date(string s)
{ char* buf = new char[s.length()+1];
  s.copy(buf,s.length(),0);  // copy C++ string s into C-string p
  buf[s.length()] = 0;        // C-strings are null-terminated
  const char* p = strtok(buf, " ,");  // see p. 213 in PWCPP
  string monthName(p);  // convert C-string to C++ string
  int m = monthNumber(monthName);
  p = strtok(NULL, " ,");  // extract day of month number
  if (isalpha(*p)) // maybe this is the month name
  { string monthName(p);  // convert C-string to C++ string
    m = monthNumber(monthName);
    p = strtok(NULL, " ,");  // extract day of month number
  }
```

```
  int d = atoi(p);
  p = strtok(NULL, " ,");   // extract year number
  int y = atoi(p);
  *this = Date(y,m,d);
  validate();
}

int Date::day() const
{ return _day;
}

int Date::year() const
{ // returns the current calendar year
  int qcn1 = quadcenturyNum()-1;
  int cn1 = centuryNum()-1;
  int qyn1 = quadyearNum()-1;
  int yn1 = yearNum()-1;
  return BASE_YEAR + 400*qcn1 + 100*cn1 + 4*qyn1 + yn1;
}

int Date::month() const
{ int d = dayOfYear();
  int y = year();
  for (int m=1; m<12; m++)
  { if (d <= daysInMonth(m,y)) return m;
    d -= daysInMonth(m,y);
  }
  return 12;
}

int Date::dayOfMonth() const
{ int d = dayOfYear();
  int y = year();
  for (int m=1; m<12; m++)
  { if (d <= daysInMonth(m,y)) return d;
    d -= daysInMonth(m,y);
  }
  return d;
}

int Date::dayOfYear() const
{ // returns the current day number within the current year
  return (_day-1)%LQC%LC%LQY%LY+1;
}

string Date::dayOfWeek() const
{ string day[] = { "Sun", "Mon", "Tue", "Wed", "Thu", "Fri", "Sat" };
  return day[_day%7];   // Dec 31 1600 was a Sunday
}
```

```
string Date::toString() const
{ ostringstream out;
  if (_day == 0) return "NAD";   // "Not A Date"
  out << dayOfWeek() << " " << monthName(month()) << " "
      << dayOfMonth() << " " << year();
  return out.str();
}


const Date Date::Y2K(145732);   // Sat Jan  1 2000

Date Date::today()
{ return Date(__DATE__);
}


Date& Date::operator++()
{ ++_day;
  validate();
  return *this;
}


Date& Date::operator--()
{ --_day;
  validate();
  return *this;
}


Date Date::operator++(int)
{ Date temp = *this;
  ++(*this);
  return temp;
}


Date Date::operator--(int)
{ Date temp = *this;
  --(*this);
  return temp;
}


Date& Date::operator+=(const int days)
{ _day += days;
  return *this;
}


Date& Date::operator-=(const int days)
{ _day -= days;
  return *this;
}
```

```
bool Date::operator<(const Date& date) const
{ return _day < date._day;
}

bool Date::operator>(const Date& date) const
{ return _day > date._day;
}

bool Date::operator<=(const Date& date) const
{ return _day <= date._day;
}

bool Date::operator>=(const Date& date) const
{ return _day >= date._day;
}

bool Date::operator==(const Date& date) const
{ return _day == date._day;
}

bool Date::operator!=(const Date& date) const
{ return _day != date._day;
}

int Date::yearNum() const
{ // returns the year number within its quadyear period
   // INVARIANT: 1 <= yearNum() <= 4
   // 1 = (Jan 1 1601 - Dec 31 1601) = (Jan 1 1997 - Dec 31 1997)
   // 4 = (Jan 1 1604 - Dec 31 1604) = (Jan 1 2000 - Dec 31 2000)
   return (_day-1)%LQC%LC%LQY/LY+1;
}

int Date::quadyearNum() const
{ // returns the quadyear number within its century
   // INVARIANT: 1 <= quadyearNum() <= 25
   // 1 = (Jan 1 1601 - Dec 31 1604) = (Jan 1 1901 - Dec 31 1904)
   // 25 = (Jan 1 1997 - Dec 31 2000)
   return (_day-1)%LQC%LC/LQY+1;
}

int Date::centuryNum() const
{ // returns the century number within its quadcentury period
   // INVARIANT: 1 <= centuryNum() <= 4
   // 1 = (Jan 1 1601 - Dec 31 1700) = (Jan 1 2001 - Dec 31 2100)
   // 4 = (Jan 1 1901 - Dec 31 2000)
   return (_day-1)%LQC/LC+1;
}
```

```
int Date::quadcenturyNum() const
{ // returns the quadcentury number beginning with 1601-2000
  // INVARIANT: 1 <= quadyearNum()
  // 1 = (Jan 1 1601 - Dec 31 2000)
  // 2 = (Jan 1 2001 - Dec 31 2400)
  return (_day-1)/LQC+1;
}


bool Date::isLeap(const int y)
{ if (y%400 == 0) return true;
  if (y%100 == 0) return false;
  if (y%4 == 0) return true;
  return false;
}


int Date::monthNumber(string s)
{ if (s.length() < 3) return 12;
  s = s.substr(0,3);
  s[0] = toupper(s[0]);
  s[1] = toupper(s[1]);
  s[2] = toupper(s[2]);
  if (s=="JAN") return 1;
  if (s=="FEB") return 2;
  if (s=="MAR") return 3;
  if (s=="APR") return 4;
  if (s=="MAY") return 5;
  if (s=="JUN") return 6;
  if (s=="JUL") return 7;
  if (s=="AUG") return 8;
  if (s=="SEP") return 9;
  if (s=="OCT") return 10;
  if (s=="NOV") return 11;
  return 12;
}


string Date::monthName(const int m)
{ switch (m)
  { case  1: return "Jan";
    case  2: return "Feb";
    case  3: return "Mar";
    case  4: return "Apr";
    case  5: return "May";
    case  6: return "Jun";
    case  7: return "Jul";
    case  8: return "Aug";
    case  9: return "Sep";
```

```
    case 10: return "Oct";
    case 11: return "Nov";
    default: return "Dec";
  }
}


int Date::daysInMonth(const int m, const int y)
{ switch (m)
  { case  1: return 31;
    case  2: return 28 + (isLeap(y)?1:0);
    case  3: return 31;
    case  4: return 30;
    case  5: return 31;
    case  6: return 30;
    case  7: return 31;
    case  8: return 31;
    case  9: return 30;
    case 10: return 31;
    case 11: return 30;
    default: return 31;
  }
}


void Date::validate()
{ if (_day<1) _day = 0;
}


const int Date::LY=365;
const int Date::LQY=4*LY+1;      //    1461
const int Date::LC= 25*LQY-1;    //   36524
const int Date::LQC=4*LC+1;      // 146097
const int Date::BASE_YEAR=1601;
```

E.6 A Deck CLASS

```
class Deck
{ //  instances represent ordinary decks of playing cards
  public:
    Deck();
    void print() const;
    void shuffle() const;
  protected:
    static const int _SIZE;
    Card** _card;  // an array of pointers
    static Random _random;  // random number generator
};
```

```
Deck::Deck()
{ _card = new Card*[_SIZE];
  int r=13, s=3;
  for (int i=0; i<_SIZE; i++)
  { if (r==0)
    { r = 12;
      s = (s-1)%4;
    }
    else --r;
    _card[i] = new Card(r,s);
  }
}

void Deck::print() const
{ for (int i=0; i<_SIZE; i++)
    cout << _card[i]->abbr() << (i%13==12?"\n":" ");
  cout << "\n";
}

void Deck::shuffle() const
{ for (int i=0; i<_SIZE; i++)
  { int j = _random.integer(_SIZE)-1;
    Card* p = _card[i];
    _card[i] = _card[j];
    _card[j] = p;
  }
}

const int Deck::_SIZE=52;
Random Deck::_random;
```

E.7 A Hand CLASS

```
class Hand : public Pile
{ //  instances represent hands of playing cards
  public:
    Hand(int);
};

Hand::Hand(int size) : Pile(size) { }
Hand::Hand() : _size(0) { }

void Hand::print() const
{ for (int i=0; i<_size; i++)
    cout << _card[i]->abbr() << (i%13==12?"\n":" ");
  cout << "\n";
}
```

```
Hand& Hand::operator=(const Hand& hand)
{ _size = hand._size;
  _card = new Card*[_size];
  for (int i=0; i<_size; i++)
    _card[i] = hand._card[i];
}


Hand::~Hand()
{ delete [] _card;
}
```

E.8 A Hash FUNCTION STRUCTURE TEMPLATE

```
template <class K>
struct Hash
{ // PRECONDITION: K == string
  int operator()(K s)
  { int h=0;
    for (string::const_iterator it=s.begin(); it!=s.end(); it++)
      h = (h<<1)^*it;
    return h;
  }
};
```

E.9 A HashTable CLASS TEMPLATE

```
template <class K,class T>
class HashTable
{ protected:
    typedef pair<K,T> Pair;
    typedef vector<Pair> Vector;
  public:
    friend istream& operator>>(istream&, HashTable&);
    friend ostream& operator<<(ostream&, const HashTable&);
    HashTable(int cap=INIT_CAP) : _(Vector(cap)) { }
    const T& operator[](Key) const;
    int size() const;
    int capacity() const { return _.size(); }
  protected
    static const float LOAD=0.75;                    // load factor
    static const INIT_CAP=109;          // default initial capacity
    Vector _;                                        // the hash table
    static int hash(Key);                     // the hash function
    int find(Key) const;                      // utility function
    bool insert(Key, const T&);               // utility function
    void rebuild();                           // utility function
};
```

```
template <class K,class T>
istream& operator>>(istream& istr, HashTable<T>& t)
{
  return istr;
}

template <class K,class T>
ostream& operator<<(ostream& ostr, const HashTable<T>& t)
{
  return ostr;
}

template <class K,class T>
int HashTable<K,T>::size() const
{ const T NULL_T=T();  // default null object for T class
  int n=0;
  for (int i=0; i<_.size(); i++)
    if (_[i] != NULL_T) ++n;
  return n;
}

template <class K,class T>
int HashTable<K,T>::find(K key) const
{ const K NULL_K=K();        // default null object for T class
  const int CAP=_.size();                    // size of table
  int k0=hash(key), k=k0;         // expected location of key
  do
  { if (_[k].first == key) return k;  // in table at element k
    if (_[k] == NULL_K) return CAP;           // not in table
    k = (k+1)%CAP;                       // use linear probing
  } while (k != k0);                    // search entire table
  return CAP;                                 // not in table
}

template <class K,class T>
const T& HashTable<K,T>::operator[](K key) const
{ int k=find(key);
  if (k == _.size()) return K();
  return _[k];
}

template <class K,class T>
int HashTable<K,T>::hash(Key s)
{ // PRECONDITION: Key = string
  const int CAP=_.size();
  int h=0;
  for (int i=0; i<s.length(); i++)
    h += s[i];
  return h%CAP;
}
```

```
template <class K,class T>
bool HashTable<K,T>::insert(Key key, const T& x)
{ int k=find(key);
  if (k < _.size()) return false;    // key is already in table
  return _[k];
}

{ const T NULL_T=T();        // default null object for T class
  int k=hash(key), k0=k;
  while (_[k] != NULL_T)          // proceed with linear probing
  { if (_[k] != key) return false;  // key is already in table
    k = (k+1)%CAP;                  // wrap around end of vector
    if (k==k0)                          // table is full
    { rebuild();
      insert(key,x);
    }
  }
  _[k] = x;                      // insert x at vector index k
  return true;
}

template <class K,class T>
void HashTable<K,T>::rebuild()
{ // Exercise
}
```

E.10 A Line CLASS

```
class Line
{ //   instances represent lines in the cartesian plane
    friend class Point;
    friend ostream& operator<<(ostream&, const Line&);
    friend bool areParallel(const Line&, const Line&);
    friend bool arePerpendicular(const Line&, const Line&);
    friend double angle(const Line&, const Line&);
  public:
    Line(double=1.0, double=1.0);
    Line(const Point&, double=0.0);
    Line(const Point&, const Point&);
    Line(double,double,double);
    double xCoef() const;
    double yCoef() const;
    double cTerm() const;
    double slope() const;
    double xIntercept() const;
    double yIntercept() const;
    bool isHorizontal() const;
    bool isVertical() const;
```

```cpp
      double distanceTo(const Point&) const;
      bool contains(const Point&) const;
      string toString() const;
      static const Line X_AXIS;     // the line y = 0
      static const Line Y_AXIS;     // the line x = 0
      static const Line DIAGONAL;   // the line y = x
  protected:
      double _a, _b, _c;   // coefficients in general form: ax+by+c=0
};
ostream& operator<<(ostream& ostr, const Line& line)
{ return ostr << line.toString();
}


bool areParallel(const Line& line1, const Line& line2)
{ return (line1._a*line2._b == line1._b*line2._a);
}


bool arePerpendicular(const Line& line1, const Line& line2)
{ return (line1._a*line2._a + line1._b*line2._b == 0);
}


double angle(const Line& line1, const Line& line2)
{ const double PI=3.1415926535897932;
  if (areParallel(line1,line2)) return 0;
  if (arePerpendicular(line1,line2)) return PI/2;
  if (line1.isVertical()) return atan(-1.0/line2.slope());
  if (line2.isVertical()) return atan(-1.0/line1.slope());
  double m1 = line1.slope();
  double m2 = line2.slope();
  return atan((m2-m1)/(1+m1*m2));
}


Line::Line(double x0, double y0) : _a(y0), _b(x0), _c(-x0*y0) { }

Line::Line(const Point& p, double m)
  : _a(m), _b(-1), _c(p._y-m*p._x) { }

Line::Line(const Point& p, const Point& q)
  : _a(q._y-p._y), _b(p._x-q._x), _c(q._x*p._y-p._x*q._y) { }

Line::Line(double a, double b, double c) : _a(a), _b(b), _c(c) { }

double Line::xCoef() const
{ return _a;
}


double Line::yCoef() const
{ return _b;
}
```

```
double Line::cTerm() const
{ return _c;
}


double Line::slope() const
{ return -_a/_b;
}


double Line::xIntercept() const
{ return -_c/_a;
}


double Line::yIntercept() const
{ return -_c/_b;
}


bool Line::isHorizontal() const
{ return (_a == 0);
}


bool Line::isVertical() const
{ return (_b == 0);
}


double Line::distanceTo(const Point& p) const
{ return abs(_a*p._x+_b*p._y+_c)/sqrt(_a*_a+_b*_b);
}


bool Line::contains(const Point& p) const
{ return (_a*p.x() + _b*p.y() + _c == 0);
}


string Line::toString() const
{ ostringstream out;
  out << _a << "x + " << _b << "y + " << _c << " = 0";
  return out.str();
}


const Line Line::X_AXIS(0,1,0);
const Line Line::Y_AXIS(1,0,0);
const Line Line::DIAGONAL(1,-1,0);
```

E.11 A List CLASS TEMPLATE

```
template <class T>
class List
{ protected:
    class Node
    { public:
        Node(const T& data=T(), Node* prev=0, Node* next=0)
          : _data(data), _prev(prev), _next(next)
        { if (_prev == 0) _prev = this;
          if (_next == 0) _next = this;
        }
        T _data;
        Node* _prev, * _next;
    };
    Node* _;   // dummy node
    int _size;
  public:
    class Iterator
    {    friend class List;
      public:
        Iterator(Node* p) : _(p) { }
        T& operator*() {return _->_data; }
        void operator=(const Iterator& it) {_ = it._; }
        bool operator==(const Iterator& it) {return _ == it._; }
        bool operator!=(const Iterator& it) {return _ != it._; }
        Iterator operator++(int)  // postfix
        { Iterator it(_);
          _ = _->_next;
          return it;
        }
        Iterator& operator++() { _ = _->_next; return *this; }
        Iterator operator--(int)  // postfix
        { Iterator it(_);
          _ = _->_prev;
          return it;
        }
        Iterator& operator--() { _ = _->_prev; return *this; }
      protected:
        List<T>::Node* _;
    };
    List();
    List(const List&);
    List(int);
    List(int,const T&);
    List(Iterator&,Iterator&);
    ~List();
    int size() const;          // returns number of elements
    bool empty() const;        // returns true iff this is empty
```

```
      T& front() const;          // returns the first element
      T& back() const;           // returns the last element
      Iterator begin();          // points to first element
      Iterator end();            // points to dummy element
      void push_front(const T&); // inserts given element in front
      void push_back(const T&);  // inserts given element in back
      void pop_front();          // removes element from front
      void pop_back();           // removes element from back
      Iterator insert(Iterator&,const T&);    // inserts element before *it
      Iterator insert(Iterator&,int,const T&); // inserts n copies before *it
      void erase(Iterator&);
      void erase(Iterator&,Iterator&);
      void clear();
      void splice(Iterator,List&,Iterator);
//    void splice(Iterator,List&,Iterator,Iterator);
//    void splice(Iterator,List&);
//    void merge(List&);
//    void sort();
};

template <class T>
List<T>::List() : _size(0)
{ _ = new Node();
}

template <class T>
List<T>::List(const List& l) : _size(l._size)
{ _ = new Node();   // dummy node
  Node* pp = _;
  for (Node* p=l._->_next; p != l._; p = p->_next, pp = pp->_next)
    pp->_next = pp->_next->_prev = new Node(p->_data,_,pp);
}

template <class T>
List<T>::List(int n) : _size(n)
{ _ = new Node();   // dummy node
  Node* p = _;
  for (int i=0; i<n; i++)
    p = p->_prev = new Node(T(),_,p);
  _->_next = p;
}

template <class T>
List<T>::List(int n, const T& t) : _size(n)
{ _ = new Node();   // dummy node
  Node* p = _;
  for (int i=0; i<n; i++)
    p = p->_prev = new Node(t,_,p);
  _->_next = p;
}
```

```
template <class T>
List<T>::List(Iterator& it1,Iterator& it2) : _size(0)
{ _ = new Node();  // dummy node
  Node* pp = _;
  for (Node* p=it1._; p != it2._; p = p->_next, pp = pp->_next)
  { pp->_next = new Node(p->_data,pp,_);
    ++_size;
  }
  _->_prev = pp;
}

template <class T>
List<T>::~List()
{ Node* p=_->_next;
  while (p != _)
  { Node* pp = p->_next;
    delete p;
    p = pp;
  }
  delete _;
}

template <class T>
int List<T>::size() const
{ return _size;
}

template <class T>
bool List<T>::empty() const
{ return _size == 0;
}

template <class T>
T& List<T>::front() const
{ return _->_next->_data;
}

template <class T>
T& List<T>::back() const
{ return _->_prev->_data;
}

template <class T>
List<T>::Iterator List<T>::begin()
{ return Iterator(_->_next);
}
```

```
template <class T>
List<T>::Iterator List<T>::end()
{ return Iterator(_);
}

template <class T>
void List<T>::push_front(const T& x)
{ _->_next = _->_next->_prev = new Node(x,_,_->_next);
  ++_size;
}

template <class T>
void List<T>::push_back(const T& x)
{ _->_prev = _->_prev->_next = new Node(x,_->_prev,_);
  ++_size;
}

template <class T>
void List<T>::pop_front()
{ Node* p = _->_next;
  _->_next = p->_next;
  p->_next->_prev = _;
  delete p;
  --_size;
}

template <class T>
void List<T>::pop_back()
{ Node* p = _->_prev;
  _->_prev = p->_prev;
  p->_prev->_next = _;
  delete p;
  --_size;
}

template <class T>
List<T>::Iterator List<T>::insert(Iterator& it, const T& x)
{ it._->_prev = it._->_prev->_next = new Node(x,it._->_prev,it._);
  it._ = it._->_prev;
  ++_size;
}

template <class T>
List<T>::Iterator List<T>::insert(Iterator& it, int n, const T& x)
{ Node* p=it._, * q = p->_prev;
  for (int i=0; i<n; i++)
    p = p->_prev = new Node(x,q,p);
  it._ = it._->_prev = q->_next = p;
  _size += n;
}
```

```
template <class T>
void List<T>::erase(Iterator& it)
{ if (_size == 0) return;
  Node* p = it._;
  p->_prev->_next = p->_next;
  p->_next->_prev = p->_prev;
  it._ = p->_next;
  delete p;
  --_size;
}


template <class T>
void List<T>::erase(Iterator& it1, Iterator& it2)
{ it1._->_prev->_next = it2._;
  it2._->_prev = it1._->_prev;
  Node* p=it1._->_next;
  while (it1._ != it2._)
  { delete it1._;
    it1._ = p;
    p = p->_next;
    --_size;
  }
}


template <class T>
void List<T>::clear()
{ Node* p=_, * q=p->_next;
  while (q != p)
  { p->_next = q->_next;
    q->_next->_prev = p;
    delete q;
    q = p->_next;
  }
  _size = 0;
}


template <class T>
void List<T>::splice(Iterator it1, List& l, Iterator it2)
{ Node* p=it1._, * pp=it1._->_prev, * q=it2._;
  p->_prev = pp->_next = q;
  q->_prev->_next = q->_next;
  q->_next->_prev = q->_prev;
  q->_prev = pp;
  q->_next = p;
  ++_size;
  --l._size;
}
```

E.12 A Matrix CLASS TEMPLATE

```
template <int I, int J>
class Matrix
{ public:
    Matrix();                                          // default constructor
    Matrix(const Matrix<I,J>&);                        // copy constructor
    ~Matrix();                                         // destructor
    Matrix<I,J>& operator=(const Matrix<I,J>&);        // assignment operator
    bool operator==(const Matrix<I,J>&) const;         // equality operator
    bool operator!=(const Matrix<I,J>&) const;         // inequality operator
    double& operator()(int,int);                       // subscripting operator
    double operator()(int,int) const;                  // subscripting operator
    int rows() const;
    int columns() const;
    string toString() const;
    void load(const double*, int);
  private:
    int _rows, _cols;
    double* _;
};

template <int I, int J>
Matrix<I,J>::Matrix()
{ _ = new double[I*J];
  for (int i=0; i<I*J; i++)
    _[i] = 0.0;
}

template <int I, int J>
Matrix<I,J>::Matrix(const Matrix<I,J>& m)
{ _ = new double[I*J];
  for (int i=0; i<I*J; i++)
    _[i] = m._[i];
}

template <int I, int J>
Matrix<I,J>::~Matrix()
{ delete [] _;
}

template <int I, int J>
Matrix<I,J>& Matrix<I,J>::operator=(const Matrix<I,J>& m)
{ for (int i=0; i<I*J; i++)
    _[i] = m._[i];
  return *this;
}
```

```
template <int I, int J>
bool Matrix<I,J>::operator==(const Matrix<I,J>& m) const
{ for (int i=0; i<I*J; i++)
    if (_[i] != m._[i]) return false;
 return true;
}

template <int I, int J>
bool Matrix<I,J>::operator!=(const Matrix<I,J>& m) const
{ for (int i=0; i<I*J; i++)
    if (_[i] != m._[i]) return true;
 return false;
}

template <int I, int J>
double& Matrix<I,J>::operator()(int i, int j)
{ return _[J*i+j];
}

template <int I, int J>
double Matrix<I,J>::operator()(int i, int j) const
{ return _[J*i+j];
}

template <int I, int J>
int Matrix<I,J>::rows() const
{ return I;
}

template <int I, int J>
int Matrix<I,J>::columns() const
{ return J;
}

template <int I, int J>
string Matrix<I,J>::toString() const
{ ostringstream out;
  for (int i=0; i<I; i++)
  { for (int j=0; j<J; j++)
      out << setw(8) << _[J*i+j];
    out << "\n";
  }
  return out.str();
}
```

```
template <int I, int J>
void Matrix<I,J>::load(const double* a, int n)
{ n = (n>I*J?I*J:n);
  for (int i=0; i<n; i++)
    _[i] = a[i];
}
```

E.13 AN OrderedList CLASS

```
template <class T>
class OrderedList : public list<T>
{ // elements are kept in nondecreasing order
  public:
    void add(const T&);
};
```

```
template <class T>
void OrderedList<T>::add(const T& t)
{ list<T>::iterator it=begin();
  while (it!=end() && *it<t)
    ++it;
  insert(it,t);
}
```

E.14 A Person CLASS

```
Person::Person(string lname)
  : _lname(lname), _dob(0), _dod(0), _yob(0), _yod(0) { }

Person::Person(string fname, string lname, int yob, int yod)
  : _fname(fname), _lname(lname),
    _dob(0), _dod(0), _yob(yob), _yod(yod) { }

Person::Person(string fname, string mname, string lname,
  int yob, int yod) : _fname(fname), _mname(mname), _lname(lname),
  _dob(0), _dod(0), _yob(yob), _yod(yod) { }

Person::Person(string fname, string mname, string lname,
  int yob, int mob, int dob, int yod, int mod, int dod)
  : _fname(fname), _mname(mname), _lname(lname),
    _dob(new Date(yob,mob,dob)), _dod(0), _yob(yob), _yod(yod)
{ if (yod && mod && dod) _dod = new Date(yod,mod,dod);
}
```

```
string Person::toString() const
{ ostringstream out;
  out << name();
  if(_dob)
  { out << " (" << *_dob;
    if (_dod) out << "-" << *_dod;
    out << ")";
  }
  else if(_yob)
  { out << " (" << _yob;
    if (_yod) out << "-" << _yod;
    out << ")";
  }
  string s = out.str();
  if (s.length()) return s;
  return "[NO NAME]";
}

string Person::firstName() const
{ return _fname;
}

string Person::middleName() const
{ return _mname;
}

string Person::lastName() const
{ return _lname;
}

string Person::name() const
{ ostringstream out;
  if (_fname.length() > 0) out << _fname << " ";
  if (_mname.length() > 0) out << _mname << " ";
  out << _lname;
  return out.str();
}

char Person::sex() const
{ if (_sex == 'F') return 'F';
  return _sex;
}

Date* Person::dateOfBirth() const
{ return _dob;
}

Date* Person::dateOfDeath() const
{ return _dod;
}
```

```
int Person::yearOfBirth() const
{ return _yob;
}


int Person::yearOfDeath() const
{ return _yod;
}


void Person::setFirstName(string fname)
{ _fname = fname;
}


void Person::setMiddleName(string mname)
{ _mname = mname;
}


void Person::setLastName(string lname)
{ _lname = lname;
}


void Person::setSex(char sex)
{ _sex = sex;
}


void Person::setDateOfBirth(int y,int m, int d)
{ _dob = new Date(y,m,d);
}


void Person::setDateOfDeath(int y,int m, int
{ _dod = new Date(y,m,d);
}


void Person::setYearOfBirth(int yob)
{ _yob = yob;
}


void Person::setYearOfDeath(int yod)
{ _yod = yod;
}


bool Person::isAlive()
//{ return (_yob > 0 && _yod == 0);
{ return ( _yod == 0);
}
```

```
int Person::age()
{ if (!isAlive()) return -1;
  if (_dob) return int((Date::today()-*_dob)/365.2425);
  if (_yob) return int(Date::today().year()-_yob);
  return -1;
}


int Person::ageAtDeath()
{ if (_dob && _dod) return int((*_dod-*_dob)/365.2425);
  if (_yob && _yod) return int(_yod-_yob);
  return -1;
}
```

E.15 A Point CLASS

```
class Point
{ // instances represent points in the cartesian plane
    friend class Line;
    friend ostream& operator<<(ostream&, const Point&);
    friend Point operator-(const Point&);
    friend Point operator+(const Point&, const Point&);
    friend Point operator-(const Point&, const Point&);
    friend Point operator*(const double, const Point&);
    friend Point operator/(const Point&, const double);
    friend double distance(const Point&, const Point&);
  public:
    Point(double=0.0,double=0.0);        // default constructor
    Point(const Point&);                 // copy constructor
    Point& operator=(const Point&);      // assignment operator
    bool operator==(const Point&) const; // equality operator
    bool operator!=(const Point&) const; // inequality operator
    Point& operator+=(const Point&);
    Point& operator-=(const Point&);
    Point& operator*=(const double);
    Point& operator/=(const double);
    double x() const;
    double y() const;
    double magnitude() const;  // the polar coordinate r
    double amplitude() const;  // the polar coordinate theta
    void rotate(double);
    bool isOn(const Line&) const;
    double distanceTo(const Line&) const;
    string toString() const;
    static const Point ORIGIN;
  protected:
    double _x, _y;
};
```

```
ostream& operator<<(ostream& ostr, const Point& point)
{ return ostr << point.toString();
}


Point operator-(const Point& point)
{ return Point(-1*point._x,-1*point._y);
}


Point operator+(const Point& p1, const Point& p2)
{ return Point(p1._x+p2._x,p1._y+p2._y);
}


Point operator-(const Point& p1, const Point& p2)
{ return Point(p1._x-p2._x,p1._y-p2._y);
}


Point operator*(const double coef, const Point& point)
{ return Point(coef*point._x,coef*point._y);
}


Point operator/(const Point& point, const double divisor)
{ return Point(point._x/divisor,point._y/divisor);
}


double distance(const Point& p1, const Point& p2)
{ float dx=(p1._x-p2._x);
  float dy=(p1._y-p2._y);
  return sqrt(dx*dx+dy*dy);
}


Point::Point(double x, double y) : _x(x), _y(y) { }


Point::Point(const Point& p) : _x(p._x), _y(p._y) { }


Point& Point::operator=(const Point& point)
{ _x = point._x;
  _y = point._y;
  return *this;
}


bool Point::operator==(const Point& point) const
{ return _x == point._x && _y == point._y;
}


bool Point::operator!=(const Point& point) const
{ return _x != point._x || _y != point._y;
}
```

```
Point& Point::operator+=(const Point& point)
{ _x += point._x;
  _y += point._y;
  return *this;
}

Point& Point::operator-=(const Point& point)
{ _x -= point._x;
  _y -= point._y;
  return *this;
}

Point& Point::operator*=(const double c)
{ _x *= c;
  _y *= c;
  return *this;
}

Point& Point::operator/=(const double c)
{ _x /= c;
  _y /= c;
  return *this;
}

double Point::x() const
{ return _x;
}

double Point::y() const
{ return _y;
}

double Point::magnitude() const
{ return sqrt(_x*_x+_y*_y);
}

double Point::amplitude() const
{ return atan(_y/_x);
}

void Point::rotate(double alpha)
{ double r = magnitude();
  double theta = amplitude() + alpha;
  _x = r*cos(theta);
  _y = r*sin(theta);
}
```

```
double Point::distanceTo(const Line& line) const
{ double a = line._a;
  double b = line._b;
  double c = line._c;
  return abs(a*_x+b*_y+c)/sqrt(a*a+b*b);
}

bool Point::isOn(const Line& line) const
{ double a = line._a;
  double b = line._b;
  double c = line._c;
  return (a*_x + b*_y + c == 0);
}

string Point::toString() const
{ ostringstream out;
  out << "(" << _x << "," << _y << ")";
  return out.str();
}

const Point Point::ORIGIN(0,0);
```

E.16 A Polynomial CLASS

```
#include <list>

class Polynomial
{ // instances represent polynomials; e.g., 2x^7 - 8x^3 + 5x^2 + 9
  // INVARIANTS: _degree == _terms.begin()._exp;
  //             it1->_exp == it2->_exp  ==>  it1 == it2
  //             *this == ZERO  <==>  _degree == -1
  //                            <==>  _terms.size() == 0;
  protected:
    struct Term
     { friend ostream& operator<<(ostream&, const Term&);
       friend Term operator-(const Term&);
       friend Term derivative(const Term&);
       friend Term antiderivative(const Term&);
       friend Term abs(const Term&);
       Term(double=0.0,unsigned=0);
       bool operator==(const Term&) const;
       bool operator!=(const Term&) const;
       bool operator<(const Term&) const;
       double _coef;
       unsigned _exp;
     };
```

```
  public:
    friend ostream& operator<<(ostream&, const Polynomial&);
    friend Polynomial operator-(const Polynomial&);
    friend Polynomial operator*(const double, const Polynomial&);
    friend Polynomial operator+(const Polynomial&, const Polynomial&);
    friend Polynomial operator-(const Polynomial&, const Polynomial&);
    friend Polynomial operator*(const Polynomial&, const Polynomial&);
    friend Polynomial derivative(const Polynomial&);
    friend Polynomial antiderivative(const Polynomial&);
    Polynomial(double=0,unsigned=0);
    Polynomial& operator+=(const Polynomial&);
    Polynomial& operator-=(const Polynomial&);
    Polynomial& operator*=(const double);
    Polynomial& operator*=(const Polynomial&);
    bool operator==(const Polynomial&) const;
    bool operator!=(const Polynomial&) const;
    double operator()(double) const;  // evaluates the polynomial
    long degree() const;
    unsigned terms() const;  // the number of terms in the polynomial
    static const Polynomial ZERO;  // p(x) = 0
    static const Polynomial ONE;   // p(x) = 1
    static const Polynomial X;     // p(x) = x
  protected:
    list<Term> _terms;    // one element for each term
    long _degree;         // maximum exponent
    void reduce();
    typedef list<Term> TermList;
    typedef list<Term>::iterator It;
    typedef list<Term>::const_iterator CIt;
};


ostream& operator<<(ostream& ostr, const Polynomial::Term& term)
{ if (term._exp == 0) return ostr << term._coef;
  if (term._coef == 1.0) ostr << "x";
  else if (term._coef == -1.0) ostr << "-x";
  else ostr << term._coef << "x";
  if (term._exp == 1) return ostr;
  else return ostr << "^" << term._exp;
}


Polynomial::Term operator-(const Polynomial::Term& term)
{ Polynomial::Term t(term);
  t._coef *= -1.0;
  return t;
}


Polynomial::Term derivative(const Polynomial::Term& t)
{ if (t._exp == 0) return Polynomial::Term(0.0,0);
  return Polynomial::Term(t._exp*t._coef,t._exp-1);
}
```

```
Polynomial::Term antiderivative(const Polynomial::Term& t)
{ if (t._coef == 0) return Polynomial::Term(1.0,0);
  return Polynomial::Term(t._coef/(t._exp+1),t._exp+1);
}


Polynomial::Term abs(const Polynomial::Term& t)
{ Polynomial::Term term(t);
  if (term._coef < 0) term._coef *= -1.0;
  return term;
}


Polynomial::Term::Term(double coef, unsigned exp) : _coef(coef), _exp(exp)
{
}


bool Polynomial::Term::operator==(const Term& t) const
{ return _exp == t._exp && _coef == t._coef;
}


bool Polynomial::Term::operator!=(const Term& t) const
{ return _exp != t._exp || _coef != t._coef;
}


bool Polynomial::Term::operator<(const Term& t) const
{ return _exp > t._exp;  // sort terms in decreasing order
}


ostream& operator<<(ostream& ostr, const Polynomial& p)
{ if (p == Polynomial::ZERO) return ostr << 0;
  Polynomial::CIt it=p._terms.begin();
  ostr << *it++;
  while (it != p._terms.end())
    if (it->_coef < 0) ostr << " - " << abs(*it++);
    else ostr << " + " << *it++;
  return ostr;
}


Polynomial operator-(const Polynomial& p1)
{ Polynomial p(p1);
  for (Polynomial::It it=p._terms.begin(); it != p._terms.end(); it++)
    it->_coef *= -1;
  return p;
}
```

```
Polynomial operator*(const double x, const Polynomial& p1)
{ if (x == 0.0) return Polynomial::ZERO;
  Polynomial p(p1);
  for (Polynomial::It it=p._terms.begin(); it != p._terms.end(); it++)
    it->_coef *= x;
  return p;
}


Polynomial operator+(const Polynomial& p1, const Polynomial& p2)
{ Polynomial p;
  p._degree = max(p1._degree,p2._degree);
  p._terms = Polynomial::TermList(p1._terms.size()+p2._terms.size());
  merge(p1._terms.begin(),p1._terms.end(),
        p2._terms.begin(),p2._terms.end(),
        p._terms.begin());
  p.reduce();
  return p;
}


Polynomial operator-(const Polynomial& p1, const Polynomial& p2)
{ return p1 + -p2;
}


Polynomial operator*(const Polynomial& p1, const Polynomial& p2)
{ Polynomial p;
  p._degree = p1._degree + p2._degree;
  for (Polynomial::CIt it1=p1._terms.begin(); it1!=p1._terms.end();it1++)
    for (Polynomial::CIt it2=p2._terms.begin();it2!=p2._terms.end();it2++)
    { int exp = it1->_exp + it2->_exp;
      double coef = it1->_coef * it2->_coef;
      Polynomial::It it=p._terms.begin();
      for ( ; it != p._terms.end(); it++)
        if (it->_exp <= exp) break;
      if (it->_exp == exp) it->_coef += coef;
      else p._terms.insert(it,Polynomial::Term(coef,exp));
    }
  p.reduce();
  return p;
}


Polynomial derivative(const Polynomial& p1)
{ if (p1._degree < 0) return Polynomial::ZERO;
  Polynomial p;
  p._degree = ( p1._degree>1 ? p1._degree - 1 : 0);
  for (Polynomial::CIt it=p1._terms.begin(); it != p1._terms.end(); it++)
    if (it->_exp>0) p._terms.push_back(derivative(*it));
  return p;
}
```

```
Polynomial antiderivative(const Polynomial& p1)
{ Polynomial p;
  p._degree = p1._degree + 1;
  for (Polynomial::CIt it=p1._terms.begin(); it != p1._terms.end(); it++)
    p._terms.push_back(antiderivative(*it));
  return p;
}


Polynomial::Polynomial(double coef, unsigned exp)
{ if (coef == 0.0)  // the "zero polynomial" has degree -1
  { _terms = TermList(0);
    _degree = -1;
  }
  else
  { _terms = TermList(1,Term(coef,exp));
    _degree = exp;
  }
}


Polynomial& Polynomial::operator+=(const Polynomial& p)
{ *this = *this + p;
  return *this;
}


Polynomial& Polynomial::operator-=(const Polynomial& p)
{ *this = *this - p;
  return *this;
}


Polynomial& Polynomial::operator*=(const double x)
{ *this = x * *this;
  return *this;
}


Polynomial& Polynomial::operator*=(const Polynomial& p)
{ *this = *this * p;
  return *this;
}


bool Polynomial::operator==(const Polynomial& p) const
{ return _terms == p._terms;
}


bool Polynomial::operator!=(const Polynomial& p) const
{ return _terms != p._terms;
}
```

```
double Polynomial::operator()(double x) const
{ CIt it=_terms.begin();
  if (it == _terms.end()) return 0.0;
  double y=it->_coef;
  unsigned e1=it->_exp;
  while (++it != _terms.end())   // Horner's Method
  { int e2=it->_exp;
    y *= pow(x,e1-e2);
    y += it->_coef;
    e1 = e2;
  }
  return y*pow(x,e1);
}


long Polynomial::degree() const
{ return _degree;
}


unsigned Polynomial::terms() const
{ return _terms.size();
}


void Polynomial::reduce()
{ // collects terms and removes those with coefficient equal to 0.0
  if (*this == ZERO) return;
  Polynomial::It it1=_terms.begin(), it2=_terms.begin();
  while (it1 != _terms.end())
  { while (++it2 != _terms.end() && it2->_exp == it1->_exp)
      it1->_coef += it2->_coef;
    if (it1->_coef == 0.0) _terms.erase(it1,it2);
    else _terms.erase(++it1,it2);
    it1 = it2;
  }
  if (_terms.size() == 0) _degree = -1;
  else _degree = _terms.begin()->_exp;
}


const Polynomial Polynomial::ZERO(0.0);   // the "zero polynomial"
const Polynomial Polynomial::ONE(1.0,0);  // the monomial p(x) = 1
const Polynomial Polynomial::X(1.0,1);    // the monomial p(x) = x
```

E.17 A PriorityQueue CLASS TEMPLATE

```
template <class T>
class PriorityQueue
{ public:
    PriorityQueue();
    PriorityQueue(const PriorityQueue&);
```

```
    ~PriorityQueue();
    PriorityQueue& operator=(const PriorityQueue&);
    int size() const;              // returns number of elements
    bool empty() const;            // returns true iff this is empty
    T& top();                      // returns the front element
    void push(const T&);           // inserts given element at back
    void pop();                    // removes element from front
  protected:
    vector<T> _;                   // dynamic array for queue elements
    void heapifyDown();            // restores the heap property
    void heapifyUp();              // restores the heap property
};

template <class T>
PriorityQueue<T>::PriorityQueue()
{
}


template <class T>
PriorityQueue<T>::PriorityQueue(const PriorityQueue& q) : _(q._)
{
}


template <class T>
PriorityQueue<T>::~PriorityQueue()
{
}


template <class T>
PriorityQueue<T>& PriorityQueue<T>::operator=(const PriorityQueue& q)
{ _ = q._;
}


template <class T>
int PriorityQueue<T>::size() const
{ return _.size();
}


template <class T>
bool PriorityQueue<T>::empty() const
{ return _.empty();
}


template <class T>
T& PriorityQueue<T>::top()
{ return _.front();
}
```

```
template <class T>
void PriorityQueue<T>::pop()
{ _.front() = _.back();   // delete the front element
  _.pop_back();           // move the back element to the front
  heapifyDown();          // restore the heap property
}


template <class T>
void PriorityQueue<T>::push(const T& x)
{ _.push_back(x);    // insert the new element at the back
  heapifyUp();       // restore the heap property
}


template <class T>
void PriorityQueue<T>::heapifyDown()
{ int n=_.size(), j;
  for (int i=0; i<n/2; i=j)
  { j=2*i+1;   // _[j] and _[j+1] are the children of _[i]
    if (j<n && _[j]<_[j+1]) ++j;
    if (_[i] >= _[j]) break;
    swap(_[i],_[j]);
  }
}


template <class T>
void PriorityQueue<T>::heapifyUp()
{ int n=_.size(), i;
  for (int j=n-1; j>0; j=i)
  { i=(j-1)/2;   // _[i] is the parent of _[j]
    if (_[j] <= _[i]) break;
    swap(_[j],_[i]);
  }
}
```

E.18 A Purse CLASS

```
class Purse
{ // instances represent purses containing coins
  public:
    Purse(int=0,int=0,int=0,int=0);
    int pennies() const;
    int nickels() const;
    int dimes() const;
    int quarters() const;
    float value() const;
    void insert(float);
    void remove(float);
    float empty();
```

```
      bool isEmpty() const;
  private:
    int _pennies;
    int _nickels;
    int _dimes;
    int _quarters;
    void reduce();
    //   INVARIANTS: 0 <= _pennies < 5
    //               0 <= _nickels < 2
    //               0 <= dimes < 3
    //               0 <= _quarters
};

Purse::Purse(int pennies, int nickels, int dimes, int quarters)
  : _pennies(pennies), _nickels(nickels), _dimes(dimes),
    _quarters(quarters)
{ reduce();
}

int Purse::pennies() const
{ return _pennies;
}

int Purse::nickels() const
{ return _nickels;
}

int Purse::dimes() const
{ return _dimes;
}

int Purse::quarters() const
{ return _quarters;
}

float Purse::value() const
{ return 0.01*_pennies + 0.05*_nickels + 0.10*_dimes + 0.25*_quarters;
}

void Purse::insert(float dollars)
{ _pennies += int(100*dollars);
  reduce();
}

void Purse::remove(float dollars)
{ _pennies -= int(100*dollars);
  reduce();
}
```

```
float Purse::empty()
{ float v = value();
  _pennies = _nickels = _dimes = _quarters = 0;
  return v;
}

bool Purse::isEmpty() const
{ return !(_pennies || _nickels || _dimes || _quarters);
}

void Purse::reduce()
{ int v = int(100*value());
  if (v < 0.00)
  { empty();
    return;
  }
  _quarters = v/25;
  v %= 25;
  _dimes = v/10;
  v %= 10;
  _nickels = v/5;
  v %= 5;
  _pennies = v;
}
```

E.19 A Queue CLASS

```
template <class T>
class Queue
{ public:
    Queue();
    Queue(const Queue&);
    ~Queue();
    Queue& operator=(const Queue&);
    int size() const;          // returns number of elements
    bool empty() const;        // returns true iff this is empty
    T& front();                // returns the front element
    T& back();                 // returns the back element
    void push(const T&);       // inserts given element at back
    void pop();                // removes element from front
  protected:
    class Node
    { public:
        Node(const T& x, Node* next=0) : _(x), _next(next) {}
        T _;
        Node* _next;
    };
```

```
      Node* _front, _back;
      int _size;
};

template <class T> Queue<T>::Queue() : _back(0), _size(0)
{
}

template <class T>
Queue<T>::Queue(const Queue& s) : _back(0), _size(s._size)
{ if (_size==0) return;
  Node* pp=0;
  for (Node* p=s._back; p; p = p->_next)
    if (p==s._back) pp = _back = new Node(p->_);
    else pp = pp->_next = new Node(p->_);
}

template <class T> Queue<T>::~Queue()
{ while (_back)
  { Node* p=_back;
    _back = _back->_next;
    delete p;
  }
}

template <class T> int Queue<T>::size() const
{ return _size;
}

template <class T> bool Queue<T>::empty() const
{ return _size == 0;
}

template <class T> T& Queue<T>::front()
{ return _front->_;
}

template <class T> T& Queue<T>::back()
{ return _back->_;
}

template <class T> void Queue<T>::push(const T& x)
{ if (_size==0) _front = _back = new Node(x);
  else _back = _back->_next = new Node(x);
  ++_size;
}
```

```
template <class T> void Queue<T>::pop()
{ Node* p=_front;
  _front = _front->_next;
  delete p;
  --_size;
}
```

E.20 A Random CLASS

```
class Random
{ // instances represent random number generators
  public:
    Random(unsigned long=0);
    void reset_seed(unsigned long=0);
    int integer(unsigned long=ULONG_MAX,unsigned long=1);
    double real();
  private:
    unsigned long _seed;
    void randomize();
    //   INVARIANT: 0 <= _seed < ULONG_MAX
};

Random::Random(unsigned long seed) : _seed(seed)
{ if (seed == 0) _seed = time(NULL);
  randomize();
}

void Random::reset_seed(unsigned long seed)
{ _seed = seed;
  if (seed == 0) _seed = time(NULL);
  randomize();
}

int Random::integer(unsigned long hi,unsigned long lo)
{ // returns a random integer in the range lo to hi
  randomize();
  return (_seed/10)%(hi-lo+1) + lo;
}

double Random::real()
{ // returns a random real number in the range 0.0 to 1.0
  randomize();
  return double(_seed)/ULONG_MAX;
}

void Random::randomize()
{ _seed = (1103515245*_seed+123456789)%ULONG_MAX;
}
```

E.21 A `RandomLine` CLASS

```
class RandomLine : public Line
{ // instances represent randomly selected lines in the cartesian plane
  public:
    RandomLine();
  protected:
    static Random _random;
};
```

```
RandomLine::RandomLine()
{ _a = _random.real();
  _b = _random.real();
  _c = _random.real();
}
```

```
Random RandomLine::_random;
```

E.22 A `RandomPoint` CLASS

```
class RandomPoint : public Point
{ // instances represent randomly selected points in the cartesian plane
  public:
    RandomPoint(double=1.0,double=1.0,double=0.0,double=0.0);
  protected:
    double _xMin, _xMax, _yMin, _yMax;
    static Random _random;
};
```

```
RandomPoint::RandomPoint(double xMax, double yMax, double xMin,
                         double yMin)
  : _xMax(xMax), _yMax(yMax), _xMin(xMin), _yMin(yMin)
{ double x = _random.real();
  _x = (_xMax-_xMin)*x + _xMin;
  double y = _random.real();
  _y = (_yMax-_yMin)*y + _yMin;
}
```

```
Random RandomPoint::_random;
```

E.23 A `Ratio` CLASS

```
class Ratio
{ // instances represent fractions
    friend ostream& operator<<(ostream&, const Ratio&);
    friend istream& operator>>(istream&, Ratio&);
```

```
      friend Ratio operator+(const Ratio&, const Ratio&);
      friend Ratio operator-(const Ratio&, const Ratio&);
      friend Ratio operator*(const Ratio&, const Ratio&);
      friend Ratio operator/(const Ratio&, const Ratio&);
  public:
    Ratio(long=0,long=1);
    long numerator() const;
    long denominator() const;
    Ratio reciprocal() const;
    void invert();
    operator double() const;
  private:
    long _num;
    long _den;
    long gcd(long,long);
    void reduce();
    // INVARIANT: _den > 0 && gcd(_num,_den) == 1
};

ostream& operator<<(ostream& ostr, const Ratio& r)
{ return ostr << r._num << "/" << r._den;
}

istream& operator>>(istream& istr, Ratio& r)
{ istr >> r._num;
  istr.ignore(1);
  istr >> r._den;
  r.reduce();
  return istr;
}

Ratio operator+(const Ratio& r1, const Ratio& r2)
{ Ratio r(r1._num*r2._den+r2._num*r1._den,r1._den*r2._den);
  r.reduce();
  return r;
}

Ratio operator-(const Ratio& r1, const Ratio& r2)
{ Ratio r(r1._num*r2._den-r2._num*r1._den,r1._den*r2._den);
  r.reduce();
  return r;
}

Ratio operator*(const Ratio& r1, const Ratio& r2)
{ Ratio r(r1._num*r2._num,r1._den*r2._den);
  r.reduce();
  return r;
}
```

```
Ratio operator/(const Ratio& r1, const Ratio& r2)
{ Ratio r(r1._num*r2._den,r1._den*r2._num);
  r.reduce();
  return r;
}

Ratio::Ratio(long num, long den) : _num(num), _den(den)
{ reduce();
}

long Ratio::numerator() const
{ return _num;
}

long Ratio::denominator() const
{ return _den;
}

Ratio Ratio::reciprocal() const
{ Ratio r(_den,_num);
  r.reduce();
  return r;
}

void Ratio::invert()
{ long temp = _num;
  _num = _den;
  _den = temp;
  reduce();
}

Ratio::operator double() const
{ return double(_num)/_den;
}

long Ratio::gcd(long m, long n)
{ if (m == n) return n;                    // basis
  else if (m < n) return gcd(m,n-m);       // recursion
  else return gcd(m-n,n);                  // recursion
}

void Ratio::reduce()
{ if (_num == 0 || _den == 0)
  { _num = 0;
    _den = 1;
    return;
  }
  if (_den < 0)
  { _den *= -1;
    _num *= -1;
```

```
        }
        if (_num == 1) return;
        int sgn = (_num<0?-1:1);
        long g = gcd(sgn*_num,_den);
        _num /= g;
        _den /= g;
}
```

E.24 A Rational CLASS

```
class Rational
{ // instances represent Rational functions; i.e., ratios of polynomials
    friend ostream& operator<<(ostream&, const Rational&);
    friend istream& operator>>(istream&, Rational&);
    friend Rational operator+(const Rational&, const Rational&);
    friend Rational operator-(const Rational&, const Rational&);
    friend Rational operator*(const Rational&, const Rational&);
    friend Rational operator/(const Rational&, const Rational&);
  public:
    Rational(long=0,long=1);
    long numerator() const;
    long denominator() const;
    Rational reciprocal() const;
    void invert();
    operator double() const;
  private:
    Polynomial _num;
    Polynomial _den;
    long gcd(long,long);
    void reduce();
    // INVARIANT: _den > 0 && gcd(_num,_den) == 1
};

ostream& operator<<(ostream& ostr, const Rational& r)
{ return ostr << r._num << "/" << r._den;
}

istream& operator>>(istream& istr, Rational& r)
{ istr >> r._num;
  istr.ignore(1);
  istr >> r._den;
  r.reduce();
  return istr;
}
```

```
Rational operator+(const Rational& r1, const Rational& r2)
{ Rational r(r1._num*r2._den+r2._num*r1._den,r1._den*r2._den);
  r.reduce();
  return r;
}

Rational operator-(const Rational& r1, const Rational& r2)
{ Rational r(r1._num*r2._den-r2._num*r1._den,r1._den*r2._den);
  r.reduce();
  return r;
}

Rational operator*(const Rational& r1, const Rational& r2)
{ Rational r(r1._num*r2._num,r1._den*r2._den);
  r.reduce();
  return r;
}

Rational operator/(const Rational& r1, const Rational& r2)
{ Rational r(r1._num*r2._den,r1._den*r2._num);
  r.reduce();
  return r;
}

Rational::Rational(long num, long den) : _num(num), _den(den)
{ reduce();
}

long Rational::numerator() const
{ return _num;
}

long Rational::denominator() const
{ return _den;
}

Rational Rational::reciprocal() const
{ Rational r(_den,_num);
  r.reduce();
  return r;
}

void Rational::invert()
{ long temp = _num;
  _num = _den;
  _den = temp;
  reduce();
}
```

```
Rational::operator double() const
{ return double(_num)/_den;
}


long Rational::gcd(long m, long n)
{ if (m == n) return n;                    // basis
  else if (m < n) return gcd(m,n-m);    // recursion
  else return gcd(m-n,n);                // recursion
}


void Rational::reduce()
{ if (_num == 0 || _den == 0)
  { _num = 0;
    _den = 1;
    return;
  }
  if (_den < 0)
  { _den *= -1;
    _num *= -1;
  }
  if (_num == 1) return;
  int sgn = (_num<0?-1:1);
  long g = gcd(sgn*_num,_den);
  _num /= g;
  _den /= g;
}
```

E.25 A SelfOrganizingList CLASS

```
template <class T>
class SelfOrganizingList : public list<T>
{ public:
    bool contains(const T&);
};


template <class T>
bool SelfOrganizingList<T>::contains(const T& t)
{ list<T>::iterator it=find(begin(),end(),t);
  if (it == end()) return false;
  if (it != begin())
  { erase(it);
    push_front(t);
  }
  return true;
}
```

E.26 A Stack CLASS TEMPLATE

```
template <class T>
class Stack
{ public:
    Stack();
    Stack(const Stack&);
    ~Stack();
    Stack& operator=(const Stack&);
    int size() const;          // returns number of elements in this
    bool empty() const;        // returns true iff this is empty
    T& top() const;            // returns the top element
    void push(const T&);       // inserts given element on top
    void pop();                // removes element from top
  protected:
    T* _;                      // dynamic array for stack elements
    int _size;                 // number of elements in stack
    int _cap;                  // number of elements in array
    static const int _CAP=4;   // initial capacity
    void rebuild();            // moves all stack elements to new array
};

template <class T>
Stack<T>::Stack() : _(new T[_CAP]), _size(0), _cap(_CAP)
{
}

template <class T>
Stack<T>::Stack(const Stack& s)
  : _(new T[s._cap]), _size(s._size), _cap(s._cap)
{ for (int i=0; i<_cap; i++)
    _[i] = s._[i];
}

template <class T>
Stack<T>::~Stack()
{ delete [] _;
}

template <class T>
Stack<T>& Stack<T>::operator=(const Stack& s)
{ _ = new T[s._cap];
  _size = s._size;
  _cap = s._cap;
  for (int i=0; i<_cap; i++)
    _[i] = s._[i];
}
```

```
template <class T>
int Stack<T>::size() const
{ return _size;
}

template <class T>
bool Stack<T>::empty() const
{ return _size == 0;
}

template <class T>
T& Stack<T>::top() const
{ return _[_size-1];
}

template <class T>
void Stack<T>::pop()
{ --_size;
}

template <class T>
void Stack<T>::push(const T& x)
{ if (_size == _cap) rebuild();
  _[_size++] = x;
}

template <class T>
void Stack<T>::rebuild()
{ _cap *= 2;  // double the capacity of the storage array
  T* temp = new T[_cap];
  for (int i=0; i<_size; i++)
    temp[i] = _[i];
  delete [] _;
  _ = temp;
}
```

E.27 A Tree CLASS

```
class Tree
{   struct Node;
    typedef string Type;
    typedef list<Node*> List;
    typedef List::iterator LIt;
    List _nodes;              // list of tree elements in preorder
  public:
    class Iterator;                       // Tree::Iterator class
    Tree();                               // default constructor
```

```
    Tree(const Tree&);                          // copy constructor
    Tree(const Type&);                       // constructs singleton
    Tree(const Type&, const list<Tree*>&);          // definition
    ~Tree();                                 // destructs all nodes
    Tree& operator=(const Tree& t);            // Tree assignment
    bool operator==(const Tree& t) const;        // Tree equality
    bool operator!=(const Tree& t) const;      // Tree inequality
    void clear();                              // empties this tree
    bool empty() const;             // true iff this tree is empty
    int size() const;          // number of elements in this tree
    int leaves() const;          // number of leaves in this tree
    int height() const;                    // height of this tree
    int level(Iterator it) const;   // level of *it in this tree
    int pathLength();               // path length of this tree
    int width(int);           // number of nodes at given level
    int width();           // maximum number among all levels
    void print(int);                   // prints given generation
    void print();                       // level order traversal
    Type& root() const;        // the root element in this tree
    void reflect();
    void defoliate();
    Iterator insert(Iterator, const Type& =Type());    // std lib
    void erase(Iterator);                               // std lib
    Iterator grow(Iterator, const Type&); // adds youngest child
    void prune(Iterator);               // deletes youngest child
    Iterator attach(Iterator, Tree&); // inserts in front of *it
    void detach(Iterator, Tree&);       // removes subtree at *it
    int generations(Iterator,Iterator);   // levels between nodes
    Iterator begin();           // inorder traversal starts at root
    Iterator end();                     // ends with null iterator
    static bool isRoot(Iterator it);            // *it is the root
    static bool isLeaf(Iterator it);            // *it is a leaf
    static bool isOldestChild(Iterator it);
    static bool isYoungestChild(Iterator it);
    static Iterator oldestChild(Iterator);
    static Iterator youngestChild(Iterator);
    static Iterator parent(Iterator it);// locates parent of *it
    static int numChildren(Iterator it);
    friend class Iterator                      // preorder traversal
    {   Tree* _tree;                    // the tree being traversed
        LIt _lit;                            // the current node
      public:
        Iterator();                         // default constructor
        Iterator(const Iterator&);          // copy constructor
        Iterator(Tree*,Node* =0);               // constructor
        Iterator(Tree*,LIt);                    // constructor
        void operator=(const Iterator& it);        // assignment
        bool operator==(const Iterator& it);        // equality
        bool operator!=(const Iterator& it);        // inequality
        Iterator& operator++();                 // prefix increment
```

```
        Iterator operator++(int);           // postfix increment
        Type& operator*() const;             // current element
        bool operator!();                 // this iterator is null
        friend class Tree;
    };
  protected:
    List level(int n);    // returns list of all nodes at level n
    LIt litn(Node*);    // the _nodes iterator for the given node
    LIt litp(Node*);     // the _parent->_children iterator for "
    LIt prevSibling(LIt);
    LIt nextSibling(LIt);
};


typedef Tree::Type Type;
typedef Tree::List List;
typedef Tree::Node Node;
typedef Tree::Iterator It;
typedef Tree::List::iterator LIt;
typedef Tree::List::const_iterator LCIt;
typedef list<Tree*> TList;
typedef TList::const_iterator TLCIt;
int n(Node*);       // size of subtree
int h(Node*);       // height of subtree
int l(Node*,It);   // level of *it in subtree
Node* clone(Node*, List&, Node*);


//////////////////////////////////////////////////////////
// definition of protected Tree::Node struct:

struct Tree::Node
{ Type _;
  List _children;
  Node* _parent;
  Node(Type =Type(), Node* =0);
};


Node::Node(Type x, Node* p) : _(x), _parent(p)
{ if (!_parent) _parent = this;
}


//////////////////////////////////////////////////////////
// public member functions of the Tree class:

Tree::Tree()
{
}
```

```
Tree::Tree(const Tree& t)
{ if (t._nodes.empty()) return;
  clone(t._nodes.front(),_nodes,0);
}


Tree::Tree(const Type& x)
{ _nodes.push_back(new Node(x));
}


Tree::Tree(const Type& x, const list<Tree*>& list)
{ Node* root = new Node(x);
  _nodes.push_back(root);
  for(TLCIt it=list.begin(); it!=list.end(); it++)
    if (!((*it)->_nodes).empty())
    { Tree* tp = new Tree(**it);      // duplicate tree **it
      Node* p = tp->_nodes.front();   // points to root of t
      root->_children.push_back(p);       // connect to root
      p->_parent = root;
      LIt lit1=tp->_nodes.begin();
      LIt lit2=tp->_nodes.end();
      LIt lit3=_nodes.end();
      _nodes.insert(lit3,lit1,lit2);  // append *tp's nodes
    }
}


Tree::~Tree()
{ for (LIt lit=_nodes.begin(); lit!=_nodes.end(); lit++)
    delete *lit;
}


Tree& Tree::operator=(const Tree& t)
{ clear();                                    // empty this tree
  Tree* p = new Tree(t);              // use copy constructor
  _nodes = p->_nodes;
  return *this;
}

bool Tree::operator==(const Tree& t) const
{ if (_nodes.size() != t._nodes.size()) return false;
  LCIt tlit=t._nodes.begin();
  for (LCIt lit=_nodes.begin(); lit!=_nodes.end(); lit++, tlit++)
    if ((*lit)->_ != (*tlit)->_) return false;
  return true;
}


bool Tree::operator!=(const Tree& t) const
{ return !(*this == t);
}
```

```
void Tree::clear()
{ for (LIt lit=_nodes.begin(); lit!=_nodes.end(); lit++)
    delete *lit;
  _nodes.clear();
}

bool Tree::empty() const
{ return _nodes.empty();
}

int Tree::size() const
{ return _nodes.size();
}

int Tree::leaves() const
{ return n(_nodes.front());
}

int Tree::height() const
{ return h(_nodes.front());
}

int Tree::level(It it) const
{ return l(_nodes.front(),it);
}

void Tree::print(int n)
{ List list=level(n);
  for (LIt it=list.begin(); it!=list.end(); it++)
    cout << (*it)->_ << " ";
  cout << "\n";
}

void Tree::print()
{ int h=height();
  for (int level=0; level<=h; level++)
    print(level);
}

int Tree::pathLength()
{ int pl=0;
  for (LIt lit=_nodes.begin(); lit!=_nodes.end(); lit++)
    pl += level(It(this,*lit));
  return pl;
}

int Tree::width(int n)
{ return level(n).size();
}
```

```
int Tree::width()
{ if (_nodes.empty()) return 0;                    // empty tree
  int w=1;
  for (int k=0; k<=height(); k++)
  { int w1=level(k).size();         // number of nodes at level k
    if (w1>w) w = w1;
  }
  return w;
}


Type& Tree::root() const
{ return _nodes.front()->_;
}


void Tree::reflect()
{ for (LIt lit=_nodes.begin(); lit!=_nodes.end(); lit++)
    (*lit)->_children.reverse();   // std lib function
}


void Tree::defoliate()
{ if (_nodes.size() < 2)
  { clear();
    return;
  }
  for (LIt lit=_nodes.begin(); lit!=_nodes.end(); lit++)
  { Node* p=*lit;
    if (p->_children.empty())
    { p->_parent->_children.clear();
      delete p;
      LIt tmp=lit;
      --lit;     // save location in _nodes list
      _nodes.erase(tmp);
    }
  }
}


It Tree::insert(It it, const Type& x)
{ // new node is new parent of *it
  // _nodes maintain preorder traversal
  Node* np = new Node(x);
  if (!it)                 // insert at (preorder) end of tree
  { Node* pp = _nodes.back();
    pp->_children.push_back(np);
    _nodes.push_back(np);
  }
  else
  { Node* p=(*it._lit);
    Node* pp=p->_parent;
    np->_children.push_back(p);
    LIt lit = find(_nodes.begin(),_nodes.end(),p);
```

```
      _nodes.insert(lit,np);
      if (pp != p)                        // *p is not the root
      { List& list = pp->_children;
        lit = find(list.begin(),list.end(),p);
        *lit = np;                   // make *np the child of *pp
      }
    }
    return It(this,np);
}

void Tree::erase(It it)
{ if (!it) return;
  Node* p=(*it._lit);
  Node* pp=p->_parent;
  if (p->_children.empty())               // *p is a leaf
  { LIt lit = find(_nodes.begin(),_nodes.end(),p);
    _nodes.erase(lit);
    if (pp != p)                          // *p is not the root
    { List& list = pp->_children;
      lit = find(list.begin(),list.end(),p);
      list.erase(lit);
    }
    delete p;
  }
  else                     // replace *p with oldest child
  { p->_ = p->_children.front()->_;
    erase(It(this,p->_children.front()));
  }
}

It Tree::grow(It it, const Type& x)
{ LIt lit=it._lit;        // locates current node in _nodes
  Node* pp=*lit;
  Node* p=new Node(x,pp);
  pp->_children.push_back(p);
  Node* ppp=pp->_parent;
  List& ppplist=ppp->_children;
  if ( (ppp == pp)                        // *pp is the root
     || (pp == ppplist.back()) )   // or pp is the youngest
  { _nodes.push_back(p);
    lit=find(lit,_nodes.end(),p);
  }
  else                // find next sibling of pp in _nodes:
  { LIt ppplit=find(ppplist.begin(),ppplist.end(),pp);
    ++ppplit;                      // locates next sibling of pp
    lit=find(lit,_nodes.end(),*ppplit);
    lit = _nodes.insert(lit,p);
  }
  return It(this,lit);
}
```

```
void Tree::prune(It it)
{ erase(youngestChild(it));
}


It Tree::attach(It it, Tree& t1)
{ // PRECONDITION: it is an iterator on this tree;
  // if t is empty, it is replaced by t1;
  // if t1 is empty, there is no change;
  // otherwise, if (it == tree.begin()), the root of t1
  //    becomes the new root of t and the old root
  //    becomes its youngest child;
  // otherwise, if (it == tree.end()), the root of t1
  //    becomes the youngest child of the root of t;
  // otherwise, t1 is inserted in front of *it,
  //    becoming its next older sibling;
  // POSTCONDITIONS: t1 returns empty;
  //    it locates the root of the subtree that was t1;
  if (t1._nodes.empty()) return it;  // no change
  // move t1._nodes list into _nodes list:
  LIt lit1=t1._nodes.begin();
  LIt lit2=it._lit;
  Node* p1=*lit1;                       // points to root of t1
  _nodes.insert(lit2,lit1,t1._nodes.end());
  t1._nodes.clear();
  // connect parent and children links:
  if (p1 == _nodes.front())        // *p1 is the new root:
    if (lit2 == _nodes.end()) ;          // tree was empty
    else     // make old root the youngest child of new root
    { Node* p2=*lit2;                    // points to *it node
      (p1->_children).push_back(p2);
      p2->_parent = p1;
    }
  else // root does not change
    if (lit2 == _nodes.end())  // t1 youngest child of root
    { Node* p2=_nodes.front();
      List& pplist=p2->_children;
      pplist.push_back(p1);
      p1->_parent = p2;
    }
    else
    { Node* p2=*lit2;                    // points to *it node
      List& pplist=p2->_parent->_children;
      LIt litp2=litp(p2);            // locates p2 in pplist
      pplist.insert(litp2,p1);
      p1->_parent = p2->_parent;
    }
  return It(this,lit1);
}
```

```
void Tree::detach(It it, Tree& t1)
{ // PRECONDITION: it is an iterator on this tree;
  // if t is empty or if (it == tree.end()),
  //    then t is left unchanged and t1 returns empty;
  // if (it == tree.begin()), then t1 is replaced by t
  //    and t returns empty;
  // POSTCONDITIONS: the previous contents of t1 are lost;
  //    t1 contains the nodes that were in the subtree of t
  //    rooted at it;
  t1._nodes.clear();
  if (_nodes.empty() || it == end()) return;      // t1 empty
  if (it == begin())
  { t1._nodes = _nodes;              // copy entire _nodes list
    _nodes.clear();                       // empty _nodes list
    return;
  }
  // move [lit1,lit2[ from _nodes to t1._nodes:
  LIt lit1=it._lit;
  LIt lit2=_nodes.end();
  for (Node* p=*lit1; lit2 == _nodes.end() && p != p->_parent;
       p = p->_parent)
    lit2=nextSibling(litn(p));
  t1._nodes.insert(t1._nodes.end(),lit1,lit2);
  _nodes.erase(lit1,lit2);
  // reset node pointers to disconnect subtree:
  Node* p1=*lit1;
  Node* pp=p1->_parent;
  List& pplist=pp->_children;
  LIt pplit1=litp(p1);        // p1's parent's pointer to *it
  pplist.erase(pplit1);
  p1->_parent = p1;        // *p1 is the root of the subtree
}

int Tree::generations(It it, It jt)
{ if (!it || !jt) return -1;
  if (it == jt) return 0;
  int n=0;
  Node* p=(*jt._lit)->_parent;
  while (jt != it && p != *jt._lit)
  { Tree* tp=this;
    p=(*jt._lit)->_parent;
    jt = It(tp,p);
    ++n;
  }
  if (jt == it) return n;
  n = generations(jt,it);
  if (n != -1 && !!it && !!jt) return -n;
  return -1;
}
```

```
It Tree::begin()
{ return It(this,_nodes.begin());
}


It Tree::end()
{ return It(this,_nodes.end());
}


It Tree::oldestChild(It it)
{ if (!it) return 0;
  Node* p=*it._lit;
  if (!p) return 0;
  Tree* tree=it._tree;
  if (p->_children.empty()) return 0;
  return It(tree,(*it._lit)->_children.front());
}


It Tree::youngestChild(It it)
{ if (!it) return 0;
  Node* p=*it._lit;
  if (!p) return 0;
  Tree* tree=it._tree;
  if (p->_children.empty()) return 0;
  return It(tree,(*it._lit)->_children.back());
}


bool Tree::isRoot(It it)
{ Node* p=*it._lit;
  return it._lit == (it._tree->_nodes).begin();;
}


bool Tree::isLeaf(It it)
{ return (*it._lit)->_children.empty();
}


It Tree::parent(It it)
{ Node* p=*it._lit;
  Tree* tree=it._tree;
  if (p->_parent == p) return It(tree,tree->_nodes.end());
  return It(tree,p->_parent);
}


int Tree::numChildren(Iterator it)
{ return (*it._lit)->_children.size();
}
```

```
bool Tree::isOldestChild(It it)
{ Node* p=(*it._lit);
  if (p == p->_parent) return true;        // *p is the root
  return (p == p->_parent->_children.front());
}

bool Tree::isYoungestChild(It it)
{ Node* p=(*it._lit);
  if (p == p->_parent) return true;        // *p is the root
  return (p == p->_parent->_children.back());
}


//////////////////////////////////////////////////////////////
//  public member functions of the Tree::Iterator class:

It::Iterator()
{
}


It::Iterator(const It& it)
  : _tree(it._tree), _lit(it._lit)
{
}


It::Iterator(Tree* tree, Node* p) : _tree(tree)
{ List& nodes=_tree->_nodes;
  _lit = find(nodes.begin(),nodes.end(),p);
}


It::Iterator(Tree* tree, LIt lit) : _tree(tree), _lit(lit)
{
}


void It::operator=(const It& it)
{ _tree = it._tree;
  _lit = it._lit;
}


bool It::operator==(const It& it)
{ return _tree == it._tree && _lit == it._lit;
}


bool It::operator!=(const It& it)
{ return _tree != it._tree || _lit != it._lit;
}


It& It::operator++()                        // prefix increment
{ ++_lit;
  return *this;
}
```

```
It It::operator++(int)          // postfix increment operator
{ It it(*this);                           // copy this iterator
  operator++();                    // increment this iterator
  return it;                             // return the copy
}


Type& It::operator*() const
{ return (*_lit)->_;
}


bool It::operator!()
{ return _lit == _tree->_nodes.end();
}


//////////////////////////////////////////////////////////
//  protected member functions of the Tree class:

List Tree::level(int n)
{ List listn;
  if (empty()) return listn;
  queue<List*> q;
  Node* root=*(_nodes.begin());                 // points to root
  if (n==0) return List(1,root);
  q.push(&(root->_children));
  while (!q.empty())
  { List* p=q.front();
    List& list=*p;
    for (LIt lit=list.begin(); lit!=list.end(); lit++)
    { Node* p=*lit;
      It it(this,*lit);
      if (level(it)==n)
        listn.push_back(*lit);
      q.push(&((*lit)->_children));
    }
    q.pop();
  }
  return listn;
}


LIt Tree::litn(Node* p)
{ // returns the LIt for _nodes that locates p:
  if (p == 0) return LIt();
  return find(_nodes.begin(),_nodes.end(),p);
}
```

```
LIt Tree::litp(Node* p)
{ // returns the LIt for p->_parent that locates p:
  if (p == 0 || p == _nodes.front()) return LIt();
  List& pplist=p->_parent->_children;
  return find(pplist.begin(),pplist.end(),p);
}


LIt Tree::prevSibling(LIt lit)
{ // returns the LIt for _node that locates
  // the next older sibling of *lit
  if (_nodes.empty() || lit==_nodes.begin())
    return _nodes.end();
  if (lit==_nodes.end()) return _nodes.begin();
  Node* p1=*lit;
  LIt litp1=litp(p1);
  if (p1 == (p1->_parent->_children).front())
    return _nodes.end();
  return find(_nodes.begin(),--lit,*--litp1);
}


LIt Tree::nextSibling(LIt lit)
{ // returns the LIt for _node that locates
  // the next younger sibling of *lit
  if (lit==_nodes.begin() || lit==_nodes.end())
    return _nodes.end();
  Node* p2=*lit;
  LIt litp2=litp(p2);
  if (p2 == (p2->_parent->_children).back())
    return _nodes.end();
  return find(++lit,_nodes.begin(),*++litp2);
}


////////////////////////////////////////////////////////////
//   local recursive utility functions:

int n(Node* p)
{ if (!p) return 0;
  List& plist=p->_children;
  if (plist.empty()) return 1;  // *p is a leaf
  int n0=0;
  for (LIt plit=plist.begin(); plit!=plist.end(); plit++)
    n0 += n(*plit);
  return n0;
}


int h(Node* p)
{ if (!p) return -1;  // the empty tree has height -1
  List& plist=p->_children;
  if (plist.empty()) return 0;
  int h0=0;
```

```
   for (LIt plit=plist.begin(); plit!=plist.end(); plit++)
   { int h1=h(*plit);
     if (h1>h0) h0 = h1;
   }
   return h0+1;
}


int l(Node* p, It it)
{ if (!p) return -1;   // the empty tree has height -1
  if (p->_ == *it) return 0;           // *it was found
  List& plist=p->_children;
  for (LIt plit=plist.begin(); plit!=plist.end(); plit++)
  { int lc=l(*plit,it);
    if (lc>-1) return lc+1;
  }
  return -1;   // *it is not in this subtree
}


Node* clone(Node* p, List& nodes, Node* pp)
{ // recursive preorder traversal;
  // creates the copy *cp of Node *p,
  // including the duplication of all its descendants
  Node* cp = new Node(p->_,pp);
  nodes.push_back(cp);
  List& l=p->_children;
  List& cl=cp->_children;
  for (LIt lit=l.begin(); lit!=l.end(); lit++)
    cl.push_back(clone(*lit,nodes,cp));
  return cp;
}
```

Index